Who Benefits from Global Violence and War

WHO BENEFITS FROM GLOBAL VIOLENCE AND WAR

Uncovering a Destructive System

Marc Pilisuk with Jennifer Achord Rountree

Contemporary Psychology
Chris E. Stout, Series Editor

PRAEGER SECURITY INTERNATIONAL
Westport, Connecticut • London

Library of Congress Cataloging-in-Publication Data

Pilisuk, Marc.
Who benefits from global violence and war : uncovering a destructive system / Marc Pilisuk ; with Jennifer Achord Rountree.
p. cm. — (Contemporary psychology, ISSN 1546–668X)
Includes bibliographical references and index.
ISBN-13: 978–0–275–99435–8 (alk. paper)
1. War and society. 2. War—Social aspects. 3. Violence—Social aspects. I. Rountree, Jennifer Achord. II. Title.
HM554.W56 2008
303.6'6—dc22 2007036174

British Library Cataloguing in Publication Data is available.

Library of Congress Catalog Card Number: 2007036174
ISBN: 978–0–275–99435–8
ISSN: 1546–668X

First published in 2008

Praeger Security International, 88 Post Road West, Westport, CT 06881
An imprint of Greenwood Publishing Group, Inc.
www.praeger.com

Printed in the United States of America

The paper used in this book complies with the Permanent Paper Standard issued by the National Information Standards Organization (Z39.48-1984).

10 9 8 7 6 5 4 3 2 1

Contents

Acknowledgments

This book represents the work of many people who have helped to locate the information, synthesize and draft summaries of diverse materials, and edit portions of the manuscript. They include Danial Durazo, Peter Christiansen, Jillian Marks, Donna Nassor, Wanda Woodward, Emmauelle Julien-Sinclair, Daphne Palliavicno, Leslie Sander, Carrie Paine, Dr. Scott Field, and Dr. JoAnne Zazzi. Jennifer Rountree helped with untiring dedication throughout the entire process, so her name is on the cover. I am grateful also for computer assistance from Norman Lau and Herb Diamond and for advice from Annamarie Weltake and Joe Marino, the Saybrook Graduate School librarians. I am deeply indebted to the alternative media for providing information not readily reported in the mainstream and particularly to Amy Goodman of "Democracy Now." I am indebted to the scholars, journalists, and professional activists who look beneath the blanket of distracting facades to the voices of the casualties of a violent social order and into the backrooms of powerful planners who orchestrate a continuing culture of violence and manipulation. Here I must thank the Corporate Accountability Project, OxFam, Global Exchange, Food First, Peace Action, Amnesty International, the American Civil Liberties Union, and the Psychologists for Social Responsibility, among the myriad of sources of information and of hope. The scholarship of two of my own mentors, Anatol Rapoport and Kenneth Boulding, has reverberated through my being, as have words of psychologists JoAnna Macy and Mike Wessells. The inspiration I continue to find in the words and deeds of Dr. Martin Luther King, Jr. encourage me to believe that a better world is possible, which is the main reason for this book.

Finally I appreciate deeply the contribution of my family. My parents, Louis and Charlotte, provided me with the chance to grow up in an environment in which social justice was truly valued. My wife, Phyllis, has listened as I shared the ideas and dilemmas in writing this book. I thank her for her understanding of my hours at work that made me less of a caregiver than I might have been as her multiple sclerosis progressed. As a parent and grandparent I want my offspring to live in a world in which love and interdependence find the resources needed to assure peace, sustainability, and justice. I hope this book will be a resource to that end.

INTRODUCTION

> During times of universal deceit, telling the truth becomes a revolutionary act.
>
> —*George Orwell*

> The trouble is that once you see it, you can't un-see it. And once you've seen it, keeping quiet becomes as political an act as speaking out. There's no innocence. Either way, you're accountable.
>
> —*Arundhati Roy*

No social scientist is value-free. I write from a deep belief that life is not only complex but also precious. Each individual is part of a web of connections to others and to the surrounding ecology, a marvelous design that sustains this experiment of life. I believe also that this complex masterpiece is in danger that is largely the result of how many humans think and behave. For life to continue there must be a balance between how we use our interconnections for our own needs and how we nurture these connections so that the entire web of life can continue. If we abuse, exploit, and conquer the world about us, we dishonor the gift of life and jeopardize the future. If we care for the web and nurture it, then the world will nourish us.

This book is about contemporary global violence. As I write, the United States is in its fifth year of an undeclared war with Iraq. It is one of the many examples of the ways that humans inflict harm upon each other. The projected cost for the United States of five years of war in Iraq is more than $1 trillion. It is an amount that I cannot imagine, but I do know that the same money might have addressed such serious problems as world hunger; the AIDS epidemic; housing for homeless people; quality health care and education for everyone; alternative energy research to combat global warning; cleanup of carcinogenic wastes from our environment; adequate warning and response systems for such natural disasters as hurricanes, floods, and earthquakes; research to prevent or heal and to rehabilitate sickness and disability; and guarantees of social security. More than 650,000 people have so far died in this war, and, of course, the Iraq war is only one part of the violence happening around the globe. If we humans are to take charge of our destiny, we will have to understand why such violence, at such a cost, recurs so often.

Violence is evident where any life is harmed or ended through the behavior or the negligence of other people. It takes many forms. We will concentrate on two of these: military violence (or war) and economic violence in which the requirements for life and livelihood are taken away or destroyed. Violence may be direct, as when one uses a gun or bomb to destroy others, or structural, as when patterns of land ownership and land use by distant corporate entities result in the starvation of children who live on that land. In this book we look first, in painful detail, at what military violence with modern weapons is inflicting and what it is able to inflict. Military violence is our most profound threat but is not, at this time, our most lethal killer. On a daily basis, even without the casualties of direct military violence, we live in ways that result in the violent deaths of vulnerable people, particularly children, as a consequence of how we exploit, consume, and dispose of the environment that sustains human life. These patterns of investment and exploitation already contribute to a loss of life greater than all wars. Moreover, the persistence of widespread violence causes us to live in a world of fear—a fear of being unable to protect ourselves or those we love. It is also a world of denial that the suffering can be so great or that the danger can be so imminent. Even among those who acknowledge the problem, we find widespread disbelief that ordinary people have the power or the wisdom to transform this world into a better place.

It is not pleasant to look at the larger picture of the violence of war and economic and environmental exploitation. But to avoid seeing the danger will remove all chances of changing it. To see how the parts fit together and what propels this dance of death is, I believe, a first step to reversing it. When we humans see instances of violence, we are often quick to respond, sometimes with efforts to assist the victims, often with efforts to punish the perpetrators. It is important that we are able to feel the pain of each individual case. It is equally important to find out why there are so many cases. For that to take place it is important to examine what common underlying levers are causing the human family to engage in such protracted and recurrent violence.

In the first chapter we examine the destructiveness of war and the extraordinary potential of modern technology to destroy. Following this, chapter 2 examines the human capacity to kill other humans. We review capacities to withdraw empathy from others, enabling them to be seen as less than human and making their destruction appear tolerable. Chapters 3 and 4 deal with the violence of the global economy to people and to their surrounding ecology. In an era of globalization, transnational corporations operate in ways that increase violence; they employ dehumanizing rules and amoral calculations to fulfill their purpose of making money. Chapter 5 deals with a taboo topic: the concentration of power. Corporations do not act alone but as part of a network of wealthy and powerful people whose personal success with the system convinces them of its inherent value. This network has become the gatekeeper over resources, lives, and livelihoods. The settings in which the most influential people come together, in secret, to chart future plans is described. Typically, however, the understandings they share are sufficiently entrenched in the day-to-day work of corporate and government agencies and in the electoral process, so conspiratorial meetings are not generally needed. Chapter 6 describes the methods and tactics used by those at the centers of power to continue a violent path and the strategic planning that provides rationales and promotes the means to exploit and to destroy. The sometimes clandestine means have ranged from persuasion to economic threats, to bribes, coups, assassinations, invasions, and torture. In chapter 7 we examine the ways that media serve powerful interests and how information is controlled to shape our views and to permit violence to appear both normal and inevitable. Chapter 8 draws from what has been presented to construct a theory of how and why this pattern of violence continues. It describes the widely shared cultural beliefs that permit powerful elites to engage in massive violence. The chapter shows how the core beliefs help to steer ordinary working people whose needs are repeatedly neglected by the economic order to find scapegoats and to allow the powerful beneficiaries to rule. It examines the tapping of such beliefs to encourage fear among common people and the dangers of fascism that such fear makes possible.

These chapters examine what common underlying levers are causing the human family to engage in protracted and recurrent violence. In viewing the enormity of the problem and the patterns that underlie it, we become able to say, and to believe, "Enough—there has to be a better way." Against the weight of the challenge presented one can examine the myriad of social actions large and small that are working to change this societal addiction to violence. The final conclusion points to what is being done and what can be done to bring peace with justice to the planet.

Looking at the deeper causes of violence is painful. Who wants to be reminded of the extent of destruction and killing? It surely has been painful for me to deal with this subject over the years it takes to write such a book. Painful as such an examination may be, that look into a dysfunctional system is our best hope and our guide to create a better way. So this book asks something of the reader. Commit yourself to do five things:

1. Stay with the disturbing facts about the forms of global violence.
2. Remind yourself that the numbers reflect real human lives.
3. Refrain from demonizing those most central to the promotion of this violence. The book names people and organizations, but the task is not to blame but to understand the system in which global violence has become a central part.
4. Retain the hope that deeper understanding will contribute to empowering each of us in what we do to create a world of peace.
5. Grapple with this book in the doses that fit your needs and with the antidotes of time for caring contact with people, with the renewing powers of meditation, reflection, exercise, music, art, food, laughter, and the beauty of the land. And if any of this restorative bounty is worth preserving, come back to grapple with the violence that threatens it and your place in securing it for the future.

CHAPTER 1

THE COSTS OF MODERN WAR

Wars throughout history have been waged for conquest and plunder . . . the working class who fight all the battles, the working class who make the supreme sacrifices, the working class who freely shed their blood and furnish their corpses, have never yet had a voice in either declaring war or making peace. It is the ruling class that invariably does both. They alone declare war and they alone make peace. . . . They are continually talking about their patriotic duty. It is not their duty but your patriotic duty that they are concerned about. There is a decided difference. Their patriotic duty never takes them to the firing line or chucks them into the trenches.

—*Eugene V. Debs*

It is only those who have neither fired a shot nor heard the shrieks and groans of the wounded that cry aloud for blood, more vengeance, and more desolation. War is hell.

—*General William Sherman, U.S. Civil War*

Mankind must put an end to war or war will put an end to mankind.

—*John F. Kennedy, Speech to U.N. General Assembly.*

If we are ever to move away from the realities of global violence, we must first face them. In this chapter we look at the practice of military violence, the circumstances that include organized efforts (usually by governments) to use lethal force to destroy and to kill others who are defined as adversaries. In this chapter we look at the extent of military violence and its consequences. There are three major problems in conveying the costs of military violence. First, the forms in which military encounters occur have changed dramatically. Wars may refer to one-sided and barely contested interventions or to engagements between the military forces of rival nations. They may be said to include individual acts of terror, such as suicide bombing, or massive bombing by missiles and aircraft. They may involve declarations of war, but not always, and they may be considered legitimate responses to defend against being attacked. Some military conflicts, however, are clandestine, undeclared, and denied. Here we will try to cover the consequences from all forms.

The second difficulty is that consequences of contemporary global violence have been of such magnitude as to be barely comprehensible. War has apparently caused more than three times the number of casualties in the last ninety years than in the previous 500. Upwards of 250 major wars have occurred in the post–World War II era, taking over 50 million lives and leaving tens of millions homeless.[1] How can that degree of suffering be acknowledged, admitted into awareness, and become a part of the process needed to change it?

The third problem, for the developed world and particularly for the United States, has been America's prominent history in contemporary war. It is difficult to accept culpability for so great a human tragedy. To acknowledge a pattern attributable to one's own nation is to accept a painful responsibility for what has occurred and a moral responsibility to make amends. Between World War II and the end of the last century, the United States led seventy-three military interventions throughout the world, almost double the total from the preceding fifty-five-year period.[2]

If we include all covert operations in which casualties occurred, the figure rises to 196.[3] The Pentagon has an ever-expanding empire of over 6,000 domestic bases, and 725 overseas. The United States' $455 billion military expenditure in 2004 was larger than the combined amount that the thirty-two next-most-powerful nations spent on their militaries.[4]

Military spending is sometimes difficult to find. Some expenditures related to nuclear weapons are in the budget of the Department of Energy, not Department of Defense. The care of veterans represents another category of expense. A major portion of interest paid on the national debt is for the unpaid costs of prior military expenditures. The Bureau of Economic Analysis (BEA) sought an accurate account for total government spending on defense. The BEA recalculated the 2004 federal outlay and concluded that the government has been understating its defense spending by hundreds of billions of dollars. Half of the discretionary budget of the United States goes for military purposes, which results in a serious lack of funding for health, welfare, and the reduction of poverty.[5]

The practice of armed conflict takes many forms. They trace back to tribal societies of which some, but not all, engaged in warfare. The emergence of kingdoms and of nation states with defined borders marked a long period in which wars were a natural outgrowth of the expressed purposes of rulers, that is, to retain and expand their influence and the territories under their control. Royal leaders and their kin led the actual battles in which rival armies faced one another directly, often in preplanned encounters. The costs were carefully considered, and a preoccupation with strategy helped to create a military caste of experienced warriors. In the western world, wars of liberation against acknowledged rulers occurred in France and in the United States. Abstract concepts of "liberty" and "consent of the governed" appeared as justifications for armed revolt. These were followed by other abstract rationales of equality, manifest destiny, democracy, communism, and fascism. Each of these provided an ultimate purpose and a rationale for greater sacrifice on the battlefields. Meanwhile, private armies of paid mercenaries were hired by wealthy interests to protect or expand their privileged status. As nation states grew sufficiently productive to maintain large military establishments, they were able to colonize much of the still tribal and agrarian world. Resistance to such colonial empires led to armies of occupation and, in response, to guerilla armies seeking to oust colonial rulers or their puppet governments. As the technology of warfare improved, the costs in lives increased, and the evolution to wars with massive civilian casualties emerged. Now over 90 percent of casualties are civilians. The firebombing of Dresden in World War II killed 135,000 civilians—more than Hiroshima and Nagasaki combined. It was carried out, according to some historians, as a demonstration of raw Allied air power to Russians moving toward Berlin. Likewise, wars generally have unintended consequences rarely confined to their original goals.[6] Along with the technological and economic progress of the developed countries in the twentieth century, portions of the militaries of these same countries descended to a level of barbarity that violated the rules of engagement set at The Hague and at Geneva. Such violations made the twentieth century the most decimated by war.[7] There have been attempts at setting limitations on the types and numbers of weapons available for use in war, both to remove provocations and to protect noncombatants, but with only modest success.[8]

The gradual independence of colonial states following World War II was accompanied by the continuation of economic colonialism in which large corporate interests retained control over the resources of countries that had been declared independent. In these countries, military bases remained to protect the economic interests, often with the support or acquiescence of puppet governments that were armed and made wealthy by such arrangements. Conflicts not between nations but between governments and large segments of their own population have produced reigns of terror. Increasingly, wars have asymmetrical opponents in which large and powerful armies with high-tech weapons are pitted against the poorest and most vulnerable people.

Particularly where tribal lifestyles were stripped of resources needed for their viability, tribal conflicts—sometimes divided on ethnic lines—emerged to battle for resources and for control over governments. The global traffic in weapons has made such conflict capable of genocide. Where the most powerful nation states have been in agreement, they have allowed the evolution of U.N. peacekeepers to take an active role in such conflicts.

The Changing Character of War

The character of war is changing from the historical image of military conflicts between nations. One study found that fewer than 10 percent of contemporary warring conflicts are between nation states.[9] In part, this reflects the transition from Cold War tensions and wars of colonial independence to the emergence of widespread internal conflict and international terrorism. War in today's world is (1) not necessarily fought between nation states; (2) most likely to be fought over control of resources; (3) more likely than before to kill civilians in large numbers and to involve widespread violations of human rights; (4) more likely to threaten or to use weapons that can irreversibly alter the opportunity for continued life on the planet; and (5) more likely to be supplied by corporations that are international weapons specialists.

The contemporary players in violent military conflicts now often include groups of hungry and displaced refugees; revolutionary groups of peasants or workers who are losing their land and their means of livelihood; and militant bands of revenge seekers espousing the tactics of terror. Scarce resources often lead to violent ethnic conflicts. Typically, smaller armed groups are pitted against more powerful elite military units with high-tech weapons, paramilitary forces, and privatized military contractors.

The emerging form of conflict is often referred to as asymmetrical, based on the pronounced difference in organization, resources, and methods on the opposite sides of a conflict. In fact, asymmetrical warfare hardly takes place on a designated battlefield but instead erupts within the domain of ordinary social affairs. Massive military superiority is faced by the ingenuity of taking hostages, suicide attacks, car bombs, blowing up pipelines, attacking symbolic targets, or nonviolent opposition. Asymmetrical warfare is similar in purpose to colonial oppression but is also different in significant ways. At present, oppression is less easily concealed, and oppressed people now have more access to information from other parts of the world that things can be different. Asymmetrical military styles and strategies are accompanied by the disintegration of a boundary that has traditionally removed violent warfare from the public landscape. This heightens public fear and insecurity, clearly a factor leading to extremism by all parties involved. The threat of biological warfare, terrorist attacks, and nuclear arms capabilities are gradually slipping beyond the control of national governments. This change in the destructive capacity of weapons, and in their distribution, has paved the way for dramatic increases in military preparedness, particularly in the United States.[10]

Where major powers have agreed, U.N. peacekeepers have played some role in limiting the scope of conflicts. Yet global corporations that provide weaponry and logistics are typically active players in armed conflict, as are those global corporations that benefit from military protection of their assets and their expansion.

A categorically distinct form of "enemy" took the industrial world by surprise on September 11, 2001, and has led to extensive military violence by the United States and a domestic turn toward suppression of dissenters and restrictions on civil liberties. Such actions on the part of a world superpower provide inducements for the recruitment of terrorists.[11] Attacks against European and U.S. targets by groups from the Middle East share a connection with popular insurgencies in Latin America and in Africa.

The driving force behind much of contemporary warfare has been the expansion of the global economy (see chapters 3 and 4). Advances in transportation and communication have made possible the emergence of large multinational corporations with interests they wish to have protected by governments, over which they exert great influence. Much of modern war reflects that corporate interest and the opposition it has aroused. Just as corporate interests have become global so also have social movements grown to thwart corporate domination. Some, in fact most, are nonviolent, whereas others have taken on tactics of inflicting terror as an expression of the injustice they perceive.

Given this evolving history of armed conflict, it is impossible to be precise about how great the toll has been upon the human community. By any measure it is enormous. With increasingly powerful weapons, the risks now extend beyond the combatants to large-scale killing of civilians and to the destruction of habitats needed to support life in any form.[12]

The ability to make war and the extent of destruction in warfare depends upon the availability of weapons. Production levels of military weapons have reached record levels in the past five years, with worldwide sales and transfer agreements totaling $37 billion in 2004. Although patterns in arms transfers have shifted since the Cold War era, weapon sales and distribution remain concentrated on developing nations.[13] This extensive world market in weapons trade provides the means by which ethnopolitical wars are being fought.[14]

Destructive Capabilities of Weapons

The ways in which wars are conducted have been changing. Dr. Rosalie Bertell[15] observes a fundamental change in the nature of warfare: there have been exponential increases in the number of civilian deaths and the amounts of indirect damage to the health of communities and to the natural environment. Technological changes include advances in chemical and biological weapons. The capacity to wage biological warfare is widespread, and clandestine forms of transmission can protect its users from detection.[16] Bertell describes the evolution of such costs of combat over the past century:

> The use of toxic gas as a weapon (WW I), poisoning of waterways or air, and using chemicals in warfare broke the taboo against widespread and indiscriminative killing of non-combatants. This trend escalated during WW II through carpet bombings, the nuclear bombs and the V2 rockets. Then chemists, using the chlorine gas, separated for a WW I weapon, developed agent-orange and an array of pesticides, herbicides and defoliants, which attacked both people and the living earth itself. The military used these in the Vietnam War. Extensive use of land mines in Korea and elsewhere, prolonged wars beyond the truce, and now we have the firing of radioactive waste, depleted uranium, at an enemy prolonging the mutilation and killing for generations after the war is over.[17]

The after-effects of the Vietnam War, in particular the effects of the chemical warfare waged, will outlast the soldiers who fought the war. The most common chemical used in Vietnam was Agent Orange, a mixture of plant hormones used to kill vegetation. Along with Agent Orange were chemicals dubbed Agent Blue, Agent White, and malathion. During the years 1962 to 1971, the United States dumped 19 million gallons of Agent Orange over Vietnam. This chemical contaminated soil, vegetation, and all human and animal life in the area. These herbicides stay in the soil for decades before breaking down, and these chemicals can be passed down from generation to generation.

At first, information about Agent Orange was not available, allegedly withheld by the U.S. government. Later studies indicated that diseases such as cancer and liver dysfunction as well as severe personality disorders and certain birth defects might be traceable to Agent Orange. Not only is the person contaminated with Agent Orange affected, but their offspring as well may be victims of enlarged livers, kidney abnormalities, and cleft palates and may suffer early death. The environment in Vietnam has suffered greatly from the effects of this chemical warfare. Large areas that were once jungle are now covered with scrub and wild grasses. It is estimated that it could take centuries to recover.

The use of biological and chemical weapons has been illegal since the Geneva protocol of 1925. However, the polarized thinking that often accompanies war results in differing interpretations of both what has occurred and what is legal. Pentagon reports in November 2005 first denied that white phosphorus had been used against people in the battle of Fallujah. Later they insisted that it was only used against enemy combatants and that it was not a chemical weapon and therefore legal to use. Earlier declassified Pentagon reports, however, had accused Saddam Hussein's government of engaging in chemical warfare using phosphorous as a weapon.[18] The occurrence raises the issue of using a double standard. In a larger sense it raises the issue of whether there are respectable and disrespectable ways to kill one's enemies.

It is not possible to fix with money the damage done by these herbicides and chemicals; however, lawsuits have been filed against companies that produced Agent Orange during the war. So far, producers have paid over $180 million in class-action lawsuits. But the anguish was borne by people.

Nuclear Weapons

With all wars so far, suffering has been great. But until the advent of the atomic bomb, war did not have the capacity to end, for all time, the continuation of human beings as a species or to threaten the continuity of life itself. The atomic bombs dropped on Hiroshima and Nagasaki produced the greatest immediate mass death from individual weapons yet known. The threat of nuclear weapons, the most frightening violent force on the planet, seems to grow with restraints wholly inadequate to the extent of the danger. That psychological reality was expressed by President Kennedy:

> Today, every inhabitant of this planet must contemplate the day when this planet may no longer be habitable. Every man, woman, and child lives under a nuclear sword of Damocles, hanging by the slenderest of threads, capable of being cut at any moment by accident or miscalculation or madness.[19]

At a meeting of the National Academy of Sciences, former Secretary of Defense William J. Perry said, "I have never been more fearful of a nuclear detonation than now. There is a greater than 50 percent probability of a nuclear strike on U.S. targets within a decade."[20] Apocalyptic dangers like this, that we know exist but still ignore, continue to have an effect upon us. They push us away from a long-term connection to our planet, pressing us to live for the moment as if each moment might be the last.[21]

With government prodding, current public attention has focused upon the possibility of a nuclear weapon attack by terrorists. The RAND corporation carried out a broad-based scenario analysis to examine the impacts of a terrorist attack involving a ten-kiloton nuclear explosion in the port of Long Beach, California. A varied set of strategic forecasting tools were used to examine immediate and long-term results. It found neither the local area nor the nation were at all prepared to deal with the potential threat of a nuclear device being brought into the United States aboard a container ship. Long Beach is the world's third busiest port, with almost 30 percent of all U.S. imports and exports moving through it. The report noted that a ground-blast nuclear weapon detonated in a shipping container at Long Beach would make several hundred square miles of the fallout area uninhabitable, and such a blast would have unprecedented economic impacts throughout the country and the world. As one example, the report noted that several nearby oil refineries would be destroyed, in turn exhausting the entire supply of gasoline on the West Coast in a matter of days. This would leave city officials dealing with the immediate gas shortages and, according to the study, with the strong likelihood of related civil unrest. Blast effects would be accompanied by intense firestorms and by long-lasting radioactive fallout, all contributing to a collapse of local infrastructure. Impacts on the global economy could also be catastrophic. There are two main reasons. First is the economic importance of the global shipping supply chain, which would be severely hampered by the attack. Second is a well-documented fragility of global financial systems.[22]

By current standards, a ten-kiloton nuclear explosion represents a miniscule sample of the power of larger nuclear weapons now in the arsenals of a growing number of countries. It is difficult even to imagine what a larger nuclear strike would mean. Another former defense secretary, Robert McNamara recalls his experience during the Cuban missile crisis when the world came close to an escalating exchange of nuclear weapons launched by the United States and the Soviet Union against each other. In his sober warning many years later, McNamara cites a report by the International Physicians for the Prevention of Nuclear War, which describes the effects of a single one-megaton weapon.

> At ground zero, the explosion creates a crater 300 feet deep and 1,200 feet in diameter. Within one second, the atmosphere itself ignites into a fireball more than a half-mile in diameter. The surface of the fireball radiates nearly three times the light and heat of a comparable area of the surface of the sun, extinguishing in seconds all life below and radiating outward at the speed of light, causing instantaneous severe burns to people within one to three miles. A blast wave of compressed air reaches a distance of three miles in about 12 seconds, flattening factories and commercial buildings. Debris carried by winds of 250 mph inflicts lethal injuries throughout the area. At least 50 percent of people in the area die immediately, prior to any injuries from radiation or the developing firestorm.[23]

There is no reason to believe that a nuclear attack would use only one such weapon. Moreover, a one-megaton nuclear bomb is much lower in destructive capacity than most bombs now available on ready alert status. These larger weapons are capable of what George Kennan[24] has considered to be of such magnitude of destruction as to defy rational understanding. One twenty-megaton bomb exploded on the surface of Columbus Circle in New York would produce a hole where twenty city blocks had been—a hole deep enough to hide a twenty-story building. All brick and wood frame houses within 7.7 miles would be completely destroyed. The blast waves would carry through the entire underground subway system. Up to fifteen miles from ground zero, flying debris propelled by displacement effects would cause more casualties. Roughly 200,000 separate fires would be ignited, producing a firestorm with temperatures up to 1,500 degrees Fahrenheit and wind velocities to 150 miles per hour. The infrastructure of water supplies, food, fuel for transportation, medical services, and electric power would be destroyed. And radiation damages that destroy and deform living things would continue for 240,000 years.[25] Such bombs, and others still more destructive, are contained in the warheads of missiles, many of them capable of delivering multiple warheads from a single launch.

Following the collapse of the Soviet Union, nuclear weapon stockpiles far in excess of what would be needed to destroy all of the world's population have been reduced. There are still 31,000 nuclear weapons in the world, most of them American or Russian, with lesser amounts held by the United Kingdom, France, China, India, Pakistan and Israel. At least 5,000 of the United States and Russian nuclear weapons are maintained on hair-trigger alert, meaning they could be fired on fifteen minutes notice.[26] We now have the capacity to destroy for all time every person, every blade of grass, and every living thing that has evolved on this planet. But has our thinking evolved to enable us to prevent this from happening?

Without enforceable controls, nuclear weapons are proliferating. The number of nations that now have or are capable of developing nuclear weapons makes the risk of their use quite high.[27] Despite a public willingness to view the nuclear threat as past, failures to curtail the development and proliferation of nuclear weapons and to move toward nuclear disarmament leave humanity vulnerable to its own rapid extinction.[28] The information technologies so central to command and control of dangerous weapons are often penetrated by unauthorized sources.[29] A study by MI5, the British intelligence agency, found more than 360 private companies, university departments, and government organizations in eight countries in Asia and the Middle East to have procured goods or technology for use in weapons programs, suggesting that the nuclear-arms trade supermarket is bigger than has so far been publicly realized. MI5 warned against exports to organizations in Iran, Pakistan, India, Israel, Syria, and Egypt and to beware of front companies in the United Arab Emirates, which appears to be a hub for the trade.[30] The central role of Pakistan's black market in selling what is needed to develop nuclear weapons to several other countries has been documented.[31]

During the Cold War, Soviet and U.S. militaries played a dangerous game of making the threat to use nuclear weapons credible. In the 1950s fallout shelters were encouraged in the United States in order to convince USSR officials that we were prepared for an attack (or a counterattack). During a subsequent period, the use of submarines as launching sites and the hardening of missile sites to assure their capacity to retaliate even after an attack were intended to demonstrate the invulnerability of our weapons. Even if the population could be killed, the weapons would still be launched, and elaborate precautions were taken to keep missiles on hair-trigger alert and responsive to any minimal indicator that an attack might be forthcoming. The policy of Mutual Assured Destruction (MAD) did produce some very close calls: some by accidents in reading radar signals and others by playing the game of chicken, as in the Cuban missile crisis. Yet it was credited with preventing an all-out nuclear war.[32] Civilian strategists, unhappy with the standoff in nuclear weapons laid out plans for a gradual escalation of warfare moving from small provocations to exchanges of nuclear weapons. Their goal was no longer to defend people, but to prevail in the horrible game plan. The use of nuclear weapons against Vietnam was seriously considered by President Nixon and his Secretary of State Henry Kissinger. Kissinger considered it immoral to ignore options to have smaller nuclear wars instead of relying upon a big one.[33] Public opposition to nuclear weapons most likely prevented their use at that time.

Few people realize that the United States spends $100 million a day maintaining its nuclear weapons. More resources now are committed to the development and testing of nuclear weapons than were spent (using constant dollar comparisons) at the height of the Cold War. The dangers of this activity are protected by a culture of secrecy at the weapons laboratories.[34]

The U.S. national obsession with nuclear weapons (an expenditure of approximately $40 billion on them annually, and more than $7 trillion to date) is a significant drain on collective resources that might otherwise be put toward education and scientific research pertaining to medical, economic, or genuine security needs. There are many sites, but Los Alamos, a $2.2 billion annual sinkhole for nuclear weapons research, design, and production, represents the most obvious example of this obsession with military spending.[35]

The Comprehensive Nuclear Test Ban Treaty was the result of endless hours of negotiation by leaders of nations with and without nuclear weapons to assure that nuclear weapons would be eliminated forever as tools of warfare. The nonproliferation treaty requires that nations without nuclear weapons refrain from developing them. It also insists that negotiations for elimination of nuclear weapons on the part of nuclear powers should be held in good faith. By rejecting the treaty, the United States is holding open the door to resumed nuclear testing. This has greatly worried many non–nuclear weapons countries and has already led to charges that the United States is acting in bad faith.

Periodically, the United States reviews its policies on nuclear weapons; it did so in 2001, the results of which have been cause for alarm. The National Resources Defense Council, a prestigious nonprofit organization of scientists, lawyers, and environmental specialists described the plan:

> Behind the administration's rhetorical mask of post-Cold War restraint lie expansive plans to revitalize U.S. nuclear forces, and all the elements that support them, within a so-called 'New Triad' of capabilities that combine nuclear and conventional offensive strikes with missile defenses and nuclear-weapons infrastructure.[36]

According to the council's analysis, the Bush team assumes that nuclear weapons will be part of U.S. military forces at least for the next fifty years; it plans an extensive and expensive series of programs to modernize the existing force. Plans include a new ICBM (intercontinental ballistic missile) to be operational in 2020 and a new heavy bomber in 2040. In addition, the U.S. administration has ordered the Pentagon to draft contingency plans for the use of nuclear weapons against at least seven countries, naming not only the "axis of evil" (Iraq, Iran and North Korea) but also Russia, China, Libya, and Syria.[37] The Pentagon, in addition, has launched programs for research and testing of a missile defense system. While technically dubious, the large program has been viewed by other nations with alarm as a signal that the United States is working toward being able to attack other countries with the security that it could intercept missiles sent in retaliation. Such planning has the obvious consequence of provoking other nations to develop their own arsenals, a process already taking place. Russia and China have responded with plans for new or updated development for nuclear weapons. Without enforceable controls, nuclear weapons technology is spreading.[38]

The danger in rejecting plans for the reduction, monitoring, and elimination of nuclear weapons is great. This is compounded by the contradictory roles of the International Atomic Energy Commission (IAEA), being at one and the same time the promoter and the policeman of nuclear energy. Promoting nuclear energy leads more states to develop technical capacities that then offer a temptation to use them for military ends. In Iraq, Libya, and North Korea, the IAEA has not been successful in detecting military programs or in preventing their development. Furthermore, it appears to be helpless when faced with a U.S.

administration that is determined to develop new types of nuclear weapons and is willing to consider using them in preemptive strikes. If the world is to avert nuclear war, the inspection powers of the IAEA will have to be reinforced and made applicable universally.[39] Why the dangers of current policy are being ignored in defense planning is the subject of chapter 6.

Human Consequences of War

The consequences of war occur during its preparations, in its actual military actions, and in its aftermath. These costs are to life, to property, and to security. They are experienced by soldiers and their families, with scars remaining long after hostilities have ended. The costs are also borne by civilians who are injured, killed, and forced to be child soldiers as well as by refugees displaced by the destruction of their homes and cities. The costs are to societies that expend their resources and their ingenuity upon the development of ever-more-destructive weapons and the training of people to use them.[40] The costs include living with realistic fear that weapons capable of levels of destruction so great as to threaten the continuation of all life will be used and will produce a final and fiery end to everything we hold dear.

Numbers are inadequate to portray the human cost of war. With every death, dreams and hopes are lost and families are broken. Yet numbers are all we have to provide a context for the size of the problem at hand. We begin with the soldiers and other victims of wars in Vietnam and Iraq. Among wars since World War II, the Vietnam War took the lives of more than 2 million Vietnamese and approximately 58,000 U.S. soldiers. It began with a U.S. effort to maintain an unpopular pro-U.S. regime in South Vietnam and ended with a withdrawal of U.S. troops. The war was approved by Congress and based upon a reported attack upon a U.S. destroyer, which did not actually occur. It would be difficult to say what worthwhile objective was accomplished or even whether something positive might have been claimed if its outcome had been different. It is also unclear what has been learned from the experience.

So far, more than 3,500 U.S. soldiers have been killed in Iraq, and more than 30,000 have been wounded. More than 650,000 Iraqis have been killed in the war, and hundreds of thousands of lives have been devastated. The reasons offered for this military action have changed several times. As with Vietnam, each setback has been met with a call for even greater military involvement.

The U.S. soldiers who fought in these wars were typically from lower- or middle-class backgrounds, distinguishing them from the government officials who had decided to engage in the war. Soldiers had either been drafted into service or, since the end of the draft, attracted to join by recruiter promises of education and job training that they could not pay for elsewhere. The highest recruitment rates (defined as the number of recruits per thousand of the eighteen- to twenty-four-year-old population) were found in counties that were relatively poorer than the rest of the nation. The top twenty recruitment counties had median household incomes below the national average. Nineteen of these ranked below the median average in their own states. The schools providing the greatest number of recruits were those offering GEDs. No part of their recruitment or training described for the recruits the likelihood of their own death, the consequences to their families, or the effects that the experience would have upon them for the remainder of their lives. In contrast, the upper classes, who benefit most economically from war, have been practically absent from military service.[41]

Soldiers after War

Soldiers who return from war do not come home unscathed. At the same time that the Department of Defense noted that reaching the figure of 2,000 U.S. soldiers to die in the Iraq war was of no special consequence, there were already 15,220 soldiers wounded, approximately half with a major injury. Johnny Dwyer's photo essay in the *New York Times Magazine* in March 2005 described what the word *casualty* actually denotes: "deep flesh wounds, burst eardrums, shattered teeth, perforated organs, flash burns to the eyes, severed limbs."[42] The images have a powerful impact that is greater than our typical images of survivors. Although the injured soldiers may have survived, their dreams—of playing sports, going to college, walking on the beach—will not. Ten percent of the wounded Iraq war soldiers had experienced head injuries, and many of these will suffer brain damage. Another 10 percent of the wounded will return with spinal cord injuries. Six percent will be amputees, double the historic norm. "You live," says Lieutenant Colonel Craig Silverton, an orthopedic surgeon, "but you have these devastating injuries." "Somebody's got to pay the price," says Colonel Joseph Brennan, a head and neck surgeon, "And these kids are paying the price."[43]

Not counted in the casualty figures are soldiers who will suffer long-term psychological trauma of combat they have experienced. During the Vietnam War these psychological effects became so common that the mental health category of post-traumatic stress disorder (PTSD) was created. The symptoms include persistent anxiety or increased arousal that were not present before the trauma, a persistent reliving of the traumatic event, hyper-vigilance, sleep disturbance, nightmares, a numbing of emotions, feelings of estrangement, an inability to experience intimacy, withdrawal from feelings of connection to the outside world, and an avoidance of frightening reminders. They sometimes involve heightened fearfulness, amnesia, irritability, and outbursts of anger.[44]

The National Vietnam Veterans Readjustment Study[45] provided a report more than a decade after hostilities had ceased. Among American Vietnam theater veterans 30.9 percent of the men and 26.9 percent of the women were found to have PTSD. This is more than six times the rate found in the general population for men and more than twice the amount found for women. An additional 22.5 percent of men and 21.2 percent of women reported having some of the symptoms of PTSD at some time in their lives. Thus more than half of all male Vietnam veterans and almost half of all female Vietnam veterans—about

1,700,000 Vietnam veterans in all—have experienced "clinically serious stress reaction symptoms."

Many years after the end of the Vietnam War, at the time of the study, 15.2 percent of all male Vietnam veterans (479,000 out of 3,140,000 men who served in Vietnam) and 8.1 percent of all female Vietnam veterans (610 out of 7,200 women who served in Vietnam) were still suffering from PTSD. The report revealed other problems: family life suffered. Forty percent of Vietnam theater veteran men were divorced at least once (10 percent had two or more divorces), 14.1 percent reported high levels of martial problems, and 23.1 percent had high levels of problems as parents.

Of the male Vietnam veterans who were presenting the symptoms of PTSD at the time of the survey, almost half had been arrested or in jail at least once, 34.2 percent had been arrested more than once, and 11.5 percent had been convicted of a felony. This might be expected, given that many returned bearing the weight of serious trauma but with training in how to use a gun. Among male veterans, 39.2 percent had experienced alcohol abuse or dependence and 11.2 percent were still reporting serious alcohol problems approximately fourteen years after hostilities had ended. Drug abuse or dependence among male veterans was also substantially higher than the national average, and treatment facilities have never been sufficient for the number of cases needing help.[46]

Because the NVVRS sample size underrepresented members of certain ethnic minorities, the Matsunaga Vietnam Veterans Project[47] undertook further research with Native American, Asian American, and Pacific Islander veterans. The project involved two studies. The American Indian Vietnam Veterans Project surveyed a sample of Vietnam veterans residing on or near two large tribal reservations, one in the Southwest and the other in the Northern Plains. These populations had sufficient numbers of Vietnam military veterans to draw scientifically and culturally sound conclusions about the war and readjustment experiences.

The Hawaii Vietnam Veterans Project[48] surveyed two samples, one of Native Hawaiians (the indigenous peoples of the Hawaiian Islands, who constitute about 22 percent of the permanent population in Hawaii) and another of Americans of Japanese ancestry (the descendants of Japanese immigrants who comprise about 24 percent of the permanent population in Hawaii). Native Hawaiians and American Indians were more likely than any other survey group to receive combat service medals in recognition of their hazardous combat duty. The Matsunaga Study's[49] key finding is that exposure to war-zone stress and other military danger places veterans at risk for PTSD up to several decades after military service. Native Hawaiian and American Indian Vietnam veterans had relatively higher levels of exposure to war-zone stress and high levels of PTSD.[50]

The Persian Gulf War was depicted in the press as an example of strategic military success with "smart" directed weapons and few casualties. But the weapons were less smart than described, and the human consequences were tragic. Approximately 697,000 U.S. veterans served in the Gulf War, and more than

263,000 have since sought medical care at the Department of Veterans Affairs.[51] Over 185,000 filed claims with the Veterans Administration for service-related medical disabilities, including significant physical and psychological distress that they attribute to their participation in the operation. A significant number of Gulf War veterans reported unexplained physical symptoms that arose during or after their service.[52] Some of these symptoms include memory and attention losses, chronic fatigue, muscle and joint pain, gastrointestinal distress, and skin rash[53]; and many veterans feared that the military's use of biological agents is the cause of these symptoms. Some research has begun to identify chemical agents and other substances as possible explanations for the physical and psychological symptoms of Gulf War illness.[54]

The unusual set of symptoms led the Centers for Disease Control (CDC) to create a classification for Gulf War illness. It consisted of three distinct symptom types: fatigue; mood and cognition problems (e.g., feeling depressed, moody, or anxious, having difficulty remembering or concentrating, having trouble finding words, having difficulty sleeping); and musculoskeletal problems (e.g., joint pain or stiffness and muscle pain).[55]

Since then, one comprehensive study examined the mental health impact of the wars in Afghanistan and Iraq.[56] Soldiers reported on their experiences in the war zones and their symptoms of psychological distress. The results indicated that the estimated risk for PTSD[57] from service in the Iraq war was 18 percent, and the estimated risk for PTSD from the Afghanistan mission was 11 percent.

Soldiers in Iraq are at risk of being killed or wounded, are likely to have witnessed the suffering of others, and may have participated in killing or wounding others as part of combat operations. All of these activities have a demonstrated association with the development of PTSD. Hoge[58] found that 94 percent of soldiers in Iraq reported being targets of small-arms fire. In addition, 86 percent of soldiers in Iraq reported knowing someone who was seriously injured or killed, 68 percent reported seeing dead or seriously injured Americans, and 51 percent reported handling or uncovering human remains. The majority, 77 percent, of soldiers deployed to Iraq reported shooting or directing fire at the enemy, 48 percent reported being responsible for the death of an enemy combatant, and 28 percent reported being responsible for the death of a noncombatant. An additional set of unique stressors stems from the fact that much of the conflict in Iraq, particularly since the announced end of formal combat operations, has involved guerilla warfare and terrorist actions from ambiguous and unknown civilian threats. In this context, there is no safe place and no safe role. Soldiers are required to maintain an unprecedented degree of vigilance and to respond cautiously to threats. There is great concern that soldiers will mistakenly think civilians who mean them no harm are actually combatants. Soldiers also need to be careful about possibly causing collateral damage to civilians in urban environments.[59] U.S. soldiers are clearly at grave risk in Iraq and continue to suffer even after they come home. Troops returning to the United States are suffering from PTSD and are even turning up in homeless shelters in cities throughout the country. Military medical officials place a premium on teams of mental health experts to help deal with the effects of engaging in battle. Lieutenant General Kevin Kiley claims that in the modern age, such mental health experts are "worth their weight in gold." Clinical scientists have now developed methods for documenting the psychological effects of engaging in battle. In the case of the war in Iraq, the army's surgeon general reports that 30 percent of troops had developed mental health problems three to four months after returning home.[60] Penny Coleman's sensitive study followed the lives of widows, like herself, of returned veterans who had received inadequate treatment for their emotional scars and had committed suicide. The long-term results for these veterans, their families, and their communities continue to be felt even across generations. Coleman also provides evidence of the government's failure to respond properly to and treat the disorder.[61] One review of this book by an Israeli woman suggests the universality of the larger issue that governments, including her own, take little heed of the long-term psychological costs of war.

Participation in combat activities is not the exclusive source of danger and stress in a war zone. There is some evidence that the stress of war is associated with an increase in sexual assault and sexual harassment with both male and female soldiers at risk for this type of victimization. In one survey 30 percent of women veterans from Vietnam through the time of the first Gulf War said they were raped in the military. A 2004 study of veterans from Vietnam and all the wars since, who were seeking help for PTSD, found that 71 percent of the women said they were sexually assaulted or raped while in the military.[62]

In addition, a variety of environmental factors specific to each mission may contribute to the risk of mental health problems in veterans. For example, factors such as poor diet, severe weather, and deficient accommodations will affect soldiers' responses to war-zone deployments. Extensive time away from family members and the disruption of occupational goals may serve as severe stressors, particularly for National Guard and reserve troops. The lengthy separations of soldiers have serious effects upon their spouses and children as well.[63] In contrast, some soldiers may find meaning and gratification in their helper roles in Iraq and Afghanistan, which can potentially buffer the impact of some war-zone stressors.

Children and War

Soldiers might arguably be said to have agreed to take part in war. This cannot be said of children, who are the largely forgotten but deeply affected victims of armed conflict. The noise, the unpredictable outbursts of weapons, the loss of parents and siblings, and the destruction of familiar settings appear in the stories and the dreams of children who have been in war zones. A UNICEF (United Nations Children's Fund) study of 5,835 children in Croatia following the war in Kosovo showed 49 percent with PTSD, a legacy of suffering and a ground for future victims and perpetrators of violence.[64] In Angola, civil war raged for twenty years. It followed a history of colonial oppression and was fanned by rivalries between superpowers and the international traffic in small arms. In some regions 88 percent of the population were displaced from their homes. An estimated 4.8 million children were affected, 1.5 million were displaced from their homes, and more than half had lost one or both parents. Famine, disease, and massive social disorganization contributed in this case to high rates of PTSD. A study of survivors confirmed that their symptoms were even more severe than those of children from other war zones, reflecting the effects of sustained and repeated trauma.[65] It is important to note that PTSD is a category designed by, and for use of, mental health professionals in a Western culture. What it describes does not apply equally to all cases. Particularly, its lack of attention to cultural factors in how people think, feel, and respond to trauma merits a precaution; its cross-cultural use in diagnosis and treatment may be severely limited without attention to the specific cultural and historic experiences.[66]

Child Soldiers

A blurred line between soldiers and civilians has extremely dangerous consequences for children who are also made to fight. Government armies, warlords, rebel groups, paramilitaries, and other militarized groups throughout the world include an estimated 300,000 children, defined under international law as people under 18 years of age.[67] The acts of recruiting, coercing, and outright forcing of children to engage in military violence are a global phenomenon. Between 2001 and 2004, children were soldiers in twenty-eight countries, in some of which multiple groups recruited children. The use of children as soldiers often reflects an explicit decision by those who recruit them. Child soldiers are targeted because they are cheap and convenient, and many children have no other options.[68] They differ from adults who elect to join in a war.

Even in the most voluntary of circumstances, can a young child really be considered a soldier? Does the decision of a ten-year-old represent the high moral ground that we so often attribute to military service? Many of these children have been born into and spent the bulk of their lives immersed in war zones, and they may become habituated to violence as a way of life. In these environments of extreme fear and powerlessness, the money, protection, food, medical care, and education afforded by military recruiters is irresistible. Subject to the deepest forms of oppression, children and young teens may also respond particularly favorably to the rhetoric of military groups attempting to overthrow unjust parties.[69]

The behavior of child soldiers is easily molded by the complete control of rewards and punishments. Where there are no alternative sources for understanding human relationships, violent behavior becomes easily hardened into the ideology of the military culture.[70]

Civilian Casualties: Collateral and Targeted

The deaths of war are not confined to soldiers. The ratio of civilian to service casualties climbed steadily over the course of the twentieth century, reaching a staggering ratio of 9 to 1 in the 1990s.[71] As many as 90 million civilian deaths occurred during war over the course of this one-hundred-year period.[72] Civilians are not asked whether they want to participate in a violent conflict that might kill them. In wars fought between the armed forces of competing nations, civilian casualties are looked upon as unintended collateral damage.[73]

Satellite-guided air-to-surface munitions were created as smart bombs to select military targets and minimize civilian damage. Of the 29,199 bombs dropped during the Iraq war by the United States and United Kingdom, nearly two-thirds (19,040) were precision-guided munitions (PGMs). In the Gulf War in 1991, 8 percent of all bombs dropped were PGMs; in Yugoslavia in 1999 approximately one-third were PGMs; in Afghanistan in 2002 approximately 65 percent were PGMs.[74] The intent was to target opposing leaders—Milosevic, bin Ladin, or Hussein—without excessive harm to civilians. A report by Human Rights Watch[75] reveals just how persistently they were used to try to kill individual Iraqi leaders in this manner, and how consistently they failed. Over the course of the war, U.S. air forces mounted fifty so-called decapitation strikes. The bombs accidentally killed dozens of civilians who happened to be near the explosions, but they killed *none* of the Iraqi leaders they were intended to strike, largely because of faulty intelligence.[76] Although both war and genocide usually result in the deaths of numerous innocent civilians, genocide is always considered a crime whereas war is often considered just.[77]

The civilian casualties that occurred in the air war in Iraq came despite the use of a high percentage of precision weapons. But in other forms of military violence, civilians are the targets. Much of contemporary military violence no longer fits the pattern of wars on designated battlegrounds by the armed forces of conflicting nations. The suicide bombing of the World Trade Center on September 11, 2001, presented the first occurrence of a tragedy of this magnitude that was perpetrated by a small group of individuals. The event highlighted the concept of terrorism in the popular culture. Certainly the bombs that exploded over Hiroshima and Nagasaki claimed many more civilian lives. But until that date, one might have taken all the individual mass murderers, all of the serial killers the world has known, and found their victims to number in the hundreds. Even with that event, the more dramatic numbers of victims of terror are killed by sources other than deranged or obsessed individuals or criminal bands. The real mass murderers, by contrast, produce victims by the thousands and tens of thousands, many times dwarfing in number the tragic losses from the attack on the World Trade Center. Bombing buildings, assassinating leaders, destroying access to food or water, and shooting people in warfare are not easily distinguished from the same acts used more sporadically by nongovernmental groups. The big-time murderers and terrorists are on the loose. They are called governments.

Neither terrorism nor formally declared wars are random violence. Terrorism is "the (calculated) use of violence for political goals."[78] It is "a form of violence (or warfare) directed primarily against civilians, rather than the uniformed military, police forces or economic assets. It is used by both governments (against their own people or other countries) and insurgents."[79]

Terrorism gained attention when the Jacobin's rule, following the French revolution, introduced a reign of terror. Robespiere noted in 1773 that "Terror is nothing but justice—prompt, severe and inflexible."[80] In the months that followed, the severe and inflexible guillotine severed the heads of 1,200 people, including Robespiere's. Since then, the power of states to inflict a domestic reign of death and terror has been expanded. The Soviet Union under Stalin, Germany under Hitler, and the United States under many administrations in the slaying of Native Americans are among the most destructive examples.[81] The regime of Mao Zedong in China, holding power over one quarter of the world's population, was claimed to be responsible for 70 million deaths in peacetime. This was more than occurred under any other regime in the twentieth century.[82] The form that took clear shape in the second half of the twentieth century was described in the "Terrorism and Human Rights" progress report prepared by Ms. Kalliopi K. Koufa, Special Rapporteur, of the United Nations, June 27, 2001:

> State terrorism in the form of "regime" or "government terror" is characterized by such actions as the kidnapping and assassination of political opponents of the government by the police or the secret service or security forces or the army; systems of imprisonment without trial; persecution and concentration camps; and, generally speaking, government by fear. . . . This type of bureaucratized terror intimidates, injures and abuses whole groups, sometimes whole nations, and it is the type of terrorism that historically and today produces the most harm. . . . A further point that deserves particular mention is the role of the law in the reification and legitimacy of "regime" or "government terror." In fact, "regime" or "government terror" is exercised according to the law that the public authorities have themselves created.[83]

The term *desaparecido* became part of the 1966 human rights vocabulary in Guatemala to describe people who vanish after being taken into custody by government officials, or with the acquiescence of government officials, and for whom the authorities claim no knowledge of their whereabouts. A second type of terrorist activity is the extrajudicial execution. These are unlawful killings performed at the behest of a government without an individual being found guilty of any crime. Such political killings are frequently performed by the government either directly or indirectly through paramilitary groups. The ingenuity of the barbarity commonly involved suggests the complete impunity of the perpetrators. It reveals also the underlying goal of intimidation of dissent. Trade unionists, human rights activists, community leaders, lawyers, and teachers are frequent targets. But often targets are bystanders, street children whose hunger and homelessness is bothersome or people who just happen to be in the wrong place.[84] Over the past half-century, there have been numerous instances of state terrorism. Here we have selected examples from Guatemala, Colombia, and Cambodia. Together they illustrate the modern face of war.

Guatemala

Following decades of colonial rule, the first free election in Guatemala produced a leftist reformer as president. This was followed by a coup, assisted by the U.S. Central Intelligence Agency (CIA), returning the country to military rule in 1954. After the invasion, the government systematically destroyed the country's former communist and social democratic leadership. Peasants, labor activists, and intellectuals by the hundreds were subjected to detention, torture, and sometimes death. Many were forced into exile or to withdrawal from political activity. Any sign of opposition was vilified and labeled communist. The Guatemalan case was one of the best documented through collaboration of the International Center for Human Rights Investigations and the American Association for the Advancement of Science.[85]

The CIA assisted successive military leaders—Armas in 1954, Fuentes in 1958, and Peralta in 1963—to gain power in Guatemala. Elections were promised again in 1966. Twenty-eight members of the labor party (PGT), lured out of hiding by hopes of a fair election, disappeared and their bodies were never found. When Mendez Montenegro, a university law professor, was elected president, he was forced to sign a decree granting the military the right to fight against its opponents without interference from civilian authorities. U.S. military advisors supervised the bombing of villages, and government forces were responsible for the killing or disappearance of many civilians. Estimates of civilian deaths between 1966 and 1968 varied from 2,800[86] to 8,000.[87] Under U.S. guidance, the army organized a powerful military force and a network of counterinsurgency surveillance that would continue for more than thirty years. It would be used both to battle guerrillas and to control, in brutal fashion, the civilian population. Paramilitary death squads carried out much of the activity. Some were security forces dressed in civilian clothes. Others were private thugs of the extreme right. The secret nature of these groups created terror but also gave the police and the army an opportunity to deny responsibility.[88]

In 1970 the army candidate, Colonel Carlos Arana, became president. He created a counterinsurgency plan to exterminate the guerrillas and their supporters, and a state of siege was declared. Legal protests against a corrupt government contract with a Canadian nickel-mining concern were met with mass arrests and with occupation of the University at San Carlos. Death squad attacks against law school professors and other leaders followed. Killings and disappearances exceeded those of the late sixties. After the leadership of the outlawed labor group PGT were tortured and killed, opposition subsided, but not before the formation of the National Front Against Violence. This group of University students, church groups, opposing political parties, and workers called for human rights and constitutional rule.[89] Arana's handpicked successor, Defense Minister Lucas Garcia, trying to gain public acceptance after a fraudulent election, permitted a degree of labor and popular organizing. State violence declined for a brief time, and a group of K'che and Ixil Indians found the courage to come to

Guatemala City in 1980 to protest the kidnapping and murder of nine peasants. They were joined by a student group but were not well received. Their legal advisor was assassinated outside of police headquarters, and when they occupied the Spanish Embassy, the police attacked, trapped them inside, and watched both protestors and hostages burn to death.[90]

Guerrillas began to harass the army and then retreat to the mountains. Typically they had substantial civilian support, since the guerrillas had worked closely with the peasant population, as many of whom had come from those communities. Increasingly, the military viewed unarmed villagers as participants in the insurgency. "Operation Ashes" clearly stated the government's program of mass killings and burning houses, crops, and farm animals as well as the scorching of entire villages.[91] The mass killings included children, women, and the elderly in a strategy that General Rios Montt called "draining the sea that the fish swim in." During almost four years under President Lucas Garcia, the government was responsible for more than 8,000 killings and disappearances in what Amnesty International labeled a "government program of political murder."[92] Ethnic factors were central, since the majority Mayan population were viewed as less than human and suffered casualties in even greater proportion than their number in the population.

General Rios Montt took power in a military coup in 1982. The U.S. Congress, which had cut off military aid to Guatemala in 1977, switched to restore aid at President Reagan's request. The aid came with assurances that the general could fight the war as he saw fit, without concern for human rights and without fear of losing the funding. With extensive military support from the United States, the military effort escalated. In remote villages the policy was toward overkill: beheading their victims or burning them alive, smashing heads of children on rocks, and commonly raping women even when pregnant.[93] In the fourteen months of Montt's rule, 10,000 documented killings or disappearances occurred, although press censorship reduced the reporting of these at the time.[94] The proportion of unnamed victims rose dramatically from the previous era. Nonetheless, President Reagan described Rios Montt in December 1982 as "a man of great personal integrity and commitment . . . who is totally dedicated to democracy."[95] The killings, torture, and kidnappings became fewer but more selective under the regimes that followed. The remarkable efforts of peasant women in Guatemala and of students have helped to bring some attention and efforts at accountability to an appalling case of state terrorism.

Colombia

The term *democra-tatorship* is used to describe the current Colombian amalgamation of democratic forms and state terror. In a continent severely marred by human-rights abuses, Colombia has compiled the worst record of the past twenty years.[96] Assistance in training and arming the Colombian military has come from Britain, Israel, and Germany, but particularly the United States.

Father Javier Giraldo, director of the Commission of Justice and Peace, published a report that documented atrocities during the first part of 1988. These included 3,000 politically motivated killings, 273 of which occurred in "social cleansing campaigns." In Colombia's cities, "social clean-up operation" is the official term for a night in which police or their collaborators murder drug addicts, homosexuals, prostitutes, vagrants, street children, and the mentally ill. In the larger cities—Medellin, Cali, Barranquilla, and Bogota—the assailants often gun down victims from motorbikes or trucks. Other times groups are rounded up and forced into trucks, their often-mutilated bodies later found in rubbish containers or on the roadside. Accurate figures on such killings are difficult to determine. Many of the victims are unknown, and most deaths go unregistered and unreported. One human rights group recorded 298 murders by death squads in the eight months of their study in 1992.[97] Despite the fact that that Colombian police use their arms to inflict terror, American aid has continued supporting the Colombian government. War against the guerillas and narco-trafficking operations is the official State Department explanation for U.S. involvement. These groups were blamed for all of the violence. In 1989 President George H. W. Bush announced the largest shipment of weapons ever authorized under the Emergency Provisions of the Foreign Assistance Act. From 1988 to 1995, 67, 378 Colombians (an average of 23.4 per day) were assassinated. The number of victims of political violence in this Colombian "democracy" far exceeds the combined number of political killings in Uruguay, Argentina, Brazil, Bolivia, and Chile during their years under military dictatorship. The Truth and Reconciliation Commission in Chile registered 2,700 politically motivated murders during the seventeen years of its brutal military dictatorship. This horrible statistic is, however, far less than the number of cases reported annually in Colombia for each year between 1986 and 1995.[98] Kidnappings by the revolutionary armed forces of Colombia have continued, as have the massacres by right-wing paramilitary groups such as United Self-Defense Forces of Colombia (AUC in Spanish), which continues even after agreements to desist, to conduct massacres of villagers.[99]

Cambodia

A similar pattern of state terror emerged in force when the United States promised not to interfere with, but in fact supplied weapons to, the military government of Indonesia in the brutal suppression of East Timor. It was seen in Iran after a CIA-initiated coup brought in the police state methods and the military support for the shah. One of the worst cases of domestic military brutality occurred in Cambodia, under a government opposed by the United States. After the massive U.S. bombing of Cambodia and U.S. assistance in the overthrow of the popular Prince Sihounuk, the United States supported the unpopular rule of Lon Nol. The Khmer Rouge overthrew Lon Nol and sought to eradicate the severe destitution by a cruel set of reforms. In a plan similar to one that had been used by the United States in Vietnam, suspect village leaders were deposed and replaced by Khmer loyalists. Angkar, or "organization on high," provided a justification to commandeer vehicles, to order people out of hospitals, and to kill. Purges and massacres were commonplace. At their center was the Tuol Sleng School in Phnom Penh, which was converted for purposes of interrogation, torture, and execution. Records found when the Khmer Rouge fled showed that many of its victims included Khmer supporters.[100]

Of 14,499 people held there, only four survived. Norkobal, the secret police system, replicated the death machine in the provinces with a far greater numbers of executions. Roughly 66,000 bodies were found in three provinces in 1981. In 1982, 16,000 bodies were found in the Kampot province in 386 mass graves. But uncounted numbers were buried in the 1,400 mass graves in the province.[101] Only a few illustrations of state terrorism are presented here. Others, including the prolonged occurrence in East Timor, will be referred to in later chapters. But the inhumanity of this form of military activity is clear. The numbers are hard to comprehend. Each victim was robbed of the right to life in a social system that orchestrated their destruction. The death and the destruction in war destroy, for noncombatants as for soldiers, the only lives that each of them will ever know.

People Displaced By War

Violent conflict forces people to leave their homes and countries. Family members are lost, and means of subsistence are destroyed. By the end of 2004 there were 13.2 million known refugees (4 million of whom are Palestinian). They represent less than half (48 percent) of a larger group including political exiles, asylum seekers, and people internally displaced within their own countries. A vast majority of refugees are women (80 percent), many with young children.[102] Today, 25 million would-be refugees from conflict are found within their home countries. A new strategy of containment has emerged that prevents many refugees from finding a welcome in developed countries. The number of internally displaced people (IDPs) is estimated at 25 million people, displaced from fifty different countries affected by conflict. More than 3 million people were newly displaced in 2002 and were forced to leave their homes because of human-rights violations or threats to their lives. In 2003, 12,800 unaccompanied and separated children applied for asylum in twenty-eight industrialized countries. The largest numbers came from war-ravaged areas in Angola and Afghanistan, both countries with a history of civil war with weapons supplied by the United States and the former USSR.[103]

Land Mines

For all those killed by war, there are many more who are seriously damaged by it. Antipersonnel land mines are particularly insidious sources of death and disability that continue long after actual combat has ended. After hostilities end, soldiers are typically demobilized and turn in the weapons issued to them, but land mines do not recognize a cease-fire. A land mine cannot be aimed. It lies dormant and concealed until a person or an animal triggers its detonating mechanism. Then land mines kill or injure civilians, soldiers, peacekeepers, and aid workers alike. Children are particularly susceptible. Mine deaths and injuries over the past decades total in the hundreds of thousands. An estimated 15,000 to 20,000 casualties are caused by land mines and unexploded ordinance each year. Some 1,500 new casualties are reported each month—more than forty new casualties a day. The numbers are an underestimate since some countries with land-mine problems, such as Myanmar (Burma), India, and Pakistan, fail to provide public information about the extent of the problem.[104]

More than eighty countries are affected by land mines or unexploded ordinance. Some of the most contaminated places are Afghanistan, Angola, Burundi, Bosnia and Herzegovina, Cambodia, Chechnya, Colombia, Iraq, Nepal, and Sri Lanka. Most of the casualties are civilians and most live in countries that are now at peace. In Cambodia, for example, there were 57,000 civilian casualties—18,000 killed and almost 40,000 land-mine survivors—recorded between 1979 and 2002.[105] From 2002 through June 2003, there were new land-mine casualties reported in sixty-five countries; the majority (forty-one) of these countries were at peace. Only 15 percent of reported casualties in 2002 were identified as military personnel. In 2002 the greatest number of reported new casualties were found in Chechnya (5,695 casualties recorded), Afghanistan (1,286), Cambodia (834), Colombia (530), India (523), Iraq (457), Angola (287), Chad (200), Nepal (177), Vietnam (166), Sri Lanka (142), Burundi (114), Burma/Myanmar (114), and Pakistan (111). Significant numbers (over 50) of new land-mine casualties were also recorded in Bosnia and Herzegovina, Democratic Republic of Congo, Eritrea, Ethiopia, Georgia, Laos, Palestine, Senegal, Somalia, and Sudan. Once triggered, a land-mine blast causes injuries such as blindness, burns, destroyed limbs, and shrapnel wounds. Sometimes the victim dies from loss of blood or from lack of timely medical care. Survivors often require amputations, long hospital stays, and extensive rehabilitation. Land-mine injuries are not accidents, since the devices are designed to maim rather than kill their victims. Survivors need care, but Landmine Monitor has identified at least forty-eight mine-affected countries where one or more aspects of assistance are reportedly inadequate to meet the needs of mine survivors.[106]

Land mines deprive people in some of the poorest countries of land and destroy infrastructure. They hamper reconstruction and the delivery of aid and delay the repatriation of displaced people. In addition, land mines kill or incapacitate the breadwinners of families and communities while assistance to land-mine survivors places an enormous strain on resources. Mines kill livestock and wild animals and wreak environmental havoc. They remove land from food production because the mere suspicion of their presence turns a patch of land into a human danger zone.[107]

As of September 2005, 154 countries have signed on to the 1997 Convention on the Prohibition of the Use, Stockpiling, Production and Transfer of Antipersonnel Mines and on Their Destruction. Forty countries, including Russia, China, and the United States, have not signed on. Some antipersonnel land mines are from earlier conflicts. They claim victims in many parts of the world. Although the situation has improved in recent years, it nevertheless constitutes a global crisis. Antipersonnel land mines are still being planted today, and mine-fields dating back decades continue to claim innocent victims. Vast stockpiles of land mines remain in warehouses around the world and a handful of countries still produce these weapons.[108]

Material and Human Costs of Preparedness

Preparedness for war has been costly. The United States spent $10.5 trillion dollars on the military during the Cold War.[109] The nuclear powers of that time spent an estimated $8 trillion on their nuclear weapons.[110] If current annual U.S. expenditures for nuclear weapons were instead invested into global life-saving measures, the result could have covered *all* of the following: the elimination of starvation and malnutrition, basic shelter for every family, universal health care, the control of AIDS, relief for displaced refugees, and the removal of land mines.[111] Money that was spent to harden missile sites or to develop missiles that might someday shoot other missiles from the skies might have been spent to strengthen the levees along the Mississippi River, already known to be inadequate long before hurricane Katrina.[112] Meanwhile, the war has meant that precious resources are being channeled toward destruction in Iraq instead of into programs that could save people's lives and meet their basic human needs. When hurricane Katrina struck, 6,000 members of the Louisiana and Mississippi National Guard were watching the catastrophe unfold from 7,000 miles away. About 40 percent of Mississippi's National Guard force and 35 percent of Louisiana's were in Iraq at the time.[113] If the National Guard troops and equipment from Mississippi and Louisiana hadn't been in Iraq, they could have responded more quickly to the devastation wreaked by hurricane Katrina, and lives could have been saved. The United States is pouring more than a billion dollars a week into the Iraq war that could otherwise be spent on health care, schools, and infrastructure here at home.

As with actual military violence, the costs of preparing for war are not just monetary. The development of nuclear weapons, apart from their use, has been a source of violence that deeply affects public health. The costs have often been concealed or minimized by public officials. On July 12, 1990, newspapers carried an announcement by Secretary of Energy James Watkins confirming, one day in advance of its official release, a report of an occurrence of dangerous exposure to radiation. The report noted that Richland, Washington, the area of the Hanford Nuclear Research Facility, had indeed been the site of a release of radioactive iodine serious enough to affect the health of people. Secretary Watkins noted that we might have placed a number of persons under health risks. An accurate estimate of how great the health consequences, and to how many, still awaits the findings of a study by the National Centers for Disease Control in Atlanta. Secretary Watkins's announcement, however, was careful to note that the particular radioactive emissions occurred during a period when hazards of radiation were poorly understood. "As years went along, we got a little smarter. I don't want you to relate it to what's going on today."[114] And surely he did not wish us to do so. What the secretary wished to assure us is that the occurrence of subjecting our own citizens to a serious risk was a singular unforeseeable incident from which current scientific knowledge and the advanced technologies of today now offer protection.

This proposition is cast into serious doubt by a long history of developing dangerous technologies with little regard for their consequences. Reviews of technological development suggest precisely the alternative to Secretary Watkins's thesis, that is, the health consequences are not isolated instances of accidents caused by an early but now corrected ignorance. Rather, these human tragedies are the sometimes intended, frequently rationalized, denied, or ignored and sometimes unintended consequences of the technological society. These consequences, rather than affecting isolated victims, are ubiquitous, and the technological hazards are contributing to our collective health problems at an accelerating and alarming rate.[115]

The report released the day following Secretary Watkins's announcement indicated that 13,700 residents or 5 percent of a ten-county population surrounding the Hanford Nuclear Reservation in Eastern Washington State had absorbed a dosage of radioactive iodine 1,200 times the level of airborne contamination that the Department of Energy (DOE) now considers safe for civilians living around its nuclear weapons plants.

The amount of radioactive absorption far exceeded the amount absorbed by Ukrainian citizens at Chernobyl and was 26,000 times the absorption at Three-Mile Island. Hundreds of thousands of residents in Washington, Oregon, and Idaho were, according to the report, continually and secretly exposed for a quarter of a century to large quantities of radiation from the air, from drinking water, and from food. Some 400,000 curies of radioactive iodine were released as a byproduct when irradiated uranium fuel rods were dissolved in acid to extract plutonium, the key component of nuclear weapons. The nine reactors at the 560-square-mile Hanford reserve were cooled by river water, returned again to contaminate major fish-hatching areas and drinking water, while airborne radiation descended upon farmlands, exposing cattle and returning radioactivity through their milk to children in the surrounding areas.[116] The report is as frightening in its implications about the government as in its conclusions about the victims.

A half-century after the Hanford facility's work on plutonium for the nuclear weapons program has ended, the site remains on the Environmental Protection Agency superfund list as among the most serious toxic sites in need of clean up. Bechtel Corporation has the contract to turn millions of gallons of radioactive waste into glasslike logs to be stored in 177 underground tanks. The project was shut down in the summer of 2005 because of seismic problems, rising costs, and delays. After it was resumed in September, 600 workers had to be sent home following the third safety problem in a week.[117]

Increases in radiation exposure beyond natural background levels have serious consequences for health. The research of Dr. John Gofman and others indicates that there is no safe dose of radiation.[118] Increases in rates of cancer and birth defects have occurred around each of the eighteen nuclear weapons facilities in the United States and around the sites in Nevada and the Marshall Islands, where nuclear weapons have been tested. Radiation is but one example of the health hazards that derive from the testing and use of substances that kill. Toxic chemicals released into the environment have similar effects. Between 1973 and 1998 cancer in the United States increased by 22.4 percent. This occurred during a time of added public awareness of the value of diet, exercise, and skin protection. In the United States more than 80,000 chemicals are produced or imported, some in the agricultural, automotive, and computer industries and some in military preparedness. Toxic chemicals, many known carcinogens and many not yet studied for their toxic effects, have found their way into our food, water, and atmosphere and then into our bodies. Increasing evidence shows that even small doses can have significant effects, sometimes causing increases in rates of sterility, stillbirths, genetic deformity, respiratory problems, and several types of cancer, particularly among children.[119] Other studies show that the risk increases directly as a result of the amount of exposure to radiation.[120]

Years after Hanford was preparing plutonium triggers for nuclear weapons, it became a clean-up project. Hanford is the most contaminated work site in the Western world, and the DOE has not performed its safety mission well. People who worked on this clean-up effort have been suffering serious health consequences and filing complaints that they had been misled. A report by the Government Accountability Project[121] documents the DOE's pattern of interference with Hanford workers' claims, its inability to effectively oversee Contract Claims Services Incorporated, and its ongoing failure to resolve concerns that workers have raised since 2000, when the compensation program became self-insured and the DOE became responsible for reviewing workers' claims. Yet, when workers seek medical care and compensation for their workplace illnesses and injuries, the DOE often challenges and obstructs their claims and fails to provide them access to objective assessment and medical treatment. One worker testified at the DOE's June 2005 state-of-the-site meeting, "I've seen people sick and lied to. You say public safety? Do you think the public trusts in you guys? Your workers don't even trust you."[122] The casualties of war preparedness come even when weapons are not used, and the casualties of work with dangerous weapons, like the casualties of war, get little attention.

The twentieth century was the bloodiest in all of human history. The astonishing scale and intensity of violence occurred at the same time when advances in science, technology, and economics were making people, on average, better off than ever before—eating better and living longer. The world in 1900 offered a prospect of greater human opportunities. The major reason for the surge of violence was likely the economic boom and bust volatility, which tore apart communities and then used racial differences to assign scapegoats. Technology made larger-scale violence possible. The century also was the stage for a struggle between decaying empires and aggressive new states. Some talk of the result as a triumph of the American century. But a stronger case can be made that the outcome is the decline of Western dominance.[123] Yet, in the new century the United States remains a key player in global violence.

United States Responsibility

The U.S. is both the largest beneficiary of global inequality and the world's specialist in weapons. Networks of key corporate and government officials perpetuate both the gross income disparities and dominance in weapons. United States policy has often been guided by an assumption that interests defined by the United States take precedence over international agreements. This has occurred first in matters that might constrain United States military activities.

For example, in August 2001, the United States withdrew from a major arms-control accord, the 1972 Antiballistic Missile Treaty. In July 2001 the United States walked out of a conference to discuss adding on-site inspectors to strengthen the 1972 Biological and Toxic Weapons Convention, which was ratified by 144 nations, including the United States.[124] Meanwhile, United States preparations to use chemical and biological weapons at Fort Dietrich and other sites have been extensive.[125] The United States was the only nation to oppose the U.N. Agreement to Curb the International Flow of Illicit Small Arms. The Land Mine Treaty (banning mines) was signed in 1997 by 122 nations, but the United States refused to sign, along with Russia, China, India, Pakistan, Iran, Iraq, Vietnam, Egypt, and Turkey. Clinton's promise that the United States would "eventually" comply in 2006 was disavowed by President George W. Bush. In February 2001 the United States refused to join 123 nations pledged to ban the use and production of antipersonnel bombs.[126]

U.S. policy also dismisses legal accountability for its international actions. The International Criminal Court (ICC) Treaty was created in 2002 to try political and military leaders charged with war crimes against humanity. The ICC treaty was approved by 120 countries, with only seven, including the United States, opposed. In December 2001 the U.S. Senate amended a military appropriations bill to exclude U.S. military personnel from the jurisdiction of the ICC. The U.N. General Assembly passed resolutions for the last ten years calling for an end to the U.S. embargo on Cuba, the last by a vote of 167 to 3 (the United States, Israel, and the Marshall Islands in opposition).[127]

The powerful position of the United States has permitted its stand as the protector of corporate prerogatives in the face of economic or environmental threats and even concerns for human rights. In 2001 the United States refused to participate in the Organization for Economic Cooperation and Development talks on ways to remove offshore tax and money-laundering havens. The United States alone opposed the G-8 group of industrial nations in a clean-energy plan. Where human rights might have some consequence for military or corporate dominance, the United States record again stood out. In the U.N. Human Rights Commission, the United States stood virtually alone in opposing resolutions supporting low-cost access to HIV/AIDS drugs, acknowledging a basic human right to adequate food, and calling for a moratorium on the death penalty. The United States was not reelected to the commission in 2001.[128]

There are over 639 million small arms and light weapons in the world today, approximately one gun for every ten people on the planet. They are used both in war and to perpetrate acts of murder, rape, and torture. These weapons often act as catalysts for cycles of conflict and poverty in many of the world's most impoverished areas. Strict control measures are needed, but weapons dealers have found an almost unlimited market. The U.N. General Assembly in 2006 approved a resolution for a global arms trade treaty by a vote of 153 to 1, with 24 abstentions. The United States cast the only opposing vote.

The United States is responsible for almost half the weapons sold worldwide, and 70 percent of those are supplied to developing countries.[129] International Narcotics Control programs provide another channel for the United States to fund military equipment and training to overseas police and armies. Serious human-rights abuses by units that receive this aid have intensified criticism of the program, requiring Congress to pass restrictions.[130] Any theory of contemporary global economic and military violence should address all of the issues raised by such data.

Wars are not accidents. They are products of a social order that plans for them and then accepts this planning as natural. The system that sustains war and other forms of global violence is the system that will have to change if we are to stop the massive killing involved both in war and in economic exploitation. A social order that humans have created must now be transformed if a world that sustains life and enriches the human experience is to survive. The study of violent conflict confronts us repeatedly with frightening facts. We gain power by considering our painful awareness as an important step in a process of change. If we choose to ignore these facts, the facts will return to haunt us.

Chapter 2

Killing: War and the Minds of Men

> The need today is for a gentler humankind, for the hand that wielded the axe against the ice and the saber-toothed tiger now cradles the machine gun equally as lovingly.
>
> —*Ethologist, Konrad Lorenz*

> And when the drums of war have reached a fever pitch and the blood boils with hate and the mind has closed, the leader will have no need in seizing the rights of the citizenry. Rather, the citizenry, infused with fear and blinded by patriotism, will offer up all of their rights unto the leader and gladly so. How do I know? For this is what I have done. And I am Caesar.
>
> —*William Shakespeare, Julius Caesar*

Chapter 1 looked at the devastating consequences of war. Unlike costs of natural disasters, these costs result from decisions by humans that inflict suffering and death upon others. Among all forms of destructiveness, war is unique in the manner in which it is justified. A declaration of war gives a state the recognized right to order people to conquer, to destroy, and to kill. Considering the consequences, why do we do it? The gains from war are questionable. Historian Barbara Tuchman's *The March of Folly: From Troy to Vietnam*[1] details a history of the human propensity to engage in violent wars. This history of bloodshed includes numerous cases in which the potential gain for any of the participants was small compared with the costs. In large measure the reason wars are fought is to be found in the institutions that humans have created. A detailed review of U.S. wars since World War II shows that most have produced unintended consequences detrimental to the United States.[2] They will be examined in later chapters. For now, we focus upon one contributing factor: the human capacity for inflicting violence.

War and Human Nature

Examples can be found of societies that have been relatively free of violent warfare for long periods of time. These cases are few, and many lie outside of the dominant societies modernized in the Western image. The Fore of New Guinea, for instance, provides an example of a society with no history of warfare and very little expression of physical violence.[3] One study selected seven examples that met five criteria of a peaceful society: no war on its territory, no involvement in external war, no civil or internal war, no standing military, and little or no interpersonal violence. All of the societies were small, and all had some exchanges with outside groups. All also contained some changing memberships. None had a strong pattern of an elite ruling lineage. Although some were able to accumulate surpluses beyond their immediate needs, the surpluses were used for the benefit of the group as a whole.[4] These exceptions from societies that engage in war may be few, but they are nevertheless important. They show that major violence in societies, although common, is surely not universal. This bears upon a question debated within the field of psychology: Does human nature make war inevitable? Cruel, selfish, and violent activities appear to be as fundamental a part of human nature as creative, caring, and cooperative actions. Aggressive inclinations may contribute to war but do not mean that wars are inevitable. Still, human aggressiveness is important. This chapter deals with one psychological aspect of what makes war possible—the capacity and the motivation of humans to be aggressive and to kill other humans.

In the natural world, animals devour other animals. But killing other members of one's own species is uncommon, and attempts to destroy an entire rival colony are rare. Competition between different bands of lemurs or chimpanzees does occur, but most of the fighting is bluff, and battles never have the ferocity or carnage of human warfare.[5] People, it appears, are distinguished as a species by their capacity to kill large numbers of their own kind as well as by their symbolic representations of reality. These two characteristics may be related. The symbols define for us a reality in which killing others is sometimes seen as necessary. Symbols are not simply word representations of objects, what Suzanne Langer has called *discursive* symbols. They include also *presentational* symbols, or larger sequences of meaning only understandable within a broader framework. The more complex of these presentational symbols include songs, stories, musical compositions, healing ceremonies, and religious rituals. The most comprehensive of these larger life symbols are the prevailing myths about who we are as human beings and as members of larger groups. Myths provide a framework for our beliefs and lead to ritual practices that are observed with the force of religion.[6]

The exceptional cognitive capacities demonstrated by humans have come late in the evolutionary process. We often fail to recognize how the systems of beliefs, or presentational symbols that human have evolved, reflect tribal origins of human societies. We evolved in small bands that were vital to our individual survival. We have only recently in our evolutionary history created formal representations of teams, corporations, social movements, and nations that sometimes replace the identifications and the loyalties to our own clan or tribe that once helped us to survive.

The Human Psyche as a Source of Killing

Humans, more so than other species, construct in memory extensive maps using symbols of whom and what they have experienced. The symbols are arranged, sometimes even distorted, to preserve congruity and a positive image of the self. Such cognitive maps provide a guide to living with safety and satisfaction of needs. From the time of infancy, the stored images are assigned to different categories, the most primitive being the distinction between what is nurturing, comforting, and good and what is stressful, distasteful, or painful.[7] As images of the world grow increasingly complex, there remains a common tendency, more pronounced in some people, to continue to divide all things about them into good or bad. This basic psychological mechanism is helpful in explaining preoccupations with good and evil as well as the need for enemies.[8]

The evolved tendency for humans to use presentational symbols to categorize ourselves into nations, religions, and other symbolic groups serves both to fortify a positive self-image and to find purpose and meaning in existence. This process, however, leads to a strong identification of the individual with the symbolic group, a connection often stronger than the individual's identification with the species as a whole. Such group attachments lead, in turn, to a sense of separation and a value judgment as to the worth of the group, with some groups clearly assigned to categories of good and others bad. The tendency to identify with one group over another sets the stage for group comparisons and rivalries. Such identities often pit one group against another and are used to justify ultimate purposes in war. These highly evaluative ideations raise the question of whether we can create belief systems in which the deep moral attachments we seek can be to all of humanity, even to all of life.

Central to each person's store of images is a concept of the self. Human selves vary greatly in the qualities we believe that we have. But almost universal is the need to look upon the self as good, worthwhile, and deserving to live. That self can be deeply threatened, but we are prone to reinterpret information that is dissonant. We seek congruity or consistency among our stored images, and we engage in much reinterpretation of experience in order to keep our self-concept surrounded by images of good people and separated from images of bad ones.

We have survival mechanisms that allow us to experience overwhelming psychological trauma, to repress such images from awareness, and then to move on. Although hidden, the buried memories continue to affect the human psyche, exaggerating fears of potential reminders and affecting perceptions of what is dangerous. The buried traumas increase our propensities both to deny danger on one hand and to picture ourselves as brave and invulnerable on the other.

Particularly when our self-concepts are deeply affected by trauma, and we are sitting atop repressed memories of our own violent or disdainful motives and behavior, we become impassioned defenders of our self-concepts and vindictive opponents of those we see as bad. One common way this occurs is through the mechanism of projection. Aspects of our own self, too ugly or reprehensible to be admitted to ourselves, can more easily be seen in the attributes of others. Meanness to scapegoats can be justified as doing away with evil while never admitting evil intentions of our own. For some, the accommodation needed to feel secure about oneself requires domination over other people. Certain conditions—the granting of permission from higher authorities, the routinization of violent practices, and the dehumanization of the targets—frequently permit this violence to occur without moral restraint.[9]

A degree of aggressive motivation appears in many species and among all cultures. Yet all cultures that have endured have fostered strongly internalized restrictions on killing other people. Sanctions against wrongdoers are universal, but most restraint from violent behavior occurs because of the sense that is not right in one's own eyes or in the eyes of one's group. People undergo disappointments, frustrations, and betrayals. They experience rage, sometimes out of proportion to the degree of inconvenience or the strength of the transgression against them. Aggressive expressions such as cursing, bullying, blaming, and ridiculing are common among humans. But most people do not, on their own, typically inflict upon others the extreme physical violence associated with war. Inhibitions against harming others do need to be learned, and this typically occurs in the immediate family environment.[10] A major aspect of such learning is the development of empathy, the ability to identify with the feelings of others almost as if they were one's own.[11] So also does the willingness to kill need to be learned. The learning process that encourages violence also occurs in families but continues in other institutions charged with molding human personalities and shaping behavior.

The antithesis to empathy is an internalized hatred of people different from oneself. Frequently found among self-trained militias are groups such as neo-Nazis or skinheads. These are typically men who have received military training, are fascinated with guns, have few options for more constructive work, and believe in a racial purification through violence.

The Contexts of Killing

There are individual differences in the willingness to inflict pain or to kill. Because we have learned that this is wrong, those who readily engage in such behavior often reflect a history that has blunted their capacities for empathy. Individuals who are more prone to violence find inducements to act violently in a culture that accentuates individual achievement and seeks retribution against evildoers. The designation of some people as evildoers who must be found, imprisoned, or killed is a major theme in the way behavior is interpreted.

But this interpretation reflects what psychologists have long studied as attribution error, the tendency to ascribe behavior to the enduring characteristics of individuals while ignoring the circumstances that are often the more important factor. The Nazis, who committed brutal and genocidal killings of unprecedented magnitude, are viewed as pathological killers. Yet, in her study of the Nazi storm troopers, Hannah Arendt noted that the most remarkable thing about the Nazis was how like the rest of us they were.[12] Compelling evidence supports the view that the capacity to engage in evil or harmful behavior lies within all of us and that surrounding circumstances play the major role in releasing violent behavior.[13]

Even when viewing killing at the level of individual homicide, we find convicted killers do not all share the same personality type. Some fit the image of strong, mean, aggressive, impulse-driven males with little sign of sensitivity or compassion for others. But another group of first-time homicides are committed by people who are more androgynous or feminine, gentle, shy and with no prior record of violence.[14] In a famous series of experiments, Milgram[15] showed that ordinary American citizens could be induced into administering harmful electric shocks to strangers under circumstances in which the experimenter explained to them that this was what they should do. Remarkably, administering even a potentially lethal shock could be induced among most subjects, males and females, across all ages and educational levels. Ninety percent of the subjects would deliver the shock if the experimenter said it was okay, if they saw their peers doing it, and if the victims were presented as being in some way inferior.[16] According to Zimbardo,[17] a contractual agreement, verbal or in writing, contributes to the willingness to justify immoral violence. One critical factor is the cover story that what is being done is for a really good cause. The depictions of Panama's Manual Noriega as a brutal drug lord and of Iraq's Saddam Hussein as a dictator stacked with concealed weapons of mass destruction are examples of cover stories that were false but nevertheless helped to legitimize violence. Another major factor is the promise that the cruel activity can be done anonymously and without individual identification. The cloak of the hangman and the uniforms of soldiers contribute to such anonymity. Societies that mutilate their victims in warfare typically provide masks to their warriors.[18]

The people behind the cloak appeared on Christmas Eve 1914 on a World War I battlefield in Flanders. As the British and French troops were settling in for the night, a young German soldier began to sing "Stille Nacht (Silent Night)." Others joined in. The British and French responded by singing other Christmas carols. Eventually, the men from both sides left their trenches and met in the no man's land between them. They shook hands, exchanged gifts, and shared pictures of their families. Informal soccer games began, and a joint service was held to bury the dead of both sides. The generals on both sides were displeased by what had happened. Men who have come to know each other's names and seen each other's families are less likely to want to kill each other. War often seems to require a nameless, faceless enemy.[19]

If we adhere to the view that severe violence is caused by evildoers or individuals predisposed to do bad things, then our responses are limited. We might choose to force the perpetrators of violence to conform to agreed-upon social norms. We might kill them in retribution or punish them as a threat, and as a warning to others, of what will happen if they continue the violent behavior. Or we may incarcerate them so that they cannot attack the rest of us. The view that violent behavior is explained by an inherent individual disposition of the perpetrator removes the option of rehabilitating the individual and allowing for a restoration for the harm committed. The view that violence is caused by personal predispositions serves a comforting function because it defines an impermeable line between good people (us) and bad ones (them). In all cases, if the individual is to blame, we take society off the hook.[20]

Dehumanization and Enemies

We humans retain long-term conceptions of others, some of whom are known personally, others known only by the images of these others offered to us by secondary sources. An intriguing experiment by Bandura[21] shows how easy it is to set up negative images of an unknown group. In this case it was just overhearing some derogatory comments. People acted upon this information by applying greater punishments (more intense shocks) to the negatively represented group than to others. To engage in killing other humans, or to sanction such killing, we make use of a capacity to withdraw a human connection to the target person or group.

Dehumanization is a composite psychological mechanism that permits people to regard others as unworthy of being considered human. On a conscious level it can be fostered by blinding hatred and by appeals to hate a particular evil adversary. Beneath the level of awareness, dehumanization permits us to resolve self-doubts by finding a scapegoat as the target for blame. Psychiatrist Robert Coles offers an insight into the psychological advantages to be obtained from dehumanizing a designated enemy: "We crave scapegoats; targets to absorb our self-doubts, our feelings of worthlessness and hopelessness."[22]

For many, dehumanization invades our perceptions by a process of desensitization. What is repulsive at first becomes barely noticeable after numerous repetitions. A distancing abstraction can also reduce the impact. Statistics may numb, but they do not bleed. The brutal destruction of a person may leave a disturbing image, but accounts of thousands killed can take on an abstract quality that is more easily put aside. Robert Lifton[23] developed the concept of psychic numbing to explain the detachment that occurs as people contemplate mass destruction in the genocidal extermination of people or in coping with the threat of nuclear war.

Dehumanization may also be fostered by the process of dissociative thinking. The symbolic worlds that we construct are not always within our own awareness. Competing images of reality sometimes coexist in the same individual. Certain states of mind provide a view of reality in which our fears, our anger, and our fantasies take the center stage of our thinking. Within such altered states we experience aspects of reality that transcend our typical thoughts and feelings. Such dissociative states can help people connect to the world in spiritual ways that promote healing at every level. Dissociative states also give people an opportunity to act out within a distorted reality in which moral inhibitions fade and killing another person becomes acceptable, even wonderful.

Olek Netzer describes a *direct causation* approach to explain how wars can happen. He looks upon multicausal theories that consider imperialistic ambitions, the deprivations of poverty and gross inequality, or historical rivalries as abstractions. In contrast, the direct and most concrete cause is that one human being pulls a trigger or gives an order that immediately destroys another. For this to occur, the target must be transformed from a complete human to a less-than-human enemy. This process of dehumanization is considered central.

> If all other contributing factors remained equal but people would just not conceive shooting, bombing, burning and killing as an option to solve their problems with other people, there could be no war. Thus, by only describing events taking place in the nonverbal world, we arrive at an awareness that is very uncommon in our and other cultures: the real causes of wars are not abstract but living people.[24]

Dehumanization constitutes a justification system within one's beliefs that destroying an inherent evil is not the same as killing a human being. People whose ordinary reality contains sharp inhibitions against inflicting violence may switch into an alternative reality that permits killing and even genocide. And because people define their identities by their connection with larger entities, a group belief can turn this alternative reality, in which killing enemies is permissible, into one that seems normal and necessary. That is an essential aspect of military training. An absolute authority structures the soldier's boot-camp reality, and killing is turned into beating enemies with the technical commission of skilled tasks. Proving masculinity is considered to be critical to the self-concept and the measure of success.[25] One American soldier told a reporter how, from the top down, there was little regard for the Iraqis, who were routinely called "hajjis," the Iraq equivalent of "gook." "They basically jam into your head: 'This is hajji! This is hajji!' You totally take the human being out of it and make them into a video game. If you start looking at them as humans, then how are you gonna kill them?"[26] The dehumanization is not restricted to enemy soldiers. Following such atrocities as the Mai Lai massacre in Vietnam, a generation before, U.S. marines in Haditha murdered twenty-four civilians, including children and infants. Examples of such barbarity are typically used to incite fear and anger against enemies. The theory that such acts are the work of a few "bad apples" is inconsistent with the circumstances that Milgram showed can release such actions from most of us. The soldiers were under heavy pressure from authorities to capture or kill insurgents. They felt pressure from peers to seem tough and to avenge the deaths of comrades. And they had been trained to dehumanize.[27] The systematic inculcation of the righteousness of a cause and the dehumanization of a grotesque enemy are needed. Soldiers would not perform as effective killers if their training helped them to recognize that they are not killing the ogre but rather others like themselves who have been oppressed by the ruler the soldiers have been taught to despise.

The process of dehumanizing the enemy, common to all training of soldiers, shares certain important elements with the training of young people to become suicide bombers. That program utilizes a variety of social psychological and motivational principles to assist in turning collective, often frenzied, hatred into a dedicated, seriously calculated program of indoctrination and training for individuals to become youthful living martyrs.[28] Distance from the target enhances such detachment. Ethologist Konrad Lorenz[29] observed that perfectly good-natured men who would not raise a hand to punish a child could nonetheless drop incendiary bombs on sleeping cities, committing thousands of children to a death in flames. Often the professional distancing of high-tech killing is contrasted to what are called barbaric practices of kidnapping people or decapitating them. This raises the issue of whether there are respectable and disrespectable ways to kill one's enemies.

The Dehumanization of the Culture

Netzer's[30] point about the importance and immediacy of dehumanization at the moment of pulling the trigger is well taken. The combat soldier is less guided by ideology than by loyalty to immediate comrades and the willingness to destroy an adversary with the necessary detachment to act quickly upon orders. However, abstract beliefs related to the self-concepts of individuals also become quite real sources of motivation, particularly for those who support a war from a distance. Nation states, like religious and ethnic groups, are abstract concepts made somehow real, and even sacred, by people's identifications with them. We are reinvested in our love for such abstractions in times of war. The display of flags jumped dramatically after the attack of September 11, 2001. The French, even french fries, were ridiculed when the French government did not support the invasion of Iraq. We are also, at such times, easily coaxed toward dehumanization of enemies. Many who do not lift a gun feel perfectly fine about calling for the blood of an enemy. Fear and hatred in the words of the larger society provide a cover for the heroic but deadly service of the actual combat soldier.

Beneath the surface recognition of courage and heroism, wars involve a form of ritual sacrifice. Joanna Bourke's[31] account of the justifications for such sacrifice during World War I is entitled *Dismembering the Male.* She supports a view about the male body in war, that it was intended to be mutilated. Although wars are looked upon as vehicles for defense, for conquest, and for legitimized violent action, their inevitable consequence is injury and death. The society, according to Bourke, encourages the soldier's delusion of masculine virility and calls him a hero in order to lure him into becoming a sacrificial victim.

Dehumanization constrains our world of experience. Macy and Brown attribute many of the ills of our culture to the blinding but compelling power of psychic numbing:

> [F]ragmentation and alienation, escapist pursuits, addiction, random violence, political passivity, blaming and scapegoating, suppression of vital information . . . a sense of powerlessness and burnout. These effects in turn create more to exclude from our consciousness.[32]

In times of war, dehumanization may become part of a larger social reality. The Dalai Lama's observations on warfare capture the basic concern:

> The unfortunate truth is that we are conditioned to regard warfare as something exciting and even glamorous: the soldiers in smart uniforms (so attractive to children) with their military bands playing alongside them. We see murder as dreadful, but there is no association of war with criminality. On the contrary, it is seen as an opportunity for people to prove their competence and courage. We speak of the heroes it produces, almost as if the greater the number killed, the more heroic the individual. And we talk about this or that weapon as a marvelous piece of technology, forgetting that when it is used it will actually maim and murder living people. Your friend, my friend, our mothers, our fathers, our sisters and brothers, you and me.[33]

Human beings are drawn to war, according to LeShan[34], because it is one of two means by which humankind is able to soothe one of its unique tensions: the simultaneous desire to belong to a group and be a unique individual. The other means is by esoteric or spiritual development, which provides a sense of connection with all forms of life and the ecology that sustains them. LeShan believes that such spiritual development, because of its rigor and discipline, is not accessible for most humans. Others see the spiritual path as readily within people's grasp but rather clouded by the complex flow of everyday commotion. War thus appears as an attractive alternative to resolve this tension.

Different Realties

Wartime and peacetime tend to involve two very different perceptions of reality. During peacetime, perceptions of reality are more likely to permit shades of gray. In wartime, reality is more likely to become one of black and white, good and evil, them and us. LeShan names three different specific perceptions of reality: the sensory, the mythic, and the magical. The *sensory* perception deals with the ordinary experience of everyday living. In contrast, the *mythic* introduces a reality in which larger-than-life forces take center stage and command an absolute dedication to a given idea. There is also a *magical* reality in which supernatural forces are felt to play a key role in our destinies. Each of these is used at different times with different effects, and most people are experts at switching from one to the next or even existing in different worlds of reality simultaneously. We are such experts that the shift between one and another takes place without our realizing.[35]

War tends to invoke the mythic reality characterized by the presence of absolute good and evil. The two forces are pitted against each other in what is experienced, as an ultimate battle, which we come to believe will result in either everlasting happiness or everlasting horror. Moreover, this reality tends to involve abundant optimism that good (generally "us") will inevitably triumph over evil. Hitler's writing and speeches used metaphors to construct a culturally shared mythic reality in which the German nation was one body, a pure living organism, that was being contaminated by a parasitic force within. The Jew was depicted as a germ, a threat to the existence of a pure and superior race, thereby making possible the death camps, gas chambers, and crematoria that followed.[36]

There are differences but also similarities between the fantasy presented as reality by the Nazis and current depictions of nationalism in the United States. The United States rides a history of manifest destiny. Shortly after the American Revolution a U.S. congressman, Giles of Maryland declared, "We must march from ocean to ocean. . . . It is the destiny of the white race."[37] Such notions of superiority are echoed in the sentiments of the document the "New American Century" that came to guide U.S. policy at the turn of the twenty-first century.[38] The document, prepared by men who rose to positions of great power during President George W. Bush's administration, set a course for U.S. policy undeterred by the needs and concerns of others (see chapter 6). Its message to the world is that we do not need to understand them; they need to understand us. We are the world's sole superpower.

Patriotism and loyalty can be consistent with healthy societies that do not encourage killing. Pride in the familiar landscapes and the idealistic heritage of a nation or group can be experiences that enrich life and provide for the common good. But much of current nationalism in the United States celebrates form over substance. On Independence Day flags, fireworks, and food are celebrated rather then the Bill of Rights or the heritage of the revolutionary idea that governments should derive their just power from the consent of the governed. "The troops" as an abstract entity are elevated to a mythic status while the realities of their work, their losses and the long-term consequences they will bear, are lost.[39] Beyond the period of outright warfare, the mythic reality is maintained by a culture espousing militarism. The economic and institutional complexities of militarism will be discussed in chapters 5 and 6. One definition includes the ideological or value dimension:

> The term "militarism" describes a society in which war, or preparation for war, dominates politics and foreign policy. Soldiers and military-minded civilians become a governing elite dedicated to expanding the military establishment and inculcating martial values.[40]

From the perspective of cultural beliefs that facilitate the process of dehumanization among individuals, militarism can be likened to a disease. We see it in a narcissism that discounts the existence of others. Its cultural symptoms include addiction to war, a timid media willing to be the propaganda outlet for officials favoring war, and the worship of soldiers through pageantry.

Sometimes both sides in a conflict invoke a magical reality, that God (or the gods) will intervene miraculously on one's side. Even without supernatural intervention war often overrides both the hassles of personal life and the disheartenment that comes with the tedious nagging problems of illness, job insecurity, a weak economy, natural disasters, and the perpetual reminders that success requires that we must have more than we already possess. When war is in the air, presidents assume the role of defenders. Sometimes the casualties and horrors of the war are reported. But in the largest media outlets, it is the excitement of cracking down upon an evil enemy that is conveyed.

LeShan[41] explains how human beings tend to shift from one reality to another. When people run out of logical solutions to a problem that they feel must be solved, they unknowingly switch to another reality. A switch into a mythic mode can quickly resolve a crisis in conscience over killing. A key example is the use of strategic language by politicians to shift public opinion towards the mythical worldview where endless battle against an evil enemy makes perfect sense. The visceral reactions of needing to fight and to win in order to survive are enhanced by a mythic reality that is itself hidden. Outside of the myth, the sensory reality might compel us to consider the human and financial costs that war will entail and the needs that will go unmet as a result. The sensory modality might call upon us to speak directly with adversaries to find options to war. Most important, the sensory reality might raise the value of human lives, each one precious in its own right, that will be destroyed by armed conflict. This might enable us to consider that the particular war being promoted would clearly be folly. The ease of moving to mythic reality, or even of using reasoning abilities selectively to justify a war mentality, is one factor that makes war so pervasive and so capable of destruction beyond its original intent.

Killing and dying may be viewed as sacrificial rituals by which absolute devotion to the state is reaffirmed.[42] The mythic reality permits a romantic version of war in which mindless euphoria pushes poorly prepared youngsters to a likely death. It permits a lust for violent bloodletting that relies upon calls for honor. It offers an opportunity for people to participate in a larger cause, and in so doing the ordinary problems of the day seem to disappear. The attractions of this mythic reality arise in part because the alternative reality includes choice, decisions, and responsibility. Many fear the uncertainties that come with freedom. Choice comes with responsibility, with a risk of failure and of blame. Reliance upon a strong authority figure provides a measure of escape and relief. War, like the stern father, provides an escape, a temporary source of certainty.[43] With such certainty, people follow the urging of leaders to indulge in massive slaughter, as was illustrated in the rise of Nazi Germany. Three groups are relevant to the permission to kill in war: those who kill as soldiers; those in an elite sector of society who plan, prepare for, and decide upon military action; and those in the larger society who support such activity.

The Experience of Combat

The path to combat as a soldier begins with their enlistment. Varying motivations for enlisting include a desire to fight, a patriotic obligation to support a leader's call to defend one's country, and the best choice available to escape from a background offering neither affordable education nor hope for a meaningful life. In poor communities military recruiters offer young people employment, training, a sense of belonging, and an opportunity for disciplined sacrifice as an escape from racial intolerance and degrading low-wage employment. The U.S. soldiers who fought in wars since the Korean War have typically been from poor or middle-class backgrounds, distinguishing them from the government officials who had decided to engage in the war. Soldiers had either been drafted into service or, since the end of the draft, attracted to join by recruiters' promises of education and job training that they could not pay for elsewhere. The highest recruitment rates (defined as the number of recruits per thousand of the eighteen- to twenty-four-year-old population) were found in counties that were relatively poorer than the rest of the nation. The top twenty recruitment counties had median household incomes below the national average. Nineteen of these ranked below the median average in their own states. The schools that provided the greatest number of recruits were those that offered GEDs. No part of their recruitment or training described for the recruits the likelihood of their own death, the consequences to their families, or the effects that the experience would have upon them for the remainder of their lives.

Once enlisted, soldiers face two realities: an emergence into the world beliefs about a hostile enemy and the systematic training to accept discipline and to kill as a professional under clear rules of engagement. Selection criteria are intended to rule out those who might not make the grade. However, to meet recruitment needs for soldiers in the Iraq war, standards have been relaxed to include noncitizen immigrants who may be desperate for work. Also included are some who have not met the mental standards. Such individuals may inflict great damage in unprofessional behavior as racist soldiers or undisciplined killers. Private Green entered the military under a lowered standard of "moral waivers" that permits recruits with criminal records, emotional problems, and weak educational backgrounds to be taught how to use weapons. Many instances of rape go unreported, but Green was described in sworn testimony by U.S. soldiers as guilty of the planned rape of Abeer, a fourteen year old, in Iraq. He was one of a group of soldiers who stalked her after one or more of them expressed the intention to rape her. They changed into black civvies; burst into Abeer's home; killed her mother, father, and five-year-old sister with bullets to the forehead; and took turns raping Abeer. Finally, they murdered her, drenched the bodies with kerosene, and lit them on fire to destroy the evidence. After repeated efforts to spin the details of the case, the military found one individual with a history of violent behavior as an effective scapegoat. If such unfit soldiers do survive their experience in war, they will be called heroes—and released back into society. Upon their return, their military training increases their danger as potential copiers of Timothy McVeigh and the Oklahoma City bombing.[44]

Not everyone is drawn into the mass fervor of war. Yet a large number of thoughtful and loving men can come to love war. For many, war is a state that gives us meaning.[45] Older veterans sometime reminisce about the sense of life-and-death involvement, the facing of horrendous danger, the loss of comrades, the camaraderie of their unit, and the acts of heroism that occurred. Their memories recall a time of their lives in which every moment mattered, and their absolute dedication to a task, ordered for them by others, provided more that was meaningful—surely more that was exotic—than what they recall of the more mundane activities that they experienced at other times. They recall the sharing of a fear and horror too great to be able to convey to others who were not there. They recall the intense moments of courage and of cowering. On a deeper level, war provides for some a value less easily talked about, an ultimate experience of the unity of beauty and destruction, of facing mortality, and of power over life and death.[46]

Sometimes the search for glory is commingled with elements of military careerism. One sergeant wrote the following from Iraq:

> I can say from personal experience in Iraq that our commanders often make soldiers carry out orders that have nothing to do with reconstruction efforts or peacekeeping. Their clear purpose is to instigate fire fights so that officers can get their combat experience, medals, and the glory they need to climb the military ladder. (Sergeant Camilo Mejia)[47]

The experiences of intense involvement also serve to cover up what might otherwise be a source of guilt for what they had done. An army staff sergeant, who was sentenced to a year in military prison in May 2004 for refusing to return to Iraq after being home on leave, talked openly about what he did there:

> What it all comes down to is redemption for what was done there. I was turning ambulances away from going to hospitals, I killed civilians, I tortured guys and I'm ashamed of that. Once you are there, it has nothing to do with politics. It has to do with you as an individual being there and killing people for no reason. There is no purpose, and now I'm sick at myself for doing these things. I kept telling myself I was there for my buddies. It was a weak reasoning because I still shut my mouth and did my job. . . . It wasn't until I came home that I felt it—how wrong it all was and that I was a coward for pushing my principles aside. I'm trying to buy my way back into heaven and it's not so much what I did, but what I didn't do to stop it

when I was there. So now it's a way of trying to undo the evil that we did over there. This is why I'm speaking out, and not going back. This is a painful process and we're going through it.[48]

A substantial number of combat veterans have returned bearing the full pain of their experience. By October 2004, the Department of Defense reported some 5,000 U.S. soldiers who were refusing to return to combat in Iraq. Their return to normalcy has given them a mission to educate others about the horror and the false justifications of war. At a July 4, 2004, memorial placing crosses for killed soldiers in the sand at Santa Monica Beach, one Marine collapsed in grief. He had been the sole survivor of a mortar attack in Iraq and had lost sixteen of his comrades. He was so bereft that he couldn't write the names of the men. The volunteers helped him, and then he gingerly kissed all sixteen crosses and sat against the Santa Monica pier completely frozen until he could finally move again.[49]

Journalist Dahr Jamail interviewed participants at a Veterans for Peace Convention in Dallas, Texas. He asked what they would tell the president if they could speak to him. One corporal from an artillery unit replied,

I don't think Bush will ever realize how many millions of lives he and his lackeys have ruined on their quest for money, greed and power. . . . To take the patriotism of the American people for granted—the fact that people (his administration) are willing to lie and make excuses for you while you continue to kill and maim the youth of America and ruin countless families and still manage to do so with a smile on your face. . . . You need to . . . take the billions of dollars you've made off the blood and sweat of U.S. service members, all the suffering you've caused us, and put those billions of dollars into the VA to take care of the men and women you sent to be slaughtered. Yet all those billions aren't enough to even try to compensate all the people who have been affected by this.[50]

Ron Kovic's memoir, *Born on the Fourth of July*, documents the transformation of one veteran who lost his legs in Vietnam. Among those soldiers whose experiences caused them to turn against the war, a number take a stand on ethical grounds while still in the service. One little-reported story from the Vietnam War is the extent of soldier rebellion. It occurred from the front lines to the stateside bases. GIs produced more than 250 antiwar committees and underground newspapers to voice their discontent. Their efforts came not only from draftees but also from poor working-class soldiers who had joined voluntarily.[51]

Glory and the Sense of Purpose

Those who glorify their experience of war help to preserve its symbolic social meaning as service to one's country. War, however destructive, is always justified by its leaders and is typically honored. William James noted, however, that the sentiments tapped by war are not all bad:

> [I]ndeed they represent the more virtuous dimensions of human existence: conceptions of order and discipline, the tradition of service and devotion, of physical fitness, of unstinted exertion, and of universal responsibility.[52]

More recently, author Barbara Ehrenreich placed mystical experience at the core of her theory of war. Her claim is that war is a sacrament, a blood ritual that draws upon humankind's oldest and deepest impulses. In the Seville statement on war, a multidisciplinary group of distinguished scholars states clearly that war (and by implication the preparation to wage war) cannot be explained as a human instinct. Although militarism is not instinctual, the religious sentiment underlying it shows characteristics of primitive programmed reactions. History provides numerous instances of the religious passions of war. The Crusades and the Islamic jihad elicited spiritual strengths of self-sacrifice, courage, and honor. During the twentieth century, nationalism provided an illustration of the same religious zeal. In Nazism, where religious rituals were specifically incorporated, but also in World War II generally, the absolute righteousness of the participants was paramount. Ehrenreich observes that "the passions of war are among the 'highest' and finest passions humans can know: courage, altruism, and the mystical sense of belonging to 'something larger than ourselves.'"[53]

The degree of immersion in the sacrament is surely different for those who are involved directly as soldiers or other victims of combat and for those who know it best in the movie version. The Dalai Lama notes,

> In modern warfare the roles of those who instigate it are often far removed from the conflict on the ground. At the same time, its impact on noncombatants grows even greater. Those who suffer most in today's armed conflicts are the innocent—not only the families of those fighting but in far greater numbers, civilians who often do not play a direct role. Even after the war is over, there continues to be enormous suffering due to land mines and poisoning from the use of chemical weapons.[54]

The Dalai Lama notes also the effects upon the dispersion of destruction. War brings a destruction of infrastructure, of roads, bridges, housing, farmlands, electricity, and medical facilities, as well as a general economic hardship. This means that with increasing frequency women, children, and the elderly are its prime victims.

The history of sacrifice and of sexual abuse of women in war is well documented.[55] Feminist scholars have frequently noted that the image of heroism in war has long been associated with proving manhood in patriarchal societies; the implicit message sent is that violence is erotic.[56] Rapes often occur in war and under military occupation. The reasons include a license to express power over a dehumanized enemy. It is also likely that the reality of imminent death drives the senses to capture the moment with sexual and romantic actions and fantasies. And rape, in many areas, has also been an explicit part of the humiliation intentionally encouraged as an instrument of war.[57]

Similarly, the Graca Machel report to the United Nations on the effects of war on children documents the disastrous effects on young people.[58] These include the loss of young lives clearly not at fault, the mutilations, the separations from family, the forced child soldiers and child sex slaves, the fear, the trauma, and the unresolved anger that will later influence the survivor's own propensity to be a perpetrator or a victim of violence.[59]

The Dalai Lama also addresses the impersonality of destruction:

> The reality of modern warfare is that the whole enterprise has become almost like a computer game. The ever-increasing sophistication of weaponry has outrun the imaginative capacity of the average layperson. Their destructive capacity is so astonishing that whatever arguments there may be in favor of war, they must be vastly inferior to those against. We could almost be forgiven for feeling nostalgia for the way in which battles were fought in ancient times. At least then people fought one another face-to-face. There was no denying the suffering involved. And in those days, it was usual for rulers to lead their troops in battle. If the ruler was killed, that was generally the end of the matter. But as technology improved, the generals began to stay farther behind. Today they can be thousand of miles away in their bunkers underground.[60]

The Decision Makers for War

The reality of being able to tap into, and to induce, a soldier's capacity to kill appears to be an insufficient explanation of the motives for war. Most of the decisions to use military force are not made by soldiers nor even influenced by their desires. Despite the frequent claim that wars must be fought, or expanded, in order to honor the sacrifices already paid by other soldiers, most of the decision makers have rarely seen a battlefield. Political officials are influenced by high-ranking military officers, by intelligence sources, and civilian strategists whose work is to investigate potential enemies and prepare to confront them militarily. They are also influenced by close ties to powerful corporate officials seeking protection for their investments and to weapons scientists whose life work has been in developing weapons and planning for their use. Such defense-planning strategists define their goals as gaining competitive advantage for their own side and are often preoccupied with strategies that enable them to outsmart or coerce adversaries. The defense intellectuals, however, display behavior that suggests their work meets deep psychological needs. Among themselves they speak with a dry technocratic language that distances their reality from the cost in lives. Military planners talk about missions, operations, securing an area, destroying a high-profile target, creating a strategic advantage, or a favorable cost-benefit ratio. The nuclear weapons laboratories develop the most lethal of all weapons. But human suffering is not part of their discussion. They exist in a culture in which every atom, every molecule, every weapon, every person, every agency, every toxic-waste product is a separate entity to be isolated, studied, mastered, and exploited. It is a symbol of a culture in which bigger is better, in which rationality prevails over intuition and feelings, in which the culture of macho bravado is provided a sophisticated form of expression and a beneficent rationale. It is connected to, indeed a creation of, the federal government in its honorable pursuit of security.

But closer studies of this elite group of men (they are almost all male) reveal that the vocations also provide gratification for masculine identities that play with a god-like power sufficient to destroy the planet. Such activities are often pursued without conscious awareness of an underlying preoccupation with the subjugation of the weak and the feminine. Images of bullying and domination of women creep through the outward rationality of their language.[61] Along with the emotionless technical language of deterrence and counterforce capabilities are the words that assure a mastery over the anxiety that might be caused by the images of radiated flesh, dying Hiroshima victims, or of incinerated cities.[62] Instead we have "clean bombs" or just "devices," "collateral damage," and "surgical strikes." But the images of extraordinary male potency break through. The Harrier II missile is described as having an "exceptional thrust to weight ratio . . . with vectored thrust capability that makes the unique rapid response possible. It is designed to maximize runway cratering by optimizing penetration dynamics and utilizing the most efficient warhead yet designed." Incidentally the French used women's names for each of the craters gouged into their test site at Mururoa Atoll. In case the imagery is unclear, the Harrier II description adds "just the sort of 'big stick' Teddy Roosevelt had in mind back in 1901." Frequently, the defense strategists ask, "Did you get to pat the missile?" Getting to pat the missile vicariously appropriates all that phallic power as one's own.[63] One strategic observer noted, after a test,

> Then just when it appeared as though the thing had settled down in a state of permanence, there came shooting out of the top, a giant mushroom that increased the size of the pillar to 45,000 feet. The mushroom top was even more alive than the pillar; seething and boiling into a white fury of creamy foam, sizzling upward, and then descending earthward, a thousand geysers rolled into one. It kept struggling in an elemental fury, like a creature in the act of breaking the bonds that held it down.[64]

The culture most difficult to see is one's own. The values of the nuclear weapons culture include the following such assumptions: Wars are inevitable; national interests justify the use of violent force; the views of scientists are correct; and the march of technology, despite its casualties, is inevitable. When we see that these views may also express deep psychological needs for masculine identity and power and may be reinforced by a clandestine organizational culture with cult-like attributes, we are able to understand better the addictive attachments that such beliefs may hold.[65]

The human needs fulfilled by war are but one factor contributing to global violence. But if war is to end as a human institution, the world may have to find ways to offer people the same sense of identity and belonging in the work of peace-building as they otherwise find in supporting or participating in war.

Although the individual capacities that enhance human willingness to engage in war are important, they are not sufficient to explain it. The aggressive behaviors of nations may bear little resemblance to the aggressiveness of their people. Reinhold Niebuhr[66] has observed that a nation of submissive robots can be led to war more easily than a nation of aggressive individualists.

War and its preparedness are institutions of society. Even in World War II, which was fought with a righteous belief in the cause, soldiers still were mainly in service because they were drafted. Most served in combat duty only for as long as their assignments required. Studies show that they were fighting more for their loyalty to their immediate squadron than to their country.[67] Continuing to fight and bear the sacrifices had to be promoted, both for soldiers and for the nation. This war, like most, was sustained by propaganda, demonizing the enemy, and extolling the virtues of our effort.

The image of a hostile enemy is a precursor to war.[68] The period of the Cold War demonstrated the continuing power of a military and economic elite, on both sides, to create so awesome an enemy[69] that its containment could justify great sacrifices to freedom and to well-being at home. In the proxy wars fought in Angola, Korea, Vietnam, Panama, Afghanistan, El Salvador, and Iran, the public was typically treated to a televised vilification of an individual and a display of war that concealed its atrocities and its costs. Even then, extended war has been unpopular. This unpopularity reflects a brutality of the experience of mutilated people that cannot be overcome by flag-waving demonstrations. James Caroll writes,

> The "bursting in air" of July 4th is an implicit glorification of war. On the day after, can we think of those combat survivors who will carry the real cost of the Iraqi war in their bodies forever? And how can we think of those American daughters and sons without thinking of their even more numerous Iraqi sisters and brothers? . . . we have become a people who wage unending war—killing and maiming our young ones and theirs—without being remotely able to say why.[70]

For ordinary people, both in and out of uniform, for people whose information comes from a mass media relying mainly upon reports from the pressrooms of government agencies and large corporations, the myth fades and the reality of war is revealed as a horror. Even with the glorification of war, the hiding of casualties, and the media acceptance of terminology that transforms war into a tactical game devoid of pain, people grow weary of war. The images of dedication, purpose, and belonging that it brings forth are often short-lived. The continuation of war requires organizational machinery to make it happen. That machinery is operated by a network of people for whom the gains of violent exploitation are greatest. Those who call for war are not evil. But they live in a world of information, rewards, and long-term practices that call forth a high level of violence and cause unspeakable harm to many.

Part of the social-psychological view of how to eliminate war has been to urge that we socialize our young people to grow up with a respect for life. The depth of the human commitment to the "other" has been viewed as a factor critical to avoiding nuclear war.[71] Within humanistic psychology both Carl Rogers and Abraham Maslow recognized that society needed to be more inviting to the development of caring and concerned individuals. Yet both placed the major emphasis upon the unfolding of the individual potential for caring engagement with the world beyond the ego.[72]

In partial contrast, Rollo May saw a darker side to human nature that made more difficult the unfolding of the human potential for replacing hatred with caring. He felt that movement toward freedom, toward participation and caring, was most realistic when it recognized the constraints of destiny. For May,[73] these included a "daimonic" human quality that was the source of both creativity and destructiveness. May's recognition of the destructive potential echoes a history of writing dating back to Sigmund Freud and his concept of the inner conflict between forces of life and love (eros) and forces of death and destruction (thanatos).[74] This is a major contribution to the debate on what is needed to deal with the potential for violence and our hopes for peace. Indeed, it is this juxtaposition between the commitment to fulfillment of the human potential and the realization of the human capacity for violence that has led to one of the most important dialogues about human nature. If people cannot always be counted upon to restrict their own belligerent inclinations, then we may succumb to the situations that bring out violence in almost all of us. Hence peace will have to be accompanied by the creation of human institutions and cultural norms that hold us accountable when we might otherwise be drawn to war. Since institutions change, this is possible.

Humans have created laws to limit the law of the jungle. The invention of the colt revolver led to an era in which one's sword could no longer define a safe space, and gentlemen gave up their swords. Now the power of nuclear weapons is such that no leaders can protect us while threatening others. Institutions like war that permit an exploitation of the earth's capacities to nurture life may destroy others first. But eventually they are likely to doom all of us. Most wars are fought because of perceived injustice. We focus next upon a set of nonmilitary institutions and practices that are increasingly seen as unjust. They are a less visible source of violence, devastating in their own right, that increase the likelihood that we humans will continue to hate and to kill others of our human family and to diminish the life-sustaining ecology so needed for our survival.

Chapter 3

The Hidden Structure of Violence

> Human beings are like parts of a body, created from the same essence. When one part is hurt and in pain, the others cannot remain in peace and be quiet. If the misery of others leaves you indifferent and with no feelings of sorrow, you should not be called a human being.
>
> —*Sa'adi, thirteenth century Persian poet*

Although individual acts of violence are readily noticed, there is often a pattern underlying them. The point of this chapter is that violence is not adequately understood by the examination of occurrences of specific violent behavior. Rather, the view is that beneath these phenotypic events there lies a genotypic pattern, often hidden, that is a fundamental factor in its occurrence. The global economy is a social structure that consigns persons, communities, and habitats to roles that enhance the likelihood of violence in many forms. Here, pathways may be traced from the global corporate economy to violence against workers, consumers, indigenous communities, and life-sustaining habitats as well as to acts of personal violence, terrorism, and the spread of AIDS among poor women. Paradoxically, globalism also offers opportunities to constrain the violent consequences of the global economy.

Author Barbara Ehrenreich once questioned President Nixon's press secretary, Ron Ziegler, about the propriety of $10,000-a-plate dinners for raising campaign funds. Ziegler's reply was that this was access and that they should have to pay for it. When asked how people who do not have that much money for a dinner might gain access to the White House, the reply was they would have to find other ways to get attention. Three days later the Los Angeles riots erupted. The message had apparently been heard by poor people. Their needs continued to be ignored and an even more serious Los Angeles riot broke out in 1992 following a brutal police beating of a black man that was caught on camera. The plight of cities lies beneath such eruptions of violence. The last of the manufacturing jobs in south-central Los Angeles departed in the early 1980s to Mexico. The area lost 70,000 such jobs in the last three decades. One might argue that the street violence was not directed toward the appropriate causes. Kids smashed windows and stole merchandise. But looting is a crude shopping spree in which people who are bombarded with messages to acquire more things find an opportunity to do so. The outbreak reflects a system that pillages and pollutes the rest of the world. The kids would explain, "Everyone was doing it." Perhaps they were right. The bankers were looters, as were the defense contractors, the Wall Street inside traders, and the corporate mergers and takeovers.[1]

I define violence broadly as any affront to the life, well-being, or dignity of a person. Any activity that increases the suffering of others is violent. Johan Galtung, a founder of peace studies, defines violence as "avoidable insults to basic human needs, and more generally to *life*, lowering the real level of needs satisfaction below what is potentially possible."[2] Since the human potential is truly amazing, Galtung's definition, including any limitations to that potential, may prove unduly broad. Still, wherever unneeded suffering or death results from preventable human actions, there is evidence that violence has occurred. Galtung's concept of *structural* violence is helpful. He sees culture—the normative beliefs and practices of a society—to be a source of violence by allowing a dehumanization of certain persons or groups. Cultural violence leads to structural violence when it is incorporated into the formalized legal and economic exchanges of the society. Although individual acts of violence have many causes, their occurrence is most frequently predicated upon a larger and often hidden structure that necessitates violence.

Structural Violence

According to Galtung, three different types of violence make up a "violence triangle": cultural, structural, and direct violence. They have different relationships to time. *Direct violence* is an event; *structural violence* is a process with ebbs and flows; and *cultural violence* is more invariant, remaining essentially the same for long periods and reflecting the slow transformation of basic culture.[3] In most cases, Galtung claims, there is a causal flow. Structural violence feeds off of the steady stream of cultural violence, which then erupts into an act of direct violence. Direct violence is used by both the underdogs and the top dogs of society, but the acts of violence by the two groups serve quite different purposes. Underdogs use violence as a way to get out of a "structural iron cage" of powerlessness and poverty or to get back at the society that put them there. The top dogs, on the other hand, use violence to keep or gain power.

Structural violence is harder to identify than direct violence. Anyone can see that an act causing direct physical harm, such as rape or murder, is violent, and we try to stop these acts from occurring. Examples of structural violence, however, look normal on the surface. The harmful effects become apparent only after close inspection. Children may die of malnutrition. The prior removal of their family's farm by a mining corporation is sometimes unnoticed. Therefore, structural violence, more often than not, is left unchanged, and the cycle of violence continues. The invisibility of the structure is frequently a function of our lack of tools to see below the surface. In the case of corporate structures in the global economy that are resulting in violence, tools to uncover the structure are present. The dissemination of the information about these structures, however, is seriously limited since the mass media (see chapter 7) are part of the global corporate structure and are less inclined to display their own downside.

Psychological and Epidemiological Perspectives

The experience of police, emergency medics, mental health professionals, and war correspondents has been with direct violence. Their tendency in explanations has typically been to look within. When we see a case of family violence, the battering or torture of a defenseless victim, or the destruction or mutilation of an enemy combatant, the line of inquiry with which psychologists feel most at home is the question of how the individual could have done this. What motivation, what state of anger or emotional arousal, what genes, what horrific childhood or adult experience, what trait of personality or pathological pattern of thought could help us to understand the case at hand? Sometimes this look within does lead us to posit hidden structures, such as repressed rage or raging hormones. Sometimes this inquiry into the person takes us far into the search for identity, for meaning, and for spiritual connections beyond the particular person. These values and connections also reveal a compelling structure; a part of what Langer has called "life symbols."[4] These are perhaps better understood in cultures with a tradition of spiritual inquiry.

The hidden structures to be found by observing and listening to individuals and by noting the symbols of their culture, although essential to understanding violence, are not, however, the topic of this chapter. Rather, following the dictum of Kurt Lewin (founder of social psychology) that behavior is a function of both person and environment,[5] the hidden structures this chapter will focus upon are part of the social order. Recall what Hannah Arendt noted, that the most shocking fact about the genocidal brutality of the Nazis was the ordinariness of the perpetrators. They were remarkably like the rest of us. What was extraordinary was the social structure that enabled people to act in brutal ways and to ignore the brutality of their neighbors.[6]

Some forms of violence, such as genocide, are obvious examples of mass evil. In such situations an understanding of one particular perpetrator or one particular victim is insufficient to understand where the responsibility really lies. In the case of genocide, one might need to discover the leaders of the effort and their powers over the individual perpetrators as well as the psychology of the bystanders.[7] There are many forms of violence in which the actual event we witness may be better understood by locating forces many steps removed. The thesis here is that the hidden force underlying a large and increasing portion of contemporary violence is the global corporate economy. It calls forth violence in the form of suffering and death from AIDS and from cancer, from street crime and from hunger, from terrorism, from ethnic strife, and from war.

Singular explanations for the roots of violence should be suspect. The goal here is not to find a scapegoat on whom to blame the ascendance of violence but rather to look at one particular contemporary structure that is an overriding and often hidden cause. In the search for the roots of complex phenomena, it is often necessary to leave the careful clinical or laboratory examination of specific cases and move to an examination of the conditions under which incidents occur. This epidemiological approach has been immensely effective in public health. In social epidemiology the findings have presented an overwhelming case for three principal factors in the explanation of breakdown in both physical and psychological health. If we forget for the moment whether the particular pathology about which we have concern is cancer, heart disease, AIDS, depression, substance abuse, child abuse, or homicide, and instead focus upon the circumstances surrounding all forms of breakdown, there are some remarkable similarities. Those people who live in poverty are at a level of risk sufficiently greater than the rest of us such that we find it necessary to control statistically for economic level when explaining any other contributing factor.[8] Perhaps an even stronger, but related, factor is social marginality. Individuals not linked into a network of supportive care and reciprocal expectations are also at risk for almost every form of pathology. Those of us who could not be considered marginal typically fall into the high-risk category when we suffer a loss or disruption in our supportive networks.[9] The third factor is a loss in control over circumstances that affect our lives.[10] Poverty, social marginality, and loss of control are all factors that, in turn, are linked to certain economic arrangements that are inevitable outcomes of the global corporate economy.

Cases of Structural Violence by the Global Economy

Some illustrations of structural violence will be helpful. A death from stabbing in Toronto and a death from AIDS in southern Florida, apparently unrelated, share a common root. An Hispanic teenager was killed in a violent fight outside a bar in Toronto. He had thrown a bottle at a man leaving the bar, accepted a challenge to fight, and was stabbed fatally with his own knife. You can conjure the precipitating circumstances, the alcohol, the gangs, the taunts, and the lack of safe recreation facilities or youth employment for minorities. A link to this horrible tragedy began ten years earlier in the Dominican Republic. Following the U.S. boycott on Cuban sugar, corporate agribusiness expanded its growth of cane sugar in the Dominican Republic. Corporate representatives of the sugar and shipping industries, closely connected to the Departments of State and Defense, engineered an intervention by U.S. Marines. It served to prevent a restoration of the democratically elected Juan Bosch, who had been overthrown in a coup but was returning with popular support to Santa Domingo. The procorporate Balaguer government followed, and the Dominican Republic has since been a haven for international capital.[11]

Capital came to the Dominican Republic, as in most places of the less developed world, with a loss of indigenous local farming and crafts activity. The work of taking from the local ecology what is needed to nourish oneself and one's family meets the most basic human need. An increase in the agribusiness hold on sugarcane forced many peasants to the cities. For those who could find it, factory work came at the lowest of wages and with no security of employment. The Toronto youngster's father lost his job and turned to alcohol. His impoverished mother avoided prostitution by finding work as a nanny in Toronto. Ten years later she had enough money to bring her son to live with her after his years of mistreatment back home.

The woman who died in southern Florida had also emigrated from a village in the Dominican Republic. Flor Alvarez was among the many Dominican young women forced to move from a small, once sustainable town to the capital city. She married a trader who made frequent trips to Puerto Rico. They lived in poverty. She never sought or received medical attention through three pregnancies until after the family emigrated to find better conditions, first to Puerto Rico and then to southern Florida. There she gave birth to a low-birth-weight baby girl, was diagnosed with tuberculosis, and was later diagnosed with candida. She was not notified about her positive testing for HIV because she had no telephone and could not be reached. She died of AIDS, leaving behind an HIV-infected infant. The corporate hand was far removed from the hospital bed in southern Florida, and from the scene of the Toronto stabbing. But it was surely a key contributor.

Another illustration is of violence against the resident rubber tapers who live in sparse tribes in the rainforests of Belize. Some of them protested the clearing of the forest that sustained them, and police were hired to drive them from their native habitat. The new proprietor was already planning to replace the rainforests with orange groves. The Belize rainforests are one of the world's most species-diverse places. They are a part of the ecological lungs of the planet, as well as home to the rubber tapers. The new owner, the Minute Maid division of Coca Cola, had sold its orange groves to developers in order to take advantage of rising real estate prices in the sunshine state. The corporate hand was not intending violence to people or the planet. Rather, it was making investments to assure its continued growth and profitability. Violence against the people of the forest was an uncalculated by-product of the decision process. Because of a public outcry and organized activity by Earth First and the Rainforest Action Network, Coca Cola accepted a compromise measure that preserved a portion of the indigenous rainforest.[12] The international expansion of large corporations like Coca Cola has led to a systematic exploitation of people who try to organize unions to assure living wages and safe working conditions. Coca Cola has been charged with aiding the intimidation and indeed murder of union leaders by government soldiers or paramilitary groups in countries as diverse as India,

Colombia, and Ireland. A number of universities in the United States have been pressured by student groups to suspend their contracts with Coca Cola in an effort to discourage this activity.[13]

There are, however, no laws protecting ancestral rights of the Mayans of Belize. Atlantic Industries, a corporation that has devastated the forests of Malaysia, has been buying out 200,000 acres (for sixty cents per acre) in Belize, in order to cut mahogany. Mayan leader Julian Co noted that if the investors are allowed a free hand in the Mayan communities, "the principle stewardship over our natural resources will inevitably be overrun by the use and run philosophy of land speculators and other commercial interests."[14] Since 1992 Belize has repeatedly made concessions to foreign companies, and in 1996 "after a closed-door meeting, the Belizean government revoked the protected status of a nature reserve in Mayan territory in order to grant logging rights to Atlantic Industries."[15] The "use and run" philosophy extends to people. This will be shown later in illustrations of plant closures in the United States as well as in poor countries where big corporations remove their facilities in favor of still poorer places.

The situation in Belize is repeated in Nigeria, where a Hong Kong–based logging company, with Nigerian governmental assistance, bypassed the country's own environmental laws to allow mahogany forests to be cut down. The project threatened the drinking water in more than 300 communities with over 2 million people. Residents of the Cross River villages were lured with promises of schools and jobs, while the habitat on which they depended was being destroyed.[16]

Global corporate investors require stable governments. Where people demand control of their local environs (through land reform) or their labor (through unions), governments able to control such discontent are valued. The training and supply of military forces to support oligarchic interests is an activity that adds to a cycle of violence. An illustration is seen in the alarmingly high rates of El Salvadoran refugee children, reported by Los Angeles case workers, who were beaten by their parents. The pattern of abuse is also replicated among migrant agricultural families torn by the needs of male mobility.[17] The perpetrators are most frequently El Salvadoran women who had lost their husbands and other family members to brutality by government forces. Most had themselves witnessed or experienced unspeakable brutalities. They are now showing the combined effects of immigration, poverty, and what psychologists see as clear cases of post-traumatic stress disorder (PTSD). When the symptoms take the form of uncontrolled violence, they reflect the cycle of violence, tracing back to an earlier trauma once acted upon the perpetrator. In El Salvador the initial trauma was typically inflicted by El Salvadoran officers, trained in counterinsurgency at the School of the Americas (SOA) in Fort Benning, Georgia. They were paid by the United States, and they represented a government by a rich oligarchy dedicated to maintaining its options for lucrative arrangements with global corporations. Paradoxically, the corporate economy in the United States, despite a period of unprecedented growth in the 1990s, has been unable to afford adequate violence prevention services to immigrant populations. Hence there is little help for the parents or for the children.[18] In 2001, when SOA opponents were forcing Congress to consider shutting down the school, the Department of Defense drafted a proposal in which the SOA was renamed the Western Hemisphere Institute for Security Cooperation—WHINSEC, which "Georgia Senator and SOA supporter, the late Paul Coverdell, characterized as a *cosmetic* change that would ensure that the SOA could continue its mission and operation."[19]

Military assistance to sustain investment-friendly governments is ubiquitous, as are its violent consequences. Much of tribal warfare in Africa has been necessitated by the fight for scarce natural resources that have been decimated by the mining and agricultural practices of giant corporations. Recall that the violence in Zaire followed the CIA-assisted murder of Patrice Lumumba. His replacement, Mobuto, protected both international mining interests and, with U.S. assistance, provided weapons to six other surrounding nations, including Algeria and Angola.

The Case of Nike in Indonesia

The workplace in the global economy produces structural violence. Modern transportation and communication have released the bond of giant corporations to any specific location. Free to move where environmental restrictions are absent, taxes low, and labor cheap, all of the largest corporations have become multinational. Details of the Nike operation in Indonesia are instructive. Cicih Sukaesih, a thirty-two-year-old woman, worked at the factory of Nike contractor P. T. Sung Hwa Dunia in West Java, Indonesia, from 1989 to January 1993. In September of 1992, almost all of the 6,500 workers went on strike over wages, benefits, and working conditions. The normal workday was 7:30 A.M. to 6:00 P.M., with one hour for lunch. Approximately three times a week, workers were forced to work as late as 9:00 P.M. The normal workweek was Monday through Saturday, but workers were sometimes required to work on Sundays. A worker who refused overtime received warnings. After the third warning, the worker was subject to firing. Additionally, the workers were financially coerced into putting in overtime hours. During the time Cicih worked at the factory, pay was about $2.10 a day in U.S. dollars. The overtime rate was double that. Only through working many hours of overtime could workers hope to cover their basic expenses.

Workers labored under a pressured quota system and under oppressive factory conditions. They were so crowded that their body heat combined with the heat of the machines made the temperature of the factory almost unbearable. Yet they were rationed only a limited amount of water to drink. Workers required a permission slip to use the bathroom. If a worker outstayed the time stipulated on the slip, guards would come to yell at her. Workers not feeling well were granted no exceptions.

Should an accident occur, there was one doctor (present only two hours a day) for 6,500 workers. A worker too ill to work still had to come in to get a permission slip from the company doctor. If she could not—even if she brought a note from her own doctor—she would be forced, upon her return, to stand in view of her coworkers for up to two hours, while a manager announced: "This is an example of a lazy worker."

The factory workforce, typical of sweatshops, was largely young females. A worker of twenty-eight was considered past her prime and could expect to be discarded. The women suffered sexual harassment. Workers were searched manually (by guards touching their bodies) upon leaving work each day to verify that they were not stealing shoe components.[20]

Nike's labor policies are bad for children. Exposing women of childbearing age to dangerous fumes harms children. Forcing mothers to work outrageous hours of overtime deprives children of nurturant care as does paying mothers poverty wages. Bob Herbert of the *New York Times* reported on the "trampled dreams" of Nike's Indonesian workers:

> Apong Herlina, a lawyer with the Legal Aid Institute, tells the heart-breaking story of women from the countryside who have come to the cities for work but do not earn enough to have their children with them. The children remain in the country, being cared for by relatives. "These women work a tremendous amount," Ms. Herlina said, "but there is not enough money for transportation or time to travel the long distances to visit their children. They see them once a year, during holiday. The rest of the year, they grieve."[21]

In April 1997 the *Sydney Morning Herald* (an Australian newspaper) reported the findings of an eight-month study of Nike operations in an outlying part of Indonesia. The young women worked an average of 11.5 hours per day and were fired immediately if they took sick leave. One young woman died from exhaustion when factory managers failed to provide her with medical attention. On March 16, 1996, the *New York Times* reported an incident in which a worker was locked in a room at a Nike shoe factory in Indonesia and interrogated for seven days by the military, demanding to know about labor activities. Independent unions are forbidden in Indonesia. Independent union leader Dita Sari received a six-year prison sentence for her peaceful union activities. Independent union leader Muchtar Pakpahan served four years in prison awaiting a trial and a possible death sentence—again, for normal union organizing activities. He was released, but only after Amnesty International had declared him a prisoner of conscience and the Canadian Auto Workers union had set up a massive postcard campaign.[22]

In Nike's hometown, the *Portland Oregonian* reported on April 22, 1997 (shortly after Nike CEO Phil Knight had signed the presidential task-force agreement on sweatshops), that 10,000 workers went on strike from an Indonesian factory that produced shoes for Nike. The workers were protesting the contractor's attempt to cheat them out of a twenty-cent-per-day increase in pay (mandated by the new minimum-wage level in Indonesia) by cutting a $7.75 monthly attendance bonus already being paid.

The official government union in Indonesia is headed by retired military officers for whom union positions are a perquisite of rank. Union dues are deducted from pay, but the government union tries to squash any actions by the workers to have their grievances addressed. Wildcat strikes frequently occur in Nike and other factories in Indonesia, when the level of frustration reaches the boiling point. Typically, such actions are brief, massive walkouts—often successful with regard to specific grievances. Also typical is that after the workers negotiate an agreement and return to work, management or the police or military interrogate workers suspected of leading the walkout. In the case of union leader Cicih, she and her twenty-three coworkers were then fired. Since losing her position with the Nike contractor, Cicih probably was blacklisted. In any case, at her age, she has no prospect of finding further employment in a global sweatshop system, which spits out women at age twenty-eight as no longer of use. Cicih was obliged to live with her sister and rely on support from her family.[23]

The workers sought help from a nongovernmental organization (NGO) that provides assistance in labor cases. Their case slowly worked its way through Indonesian courts and review boards. In November 1995 a court ruled against the company and ordered that the workers be reinstated with back pay. This was a remarkable decision, given the repressive nature of Indonesian government. But the decision was contested and not fully implemented.

Nike headquarters has refused to act for these workers by taking the neutral position of leaving the case up to the Indonesian Supreme Court. Nike's neutrality means that Cicih may never live to see her case decided, since the Indonesian Supreme Court last year ruled on only twenty-four cases out of a backlog of some 2,000. The company claims to pay more than the minimum wage in Indonesia. But Indonesia sets the minimum wage below the poverty line to attract investment. Only through overtime do Nike workers make more than the minimum wage and then, in a manner similar to Wal-Mart employees in the United States, they are not paid for all of their hours.

Nine Indonesian NGOs have offered truly independent monitoring of Nike factories in their country, but Nike refuses to allow independent monitors to verify hours and pay levels. Recently, Nike was sued by a California man for misrepresentation of facts relating to its labor practices in factories overseas. Deciding that allowing independent monitoring of its factories would be better than a lengthy litigation process, Nike reached an out-of-court settlement with the plaintiff, Mark Kasky, part of which involved paying $1.5 million to the Fair Labor Association, a Washington DC–based organization dedicated to independently monitoring labor standards.[24]

Despite its record, Indonesia, like South Korea and Taiwan, is sometimes suggested to illustrate the value of the global marketplace in raising the living standards of less-developed countries. All have had atrocious records for human rights, and in no case has the economic development improved the conditions of the very poor. The jobs in oppressive textile, toy, or computer chip factories require long hours and pay below the minimum wage. They carry no benefits and lack the rudiments of workplace safety or decency. Many of those jobs are now being lost because people can be found who work for even less in Vietnam or Haiti. A public relations consultant for the Nike corporation told critics that Nike's continuing production (albeit at a reduced level) in Korea and Taiwan "demonstrates our commitment as a good citizen." Yet his boss, Phil Knight, said in the December 30, 1996, issue of the *Washington Post,* "We're the last ones in Korea and Taiwan, and in five years we won't be there."[25]

Companies like Nike push for standards so low as to make a "no sweat" label meaningless. Nike uses its presence on the commission to depict itself as concerned and progressive. Transnational corporations like Nike benefit from U.S. promotion of the free market. China, Bangladesh, Pakistan, Honduras, and many others compete in a race to the bottom, each forcing workers to work fourteen-hour days, seven days a week.[26]

Corporate Movement into Vietnam, Haiti, and China

What makes Vietnam a better choice for global corporations such as Nike? An envoy from the International Monetary Fund spoke on the *Lehrer NewsHour* of a successful visit to Vietnam in April 1997. The barriers to trade, mainly the politics of unaccounted, missing, or imprisoned U.S. soldiers from the war, were being handled with full cooperation from Vietnamese authorities. The leaders conveyed no hostility over the past and were quite interested in capital investments from the United States. The envoy was asked why he had not accepted an invitation to a tribunal on crimes of the Vietnam War during his visit. He replied that he did not have time for the tribunal. The envoy bypassed a war-crimes tribunal for a war in which the United States was the aggressor and in which it killed 2 million Vietnamese. He did, however, attend the Carnegie-sponsored program teaching entrepreneurial skills to interested Vietnamese. It would appear that in the minds of the developers, market interests readily supersede accountability for violence and that corporate contracts are a fair substitute for the reconciliation, necessary to preclude future violence.

On October 17, 1996, the CBS program *48 Hours* exposed Nike labor abuses in Vietnam, including beatings, sexual harassment, and forcing workers to kneel for extended periods with their arms held in the air. On March 28, 1997, *New York Times* columnist Bob Herbert reported that fifty-six women employed at a factory making Nike shoes in Vietnam were ordered to run around the factory in the hot sun because they hadn't worn regulation shoes to work:

> The women ran and ran and ran. One fainted, and then another. Still they ran. They would be taught a lesson. . . . More women fainted. The ordeal didn't end until a dozen workers had collapsed.[27]

This incident occurred on March 8—International Women's Day. On this day some Vietnamese companies give women workers flowers, but these "12 Vietnamese women had to spend the day in the emergency room."

McDonald's and Disney in Vietnam

Located in Da Nang City, the Keyhinge Toys Co. factory employs approximately 1,000 people, 90 percent of whom are young women, seventeen to twenty years old. They make the popular giveaway promotional toys for McDonald's Happy Meals. Included in the Happy Meals sold at McDonald's are small toys based on characters from Disney films. According to McDonald's Senior Vice President Brad Ball, the Happy Meals characters from the *101 Dalmatians* movie were the most successful in McDonald's history. Ball added, "As we embark on our new global alliance, we anticipate ten great years of unbeatable family fun as customers enjoy 'the magic of Disney' only at McDonald's."[28]

As in Indonesia, overtime is mandatory in the Vietnam factory with shifts of nine to ten hours a day, seven days a week. The effects of fatigue are heightened by poor ventilation. On one day in February 2000, a large number of women fell ill, twenty-five collapsed, and three were hospitalized as a result of exposure to the chemical solvent acetone. Exposure to acetone can cause dizziness, loss of consciousness, and damage to the liver and kidneys as well as chronic eye, nose, throat, and skin irritation.

All appeals from local human and labor rights groups were rejected by Keyhinge management, which refused to improve the ventilation in the factory or remedy other unsafe working conditions. Along with demanding forced overtime, Keyhinge management did not make legally mandated payments for health insurance coverage for its employees, who receive no compensation for injury or sickness. Many of the women making McDonald's Disney toys at Keyhinge were paid well below subsistence levels. After working a seventy-hour week, some of the teenage women would take home a salary of only $4.20. In a 1996 study, they earned from six to eight cents an hour. Some earned just sixty cents after a ten-hour shift. The most basic meal in Vietnam—rice, vegetables and tofu—costs seventy cents. Three meals would cost $2.10. Wages cover less than 20 percent of the daily food and travel costs for a single worker, let alone her family. By contrast, the CEO of Disney that same year earned $203 million.[29]

Indonesia and Vietnam are not the only places where violence toward workers is found. Haiti, Guatemala, China, and Pakistan provide equally tragic examples of this structural form of violence. In June 1996 *Life* magazine carried a story by Sydney Schanberg that depicted children sewing soccer balls for Nike in Pakistan for sixty cents a day. Nike started production in Pakistan (one of the most notorious countries for child labor) without taking measures to monitor hiring practices by contractors. Only after the *Life* magazine article did the company promise to correct the situation.[30]

The violence of the global economy does not apply solely to workers; consumers are also affected. Avon has an aggressive campaign that brings expensive beauty products to the poor areas of Brazil. Avon saleswomen are making house calls in the remote village of Santarem, where most people do not read or write and the average household income is $3 a day. The product they sell is called Renew, a cream that burns off the top layer of skin and magically takes away wrinkles. Rosa Alegria, communications director for Avon Brazil says

> Women do everything to buy it. They stop buying other things like clothes, like shoes. If they feel good about their skin they prefer to stop buying clothes and buy something that is on television. People think it is a real miracle.[31]

Multinational corporations add to structural violence in the United States as well. An example of this is Channel One, an advertiser-sponsored school television program. Channel One is shown twelve minutes a day in 12,000 schools. In exchange for satellite dishes and video equipment, schools must show the program, which is filled with ads for sneakers, candy, and fast food, to 90 percent of the children at least 90 percent of the school days. The teachers are not allowed to turn off the program. Since Channel One was shown in school, children believed that the advertised products must be good for them.[32] In such situations, multinational corporations are using advertising to get poor people to spend beyond their means by telling them that they cannot get along without their products. Both internationally and domestically, the most common victims of structural violence turn out to be poor women and children.

Women, Children, Violence, and AIDS

Several serious illnesses are preventable but are not prevented. In Africa, where indigenous tribal economies have been sacrificed to allow exploitation for mining and export agriculture, basic public health practices are often lacking. Every day in Africa 3,000 people die of malaria, 5,000 from measles, and 8,500 from AIDS.[33] Death from AIDS among poor women represents yet another form of structural violence enhanced by the global economy. The sale of female children from Asia and the Philippines into roles as sex slaves reflects upon the lack of options for parents to feed their families. For ordinary families, destitution makes people vulnerable to prostitution and even to the sale of their children to traders who promise them jobs and sell them into slavery. This is disturbingly common in countries where the local wealth is usurped for export and is unavailable to feed poor families. The United Nations estimates that there are currently 57 million female and child prostitutes. The Subic and Clark military bases in the Philippines were served by a massive prostitution industry. With the bases closed, the industry has been retained to serve soldiers on military training missions and increasingly to serve tourists and businessmen. Roughly 30,000 hospitality girls are registered in the Philippines, but the actual number is closer to 75,000. This comes at a time when the Philippines is said to have prospered.[34] Its income growth is 4.5 percent per year, and a survey of the

Asia-Pacific Economic Forum considered the Philippines one of the best places for investment among ten Asia-Pacific countries.[35] This reflects an early agreement to turn Subic Air Force Base into a free-trade zone, bringing in 150 large corporations. The benefits, however, have not reached the women who still sell their bodies, even with the increased risk of HIV infection.

The roots of this problem in the Philippines go back to the Philippine-American War of 1899 to 1914. The war lasted fifteen years and killed at least 100,000 people. Yet it is hardly mentioned even in history textbooks and has been all but erased from the public memory. The war marked a pivotal episode in the intertwining of U.S.-style racism and empire building. It was openly touted in the press and by the McKinley administration as the moment when the United States supplanted both Britain and Spain in "taking on the white man's burden."[36] Much of the subsequent history of the Philippines has been one of military and economic exploitation abetted by U.S. support for oppressive regimes and military opposition to the Philippine independence movement.

Later the exploitation of Philippine workers was enforced by martial law made possible by loans from the World Bank.[37] The current economic oppression of Philippine women is accompanied by efforts to eliminate any efforts to improve the conditions of work. In August 2005 the International Solidarity Mission (ISM) investigated human-rights violations in the Philippines. Over eighty-five foreign delegates from sixteen countries joined local delegates and organizations. Among the main conveners of the ISM are Karapatan (Alliance for the Advancement of People's Rights), Bayan Philippines (New Patriotic Alliance), Ecumenical Movement for Justice and Peace, and Public Interest Law Center. Their report noted that the effort to maintain cheap labor has taken the form of killing labor leaders. On September 22, 2005, Nestlé Union Leader Diosdado Fortuna was shot dead; on September 30 the head of the teachers' union in Surigao del Sur was stabbed to death; on October 7, Former Union President Rollie Mariano was killed; on October 10, 2005, Atlas Mining Corporation Union President Tony Cuizon was assassinated.[38]

Sweatshop labor has become the only employment in many areas,[39] and environmental degradation inevitably follows single-crop agriculture.[40] The human casualties include indigenous peasants and labor leaders who seek protection of their wages and their habitat.[41] Consistent with maintaining low labor costs, one of six children in today's world is involved in labor. The global economy includes 246 million child laborers, 73 million of whom are below the age of ten. They are robbed of childhood, of education, and, because of unsafe and contaminated work conditions, of their health. Nearly 22,000 of these children die yearly in work-related accidents. More than 1.2 million children are trafficked across international borders each year. Many are captured and delivered by smugglers. About 8.4 million children are trapped in slavery, trafficking, debt bondage, prostitution, pornography, and other illegal activity. Some 200,000 people live enslaved in ninety-one cities in the United States today. Although many wind up in brothels, a large number work as an underclass of nannies or nursing home aids, or in jobs with unhealthy working conditions.[42] The voices of these modern-day slaves deserve to be heard. Some have been captured in Batstone's important book, *Not for Sale*.[43]

AIDS among exploited women is another example of structural violence. The spread of AIDS is rampant where families can no longer stay together for the task of feeding and raising children.[44] Conservative thought sometimes favors a theory of AIDS prevention that hides the role of social structure. For example, cognitively based theories often assume that AIDS may be prevented if some new way can be found to teach that unsafe sex is really dangerous. The approach is seriously limited where the participants have few options. In the areas of Southeast Asia, the Philippines, sub-Saharan Africa, Latin America, and central cities of the United States, the life and livelihood options open to poor women are increasingly restricted. Some find manufacturing or service-sector jobs that lack health benefits and pay too little to survive. Others turn to prostitution, relationships with drug traffickers and transients, addiction without safe needle exchange, and even sale of children into the sex slave trade. Wherever the global economy expands into poor areas and replaces the means for local livelihood, we find the HIV epidemic to be spreading among women. The increase is usually combined with minimal access to treatment.

> As is the case internationally, the incidence of HIV infection (in the US) is, like the incidence of addiction, heavily skewed by class. . . . HIV has disproportionally affected women of color. As early as 1987, AIDS was the leading cause of death among 15–45 year old Black and Latina women living in NYC.[45]

The health behavior model (trying to modify the risky behaviors) falls short precisely where it fails to examine the behavior of those who are responsible for these conditions. Anthropologist Martha Ward observes,

> For poor women AIDS is just another problem they are blamed for and have to take responsibility for. . . . (Poor women's) sickness may be thought of as structural violence because it is neither nature nor pure individual will that is at fault, but rather historically given (and often economically driven) processes and forces that conspire to constrain individual agency. Structural violence is visited upon all those whose social status denies them access to the fruits of scientific and social advances.[46]

AIDS is hitting the most disadvantaged communities the hardest. Women, especially drug-addicted women, bear a major burden of this disease. Poverty is a condition that puts women at great risk of contracting AIDS:

> Sex and drugs tend to be linked in drug-using women's lives. It is not uncommon for women to provide sexual favors to drug users out of desperation for drugs, a circumstance to which women crack users appear to be particularly susceptible. In NYC, research suggests that 75% of crack addicted sex workers engage in oral sex exclusively for drug money, an activity that clearly puts women at greater risk than

> men. The virus gains easy entrance into the bloodstream through mouth lacerations from crack smoking as well as higher rates of genital ulcerations among female crack users.[47]

High rates of physical and sexual abuse among poor women are higher still amongst drug users. A New York City study of female intravenous drug users (IDUs) found that more than 60 percent had been physically abused at some point in their lives. Long periods of physical abuse, combined with drug use, leave many women feeling powerless about situations in their lives that involve drugs and sex.[48] Women have unequal access to clean needles. Women IDUs are more likely to borrow needles to avoid arrest for possession and more likely to lend needles as a form of life insurance in order to secure help in event of an overdose. This need for protection from male IDUs is why women are more likely to be in a sexual relationship with another IDU, again increasing their risk of infection. Connors observes, "The absence of a critical analysis of the role of poverty as a driving force in accelerating rates of HIV among women limits the development of programs to address the fundamental determinants of risk."[49]

The violence inflicted upon the mother is not confined to her. The parent with AIDS is typically indigent, with no prospect of employment. The families with seropositive mothers are in need of accessible and affordable health care, of welfare for living expenses, and of legal assistance to secure custody or guardian services. Between 7,000 and 10,000 American children are orphaned each year when their mothers die from AIDS.[50] Yet foster care and adoption assistance programs are among those least adequately funded in relation to the rise in cases. The redirection of income, related to globalization, has meant legislation cutting the government safety net of entitlements that sustain these families. The *New York Times* reported that the Welfare Reform Bill of 1996 provided a combined total from block grants for child care, from workfare, and from cash assistance of less than $15 per poor child per week in poor Southern states such as Mississippi and Arkansas.[51]

Several trends lead to institutionalized poverty of women. These include cuts in Aid to Families with Dependent Children (AFDC), minimum-wage employment, and the incarceration of black men. Prison construction has become a highly lobbied growth industry. When the men are sent to jail, it also hurts the women who have to take care of the family. Minimum-wage jobs do not make ends meet. Often, the only viable money-making options are to sell sex or drugs. Crime increases when better life options are restricted.

A study of Latino murders in 111 U.S. cities found links between homicide rates and Latino poverty, lack of educational opportunity, economic inequality, and the concentration of exclusively Latino ghetto communities. The importance of economic over racial factors could be seen in the diversity of the data. In Dallas, Texas, the Latino homicide rate was 67.9 per 100,000. This was sixty times greater than their rate in San Francisco.[52] Homicides rise where the local community has lost its assets to remote corporate interests. The ensuing poverty generates crimes of despair just as it generates the spread of HIV. And the globalization of the free-market economy ensures poverty and ecological devastation just as surely as it assures economic growth.

Clinton in Mexico

The North American Free Trade Agreement (NAFTA) and the neoliberal economic program that preceded it were presented in Mexico as the solution to sluggish growth rates experienced in the wake of the 1982 debt crisis. This promise has not corresponded to the reality that followed. Instead, the Mexican economy contracted and the country's productive capacity was seriously weakened. Mexico's trade deficit was filled by foreign investors who would then leave to find cheaper labor elsewhere and who would not renew short-term bonds, thereby creating a financial crisis. Free-trade agreements affect community well-being on both sides of the U.S.-Mexican border. President Clinton paid a visit to Mexico on Cinco de Mayo of 1997. His purpose was to promote the next phase of NAFTA, and he spoke to thousands of Mexican businessmen about the success of free trade. Mexico, like the United States, has experienced the benefits to a new group of multimillionaires. Mexican unemployment, however, has reached all-time highs. Massive Mexican military assistance was needed to buttress the police efforts to clear out a protest that appeared large enough to bring the largest city in the world to a close. The use of the military and a virtual press blackout is not surprising when considering the corporate stakes on both side of the border. The size of the protest should also not be a surprise because real wages in Mexico have dropped by half since the General Agreement on Trade and Tariffs (GATT) were put into place. The extent of desperation leads to violence.[53]

Recall the peasants of northern Tabasco, who organized the hunger strike until death. Recall also the more organized efforts of the Zapatistas. In a declaration at the outset of the revolt, the rebels noted that "in Chiapas, 14,500 people die a year, the highest death rate in the country, mostly from curable diseases." Mexico's first uprising in decades began on the day that NAFTA was signed. The rebellion in Chiapas pitted the indigenous rural poor against the Mexican government. Statements by Zapatista rebels indicate they were part of a larger movement for social and economic rights. On January 18, 1994, Zapatista leaders replied to the Mexican government's offer of conditional pardon:

> Who must ask for pardon and who can grant it? Why do we have to be pardoned? What are we going to be pardoned for? Of not dying of hunger? Of not being silent in our misery? Of not humbly accepting our historic role of being the despised and the outcast? Of having demonstrated to the rest of the country and the entire world that human dignity still lives, even among some of the world's poorest peoples?[54]

By the time of Clinton's visit, there had been a 45 percent increase in the number of maquiladoras working just over the border. Their average earnings had dropped from $1 an hour to seventy cents. The leaders of their protests were in jail. The maquiladora sector at the northern border has grown at the expense of manufacturing in other parts of Mexico. Still, China and India have overcome the Mexican lead for textile and clothing manufacture. For the United States, China has become the world's most powerful sweatshop provider. This goes with its abysmal working conditions, strict controls prohibiting worker organizing, lack of enforcement of labor laws, and a deliberate strategy by the Chinese government to convert a once-protected workforce, employed in state-owned factories, into a mobile and extremely vulnerable migrant labor force.[55] With economic decline and high unemployment in Mexico, immigration, both legal and illegal, has increased. Immigration has been blamed for loss of jobs in the United States and anti-immigrant groups have participated in vigilante activities against Mexicans coming over the border into Arizona.[56]

Domestic Terror

Mexicans, other immigrant groups, and racial minorities have been the target of serious racist scapegoating in the United States. Acts of direct violence such as church burnings reflect not only hatred but also the frustrations that permit it to take such forms. Some of the violence labeled terrorism is linked to the loss of personal control precipitated by the increasingly centralized control over local resources. The Unabomber, citing globalization, provided a more educated expression of this exclusion, but Timothy McVeigh, convicted of the Oklahoma City bombing, and the numerous militias are more typical. Their popular depiction as deranged individuals conceals some symmetries of their ideologies and of the options that have been left to them by the global economy.

A splinter faction of one such group, who call themselves the Republic of Texas, held two hostages near Fort Davis, Texas. Their claim was that Texas was never legally a part of the union, and they want it to act like an independent nation. Their weapons make their beliefs more than bothersome misperceptions. The Republic of Texas hostage-taker Richard McLaren was criticized by his own group for having "gone completely off the deep end" and was impeached as its ambassador.[57] The evolution of the Republic of Texas is instructive: The group is an offshoot of the property-rights movement, which itself shades gradually from people who are disgruntled with a government they see as not serving them to others obsessed with guns, military maneuvers, "The Turner Diaries," race war, and blowing up government buildings. The common themes are that wealthy Jewish bankers have control over the government and are taking away the rights and property of local citizens. They blame the government's affinity for racial minorities and immigrants who are getting the jobs deserved by "true" Americans. It is too easy to dismiss them as sociopaths or individuals unable to find a useful purpose in their own lives. The problem is that they cannot find a life with a useful purpose, and that is what accounts for the anger that winds up taking such bizarre turns.[58]

Terrorism reflects a political and economic problem. Half the working population of the United States has had falling or stagnant wages for thirty years. There is no future for young people who are not headed for college. The only time they are told that they are needed is as soldiers in meaningless wars, and they return with skills to shoot a gun but not to be part of the nation depicted for them on TV. They hear in the media how well people are doing, how the economy is booming, how the good life can be bought on credit. But millions of people lack the education or skills to participate in a high-technology global economy. Few of them know how much of the land they see as rightfully theirs is actually owned by international corporate interests in mining and forestry with headquarters in South Africa, Japan, or an offshore island tax shelter.

Republicans in the G. W. Bush administration are often blamed for the economic distress of poor people. However, hope that the Clinton administration might have done something substantial for working-class people had long since disappeared. Clinton's notable trip to Philadelphia in 1997 was to announce that government programs would not solve our problems—that we need volunteers. To provide the austerity to be competitive, the United States under the Clinton administration cut support for low-income housing by more than 90 percent. More people got arrested, and the prison construction industry grew to reflect the increased violence, one consequence of hopelessness. Jimmy Carter, who knows about volunteerism, tells us that the thousands of homes built by Habitat for Humanity are only a drop in the bucket of what is needed.[59]

Former Labor Secretary Robert Reich acknowledged that Bill Clinton's "Putting People First" plan, which would invest $50 billion a year in training people for skilled jobs that might support a purpose in life, is in the past. The political reality of bond traders during the budget surplus of the late 1990s called for balancing the budget, decreasing the debt, keeping interest rates at a level that satisfies Wall Street, reducing trade barriers, and cutting the safety net that prevents people from becoming victims of violence. These were neither nefarious schemes nor accidents of shortsighted policy. They were direct consequences of corporate-dominated economic globalization. Agencies of government seriously concerned with job creation or living wages no longer have the ability to enact programs that could achieve these ends. Now, in the twenty-first century, debt rates have been allowed to rise to historic levels. The borrowed money is not being used for education or for health care. Schools, enrichment programs, and libraries are closing and medical facilities are understaffed. The beneficiaries of the debt turn out to be the wealthiest investors of global corporations whose taxes have been reduced markedly. Social movements the world over have turned against the domination of their lands by global corporations and the military forces that protect them. In response, the weapons development and production sector of global corporate activity has grown, as has the recruitment of soldiers. This contribution to debt provides one more path by which wealth is transferred to the largest corporations at the expense of poor and middle-class people. Since the 1980s the United States has witnessed a serious assault on the concept that government provides for the well-being of its people. A middle-class lifestyle is often maintained by extensive debt and requires several incomes to sustain it. Many are just one job loss or one illness away from poverty.[60]

Is Global Corporate Growth Needed for Jobs or for Investments?

The theory of comparative advantage is an unquestioned assumption underlying one of the major tenets in trade theory. It contends that each country should enter the world market selling the products that they produce best or have a comparative advantage in producing. In theory, comparative advantage will have everyone working efficiently; production and consumption will increase, which should provide more goods for all. In practice, this means that countries well-endowed with raw materials and unskilled labor are to extract raw materials and provide labor for menial tasks of assembly while those well-endowed with capital, technology, skilled labor, and scientists are to process them. The doctrine serves as justification for a division of nations and communities according to what they bring to the production process.[61] This law traps countries in the place where their production profile has landed them, for historical or geographical reasons. It legitimizes an intolerable status quo and is itself a piece of structural violence.

The *National Security Strategy of the United States of America* turns such inequality into official policy. It notes, "History has judged the market economy as the single most effective economic system and the greatest antidote to poverty." Therefore, "the United States promotes free and fair trade, open markets, a stable financial system, the integration of the global economy, and secure, clean energy development." In this view the United States justifies invading the economies of many developing countries, sometimes with money, sometimes with military force.[62]

Proponents of the global economy argue that a rising tide raises all boats and that increased efficiency in productivity raises the standards of living for all nations and all peoples. It is likewise argued that international corporations bring in the jobs necessary in already impoverished areas and such jobs, even at low pay, provide a bridge for the country into the productive advancements of the industrially developed world. The nature of the jobs being produced should be examined. People are making garments, shoes, toys, and electronic components. Young females have the needed dexterity and the lack of options for other work and are the most frequent employees. Like the farm workers who are exploited by agribusiness in California and Texas, these women are recruited by subcontractors. This removes responsibilities for their pay or working conditions from the corporations. Although they may work ten to twelve hours a day for long periods, they are treated as casual employees without benefits or job security. They work with informal agreements rather than contracts on highly fragmented tasks for which they can be easily replaced. In fact, displacement is what is occurring. Destitute women in the Philippines are losing these awful jobs as companies move to Vietnam or China, where the work can be done even more cheaply and where worker organization would be more difficult.[63] One problem in protecting human rights against oppression has been the mobility of capital. If a massive corporation can pick up and move when labor gets too uppity in one country, then labor has no leverage. Mexico's maquiladoras plants have seen this happen with corporations moving to China.

Corporations have found another means to keep labor costs down while cutting the temporary costs of relocating their factories. The *mobile work force* refers to a process by which a company may remain in one area while importing workers, through a contractor, from more destitute regions anywhere in the world. Pakistanis wind up in China or in Mexico. These migrants, who are poorer than the local population, are housed in cheap hovels. Cut off from close familial ties, they are entirely dependent upon the contractor.

The market is considered the primary source for economic entrepreneurship and technical innovation. However, markets do not instruct people with large incomes to consume no more than their rightful share of natural resources. They do not prevent retailers from selling guns to children. They do not require producers to recycle their waste. They give no priority for the allocation of scarce resources to meet the basic needs to those who have little or no money before providing luxuries to those with great wealth. In fact, the market does just the opposite. Civil societies create governments precisely for citizens to establish and maintain rules that might restrict the forces of the market.[64]

The shoe and apparel industries utilize low-capital investment (labor-intensive work) with little expenditure for technology that would improve the work environment. Such practice does not promote vigorous national industries. Nike claims credit for higher wages eventually won by workers in Taiwan and South Korea. Those wage increases were a product of popular movements for democratization. As repression lessened, workers were able to unionize and win better wages and working conditions for themselves. Large corporations are not generous. As conditions improve for workers, the company finds other locations and moves on.

The global economy rewards repression through investment and punishes freedom through disinvestment. The low-wage havens sought by corporations are also, not coincidentally, havens of repression. When South Korea and Taiwan began to democratize, Nike looked to Indonesia. Now China and Vietnam are the new magnets for investment. These corporations do not overtly support repression, but they most certainly profit from it. Multinational corporations conduct extensive research and can quickly move capital wherever the conditions of low wages, weak environmental laws, or assured profits can be found. Multinational corporations are currently engaged in a race to the bottom, where in order to be competitive they outsource their production facilities to countries with weak environmental and labor laws.

The movement toward corporate globalism, although accelerated today, is surely not new. The earliest corporations, such as the Hudson Bay Corporation, were created for the exploration and exploitation of new lands on behalf of imperial powers. What is new is the ability of the global economy to command the resources of almost every locality.[65]

Global corporations benefit from policies of the U.S. government and the World Bank (in which the United States has a controlling interest). Policies include supporting repression and loaning huge sums to swindlers who can deliver cheap labor. The result is that many countries are hopelessly in debt and at the mercy of the World Bank and International Monetary Fund, whose actions have proliferated low-wage, export-oriented economies. By the World Bank's own criteria, 37.5 percent of bank-funded projects in 1991 were failures at time of completion. An earlier study of four- to ten-year follow-up evaluations found that twelve of the twenty-five projects that were rated successful when completed eventually turned out to be failures. This means that less than a third of the projects provided an economic return sufficient to justify the original investment.[66] At least one country, Eritrea, has refused such loans and is slowly using its own resources to rebuild a railway that was destroyed by civil war. Its cost will be less than one-fifth of what international contractors would have charged. Perhaps not by coincidence, the United States has supported Ethiopian military efforts to destabilize Eritrea. Failure or not, the World Bank has no liability for its errors. The loans must be repaid by poor countries in scarce foreign exchange. This means absolute austerity in programs that might improve the lives of people. It is a great deal for corporate giants but a disaster for most of the world. The continuing, misguided approaches of the World Bank have been documented by former World Bank economist William Easterly.[67] World Bank and International Monetary Fund policies have left the poorer countries in such debt that they have no choice but to allow international commerce to exploit their natural resources, pay their workers at poverty levels, and accept the toxic wastes of the developed world.[68] The global economy is creating populations with no measure of control over the local material and human resources they need to survive.[69]

The Continuum—from Slaves to Billionaires

How bad a deal this is for poor people may be seen in the fact that poverty tends to increase regardless of whether the economy for investors is growing or shrinking. As a general rule, women are more vulnerable than men. Women constitute 75 percent of the poorest people in the world today. They produce half the world's food, but own only 1 percent of its farmland. Two-thirds of illiterate adults are women. In some developing countries, women are more likely to die in childbirth than reach the sixth grade. A large number of these people currently live not merely in poverty but in slavery.[70] The estimated number of human slaves today in all continents is 27 million. Debt bondage is the most common form in which families with nothing are forced to work merely to repay unjust debts to a landowner.[71] The debt of poor countries is being taken over by vulture fund companies. They buy the debt of poor countries, such as Zambia, at hugely discounted prices and then sue for the full amount plus interest and punitive damages. It is completely legal, but it dooms people in these countries to endless bondage. The vulture companies have no moral and legal obligations. Beyond debt forgiveness, a comprehensive debt-relief system would require companies to follow ethical and legal guidelines.

How great a deal is this economic structure for the global investors? There were 793 billionaires in 2005, up 15 percent from the previous year. Their combined net worth was $2.6 trillion dollars with U.S. billionaires accounting for almost half of the amount.[72] Earnings of these billionaires are greater than the income of the poorer half of the world's population. During the past year there has been an 11 percent increase in corporate growth, and CEOs from the major corporations increased their incomes by 50 percent. The U.S. Congress, which cut 90 percent of funds for low-income housing, could not pass a law preventing corporations from deducting incomes in excess of $1 million as ordinary business expenses. Of the 100 largest economies in the world, fifty-one are now not nations but corporations.[73] The 100 largest corporations are still the source of employment for just one-third of 1 percent of the world's population.

Risk and the Market

One basic rule of market economics is that the participants in transactions must bear the full costs of their decisions in addition to reaping the benefits. However, the best way to avoid losses is to find another party who can be tagged with the responsibility for assuming risk from which you benefit.[74] Larger corporations go to considerable lengths to reap the benefits for themselves and to pass the costs on to others. They do not provide adequate health insurance for their employees. Wal-Mart is the world's largest and most profitable retailer and its largest employer. At the end of 2005, the company ranked second on the Fortune 500 with sales of $312 billion and net profits of $11.2 billion. Yet Wal-Mart failed to provide company health care to half of its employees and instead offered advice on how their low wages could get them government coverage. The practice left nearly half of its workers either uninsured or on public assistance at a cost of $1.4 billion to taxpayers. In 2005 Wal-Mart failed to provide health care for 15,693 of its California workers and their dependents. Instead, these employees were forced to rely on government programs, which cost California taxpayers over $39,141,590.

The success of larger corporations has been based largely upon their ability to have the risks associated with their expansion underwritten by governments, and ultimately by taxpayers. Hence the $20 billion development of a satellite system from government funds was transferred to AT&T. Nuclear energy, electronics, aeronautics, space communications, mineral exploitation, computer systems, agricultural technologies, and medical biogenetics are all areas of research subsidization.

Costs of environmental damage are also transferred. The government not only fails to stop environmental damage but also contributes to it. There are over 20,000 radioactive and toxic chemical sites in U.S. military bases, contaminating air, water, and land. The Department of Energy has no safe way to dispose of radioactive waste, yet it failed to stop the leakage of uranium into underground water supplies adjacent to several nuclear-weapons facilities. The government has also let the military and the private sector dump radioactive nuclear waste into the ocean, near fishing areas along the East and West Coasts.[75]

In *Democracy for the Few*, Michael Parenti states the essential problem:

> Serious contradictions exist between our human needs and our economic system, a system whose primary goal is to maximize profits regardless of the waste, cost and hazards. We see that government is an insufficient bulwark against the baneful effects of giant corporate capitalism and often a willing handmaiden.[76]

Global poverty is tragic, but it is not an accident. A closer look suggests a

> system-driven global impoverishment and poverty-creation, a process of high crime and grand fraud made all the more pernicious by its patent exploitativeness and extreme social injustice but also by its invisibility and concealment by the blinders of the market. It is thus a perfect crime, until of course it is exposed. But until then it is the world's best-kept secret.[77]

If one takes the perspective that violence is created by the blocking of human-needs fulfillment, the global economy presents some long-term problems. We are experiencing astounding economic expansion. But where do the resources come from that allow for exponential economic growth? Where will the wastes be stored? What will happen to the farmers who are displaced? How many roads will have to be built for how many cars, and how much of the earth's limited resources will be consumed? Where will we look for wisdom once global consumerism has produced a monoculture of the mind? How will we count the costs of the loss of wetlands and songbirds? When only growth and marketability are valued, how then will we cope with overcrowded cities with sporadic employment? How will we cope with inadequate care for children, elders, the disabled, poor single parents who raise their children, and other members of society whom we have labeled dependent? How will we cope with the stress of work sped up for the holders of temporary jobs? How much violence will be generated by this success of the global economy? When the key players are multinational corporations, then it seems economic growth is not a valid indicator of anything that we should care about.

Increasing trade is not something to be feared. Neither is technology the culprit. Globalization has potentials for creating a culture in which all humans are viewed as family. The problem is a process of integration into the global market carried out, at least since 1980, under circumstances of unsustainable finance. Wealth has flowed upward from the poor countries to the rich, and mainly to the upper financial levels of the richest countries.

> In the course of these events, progress toward tolerable levels of inequality and sustainable development virtually stopped. Neocolonial patterns of center-periphery dependence, and of debt peonage, were reestablished, but without the slightest assumption of responsibility by the rich countries for the fate of the poor.[78]

The global economy is creating a borderless world shaped by capital efficiency and military and technological superiority.[79] The good news is that globalization has also contributed an amazingly powerful global movement to retake control over the basic resources needed for human well-being. Breakthroughs in communication have combined with the diminution of power and the malleability of boundaries of the nation state. An international global network of NGOs and local grassroots groups is taking shape.

CHAPTER 4

PEOPLE, FARMLAND, WATER, AND NARCOTICS

Each generation has its own rendezvous with the land, for despite fee titles and claims of ownership, we are all brief tenants on this planet. By choice or default, we will carve out a land legacy for our heirs. . . . History tells us that earlier civilizations have declined because they did not learn to live in harmony with the land.

—*Stewart Lee Udall, The Quiet Crisis*

This we know. The earth does not belong to man: man belongs to the earth. All things are connected. . . . Man did not weave the web of life; he is merely a strand in it. What he does to the web, he does to himself.

—*Chief Seattle*

Economic globalization has been shown to create extremes of wealth among a few and serious poverty for many. This chapter examines an even greater impact of the same corporate economic forces upon the land, cultivation of food, and the precarious link between the ecological system and the continuation of life.

Ancient migrations were common as hunters and gatherers sought food and hospitable surroundings. Then, agriculture contributed to a sense of permanence and of place that lasted across generations, sometimes even providing a surplus for trade and for more complex cultural development. People were once closer to the acre of land that fed them. The variety of products and the level of care that preserved the land for future use made these one-acre farms from 200 to 1,000 times more efficient than the corporate farms that have replaced them. Farmers nurtured the 2 billion microorganisms found in a spoonful of soil and saved the best seeds to improve their produce. The seeds, the values of attachment to the land, and the farmers themselves are being replaced.[1]

Farmers whose families have been farming for up to six generations are being forced to leave the land, but they cannot sell their farms for a price high enough to pay even the taxes on the land. A sense of failure has increased farm suicide rates in the United States and around the world. Farmers can no longer feed their families on what they produce.

The change in agriculture from small and medium-sized family owned farms to corporate, plantation agriculture has devastated millions throughout history. Modern agricultural firms such as Cargill, ADM, and ConAgra have bought up their smaller competitors and now constitute an agribusiness that maximizes profits with high pesticide and technology use and very low labor costs. They produce mono-crops for global distribution and are subsidized by acreage. They do not pay for the long-term costs of the devastation of the soil or of the communities they have transformed.[2]

Large agricultural production facilities meet the needs of a few international food companies, which control the processing and distributing of most food. Nestlé, the world's largest food corporation, has been involved with the marketing of infant formula to areas of the world where people had neither the money to continue using the formula once breast milk had stopped nor clean water to mix it. The second largest food company, Phillip Morris (which owns Kraft Foods), still targets children for cigarette markets outside of the United States.

Contemporary agriculture does produce a plentiful and sometimes inexpensive supply of food for supermarkets. However, with the food supply driven by criteria of profitability, much of the world's population (including many who used to be small farmers) is not getting this food.[3] Driven from once-viable farms to rocky hillsides, farmers in poor countries are forced to abandon the land and move into the money economy to support their families. Some find low-paying jobs producing for supermarkets and fast-food chains. Forty percent of the world population lives on less than $2 a day. There is more food, more waste, and more hunger now than ever before. The psychological consequences have been devastating. Before colonial control over agriculture, men had meaningful jobs to do and the freedom to do them. Colonial expansion routed men and women from work with clear meaning to jobs defined by others, often leaving deep wounds in the identification with what it means to be human.

Food Production: The Impact of Globalization

Over 75 percent of the world's poorest people rely on farming as their way to earn a living. Paradoxically, many of them go hungry. There are 840 million hungry and malnourished people in the world today.[4]

The human population is growing exponentially, with a quarter of a million people added daily; yet food production is only able to increase at a linear rate. Providing food for the increasing numbers is an overwhelming challenge.[5] People are not starving because there is too little food. Currently, there is enough food to feed everyone on the planet. In the United States there is such abundance of food that one in every five adults is obese, and obesity among children (and even among pets) is increasing.[6]

A common myth is that economic development removes malnutrition. India, with the second largest population in the world, has experienced remarkable rates of economic development. The U.S. Congress has approved an agreement for U.S. corporations to develop nuclear power plants in India, thereby promising an increase in electricity to promote future development. As President Bush and Prime Minister Manmohan Singh shook hands on the landmark pact, the World Bank released a study showing that almost 40 percent of the world's malnourished children live in India. "I think the Western world, and perhaps more so the United States of America, has a feeling that India is a highly developed country," noted Babu Mathew, Indian director of the development agency ActionAid. "They are reluctant to face the reality of the other side of India, which is millions of people living in poverty." An estimated 300 million of India's 1.1 billion people live below the official poverty line of less than $1 a day. According to Mathew, the number of poor is actually much higher because the government underestimates the daily minimum of calories each Indian needs when measuring poverty. Although the right to adequate nutrition is enshrined in the Indian Constitution, the World Bank study found more than 38 percent of the nation's children are undernourished, compared with 26 percent in sub-Saharan Africa.[7] The conditions of food insufficiency underlie movements for radical change in how the necessities of life are distributed.[8]

Hunger in the United States

Hunger is defined as "the uneasy or painful sensation caused by lack of food due to constrained resources"; food insecurity refers to the lack of access to enough food to fully meet basic needs at all times.[9] Adults living in food-insecure households, for example, will skip meals so their children can eat and will feed their family with low-quality, unbalanced diets. Based on U.S. Census Bureau surveys, those at greatest risk of being hungry live in households that are (1) headed by a single woman, (2) Latino or Black, and (3) with incomes below the poverty level. Households with children face food insecurity at more than double the rate of those without children. Food insecurity is also more common in central city households than in suburban or rural areas.[10]

In the world's richest country, well over 20 million Americans do not have enough to eat. The number rose by 50 percent between 1983 and 1997 and continues to rise. According to FRAC, a national nonprofit research and public policy center working to eradicate hunger, nearly 35 million people—including 13 million children—in the United States were hungry or living on the edge of hunger in 2002. In 2003 over 36 million Americans were living in food-insecure households. Between 1999 and 2002, food insecurity increased in total by 3.9 million individuals (2.9 million adults and over 1 million children).[11]

In 2001 America's Second Harvest, the largest hunger relief organization in the United States, conducted a nationwide survey consisting of more than 32,000 face-to-face client interviews. Their research concluded that over 23.3 million Americans per year are served by their network of service providers—an increase of over 9 percent since their previous survey in 1997. Children make up 39 percent of those served. The most disturbing trend identified by their research was that the greatest increase in hunger and food insecurity is among the working poor. During 2001, 39 percent of food recipient households (those served by emergency shelters, soup kitchens, and food pantries) had one or more adult working.[12] Well over 21 million Americans turn to food banks or soup kitchens each year, and more than 70,000 people are turned away when supplies run out.[13]

Each year, the U. S. Conference of Mayors (USCM) presents an annual survey of cities' requests for emergency assistance. In December 2004 requests for emergency food assistance had increased in 96 percent of the twenty-seven cities surveyed from 2003. The report also concluded that an average of 20 percent of the demand for emergency food is estimated to have gone unmet in the surveyed cities. Almost half of the cities reported that emergency food assistance programs were not able to provide an adequate supply of food.[14]

In the poorer half of the world, where neither nutrition nor potable water is assured, 12 million children under five years of age die each year (33,000 per day), the overwhelming majority from preventable conditions. An equal number survive with permanent disabilities that could have been prevented.[15] The toll from malnutrition occurs because people have neither the means to produce food nor enough money to buy it. "Further, farmers in the leading grain-producing regions of the world are going broke because grain surpluses keep prices below the cost of production, a deficit met by about $28 billion in direct farm subsidies in the United States alone in 2000."[16] Farmers in the United States and Europe have been suppressing the world price of grain by subsidizing agribusiness. The United States alone issues $28 billion a year in direct farm subsidies, leading the farmers to overproduce grain.[17] This surplus grain from the developed countries, in turn, significantly lowers the world price, making it very difficult for poorer, mainly agriculturally driven, countries to compete in the grain market. In fact, in many poor regions such as Africa and South America, and even in some middle-income countries such as Egypt, the grain market has been wiped out because of the heightened competition.

Most American grain is produced to sustain a highly inefficient meat-centered diet. Livestock must be fed before they are killed. A pig in the United States consumes about 100 pounds of soybean meal and 600 pounds of corn and will weigh about 240 pounds when slaughtered. The meat from this pig will provide one person with enough food for forty-nine days. However, the person who eats the soybean and corn directly will have more than enough food for 500 days.[18] Much of food production is for the fast-food industry, growing most rapidly in China where the first McDonald's opened in 1992. The globalization of McDonald's is visible almost everywhere, including the entrance to Dachau, a German concentration camp during the Holocaust.[19] The global fast-food industry fuels the cruel treatment of animals, which are subject to rampant disease, fed on grains that could feed people, and dosed with more antibiotics than are used by human beings.[20]

Economic Globalization

Globalization means the spread of free-market capitalism to virtually every country in the World.[21] Its core assumption is that trade, unrestricted by national or local regulation, is good. International standards, determined by the World Trade Organization, aim to provide free reign to market forces. Globalization is the "result of conscious political decisions that place international trade above other priorities."[22] Trade once reinforced nationalism. With globalization, trade undermines it.[23] Acquisitions, consolidations, and mergers, however, reduce free-market competition and concentrate power in the hands of a few.[24] A small number of large global corporations are now as powerful, if not more powerful, than many small- and medium-sized nation states.[25]

World Bank structural adjustment policies allow poor countries to address their development loan debt by extending terms of repayment. Restructuring is contingent upon the nation's acceptance of free-trade agreements and substantial restrictions in government spending. This has meant serious restrictions in education, aid to local farmers, and health care. Structural adjustment creates long-term debt that removes hopes for future solvency, leaving poor countries at the mercy of private corporations for meeting basic needs.[26]

One of the downsides of corporate globalization is the polarization of income. While the gross domestic product (GDP) in poorer countries may be growing, very little of this growth is expressed accurately in GDP per capita. Indeed one of the biggest problems of economic development has been the uneven distribution of profits and rising inequality. The poorer half of the world's population has a decreasing share, while the upper 5 percent has a markedly increased share.[27]

Other problems of globalization and the proliferation of multinational corporations include an increase in the slave trade. Poor women from Thailand, Ukraine, and other areas in which the local economy has been displaced have been lured by false promises into the sex slave industry, while children have been kidnapped and forced to harvest chocolate in the Gold Coast of Africa or to make rugs in Pakistan.[28] This chapter, however, will focus primarily upon changes to patterns of sustainable agriculture that have existed since the first cultivation of vegetation or animals.

"Globalization has changed the entire food chain, including suppliers of fertilizers, pesticides, hybrid seed and tractors, as well as grain traders, transportation companies, processors and supermarkets."[29] ConAgra, the largest multinational food production corporation in the United States, is involved in every part of the food chain that begins with the seeds and ends in the shelf of the supermarket. Its profits have been increasing at approximately 14 percent per year.[30] Six grain companies control the grain trade in the United States. There are about the same number around the world. Four meatpacking companies slaughter 79 percent of all the beef in the United States. Lacking economic power, farmers are being reduced by giant grain companies to a minimal role in the food system, whereas supranational corporations now rule world food production.[31]

In the United States, 50 percent of the farmland is owned by 4 percent of farm owners. Typically, farmers who own the land do not farm it but hire others. About 38 percent of the farm laborers hired to work the farms are paid either at, or below, the federal poverty level while working an average of forty-six hours per week. We have long had studies to show that towns with absentee ownership of the land have a lower quality of life on many dimensions—worse schools, fewer libraries, inferior community services, and shorter life expectancies.[32] Conditions are much worse for the landless in less-developed countries. Clearly the profits from the multinational food production companies are not being passed on to workers.[33]

Most of the world's 183 nations depend upon imported food. Canada, France, Australia, Argentina, and the United States export 80 percent of cereal grain. With the U.S. population expected to double in seventy years, the cereal grain now exported to poor countries would be used to feed the addition of 540 million Americans. When American exports cease, countries in Africa and Asia, now dependent upon the imports, will be without food that is essential to their survival.[34] China is expected to become the largest importer of food in the world within the next decade.

People are starving because of the uneven distribution of food and the inability of the people in poor countries to afford it. The harsh fact is that food is not reaching the 840 million hungry people in the world who need it.[35] "Economic globalization in the absence of civic and political globalization means we have globalized our vices without globalizing our virtues."[36]

Biotechnology

Scientific breakthroughs are often heralded as the answer to world hunger. The biotechnology industry is booming. As of April 2005, the total value of publicly traded U.S. biotech companies was $311 billion.[37] In 1994 industry sales were $7.2 billion, and in 2004 industry sales were up to $33.3 billion.[38]

In agriculture, biotechnology is focused upon efficiency. This is driven by supranational corporations, such as Monsanto, that have entered the biotechnology industry with genetically modified seeds. The justification for adding fish genes to a tomato has nothing to do with its nutrition or taste but only with its shelf life. Shelf life is important only if we destroy local farms and replace them with transnational farm factories. Nearly $500 million a year is spent on media campaigns to tell us that this is good.[39]

According to the International Service for the Acquisition of Agri-Biotech Applications (ISAAA), biotech crops increased more than forty-seven-fold, from 1.7 million hectares in 1996 during the nine-year period between 1996 and 2004. Acreage of biotech crops increased 20 percent between 2003 and 2004, which amounts to an increase of 32.9 million acres, or 13.3 million hectares.[40] The estimated global area of biotech crops for 2004 was 8.1 million hectares (200 million acres). The ISAAA notes that in 2004, for the first time, growth in biotech crops in developing countries outpaced that of industrial countries by 35 percent.[41]

These figures, however, have been disputed. The industry coalition Agriculture Biotechnology in Europe says the ISAAA's claims of 500,000 hectares of biotech crops in South Africa are grossly exaggerated. According to the international environmental organization Grain, the number of farmers in South Africa growing GM Bt (genetically modified, insect-resistant) cotton has declined from 3,000 to 700. Of the remaining 700 farmers continuing to grow the GM Bt cotton, 90 percent are in debt. The total debt among small-scale cotton farmers in Northern KwaZulu Natal was estimated at over $3 million (U.S. dollars) in 2004.[42]

The agri-biotech industry claims that their mission is to increase production for farmers everywhere and to end poverty and world hunger. The mission of CGIAR (Consultative Group on International Agricultural Research), the mammoth alliance of fifty-eight countries, international and regional organizations, and private foundations is to "achieve sustainable food security and reduce poverty in developing countries through scientific research and research-related activities in the fields of agriculture, forestry, fisheries, policy, and environment."[43] The fifteen centers and programs under CGIAR include the International Food Policy Research Institute, the International Water Management Institute, and the World AgroForestry Centre. The two top contributors to CGIAR in 2004 were the United States ($54.2 million) and the World Bank ($50 million). Total revenues for CGIAR in 2004 were $453 million. Ismail Serageldin, vice president of the World Bank, is also chair of CGIAR. The consortium produces regular reports of its activities. It is revealing that with all of the elaborate documentation of financial reports and returns for investors, little or no evidence is given to show actual benefits to the farmers themselves—for whom these projects are purportedly designed.[44]

Mergers and acquisitions in the biotech industry have created a vertically integrated supply chain. Large multinational firms, such as Monsanto, DuPont, and Novartis, team up with small genetics firms that supply the large firms with services and supplies. The smaller firms are protected by licensing agreements, the large firms by patents.[45] With the introduction of genetically modified (GM) seeds, farmers are asked to sign licensing agreements to use the seeds. They must agree not to share the seeds with family or neighbors, and not to save any seeds for future harvests.[46] For additional protection for the multinationals, a researcher with the U.S. Department of Agriculture has developed a "terminator" gene, backed by Monsanto, to avoid seed piracy. The terminator prevents a seed from germinating. In essence the seed is sterilized and can only be used by the party signing the licensing agreement for that particular seed.[47] The farmer who once saved the best fruits for next year's seeds is then obliged to purchase seeds anew.

Biotechnology and Intellectual Property

Before 1930 the concept of intellectual property over living organisms did not exist. Plants were viewed as being part of the public domain, and their use could not be restricted. The passage of the Plant Variety Protection Act in the United States established intellectual property rights for plants.[48] Intellectual property rights result when ownership can be claimed for ideas and knowledge. Corporations have been accused of scientific poaching,[49] benefiting from the use of over 70 percent of the genetic pool of agricultural seed and livestock of developing countries without any compensation for the developing country.[50] Traditionally, one could gain a patent for an invented device, but the ideas on which the device was based were public. Watson and Crick did not patent their theory about the molecular structure of DNA. Gene splicing made this patentable because it is the application of the basic theory of the molecular structure of DNA. However, the distinction between public and private domain is becoming blurred.[51]

> The continuous squeezing of biotechnological inventions—particularly the patentability in Europe of inventions related to living matter—into the framework of patent law has obliged the introduction of rather strained legal concepts or blatant irregularities in the application of the law. Much of this tinkering has been prompted, of course, by transnational companies' needs to obtain cross-border protection.[52]

Rice is the single most important crop for feeding humans. Most rice has been grown through history in small paddy fields in China, India, and Indonesia. Now it is being genetically mapped by Syngenta, the world's largest agrochemical firm, just ahead of Bayer. It is also a major seller of seeds, just behind Monsanto and Dupont. The patent sought for rice could apply to flowering plants in general, giving the firm a key foothold for control over agriculture. The firm's extensive lobbying budget and close connections with CGIAR and the U.N. Food and Agriculture Organization make it well placed to increase its fortunes through genetic modification and patents over seeds.[53]

Genetically modified seeds do not increase the farmer's yield. Monsanto has developed, licensed, and sold a GM soybean crop called Roundup Ready. It actually yields far less than other soybean seeds that are not genetically modified. But promotion by such companies as Asgrow, a Monsanto subsidiary of GM seeds, abounds in seed catalogues. This propaganda is also presented to farmers by major agribusiness through forums. It is also propagated by researchers at the universities who receive government funds for agricultural research.[54] As a result, farmers are placed under great pressure to buy the GM seeds even if they yield less than seeds not genetically modified.

The green revolution of the 1960s and 1970s created designer hybrids of such basic crops as corn, soybeans, and wheat for higher yields and disease resistance. The resulting monoculture places the world's harvest at risk to unknown diseases. "The greater the diversity of seeds and crops, the less likely it would be that the system as a whole would be at risk."[55] When Hurricane Mitch hit Central America in 1998, traditional land management systems were found to be much more resilient to this natural disaster. Farms that used the monoculture method had 60 to 80 percent more crop damage, soil erosion, and water loss than those that used traditional farming techniques, such as water conservation, crop mixing, and biological pest control. A focus on this type of resilience from traditional farming methods protects the farmer's future livelihood just as diverse crops reduce the risk of agricultural blight.[56] Diverse crops reduce the risk of agricultural disasters just as diverse investment portfolios reduce risk of financial setbacks.

Seeds are the basis of life but are no longer viewed as part of the public domain. Once patented, no one can use the seeds without paying a royalty. This is true for an organic seed, such as for colored cotton from Latin America,[57] as well as for a genetically engineered seeds for corn, cotton, soybean, and canola owned by Monsanto.[58] Biotechnology has proven to be another tool for the domination of food production by corporate agriculture. As such, it has contributed to the erosion both of the soil and of people's capacity to provide food for their families. Unable to farm their traditional crops in a sustainable manner, they are either driven from the land or forced to produce for the drug trade.

The Privatization of Water

Beyond the sales of patented seeds, corporations have found other ways to commodify gifts of nature and thereby affect the viability of local communities. Consumption of water, worldwide, is doubling every twenty years, more than twice as fast as population growth. "Groundwater is being pumped faster than nature is recharging it in many of the world's most important food-producing regions—including parts of India, Pakistan, the north China plain, and the western United States."[59] Forty percent of the human food supply comes from irrigated land; yet more than a billion people live in areas that lack the water resources to meet basic food and material needs. One-fifth of irrigated land is losing productivity due to soil salinization. And in many of the world's river basins there is little water left to tap for agriculture. In Bangladesh a farmer was killed by a corporate aquaculture group for protesting the destruction of farmland from saltwater seepage. Similarly shortsighted applications of corporate aquaculture are destroying wetlands and local agriculture in India, Malaysia, and Ecuador.[60]

According to the United Nations, more than 1 billion people already lack access to fresh drinking water. Fresh water is a finite resource that accounts for less than one-half of 1 percent of the world's total water stock. It is rapidly being diverted, depleted, and polluted, largely by corporate agriculture. Every fifteen seconds a child dies from a condition associated with unsafe water. By the year 2025, two-thirds of the world's population will be living with serious water deprivation. By that time, fresh water demand is expected to rise to 56 percent more than is currently available. Technologies exist to increase water efficiency, but the global economy does not assure that they will be affordable to farmers.[61]

Recognizing an emerging market for water, global multinationals, such as Monsanto and Bechtel, are seeking control of world water systems and supplies. Monsanto plans to earn revenues of $420 million and a net profit of $63 million by 2008 from its water business in India and Mexico. The company estimates that water will become a multibillion-dollar market in the coming decades.[62] The World Bank has accommodated to this new market by a policy of water privatization and full-cost water pricing. Governments are signing away control over water supplies by participating in the North American Free Trade Agreement and in the World Trade Organization. These agreements give transnational corporations the unprecedented right to the water of signatory countries.[63]

While companies have expanded their profits, grassroots resistance to privatization of water has emerged. Recently, a civil society movement has been created to wrest back control of water and claim it for people and nature. The Blue Planet Project is an alliance of farmers, environmentalists, indigenous peoples, public sector workers, and urban activists whose pressure brought the issue of water as a human right to the March 2000 World Water Forum in The Hague.[64] One focal point of the effort has been in Bolivia. At present, 70 percent of the 8.4 million Bolivians live below the poverty line. Most rural communities lack electricity and running water, and the country's rates of infant and child mortality are the highest in South America. Coca eradication strategies cost Bolivians a total of $500 million each year. It is little wonder that the most marginalized populations in the Andean nation resent the United States for dramatically altering peasant livelihoods in an ineffective effort to curb an epidemic of cocaine addiction that the United States has failed to competently address back home.[65]

This policy of water privatization is leading to major distress in poor countries. The fear is that their citizens will not be able to afford water sold for profit. Studies have shown that when water is sold in the open market, it is delivered only to wealthy individuals and cities.

Bechtel vs. Bolivia

In 1999 the Bolivian government granted a forty-year concession privatizing the water system of its third largest city, Cochabamba. A consortium led by the Italian Water Limited and U.S. Bechtel immediately raised water prices. With many Bolivians working at a minimum wage of $65 month, water bills of $20 or more proved an extreme burden. Some could not even afford the permits required by the company for water collection. Thousands of citizens protested for weeks. The Bolivian army killed one, injured hundreds, and arrested coalition leaders. In April 2000 the Cochabamba citizen coalition known as *La Coordinadora* won its demands, and the consortium of corrupt government managers and transnational corporations was obliged to withdraw.[66]

Eighteen months after being forced to leave the country, Bechtel and its coinvestor, Abengoa of Spain, filed a $50 million lawsuit against Bolivia to compensate for its investments (estimated at less than $1 million) and lost future profits. The lawsuit was brought before a closed-door trade court operated by the World Bank. The trade court, the International Center for Settlement of Investment Disputes (ICSID), operates in a highly secretive manner; the public and the media are not informed as to where or when the case tribunals meet, who testifies, or what they say. As a report by the Institute for Policy Studies and Food and Water Watch describes it, the World Bank/ICSID dispute resolution process "has given global companies unprecedented power to undermine governments' authority to protect human rights and natural resources and pursue national development strategies."[67] In May 2007, three Latin American countries—including Bolivia—announced that they were ending their participation with the ICSID.

International trade courts aside, it is not easy to win a lawsuit against Bechtel, which *Engineering News-Record* magazine ranks as the largest construction company in the United States. The company's projects have included the Alaska pipeline, the Hoover Dam, and the San Francisco Bay Bridge. Their work on natural gas pipelines in Algeria has displaced large numbers of people and contributed to a history of violence, as have their refineries in Zambia. In the past century, Bechtel has worked on 19,000 contracts in 140 different countries. The company signs new contracts around the world on a daily basis. Environmental and social impacts of the company's construction activities, such as the Bolivian water project, are rarely reported. Hopes to contest Bechtel's suit against the cooperative water project in Bolivia centered on the company's desire to avoid bad publicity.[68]

On January 19, 2006, Bechtel and its coinvestor, Abengoa of Spain, agreed to drop their case in ICSID for a token payment of 2 bolivianos ($30). Sources directly involved in the settlement negotiations cited continued international citizen pressure as the reason the companies decided to drop the case.[69]

This is the first time that a major corporation has ever dropped a major international trade case as a direct result of global public pressure. The case illustrates the importance of information exchange that goes beyond mainstream media. Equally important, it shows that citizen's groups provide local voices with an opportunity to be heard in the promotion of effective water conservation.

Agriculture and the Production of Narcotics

Factory farms, accompanied by the domination of seeds and water by transnational corporations, have made small farms unprofitable. Former farmers the world over have been transformed into farm laborers, refugees, and pawns in the growth of crops for illegal drugs. The pattern has historical roots.

The concept of war between nation states is overshadowed in history by the conquest and colonization of most of the world by European nations, particularly Great Britain. In many instances the conquests came against tribal societies, sometimes bribed and often coerced into accepting colonial domination. One major mechanism for control over colonized people was through the distribution of narcotics. In India in the eighteenth century, small-scale farming was forcibly replaced by the British East India Company, with larger cotton plantations and with the massive cultivation of poppies. The extracted opium was shipped to the coastal cites of China, Canton, and Hangchou, where it was initially given away. By 1906, 27 percent of the Chinese male population were users. As production and distribution expanded to create a passive and servile underclass, a worldview created by royal elites espoused their divine rights to rule over this depraved group and to justify their own extreme privilege.[70]

The War on Drugs

The more recent war on drugs has left big narcotics cartels untouched and has not stopped drug laundering through established financial institutions. It is instead a war on drug addicts. Nonviolent first offenders in drug cases are in jail longer, on average, than murderers and other violent criminals. There has been an influx of police officers, National Guardsmen, and other federal agents into certain U.S. inner cities because of a program called "Operation Weed and Seed." By way of aerial and video surveillance, antigang and antidrug sweeps and making residents carry special identification, the government tries to "weed" criminals out. The main accomplishment of this exercise has been to violate the civil liberties of the residents. The drug war is supported by the pharmaceutical industry, which has historically marketed narcotics and which now markets its own legal forms of barbiturates, painkillers, and mood-altering substances. Their lobby, Pharma, is a supporter of the war on drugs, which helps to criminalize a strong competitor.[71] The most ironic thing about the program is that the money used to operate Weed and Seed had previously been allocated to human services, where it could have been use to improve the infrastructure of the inner cities and to work on correcting the root causes of crime.[72]

Three case studies—in Colombia, Afghanistan, and Burma—illustrate what globalization has caused in the transition from local farming to reliance upon drug cartels.

Colombia: Militarizing a Social and Economic Problem

Colombia has 40 million people, 50 percent of whom live in abject poverty with a yearly wage of less than $500. In the rural areas, the number living in poverty increases to 80 percent. Although there is arable land, the farmers are unable to grow legal crops, in part because they are undersold by imports but also because there are few roads to take the crops to market. Colombia receives extensive aid from the United States, but instead of using this for infrastructure, it is spent on buying military assistance for the government. However, coca (cocaine) can be harvested four or five times a year, and once it is reduced to paste can be carried out on horseback. After expenses and taxes paid to the paramilitary or the guerillas, the farmer nets less than $150 a month for growing coca.[73]

The Colombian government has favored privatization and major World Bank projects. As a result Colombia is now importing much of its food from abroad. Two million internally displaced Colombians are homeless, unemployed, and have no government support. Local farmers, disproportionately Afro-Colombians, have been forced out of growing corn, yucca, and other agricultural products by low-cost imports. Coffee plantations have not been touched by the movement for Fair Trade coffee (which would assure workers a living wage), and workers do not earn enough to feed their families. Farmers have been displaced in every area except one: coca.

In return, farmers have become the targets of Plan Colombia, a $1.3 billion aid package as the latest plan in the U.S. drug war. In 2000 this plan was passed in Congress after hearing testimony predominantly from governmental and military sources. The European Union, Human Rights Watch, Amnesty International, and the National Council of Churches strongly opposed Plan Colombia because of the military emphasis of the project.[74]

Seventy-five percent of the aid package was designated for military and police activity. The big beneficiaries are Sikorsky (helicopters), Lockheed Martin (radar surveillance), Monsanto (pesticides), and their strongest promoter, Occidental Petroleum, which sees military action as a way to secure both oil exploration and the pipeline. Occidental Petroleum has operated in Colombia for over thirty years. During the congressional testimony in 2000 for Plan Colombia, Occidental lobbied for the plan stating that Colombian oil was very important to the United States because it would reduce the oil imports from the Middle East, which was an unstable area,[75] as if Colombia was not. Occidental Vice President Lawrence Meriage stated that oil drilling could be an alternative to drugs in developing the economy of Colombia.[76] It also appeared that Occidental Petroleum was looking for governmental support in its battle against the U-wa tribe to drill oil on its sacred land.

Occidental Petroleum received drilling rights in 1992 on the U-wa tribe ancestral lands in a remote area of Colombia. However, the U-wa tribe believed they were signing a document stating their presence at a meeting and not an oil-drilling agreement on their sacred land. In 1997, 5,000 members of the U-wa declared they would commit collective suicide if Occidental Petroleum proceeded to drill on their land.[77] U-wa means "the thinking people." To them oil is the "blood of mother earth." They believe that removal of the oil would be violence to their land and would be a violation of their sacred beliefs.[78] After almost nine years of nonviolent protests, the death of three American activists, and the confrontation of major shareholders of Occidental Petroleum, including Al Gore, Occidental Petroleum removed their drilling equipment from the U-wa land in July 2001. The removal, however, may have occurred because they were unable to find oil from a test drill.[79]

Plan Colombia's war on drugs interfaces with a civil war in Colombia that has been going on for over forty years. The war is on multiple fronts and is driven by cocaine and heroin. The various groups consist of drug lords, right-wing paramilitary death squads known as AUC (United Self-Defense Groups of Colombia), insurgent left-wing guerillas known as FARC (Revolutionary Armed Forces of Colombia) and ELN (National Liberation Army), and a government army that aligns with the paramilitaries. The guerillas kidnap for ransom, bomb pipelines, and murder security forces and civilians. They also extort money from the heroin poppy and coca farmers in exchange for protection.[80] The FARC recently announced a "peace tax" against all businessmen and individuals who have more than $1 million in assets. Otherwise they risk being kidnapped.[81] There are ten kidnappings a day for ransom in Colombia, a figure equivalent to half of the world's kidnappings in 2000.[82]

The AUC and the illegal paramilitary death squads traffic in drugs and invade villages under the pretense of looking for those who support the guerillas. Their main targets, however, are labor and community leaders, human rights workers, and teachers. They massacre, torture, and murder these people no matter how nonpolitical they may be. It is believed the AUC is financed by drug lords, large landowners, and possibly multinational oil firms who may be trying to do business in Colombia.[83] They have also been financed by the American banana-producing corporation Chiquita. Between 1997 and 2004, Chiquita made almost monthly payments to the AUC, totaling at least $1.7 million. The company claims it had to make payments under the threat from the AUC in order to protect its employees and property. Colombian officials are investigating reports that Chiquita may have also supplied the AUC with arms. In 2001 a Chiquita-owned ship was used in Colombia to unload 3,000 Kalashnikov rifles and more than 2.5 million bullets.[84]

The Colombian military has used the AUC as an unaccountable force against villages that support the guerillas. In a continent severely marred by human-rights abuses, Colombia has compiled the worst record of all South American nations.[85] In describing the consequences of war (chapter 1) we noted the displacement of people from their homes and communities. A report by Human Rights Watch[86] stated that Colombia has the world's largest internal displacement crisis after Sudan. In the last three years alone, more than 3 million people have been forcibly displaced because of the country's war between right-wing paramilitaries and left-wing guerillas. More than half of all displaced persons in Colombia are children under the age of eighteen. The Colombian government does little by way of assistance for these displaced peoples. They are often denied medical care, and even those enrolled in the subsidized health-care system must pay for medications. Displaced children may be denied access to schools because other schools have no room for them or demand that they produce school records that they no longer possess.[87]

President Uribe, with U.S. approval, has responded to world criticism by creating a law permitting extradition of human-rights abusers. The law, however, would demobilize and grant partial amnesty to members of the AUC who have been guilty of the most heinous atrocities, along with the promotion of the drug trade. Human-rights organizations point to this law as a phony effort that permits both the killing and the drug trade to continue.[88]

Some believe that Plan Colombia is intended to destroy the political movement for land reform in Colombia. The stated goal of Plan Colombia, however, is to fumigate and destroy the coca and poppy farms that will become the ingredients for 90 percent of cocaine used illegally in the United States and most of the heroin.[89]

But it is the small farmers in Colombia who are caught in a military and political nightmare. The province of Putumaya, for example, has become the first target of Plan Colombia. Putumaya, in the middle of a southern Colombia jungle, has 330,000 residents, mostly farmers. These farmers colonized the area after fleeing the economic poverty and violence in other areas of the country. They grow coca in huge quantities and sell the processed paste to middlemen who distribute it to the United States and Europe. The coca production is in large fields, and the farmers grow legal crops as well and even raise cattle, thereby providing food for the community. The toxic spraying continues despite protests by the farmers that fumigation kills the legal crops along with the coca. Putumayo province is caught in the middle of a war between the FARC, the guerillas, and the AUC. This war is financed by the forced taxes on the farmers.[90] Once again, the farmers are subjected to the same economic poverty and violence they previously fled. There is no substitute crop for the small farmers, and funds in Plan Colombia are reaching few farmers. Even if Plan Colombia successfully eradicated coca in the Putumayo province, the small farmers, large growers, and rebels are capable of replicating their massive operation and moving farther into the Colombian jungles to avoid the aerial-launched chemical crop dusters.[91]

The efforts of lobbyists for Occidental Petroleum were key in the creation and implementation of Plan Colombia. Occidental International Corporation, the company's Washington-based lobbying firm, spent $8.6 million to lobby the U.S. Congress for military aid to Colombia. In 2003 and 2004, $98 million and $110 million, respectively, of Plan Colombia's funds were allocated specifically for the protection of the Cano-Limon pipeline with a brigade of U.S.-trained Colombian Special Forces.[92]

The war in Colombia is fueled both by military supplies from the United States, Britain, Israel, and Germany and by cocaine and heroin.[93] The war is not serving the needs of the Colombian people, nor is it supported by them. In November 1996 nearly 3 million Colombian girls and boys voted for the Right to Peace, a movement that was cofounded by Farliz Calle, a fourteen-year-old girl. Inspired by Calle, the following year, 10 million adults demanded that the participants in the armed conflict in Colombia stop involving the children in war and end the use of murder, massacres, torture, kidnapping, and the displacement of civilians of Colombia from their homes.

> In this world, life is becoming increasingly difficult for children. Despite advances in technology, war and armies have become more sophisticated and children are increasingly involved in this culture of death. Crimes against humanity are even more inhuman when they are inflicted on children.[94]

Colombia remains in a struggle. Both FARC and paramilitaries are taxing farmers. The paramilitaries kill those who try to organize, and FARC takes hostages from anyone with money. This children's movement arose to demand that people not participate. It became a women's movement so large that both sides had to accommodate some of its demands.

Afghanistan: Opium and Intervention

Afghanistan's inhospitable terrain has steep mountains and sweeping deserts; yet it remains a strategic gateway to the trade route between Europe and India. As a result, Afghanistan's history has always been a battle of invaders, from Alexander the Great in 328 B.C. to the Huns, the Turks, the Arabs, and Imperial Britain. In 1979 the Soviet Union invaded Afghanistan. The Soviets were met with Afghani resistance fighters known as the Mujahedeen, who were supported by the United States, Britain, Pakistan, Saudi Arabia, and the United Arab Emirates. In 1989 the USSR withdrew, leaving the land in ruin and the warring factions in chaos. Civil war ensued in which tribes fought for control. By 1996 the fundamentalist Islamic Taliban movement ruled most of Afghanistan but was met with resistance from the Northern Alliance, supported by Russia, Tajikistan, and Uzbekistan.[95] The legacy of that war includes a country with a 64 percent illiteracy rate, a reported 48 percent of its children suffering from malnutrition, and a life expectancy of forty-six years.[96]

Afghanistan is composed of a complex group of people, worldly through their contacts with traders and conquerors, yet isolated by their terrain and tribal structure. The existing tribal system emerged 250 years ago from the province of Iran. At that time, it was agreed that each tribe would be governed by its own leaders. This type of tribal federalism remains even as the U.S.-led coalition attempts to superimpose a central government.[97] Over the last 250 years, there has been an intermixing of many different groups. More than thirty distinct languages are native to Afghanistan, and there are ten major tribes.[98] Afghans have never moved from an agricultural tribal existence, and as a result have not acquired a sense of nationalism. Each Afghan is either a Pashtoon (about 40 percent of the population) or a member of a smaller tribe such as the Uzbek, Tajik, or Hazareh tribes. Lacking a national identity, Afghans do not refer to themselves as Afghans until they leave Afghanistan.[99]

Despite their difficulties, most Afghans continue to live as farmers and herders of sheep and goats, as they have for centuries. Many are nomads with no permanent homes, and they move with their herds. Their sparse existence is upon a land that has been destroyed by years of war. As a result of the ten-year war with the USSR, there are 10 million land mines that must be avoided by children and adults. Afghanistan continues to be one of the poorest countries in the world. Following a three-year drought, the worst in thirty years, only 12 percent of the people had safe drinking water.[100] This has been devastating to a country where 85 percent of the population, estimated at 21 million people, is dependent upon agriculture. As a result of the drought, rivers used for drinking water and irrigation are almost dry, livestock have perished, and rural economies have collapsed.[101] There are few economic options in Afghanistan beyond labor migration, becoming a mercenary or cultivating opium.[102] In 1990 Afghanistan was the world's second largest producer of opium. The global trade in illegal drugs generates billions of dollars in profits for the refiners and distributors, but not for the growers. In early 2000, Afghanistan became the largest opium producer, cornering 75 percent of the world's market. The CIA estimated that 39 percent of the world's opium supply came from just a single province in Afghanistan. The poppy plant is a much better crop than wheat because it is drought resistant and every part of the plant can be used. Its cultivation is also labor intensive so that jobs are provided, and it can be harvested several times a year.

In July 2000 Taliban's leader, Mullah Mohammed Omar, for religious reasons, banned opium poppy cultivation in Afghanistan. His edict became the greatest drug moratorium in modern history.[103] The CIA estimated that drug production dropped from 4,042 tons to 81.6 tons. Many believe that substance abuse can only be addressed by providing treatment for addicts and offering meaning in life for young people. But to the extent that production of illicit drugs contributes to the problem, the change in Afghanistan might be acknowledged as one of the greatest accomplishments of drug enforcement.[104]

The paradox of the militarily mandated solution may be seen in other outcomes of imposed poverty and degradation. One of these is the incitement to strike back violently. Six months before the suicide bombings of the World Trade Center, President G. W. Bush's administration provided assistance to the Taliban as part of its own crusade, the militarization of the war on drugs.[105]

The economic result of the cut in poppy cultivation was catastrophic. Since July 2000 the poppy fields have been replaced with wheat. Farmers state they are unable to break even and unable to pay their workers. Farm workers who left to find jobs in the cities have returned without finding work.[106] With the Taliban no longer in power, opium farmers have been returning to their fields to plant poppies once again.[107] A fifty-four-year-old farmer tells us that with ten children and twenty-eight people in his household, there is no other way to survive. From his 2.5 acres of land, he can sell the opium base at $100 per pound. This is 100 times more than what wheat and vegetables will bring. Without opium his entire family would starve. In the global market, the opium will be worth billions of dollars and will supply millions of addicts worldwide.[108]

The farmers agree that poppy cultivation violates Islamic beliefs, but they also point out there is no industry; they are hungry, impoverished, and without choices.[109] One poppy farmer said that his message to the world is to help establish industries in Afghanistan. He views the Afghani people as diligent workers who would welcome the chance to work in factories. But there are none.[110] What the poppy farmer may not realize is that sweatshop factories in Mexico, Indonesia, and Vietnam have increased the poverty in those countries for all but a few. In Afghanistan, unlike Iran, which is buoyed by the production of oil, poverty will continue to be a strong incentive for the cultivation of opium.[111]

Conservative estimates indicate that the opium trade represents about one-third of Afghanistan's total economic activity. Hundreds of millions of dollars' worth of U.S. and British taxpayers' money have been spent on the eradication of the drug trade, but with hardly any effect. The region of Helmand, for example, in 2005 saw a 10 percent decline in opium cultivation; in the neighboring region of Nimroz, however, opium cultivation increased by 1,370 percent. In other words, growing operations simply relocated.[112]

Some scholars argue that the U.S. and U.K. program of eradication is ill-conceived and undermines its own objectives. Crop eradication hurts poor farmers (who use cash from opium futures contracts to feed their families over the winter) and makes drug traders richer. After the announcement of crop eradication, prices increased from $90 to $400 per kilo.[113] And because opiates—raw or refined—have a long shelf life, traders stockpile crops for resale at higher prices.

In November 2004 an unidentified aircraft sprayed herbicide on opium crops (and everything else, including children) in eastern Afghanistan. Both the United States and Britain denied involvement. Since this incident, the U.S. administration has been pressured to reallocate the $152 million set for aerial eradication to community development and alternative livelihoods for rural communities. Only 15 percent of a total program of $778 million was originally earmarked for such programs.[114]

As in the cases of Colombia and Bolivia, eradication of crops has only succeeded in hurting poor farmers and in making traders, warlords, and traffickers richer. Researchers explain that if stabilizing the economy and democracy in Afghanistan are truly the goal, rural communities need alternatives to the credit, employment, and cash incomes that opium provides. Opium has been a cornerstone of the Afghani economy for decades. It continues to be a much more important source of revenue for the poor than the aid economy. For example, during 2002 and 2003 the income to Afghans from opium (estimated at $4.8 billion) was more than 70 percent greater than the international aid disbursed for projects in Afghanistan ($2.8 billion).[115]

In the world market, drugs are the only item that Afghanistan has to exchange. Afghanistan does have the location for a pipeline for oil to the Caspian Sea, but the short booms created by massive construction projects replace what viable resources people had before. Such projects do not support small farms, schools, or medical facilities. Instead they devastate the ecology, leaving people as impoverished as they were before.

Both the United States and Britain see the drug trade as a threat to Afghanistan's economy and burgeoning democracy.[116] But a military occupation, insensitive to the history and culture of the region, has cast into doubt the idea that either democracy or legitimate economic development can be attained by military force.

The continuing war and the extreme poverty in Afghanistan have sent more than 4 million people to take refuge in other countries, and several hundred thousand have been displaced within their own country.[117] Many Afghani refugees live in tents in refugee camps. There they witness family members die of starvation, particularly when winter sets in. One refugee says he prefers to die only once instead of a little at a time, and the Americans should have bombed them as well.[118] The U.S.-led war of retaliation against al Qaeda has killed as many civilians as were killed in the bombing of the World Trade Center. As the bombing subsided, 6 million people in Afghanistan were left in need of food, and many continued to die as the winter temperatures drop to five degrees, leaving the ground too hard even to bury the dead. Children die first, then the others.[119] Joseph Stalin stated, "The death of one person is a tragedy, but the death of one million is only a statistic."[120] Disrupted international aid has not yet been fully resumed. The publicized postinvasion gains in education for girls and voting in elections have affected only a small number of people in the cities. For the rest, Afghanistan is in danger of becoming another global statistic.

Burma (Myanmar): Oppressive Government, Pipelines, and Opium

Burma is a country rich in resources and fertile farmland. Yet, one-third of its children under age five are malnourished. Burma, the largest country in mainland Southeast Asia, is one of the most needlessly miserable countries in the world. Its population estimated at 48 million consists of 65 percent ethnic Burmese with the remainder from various other ethnic groups. As a result of British rule, there has been bitter hatred between lowland Burmese and the highlanders, which has kept the country divided, isolated, and therefore prone to military takeovers.[121]

Since 1988, Burma has been ruled by a brutal military regime, which came to power after killing thousands of prodemocracy activists, including university students, women, and children. The new military government called itself the State Law and Order Restoration Committee (SLORC) and changed the country's name from Burma to Myanmar.[122] Officially, the SLORC was euphemistically changed to State Peace and Development Council (SPDC).[123] The Burmese people voted to oust the military through free elections in 1990. The regime, however, refused to yield and continues to dominate by using forceful tactics, such as torture and slave labor, to suppress dissent. Aung San Suu Kyi, the prodemocracy movement leader and Nobel Peace Prize winner has been repeatedly placed under house arrest by the military regime.[124]

Burma has been repeatedly condemned by the United States and the United Nations for its human-rights violations. The country has the worst human-rights record in the world. However, the SPCD does not recognize the concept of human rights, and there is no freedom of assembly, press, or religion. The U.S. government forbids new investment by American corporations, and the International Labor Organization has found that "a modern form of slave labor" is practiced by the Burmese military. From 1992 to 1996, 2 million people were forced to work without pay, some in leg shackles. The workers included women, children, and the aged.[125] The Burmese military systematically rapes ethnic minority women. It is a form of ethnic cleansing because it redistributes the ethnic balance as a result of the children born from the rapes. For the Burmese military, rape is viewed as a legitimate behavior and as a weapon of war. But the violent raping of ethnic women by the Burmese military fits the description of a war crime as outlined in the War Crimes Tribunal of the former Yugoslavia as well as the Geneva Conventions.[126] To understand why Burmese military rule is tolerated by powerful nations such as the United States, it important to mention that natural gas deposits were discovered in 1982 in an area later named the Yadana field. The Yadana pipeline was begun in 1994 and completed in 1998 by a consortium including Unocal, an American corporation, and the French oil company Total.[127] Premier Oil, a British company, was also heavily invested, primarily in a joint venture with the Burmese military government for the Yetagun natural gas pipeline. Following strong international protest Premier divested, but companies from ten countries still remain as contractors. The Yetagun natural gas pipeline runs parallel to the Yadana pipeline. It is one of the largest sources of income for the Burmese regime.[128]

Villagers in the pipeline region live a miserable, oppressed, precarious existence, in part due to Unocal, now owned by Chevron, Total, and Premier. Entire villages have been relocated at gunpoint, women have been raped, and children killed by Burmese military units providing security for the gas pipelines.[129] Whole families have been forced into slave labor to construct infrastructure used by foreign oil companies. For the past fifty years, Burma's infrastructure has been ignored. The roads are in such bad repair and are so primitive that no amount of forced labor will upgrade them for use by foreign enterprise.[130]

The pipelines cut directly through the Tenasserim rainforest, one of the largest intact rainforests in Southeast Asia, and home to diverse peoples and numerous endangered species, including Asian elephants, tigers, and rhinoceroses.[131] The environment has been permanently destroyed by the pipelines. Yet analysts suspect the money payable by Thailand for gas from the Yadana pipeline will probably go directly into the pockets of the military. This will further increase the inflation and poverty in Burma.[132] The displacement of forests and farmlands by oil pipelines and military forces to protect them has become a frequently repeated pattern.

There are 45 million acres of potentially arable land in Burma. This is about 25 percent of the total land mass. Half of the arable land is cultivated by families who have small plots of land. It is estimated that 77 percent of the main source of income of rural households is agriculture. For subsistence living to occur, each farm must be approximately five acres. Of the 4.7 million farm households, over 60 percent had less than that. Of the rural households surveyed by the U.N. Land Development Program, 35 percent were landless, 40 percent owned no livestock, and 24 percent owned neither land nor livestock.[133]

Legally, all land in Burma is state owned. Use rights are given to farmers, who must not leave the land idle for more than three years; otherwise the land reverts back to the state. Because farmers do not own the land, they are unable to obtain loans using the land as collateral. Instead they may only receive small loans at high interest rates. The farmer's inability to own and mortgage land has had a severe impact on agricultural production.[134] Land tenancy results in a reduced incentive for investment or improvement in the land.[135]

Beyond lack of ownership of land, there is inadequate incentive structure for farmers to produce. There is a tax on the use of the land to produce rice. Also, an export tax on rice is enforced by a legal monopoly, the Myanmar Agricultural Produce Trading (MAPT), a government-owned enterprise. A government monopoly also controls exports of cotton, jute, sugar, and rubber. Since 1995, a decline in the growth of agriculture has resulted in static yields of crops relative to other Southeast Asian countries such as Thailand.[136]

In 1998 the government began using forced labor to develop 22 million acres of wetlands and pristine untouched lands. In order to develop these lands, "labor villages" were established to assist private entrepreneurs and foreign investors. Over a million acres of this reclaimed land is owned by eighty-two business groups. The local people are now denied access to these lands, which has the potential for future conflict between the local people and the business groups who, with the aid of forced labor, attend to these large agricultural estates.[137] The Free Burma Coalition (FBC) estimates that, at present, 1 million Burmese are internally displaced by the government and are being used as forced laborers. Their whereabouts are unknown to their families; their length of service indefinite. General Khin Nyunt, the SPDC leader, has denied government involvement in forced labor and claims that the people have contributed their labor voluntarily so government projects can be completed sooner.[138]

Burma's government-controlled agricultural economy presents a looming agrarian crisis where the only agricultural success is the illegal opium industry, much like Afghanistan and Colombia (with coca). Burma continues, with the collusion of the military, as the world's largest source of illegal opium and heroin, about 60 percent of the world market. Not only is valuable farmland being used to grow the opium poppy, but because heroin is so easily available, it is now being used inside the country. In some townships as many as 25 percent of the people are injecting heroin. Since it is a crime to carry needles in Burma without a medical license, needles are at a premium and are shared. As a result of needle sharing, HIV infection among drug users in Burma is the highest in the world.[139]

Burma, once the wealthiest country in Southeast Asia is now the poorest in the region with the highest infant mortality rate and the least expenditure on health care and education. Meanwhile, 40 percent of the national budget goes to the military, which views the independence movement as a constant threat.[140] The continuing enforced poverty and a serious food shortage in Burma may become the catalyst to topple the corrupt and illegal regime presently in power, although it is a regime tolerated by its Western trading partners. In the meantime the horrible economic conditions have led to a migration to Thailand, where global corporate expansion has created cheap-labor jobs that provide goods for export. Many have been lured by brokers and sold into slavery or bonded into indebtedness. The migrants become an underclass of noncitizens. The pattern is similar to the situation of migrants from Mexico and Guatemala to the United States (see chapter 8).[141]

The Evolving Story of People and Land

If a time line of how long human beings have been on earth is represented as twenty-four hours, then agriculture has been on earth for five minutes. Prior to that, humans were hunters and gatherers, and each family related to others in an interdependent way for food, shelter, and clothing. With the advent of agriculture, human beings have increased 10,000-fold during the last five minutes, and most of the increase has occurred in the last ten seconds. However, in the last few seconds, food production has gone from a community partnership to global domination, partly through the use of biotechnology and patents.[142] Land, food, and water, throughout history were considered the sacred gifts of nature that existed to support life. Rapidly and without reflection, we are allowing a small number of companies to assume control over them. The ways to restore viability to the world of food production are known, but there must be a will take the steps.

When people are displaced from viable local enterprises, they seek such options as living-wage jobs that the global economy has not been willing to offer. To survive, many will try to emigrate; some may engage in drug production or other illegal enterprises, including prostitution; some will join violent revolutionary groups; and others will try to organize protests to obtain food and justice. A military response to any of these activities ignores the prime cause of displacement by the global economy and can only make matters worse.

Separating people from food is violence. There are millions of people in impoverished countries such as Colombia, Afghanistan, and Burma who are starving because they are unable to grow food or are too poor to buy food that is available. In order to survive, they are forced to use the land to grow opium or coca to supply the global markets. Colombia, Afghanistan, and Burma are the major suppliers of all the illegal opium and heroin in the world. To avoid hunger and death from starvation, the poor people of these impoverished countries must grow an illegal substance that will ultimately kill many people in all parts of the world.

Separating people from the land is costly. We can sustain such activity only by turning our heads away from the violence it is inflicting upon people. When we stop treating nature as precious and see it only as something to be exploited, then we are in danger of losing it. Separation threatens to reduce the spiritual renewal that the land and the waters have given us.

The issues of globalization do not have to do with the increasing interdependence of the global community, nor even with whether regulations that affect international trade are good or bad. Rather, the issue is who participates in the decisions and whether values that reflect the long-term sustainability of communities and of the planet are heard.[143] Taiwan and South Korea are sometimes looked upon as early successes of economic globalization, but both have paid a heavy price in environmental destruction, another common casualty of market-driven development.[144]

A change is needed from the values of the market to the values of participation and caring. The task will require a strong sense of solidarity with our sisters and brothers whose exploitation benefits us in the developed world. In the United States and in other affluent countries, we will have to examine and reduce our own consumption of valuable and finite world resources so that they will be available for others on this planet and for future generations. Included in the task is a need to renew our love for the land and for its fruits. There will be a need to support local alternatives that honor the environment. Finally, it will require us to pressure or persuade those with great wealth and power that people, along with all the species who share our planet, deserve a viable habitat and a voice in how it is to be used.

Chapter 5

Networks of Power

> Behind the ostensible government sits enthroned an invisible government owing no allegiance and acknowledging no responsibility to the people. To destroy this invisible government, to befoul the unholy alliance between corrupt business and corrupt politics is the first task of the statesmanship of the day.
>
> —*Theodore Roosevelt, April 19, 1906*

This chapter examines the topic of power. Power is a phenomenon that is invisible to the naked eye, and one that is more deeply surrounded by taboos than was the topic of sex in Victorian days. This chapter focuses on the movers and shakers, the concentrations of power, from which flow decisions that contribute greatly to global violence. The lens of power is not the only one that frames our reality. There is also a reality that is captured in the daily lives of people finding joy and meaning often under circumstances of war, displacement, illness, and loss. There are larger cultural and spiritual realties that connect us to the shared symbols of religion, community, supernatural deities, chiefs, people who achieved stardom, and to special places. There is also a marketed reality of goods, sales pressures, demands for competitive success, and admonitions to blame hapless outsiders or petty criminals for what is missing in our own lives. Each of these realities is important and visible on a daily basis. The reality of large corporate decisions that determine how much we earn, who gets to eat, what dangers to our health will be removed, what candidates and issues will be on the public agenda, who will benefit from the human and natural resources of our communities, whether and where we shall go to war—these are part of the reality of concentrated power that are mostly out of view. This chapter brings them into view.

What Is Power?

Power is the capacity to exert the effort we need to attain our wishes and to meet our needs. There is a dearth of power among most of the displaced people of the world. Power is severely lacking among those who have no choice but to live in a highly toxic environment or in a war zone, or who have no chance to attend college without joining the military. We speak of empowering such people as a means to enhance their choices. Some who are well positioned have extreme power to make decisions that will affect the lives of many others, thereby seriously limiting the amount of power or choice that others will need merely to live with dignity. Power can be abused, and power can be corrupting both for those conferring it and for those seeking it. The creation of the modern nation state with great autonomous powers brought with it a critical distinction in social classes in which some few had special access to authorities and others did not.[1]

Networks of Power

One way to look at power is as an attribute of a person—big muscles, big weapons, a big bank account, or an unrelenting motivation to compete. Looking at power in that way conceals the fact that an individual can only express power in relation to others and that power is itself embedded in a set of relationships, often hidden relationships. Just as chapter 2 discussed that destructive behavior was not merely an attribute of individuals but rather a function of circumstances, so do we find power to be better understood as something that resides within a network of connections rather than within individuals.

Bill Domhoff argues that the critical players are organizations. Organizations are little more than a set of positions and rules. The rules are agreed-upon ways of doing things to achieve some specific purpose. Organizations may be informal, such as a family or a support group, or formal, such as a corporation or a government agency. In either case, they are typically defined as having identifiable boundaries and memberships. But in actual practice we find family members sometimes relating to nonkin in ways more associated with the bonds to members of one's own family. And with agencies we often find key transactions with representatives of other organizations, sometimes proving more important than those within the agency. It is useful to study actual exchanges, transactions, interactions, and even attachments without making reference to a particular defined entity such as the family, the neighborhood, the workplace, or the church, club, or company to which an individual claims membership. The concept of networks can clue us to the actual transactions that take place.

Network Analysis: Revealing Networks of Power

Borrowing from an abstract mathematical theory and from efforts by anthropologists to study the latent social groupings that western biases might conceal, the theory of network analysis has been revived. The concepts are seductively simple. It will be helpful to ignore, for the moment, the qualities of individuals and instead to focus upon a web or network of exchanges between individuals. Pretend that each person is but a dot in a big matrix. Each dot has connections with some other dots. The lines that connect them represent actual exchanges, transactions, interactions, and even attachments from one to another. They might consist of information, or exchanges of money or goods, or of loving care, or any of the many forms of social support. The transactions may be symmetrical, or they may go in only one direction. Some of the links are used continually, some rarely, and some only indirectly through connections to a third or more distant party. Some are ongoing connections, others singular happenings. The exchanges might as easily be applied to diffusion of new ideas or to transfers of small arms, of cocaine, or of political favors. The links might be reciprocal or unidirectional, frequent or rare. Network maps can be drawn from the point of one individual, your grandma or the secretary of state, or with a defined group such as your household or the Defense Department, as the point of origin. Most important, the framework places no restrictions on what links might arise. This web or network will help to uncover a latent structure to show who, whether formally or informally, is linked to whom. Modern society is marked by rapidly changing acquaintances, marriages, residential locations, and jobs. Mapping a network of actual interactions can be an important tool in determining whether the old familiar sources of identity, caring, and support have been lost or were merely being replaced by newer and more flexible arrangements. The potential to reveal the less obvious underlying networks is particularly useful in the study of power.

For the purpose of this chapter, we examine networks of power in order to see who is central to them as well as who is excluded. Whose special interests are intrinsically protected by their network connections, and who gets left out of the vital connections needed to thrive in today's world? To find out who is central in a powerful network, one would start with an examination of the multiple positions held by the occupant of an important political office. Take Secretary of the Navy Gordon England. Secretary England was appointed the seventy-second secretary of the U.S. Navy in May 2001. In this position England led America's Navy and Marine Corps and was responsible for more than 800,000 military and civilian personnel and an annual budget of more than $120 billion. He joined the Department of Homeland Security in January 2003. Prior to joining the administration of President G. W. Bush, England was executive vice president of General Dynamics Corporation (GD), where he was responsible for two major corporate sectors: information systems and technology and international contracting. Previously, he had served as executive vice president of the Combat Systems Group, president of General Dynamics Fort Worth aircraft company (later Lockheed), president of General Dynamics Land Systems Company, and as the principal of a mergers and acquisition consulting company. Such corporate-government connections are common. But corporations are also connected with one another. One can track the board memberships of England's GD colleagues as well as the accounting and law firms that serve GD. Among the GD board are retired generals and admirals, directors of major financial firms (Morgan Chase, LLC investment banking), the food industry (Sara Lee), and pharmaceuticals (Schering Plough). The web of interconnections extends even farther. With high-level government and corporate officials, one finds multiple links to certain financial institutions, law firms, accounting firms, and trade organizations such as the Petroleum Institute or Pharma. The networks include links to managers of major media corporations, to research centers, and to think tanks. People central in these powerful networks are sought after for boards of universities and major medical centers, where they can help to attract donors as well as play a part in assuring the supply of trained persons to run and to serve the greater society.

Network analysis provides an excellent tool for examination of the social exclusivity of the super-rich who have used their networks to amass ever-greater portions of wealth. They conceal their power over policy by making governments dependent upon their economic decisions and candidates dependent upon their financial support. In one example the U.S. Supreme Court had decided that the identities of those who met secretly with the U.S. vice president to draft an energy policy need not be revealed. The consequences of such collaboration are that governments find it perfectly legal to provide major tax loopholes for multinational corporations. The fact that voices of local projects that provide low-cost services and barter exchanges are not in attendance at such meetings explains why government agencies treat them less generously. Lacking a seat at the table, local projects are frequently harassed for evading taxes or violating ordinances even while the government subsidizes the efforts of the largest corporations and does little to curtail their environmental abuses or tax evasions. We shall return later to the issue of exclusive elite groups that exercise unaccountable power.

Creating Authority

Those who hold great power over others rely less frequently upon brute force than upon claims that their positions give them legitimate authority. They renew this authority by reiterating their ability to control the rewards and the punishments of others, but also by claims to their legitimacy in accordance with cultural beliefs. In a democracy the belief is that the rules and decisions made are accountable to the wishes of the people. The belief is at best an ideal and often a myth, fanned by those with power. It is a myth that enables the largest purveyors of power to pass unnoticed.

In the United States the myth has been fueled by three important Supreme Court decisions. The first, *Santa Clara v. Southern Pacific Railroad* (1886), was the original case extending to corporations the Fourteenth Amendment due process and equal-rights protections originally intended for former slaves. Two other decisions, *Buckley v. Valeo* and *Bellotti v. First National Bank of Boston*, in the 1970s established that money for use in political activities is a form of free speech protected by the first amendment of the Bill of Rights and therefore may not be restricted. Other cases based on this are affecting campaign spending and making it impossible to elect persons to state and national office who are unable to attract massive funding. These Supreme Court decisions remove much of the power of people to have their governments protect them against abuses by corporations.[2] These decisions ultimately have allowed corporations to become powerful, autonomous entities.

Effects of Concentrated Corporate Growth and Expansion

A business in which a local owner in a small town must face customers and employees on a daily basis will want to combine entrepreneurial ingenuity with an accountability to the community. Such businesses do not typically sell shares in the financial markets and, unless squeezed by low-cost chain stores, do not have to expand continuously for their survival. Large corporations, by contrast, are designed to require continued growth of profits. By accumulating capital they provide options for exploration, investment, technology, mass production, and exploitation on a level that created the industrialized world. During some periods of this expansion, corporations were obliged to share the rewards of their success. A balance between the power of the largest automakers and the unions supplying their workforce, for example, permitted a period of great profitability while assuring workers a doorway into a world of reasonably secure employment, a five-day workweek, paid vacation time, and health insurance. However, with an increasingly global workforce and continued pressures to increase profitability, patterns of destructive use of resources and people could be predicted.

The need to expand required that all countries should be available as sources of needed raw materials and as markets for consumer products. State-owned or socialist enterprises limited such expansion and were viewed with great alarm. In contemporary market economies, the welfare state has, however, provided a measure of free or inexpensive education, housing, and public parks for the entire society. The welfare state served to limit the desperation of people who work for meager wages, but it was also viewed as a burden to corporate taxpayers. The declining power of the individual companies and declining rates of profitability were accompanied by other corporate fears. In Great Britain the threat of nationalizations and of worker participation in corporate governance seemed real. In the United States, government intervention to improve public welfare was viewed as an obstacle to corporate growth.

In the 1970s major officers of large corporations in the United States and Great Britain responded. They formed what Michael Useem calls the "inner circle," a semiautonomous network designed to provide a centralized corporate force to mobilize the interests of corporate capitalism.[3] Since corporations are legally autonomous entities, this network helped to provide an institutionalized form of corporate capitalism. It clearly distinguished the interests of the large corporate investors as a class and provided a corporate logic for a centralized and concerted advocacy.

A select group of corporate officials were, according to Useem's evidence, able to take on a leading role in consultations with the highest levels of national governments. They worked in the support of political candidates and in the governance of foundations and universities. They created a highly visible public defense of the free-enterprise system. One major goal of this network was, and continues to be, the promotion of a better political climate for big business. It engages in image building through philanthropy, including generous support for cultural programs. It also works by issue advertising, not tied to selling their product but to shaping public opinion in their favor. Finally, the inner network took on a major role in financing political campaigns. A main goal was to control the power of the media which, in the United States, were considered far too liberal.

On the media front, the influence of corporate America is highly enhanced, directly through media mergers and indirectly through the high corporate advertising budgets. The corporate resources for advertising, public relations, and sales have permitted their extensive involvement in the packaging and selling of legislation and of candidates. The interventions of this "inner circle" were (and are) extremely successful. President Reagan and Prime Minister Thatcher were partly products of business mobilizations. They lowered taxation, reduced government (except military) spending, lifted controls on business, and installed cutbacks on unemployment benefits and welfare.

The symbiotic relationship between corporations and legislative government are but one example of "overlapping and intersecting socio-spatial networks of power."[4] Mann's Four Networks Theory of Power defines ideological, economic, military, and political realms of power; in each case it is the organizational resources for action that makes one realm or another dominant. However, as in the case of the relationship between corporations (economic) and government (political), when two organizational realms come together in a symbiotic relationship, it not only benefits but strengthens them both.[5] Such has been the case of the military and economic realms in modern times.

The Military-Industrial Complex

In his farewell address in 1961, after eight years in the White House, Dwight Eisenhower warned of the "grave implications" of the conjunction of the military establishment and the arms industry.

> In the councils of government, we must guard against the acquisition of unwarranted influence, whether sought or unsought, by the military-industrial complex. The potential for the disastrous rise of misplaced power exists and will persist.[6]

The danger of this centralized power is that it directs U.S. foreign policy in a way that assumes the legitimacy and the inevitability of armed conflict and the absolute requisite of military spending for preparedness—without taking into account the full range of domestic issues.

The Military-Industrial Link

In modern times the military-industrial linkages have emerged as major concentrations of power. Contracts and subcontracts for military supplies, equipment, and bases are extremely widespread. Local communities that need the jobs will fight against the reduction of military spending. The Defense Department contracts provide opportunity for risk-free investments. The federal government is the sole customer, and contracts cover cost overruns in which profits increase when the contractor spends, or wastes, more than the estimate of the original bid. Equipment that is defective, used, or destroyed needs to be replaced by extending contracts. The details of these transactions are typically out of public view. Corporate facilities are sometimes employed directly for covert military operations, and contractors have become mainstays of a privatized military force. Most important, there is a revolving door of individuals moving from high-level military positions and from military appropriation positions in government to corporate boards, and from corporate contractors to government.

Career military professionals and corporate contractors create a specialized lobby. They serve both as a provocateur for military actions and an opinion force for the assumption that military force is the essential ingredient for national security. The military-industrial centers support groups that are ideologically driven by justifications for violent defense of God and country. The language of evangelical leaders helps to sustain the essential image of a godless enemy, while veteran's organizations are used to glorify and provide justification for the sacrifices of soldiers. The military-industrial complex is perpetuated by a massive federal defense budget and driven by a private industry reaping excessive profits from military activities. Opportunistic relationships between political leaders, military personnel, and defense contractors grease this well-oiled machine.

National Defense Budget

This conjunction of the military and industry, which began with World War II and expanded throughout the years of the Cold War, is reaching an apex with the G. W. Bush administration. The U.S. military budget request for fiscal year 2007 is $462.7 billion.[7] This figure includes the Department of Defense budget, funding for the Department of Energy (nuclear weapons development), and "other" beneficiaries who are not defined. This figure does not include spending for the Iraq and Afghan wars. As of early 2006, Congress had already granted $300 billion for operations in Iraq and Afghanistan.

To put these extraordinary numbers in perspective, for 2005 the U.S. military budget (not including spending for Iraq and Afghan wars) was seven times larger than the next biggest military spender—China. Adding together the military budgets for China, Russia, and the six "rogue" states (Cuba, Iran, Libya,

North Korea, Sudan, and Syria), a total of $139 billion was spent in 2005, only 30 percent of U.S. military spending in the same year.[8]

Compared to other departments within the United States in 2005, the next largest budget requests were for education and health, $60 billion and $51 billion, respectively. Over half of all federal spending is allocated for the military.[9]

The union of military and industry during World War II initiated a boom in the military budget to meet the demand for development and production of weapons, ships, submarines, and aircraft. During the years of the Cold War, the budget for national defense increased as billions of dollars went into the development and production of nuclear weapons. But the G. W. Bush administration has taken spending far beyond that of the Reagan administration. The Afghanistan and Iraq wars, according to a Nobel-prize-winning economist, are likely to cost between $1 trillion and $2 trillion, a much greater figure than the Bush administration's projection of $60 billion.[10]

American taxpayers are paying these costs. The average American taxpayer, however, may not be outraged or even aware of this expense because such information is not clearly or accurately presented to them (see chapter 7). The name War Department was changed to the Defense Department to accentuate its continuing role. Its actual activity might more accurately have earned the name "Department of Foreign Intervention."

The Industry of Defense

The defense industry is quick to point out that military research and development (R&D) programs have driven the rapid advancement of technology. These military R&D programs push development in the private sector, which leads to mass production and lower prices for such items as computer processors, cell phones, high-tech cars, and appliances. As the argument goes, technological advancement is valuable—not just profitable—because it makes the military more efficient and safe, presumably saving lives.

> It takes far fewer people to fight and direct wars today than it did even a decade ago. That's because the speed and power of the front-line soldier have been so greatly amplified by smart weapons and smart delivery systems, and because accurate information now moves so easily up the chain of command . . . our civilian sector gave our soldiers the tools they needed to bring this war to its mercifully quick conclusion.[11]

There has, however, been no "mercifully quick conclusion" to the U.S.-led war in Iraq. One tragic irony is that the technological advances most basic to the protection of U.S. troops—body armor—have been denied to them.[12] In light of this evidence, it appears safety is not the primary motivation for the advancement of technology.

Another argument in favor of technological development and private industry is that outsourcing as many tasks as possible to private contractors allows the military to be more efficient by focusing on combat. From the design and maintenance of high-tech helicopters to laundry detail, recruiting, even combat itself—all of these are now performed by private companies. In the late 1990s, KBR (Kellogg, Brown, and Root), a Halliburton subsidiary, provided nearly all the food, water, laundry, mail, and heavy equipment to the roughly 20,000 U.S. troops stationed in the Balkans. During the last Gulf War, there was approximately one contractor for every one hundred soldiers. A year into the Iraq war, there was approximately one contractor for every ten soldiers.[13]

Having so many civilians "in the field" has prompted complicated questions for which military officials have no definitive or consistent answers. For example, should information-technology consultants carry arms? If employees of private companies run from their posts, are they considered deserters? If taken prisoner, will they be considered POWs covered by the Geneva Convention? Or, if they detain prisoners, are they responsible to comply with the directives of the Geneva Convention?

Profit is a clear motivation in the rise of the defense industry. For its service in the Balkans in the late 1990s, KBR was paid $3 billion.[14] Between 2002 and July 2004, KBR was paid over $11 billion for their services in Afghanistan and Iraq.[15] Nearly half of the worth of these contracts was handed to corporations through no-bid contracts. Auditing for the Department of Defense is also outsourced to private accounting firms; many of these accounting contracts have similarly been awarded through no-bid deals. The amount of sheer unaccountable waste and giveaways is astounding.[16]

Over the six-year period between fiscal year 1998 and fiscal year 2003, the Center for Public Integrity examined more that 2.2 million defense contract actions totaling $900 billion in authorized expenditures.[17] After nine months of research, the center determined that half of the Defense Department's budget goes to private contractors. Only 40 percent of Pentagon contracts were conducted under "full and open competition". In other words, over half of them fall under the category of no-bid contracts. Out of tens of thousands of contractors, the biggest 737 collected nearly 80 percent of the contracting dollars; the top fifty contractors got more than half of all the money. Topping the list for this fiscal period was Lockheed Martin ($94 billion) and Boeing ($82 billion). By fiscal year 2003, 56 percent of the Defense Department's contracts paid for services rather than goods.[18]

Not surprisingly, many companies have been accused of overcharging.[19] When auditors discovered that KBR, the Halliburton subsidiary, was overpaid $208 million to transport oil in Iraq, they also discovered that government employees doing the same job (in this case, the Defense Energy Support Center) were much more efficient. A Columbia University economist describes this phenomenon in one word: incentive.[20] A government worker's paycheck is the same no matter what he or she does. But for someone working on a cost-plus contract (a contract in which all services are reimbursed plus interest), efficiency may not be in his or her best interest. What is most troubling, however, is that even though the discrepancy was discovered, the U.S. Army paid nearly

$204 million of the $208 million overcharge. Was this because the army recognizes Halliburton as being in favor with Vice President Cheney, the former head of Halliburton? Or were army personnel hoping to find work with the company after retiring from duty? The vice president's influence was prominent in Halliburton's contracts with an oppressive government in oil-rich Nigeria.[21]

Other companies have made their fortunes by subcontracting. Chenega Technology Services, owned by native Alaskans from the small coastal village of Chenega, was awarded a no-bid contract by the Department of Homeland Security, much to the shock of executives at Lockheed and DynCorp. For a project to upgrade and maintain X-ray machines at U.S. port and borders stations, Chenega, a company little experienced with such machines, seemed an especially unlikely choice. Chenega, however, subcontracted to two other companies—SAIC, Inc. and American Science and Engineering, Inc.—to do the high-tech work.

Alaskan native corporations maintain their small-business status in spite of their $million+ revenues. These "native" corporations do not have to be run by Native Americans (only 33 of Chenega's 2,300 employees are Alaskan natives). The company headquarters, in fact, are not in Alaska but in Alexandria, Virginia. After 9/11, the demand for X-ray and gamma-ray equipment skyrocketed. In 2001 Chenega recorded $42 million in revenues; in 2004, $481 million.[22] In 2004 about $1 million was distributed to native shareholders and cultural and educational programs for native Alaskans. Not one Alaska native has worked on the Chenega contract. When asked about his company's success, Chenega's chief operating officer described it as "an American success story that benefits from preferential laws based upon the trust relationship the United States Government has with its indigenous, aboriginal people."[23]

If private companies are overcharging and profiting from loopholes in state and federal laws, how does the military-industrial complex benefit government? There are multiple ways that private industry benefits government—or more specifically, benefits politicians and ranking military personnel—campaign and political party contributions, lobbying, investment, economic stimulus, and high-paying corporate jobs. But those who benefit most of all by the marriage of military and industry are those who represent both sides—they are the military-industrial complex.

The Government as Contractor: Bechtel, Carlyle, and Halliburton

Former Congressman Ron Dellums once remarked that he had to come to Congress to understand the difference between welfare and subsidy. Subsidy is a big check that goes to a few people. The degree to which wealthy interests are subsidized has been documented.[24] Nowhere is this more pronounced than in the defense sector.

> In this charmed circle of American capitalism, Lockheed Martin-, Boeing-, and Raytheon-manufactured munitions destroy Iraq; George Shultz's Bechtel Corporation and Dick Cheney's Halliburton rebuild Iraq; and Iraqi oil pays for it all.[25]

Like England, who was introduced earlier, many U.S. military and political officers move between positions in government and the private sector. The transition from positions in governing bodies to the companies soliciting contracts creates enormous conflicts of interest. But it is the connections between the officers of government agencies and the defense industry that are most egregious. With their connections to the upper echelons of government, these companies have had a tremendous impact on foreign policy.

The Bechtel Group

The Bechtel Group is one of the world's largest engineering, construction, and project management companies, including nineteen joint-venture companies and numerous subsidiaries. Based in San Francisco since 1899, four generations of the Bechtel family have led their business through more than 22,000 projects in 140 nations on all seven continents. Beginning with their part in the building of the American railroad system, such projects include the Hoover Dam, Bay Area Transit (BART) in San Francisco, and presently the management and operation of Los Alamos National Laboratories.[26] The company plays a major role in the nuclear sector, with its early involvement in the Manhattan Project and its construction or design of over half the nuclear power plants in America.[27] As explored in chapter 4, it is also one of the premier water-privatization companies in the world.

The company also has a long history in the Persian Gulf. Since World War II, Bechtel has built oil refineries and pipelines, as well as major infrastructure such as highways and airports. During the 1980s, a subsidiary of Bechtel had a major Saudi Arabian client that invested $10 million in the company, Bin Laden Construction.

The U.S. government, however, is the biggest financier of Bechtel and its subsidiaries. From fiscal years 1990 to 2002, the company received more than $11.7 billion in U.S. government contracts. Between 2002 and July 2004 Bechtel received nearly $3 billion from the agency USAID.[28]

Bechtel's ties to the U.S. government facilitate this process. The company's relationships with U.S. policy makers and officeholders began when Stephen Bechtel partnered with John McCone, who later became head of the CIA under President Kennedy. In the 1970s Bechtel hired numerous government officials, including Secretary of Health, Education, and Welfare Caspar Weinberger (who in 1980 left the company to become President Reagan's defense secretary), former Atomic Energy Commission Chief Executive Robert Hollingsworth, former Marine Four-Star General and NATO Commander Jack Sheehan, and Richard Helms, who consulted on Iranian and Middle Eastern projects in 1978 after serving as the CIA director and the ambassador to Iran. Helms is known for his involvement with the attempted assassination of Fidel Castro and the overthrow of Chilean leader Salvador Allende.[29] The exchange has been in both directions, with government officials moving into Bechtel positions and Bechtel officers moving into government. Many former Bechtel executives have left the company and gone on to hold positions in government or become government consultants.

The highest-profile government officeholder was George Shultz, former treasury secretary to Nixon. Shultz bounced back and forth between an executive vice president position in Bechtel to the position of secretary of state under Reagan and back to Bechtel's board of directors. Shultz's involvement with Iraq is long and deep. As secretary of state, Shultz sent Donald Rumsfeld to meet with Saddam Hussein to advocate for the building of a pipeline from the oilfields of Iraq to the port of Aqaba in Jordan. Also during this time, as the chairman of International Council of JP Morgan Chase, Shultz loaned $500 million to Saddam Hussein to buy weapons; Bechtel was one of the companies that sold the weapons.[30] As chair of the Committee for the Liberation of Iraq, Shultz wrote a piece in the *Washington Post* entitled "Act Now: The Danger is Immediate," advocating a preemptive strike on Iraq.

Carlyle Group

Unlike Lockheed Martin and General Dynamics (who manufacture weapons) or Bechtel and Halliburton (who design, build, and manage large enterprises), the Carlyle Group specializes in investing. Since its founding in 1987, this Washington DC–based corporation has made billions on investments, mergers, and acquisitions with defense manufacturing companies. As the military began to increase outsourcing of manufacturing and services to private companies, a new niche market was created for private-equity firms. The Carlyle Group found its initial success by purchasing underperforming defense companies, installing their own management team, encouraging investment, and then selling the companies at a large profit. With the 1997 sale of BDM International, Inc., the group made a 650 percent profit.[31]

Carlyle's biggest transaction was the sale of United Defense in 2002. Only a year earlier, the company had vigorously lobbied the Pentagon over United Defense's Crusader artillery system and garnered $2 billion for it. Secretary of Defense Rumsfeld, who disliked the expensive system, announced his lack of interest in purchasing the Crusader, but only after the Carlyle Group had sold United Defense at a profit of over $247 million.[32] Critics have proposed that the profitable sale was facilitated by insider information.

Links between high-ranking government offices and Carlyle are profuse. Former Secretary of Defense Frank Carlucci, chairman of Carlyle at the time of the United Defense sale, was the college roommate of Donald Rumsfeld at Princeton. Other notable links include William Kennard, former Federal Communications Commission (FCC) chairman, who under Carlyle directs the business investments of the companies he once regulated. Former Secretary of State

James Baker and his former boss, George H. Bush, have also worked for Carlyle. Bush commands over $500,000 for his speeches in support of the company. Bush and Baker are particularly valuable to the company as emissaries to investors in the Middle East, most notably the Saudi Arabian Bin Laden Group.

Halliburton

Founded in 1919, Houston-based Halliburton is one of the world's largest providers of products and services to the oil and gas industries. This company has made billions of dollars in no-bid contracts with the U.S. government (particularly the Pentagon) to build and repair oil wells and pipelines and construct military bases. More recently, the company has become a "privatized" sector of the military, offering all sorts of services from laundry and mail to information technology and intelligence. Halliburton has gained special notoriety among government contractors for two reasons: (1) the company's ties to Vice President Dick Cheney, and (2) its track record of overbilling.

Overbilling

In 1992 the Halliburton subsidiary KBR was awarded the U.S. Army's first Logistics Civil Augmentation Program (LOGCAP) contract. LOGCAP is a U.S. Army initiative for peacetime planning for the use of civilian contractors in wartime and other contingencies. Under the "cost plus award fee" contract (a fee on top of the cost of service ranging from 2 to 5 percent) was awarded to KBR to provide support in all of the army's field operations, including combat and intelligence. KBR came under scrutiny by the General Accounting Office (GAO), which reported that the company had padded its estimated costs by 32 percent. The company boosted its bottom line by charging $84 for a $14 piece of plywood.[33] In another case, Halliburton spent $82,000 for a shipment of natural gas from Kuwait to Iraq, but charged the government $27.4 million.[34] In 2000 the GAO released another report claiming the army had done nothing to curb inflated contractor costs estimated at $2.2 billion in the Balkan conflict.

Since 9/11, Halliburton and KBR have received billions in no-bid contracts in Afghanistan and Iraq, the most dubious perhaps being the two-year $7 billion contract to rebuild Iraq's oil infrastructure. What is interesting about this deal is that this no-bid contract is for fighting oil fires and reconstructing oil fields after the U.S. invasion, even though only eight gas wells and pipelines caught fire, and all but one was extinguished by the time the contract was made.[35] Incidentally, KBR wrote the army's contingency plan for the Iraqi oil-well repair.

The Pentagon's own auditors accused Halliburton of overcharging by over $100 million on just one of their task orders in Iraq. This investigation by the Defense Contract Audit Agency, released in October 2004, was not released to Congress until March of 2005. Congressman Henry Waxman from California initiated a congressional investigation. The Pentagon rejected twelve separate requests for information by the congressman.[36] The Pentagon similarly thwarted an investigation by the United Nations regarding oil-contract profiteering. Waxman suggested that Iraqi oil proceeds were used to pay (or overpay) Halliburton. With the early 2007 announcement of the company headquarters move to Dubai, a case can be argued that Halliburton's top executives would be out of reach of U.S. law-enforcement agencies in the event that indictments are handed down. Dubai, part of the United Arab Emirates and located in the heart of the world's biggest oil-producing region, has no extradition treaty with the United States.

Halliburton has a long-standing history with the U.S. government. In World War II the company was contracted to build the infrastructure for the oil fields of Saudi Arabia, Bahrain, and Kuwait. In the 1950s, with millions of dollars at stake when Mohammed Mossadegh planned to nationalize Iran's oil reserves, Halliburton and the American oil consortium appealed to the U.S. government to take action. This ultimately led to the assassination of Mossadegh and the CIA-orchestrated reinstallation of Reza Pahlavi as the American-business-friendly Shah of Iran (see chapter 6). Under the Johnson administration in the 1960s, the company was contracted to build military bases for the Vietnam War. In 1967, the GAO disclosed that Halliburton could not account for nearly $120 million worth of materials that had been shipped from the United States to Vietnam.[37] Similar to the release of more recent accounting reports, the document was essentially buried by the Pentagon and left untouched by the press.

In the 1970s the company was contracted by Saddam Hussein to build two enormous oil terminals in the Persian Gulf off the coast from Umm Qasr. For the next thirty years, Halliburton has been called upon again and again to repair the terminals and pipelines that have been repeatedly bombed by Iranian and later by U.S. forces. Just weeks before Saddam Hussein invaded Kuwait (which led to the first U.S. Gulf War), the Iraqi government paid Halliburton $57 million for work on one of the country's terminals and for assistance with exploration technology; only weeks later, the Pentagon paid the company $3.9 million to put out oil fires, while KBR was contracted to construct the bombed-out buildings of Kuwait City.[38]

In 1992 as defense secretary under President George H. W. Bush, Cheney hired KBR to write the privatization report that initiated the LOGCAP program. Three years later, Cheney became CEO of the company and remained there until 2000, when he left to become vice president. Upon leaving his position as CEO, Cheney received $30 million in stock options and is paid up to $1 million per year in deferred compensation. As CEO, Cheney doubled the size of the company through business mergers as well as deals with the Pentagon. During this time he landed a $1.1 billion Pentagon contract for services in the Balkans, as well as billions in government loans.[39] During Cheney's years as CEO, the company donated $1.2 million to political parties and Congress, and spent over a half a million on lobbying.

Caldicott makes two important points about Halliburton's influential position. Between 1997 and 2000, while Cheney was CEO of Halliburton, the contracts signed with Hussein by two Halliburton subsidiaries were in clear violation of U.S. sanctions against Iraq. Second, in the years before Cheney became CEO, the U.S. Import-Export (IE) Bank (which secures loans for Halliburton's foreign customers) guaranteed loans of $100 million. During Cheney's time as CEO, the IE Bank guaranteed loans up to $1.5 billion.[40]

A vast military-industrial complex includes excessive corporate profiteering from military activities. Militarism also brings the inevitable widespread public corruption that is needed to conceal the real beneficiaries of the war and the deceptions needed to promote it.

For a powerful industrial elite to steer a policy process with self-serving deals of this magnitude, one needs more than the pressures of independent corporate lobbyists. One also needs three other elements: (1) groups such as think tanks and advisory boards that meet together in the role of architects for new policy; (2) groups with resources to influence and implement policies; and (3) elite clubs to assure camaraderie and loyalty to their class.

Elite Clubs: Building Networks of Power

For elite brokers of power to transact business, there is a need for an underlying appreciation of the unspoken rules. What is best for the corporations is assumed to be in the national interest. They know what is best for others. Their private transactions are better hidden behind a public mask and are conducted in secret societies they have created. These societies create face-to-face familiarity that eases the flow of favors and positions across the inner network and promises confidentiality.

The Order of Skull and Bones

The Order of Skull and Bones, formally known as the Brotherhood of Death, is a secret society dating back to 1832. The Ivy League has many societies and clubs, but this one at Yale University is especially notable not only for its gothic ritual and utmost secrecy, but because of its membership. Former bonesmen have included many of the most powerful families in politics and business, including the families Rockefeller, Taft, Harriman, and Bush. Bonesmen have filled the Senate, the Defense Department, the CIA, and the Council on Foreign Relations (CFR); have owned and managed banks and investment firms; and have owned major newspapers and communications companies.

The society's iconography (a skull and bones with the numbers 322) and rituals (which occur inside a building known as "the Tomb") have added to the secret organization's mystique, providing fodder for conspiracy theorists and Hollywood films. With initiation rites rumored to include masturbation and coffins, one can understand why. Whatever their initiatory and psychological conditioning procedures, they appear to have served a purpose: The fraternal bonds between initiates and the legacy of the patriarchs that came before them indefinitely perpetuate this network of power. One anonymous bonesman, in an interview with Alex Robbins, a Yale graduate who investigated the underground society, described that networking:

> The biggest benefit to Skull and Bones . . . is the networking. In the rest of the world you get to know people through accident or through choice. In Bones you meet people whom you otherwise wouldn't get to meet. It's a forced setup among a group of high achievers, even the legacies.[41]

One example of how this setup has played out among the elite involves the Bush family dynasty. When asked why he had chosen to attend Yale, George Herbert Walker Bush explained that his family had a Yale tradition. Indeed, Skull and Bones alumni included his father (Senator Prescott Bush), brother Jonathan Bush, uncles John Walker and George Herbert Walker, III, great-uncle George Herbert Walker, Jr., cousin Ray Walker, his son (George W. Bush), and of course himself. For generations, the family has called on, and been called upon by, the Brotherhood.

At age thirty-one, Prescott Bush was hired by club members Averell and Roland Harriman to work at what was then the largest private bank in the United States. (The Harrimans had formed their company with the help of another bonesman, Percy Rockefeller). After graduating from Yale in 1948, George Herbert Walker Bush went to work for bonesman Neil Mallon at Dresser Industries; in 1950 Bush left to form Bush-Overby Oil Development Co. with financial support from bonesman uncle George Herbert Walker, Jr., and bonesman Lud Ashley.

His relationship with Ashley later came under fire during his presidency, when Ashley, then president of the Association of Bank Holding companies, helped write and lobby for Bush's banking deregulation bill. Of their relationship, Kenneth Guenther, executive vice president of the Independent Bankers Association of America, commented, "It is almost unprecedented that the head of a narrow private-interest lobby directly and immediately influences presidential policy to the direct financial benefit of the group's members."[42] Later, Ashley would help George H. W.'s son Neil, who became involved in a savings and loan scandal, to receive the lightest possible punishment.[43]

Three of George H. W.'s fellow bonesmen, George H. Pfau, Jr., Jack Caulkins, and William Judkins Clark raised significant funds for his presidential campaigns. As president, he named Pfau to be director of the Securities Investor Protection Corporation. Numerous bonesmen were granted positions as speechwriters and department secretaries. Several bonesmen were appointed as foreign emissaries: Richard Anthony Moore as ambassador to Ireland, Paul Lambert as ambassador to Ecuador (although he had no diplomatic experience), and bonesmen classmates David Grimes and Thomas W. Moseley represented Bush in Bulgaria and Uruguay, respectively.[44]

George W. got into Yale despite a weak academic record and has utilized Skull and Bones member connections just as his father and grandfather before him.

When he formed his first company, Arbusto Energy, Inc., he sought the financial assistance of bonesman uncle Jonathan Bush and William H. Draper III (Bones 1950). Bonesman Stephan Adams spent $1 million on billboard ads for Bush's 2000 campaign. At least fifty-eight bonesmen contributed at least $57,972 to Bush's campaign, while others donated money in their wives' names.[45]

Not unlike his father and grandfather, George W. has also returned the favor to his clubmates. In November 2001 he appointed Edward McNally (Bones 1979) to the newly formed Office of Homeland Security. Robert D. McCallum, Jr. (Bones 1968) was named assistant attorney general of the Civil Department. This position, notably, represents the federal government in cases such as fraud, international trade, patents, bankruptcies, and foreign litigation.

The Bilderberg Group

This elite, private club is especially noteworthy for two reasons: (1) members of the group (selected by invitation only) are among the most prominent leaders in the world in financing, business, academia, and politics; and (2) because of the group's complete secrecy. Not only are the meetings sheltered from the public and the press, but the entire event is managed by its own staff—taking over as hotel, catering, and security staff several days before the onset of each meeting.

In 1976, in a column of the British Financial Times, C. Gordon Tether wondered if there was so little to hide, why so much effort is devoted to hiding it.[46] The column, however, was never printed; it was censored by *Financial Times* editor Mark Fisher (member of the Trilateral Commission). Tether was dismissed from the column later that year.

Structure and Membership

At the core of the Bilderberg organization is a steering committee consisting of a permanent chair, a U.S. chair, European and North American secretaries, and a treasurer. Members, again, are solicited by invitation only and are distinguished by their knowledge, experience, and influence in their respective fields. Membership is extended only to residents of Europe and North America. They gather once, or sometimes twice, a year, each time at a different European or American five-star resort. The meetings operate as discussions on various timely subjects. (At a recent meeting, one prominent topic was what to do about Venezuelan president Hugo Chavez.) Rather than voting on any particular action, the meetings are organized on the principle of reaching consensus.

Origins of Bilderberg

The manner in which the initial Bilderberg group members formed illustrates the network of corporate power. The first relationship between the founders and corporate invitees occurred when Joseph Retinger, a political advisor, befriended Paul Rijkens, at that time president of Unilever, one of the largest and most powerful multinational corporations in the world. Rijkens was also at that time on the board of Rotterdam Bank. Based on that relationship, other board members of Rotterdam Bank, such as H. M. Hirschfield, K. P. Van der Mandel, and H. L. Wolterson became part of a clique. Wolterson was also chair of the Philips electrical corporation, and Hirschfield was on the board of Philips. These associations brought in P. S. F. Otten, then president of Philips. In addition to his corporate positions, Hirschfield had worked for the Dutch Ministry of Economic Affairs during World War II and afterward served as commissioner for the Marshall Plan in the Netherlands.[47]

To garner interest for membership in the United States, Prince Bernard, cofounder with Retinger, enlisted the help of his close friend Walter Bedell Smith, director of the CIA. Smith then turned to Charles D. Jackson, special assistant for psychological warfare to the president, and president of the Committee for a Free Europe (anticommunist) organization. Jackson was formerly a publisher of *Fortune* magazine as well as director of *Time/Life*. Jackson appointed John S. Coleman, president of the Burroughs Corporation and member of the Committee for a National Trade Policy, as U.S. chair of the Bilderberg group.[48] Retinger, Prince Bernard, and Rijkens selected the invitees (drawn from corporate and government officials in the European NATO countries plus Sweden) to the first Bilderberg conference.[49]

The original members on the American side include names and entities recognizable to American readers: George Ball, head of Lehman Brothers, a former State Department official and future member of the Trilateral Commission; David Rockefeller, key American member of Bilderberg and head of Chase Manhattan Bank, member of the Council on Foreign Relations, member of the Business Council, member of the U.S. Council of the International Chamber of Commerce, and future founder of the Trilateral Commission; and Dean Rusk, future U.S. secretary of state (1961–1969), former president of the Rockefeller Foundation.[50]

Even more recognizable to American readers are these former and current members of Bilderberg: Donald Rumsfeld, former U.S. secretary of defense; Paul Wolfowitz, former U.S. defense secretary and president of the World Bank; Peter Sutherland, chairman of Goldman Sachs and British Petroleum and former commissioner of the European Union; and Steven Harper, right-wing Prime Minister of Canada.[51]

The Bohemian Club

For two weeks every July, 2,000 to 3,000 men gather together for "summer camp" in the redwood forests of Northern California. These are not ordinary men but rather government leaders; military officials; CEOs of oil companies, financial institutions, and weapons manufacturers; owners of corporate print and television news media and utility companies; and directors of policy councils or major philanthropic foundations.

The Bohemian Club began in San Francisco in 1872 as a small group of artists and writers who wished to celebrate arts and culture in the post-gold-rush era of

San Francisco. For financial purposes, the club extended its membership to wealthy members of the business elite, who dominated membership soon thereafter. Prominent leaders of government became members as well; in fact, all U.S. Republican president since 1923 (as well as several Democrat presidents) have been members. Members and member emeriti include former secretaries of state Henry Kissinger, George Shultz, and Colin Powell; Secretary of Defense Donald Rumsfeld; David Rockefeller and David Rockefeller, Jr.; S. D. Bechtel, Jr. (Bechtel Corporation); Thomas Watson, Jr. (IBM); Phillip Hawley (Bank of America); Ralph Bailey (Dupont); and A. W. Clausen (World Bank).[52] High-ranking officials from foreign countries also attend.[53]

Membership

Membership is by invitation only and is distinct from the thousands of people who are invited to the two-week camp-out as guests. Membership lists are private and have only recently been obtained by a watchdog group, the 2004 Bohemian Grove Action Network. New members must be nominated by two current, active members who write letters of recommendation to show "good Bohemian" character. The application form requires a prospective member to list his other club memberships and professional connections. It includes the wife's maiden name and asks him to name at least five other club members who know him. After collecting the information, a letter is circulated to all current members, who then vote on the new members. It is a lengthy and time-consuming process. Some are put on waiting lists to join—with some waiting as long as ten years. As a recent club president used to say in his letter of congratulations to new members, "You have joined not only a club, but a way of life."[54]

Activities

The general atmosphere at the two-week event in Monte Rio, California, might best be described as combination of fraternity party and summer camp. It has been called "the greatest men's party on earth." The yearly outdoor event includes lectures, plays (with men playing female roles, because women are not allowed), music performances, political discussions, and heavy ritual, centered on an endless bacchanalian feast of food and alcohol.

The lectures, called "lakeside chats," are off-the-record presentations on world issues such as military budgets or global free trade. One such chat, given by a University of California political science professor in 1994, warned club members of the dangers of multiculturalism, Afrocentrism, and the loss of family boundaries. "Elites based on merit and skill are important to society," he explained. The "unqualified" masses, he concluded, cannot be allowed to carry out policy—the elite must set values that can be translated into "standards of authority."[55] Whatever the subject, such issues are presented in the manner of one "insider" to another, as members of the elite. The topics may never be publicly presented.

Numerous theater performances enhance the overall carnival atmosphere. The elaborate, original theater productions, known as "High Jinx," are often based on a mythical theme (such as "The Man of the Forest" or "A Jest of Robin Hood"). These are sophisticated productions, with casts typically around 75 to 100 men, professional lighting and sets, and with costs as much as $150,000.[56] None of this exorbitance is for salaries. The production is performed by associate members who dabble in the arts. The musical comedies are known as "Low Jinx." These are bawdy and lewd acts that usually refer to the prostitutes who are flown in from all over the world to perform their services for members. Homosexual encounters are also reportedly frequent.

The Cremation of Care Ceremony

Perhaps the most bizarre aspect of the Bohemian Grove is the ritual Cremation of Care ceremony on the opening night of festivities. It begins with members in flowing red robes and pointed hoods carrying a coffin containing a life-like human effigy, the Body of Care. This symbolizes all the cares and woes that distinguished club members carry in their heavy hearts day after day. The funeral dirge marches to the foot of a forty-foot-tall owl statue, amid chanting and torches of fire. Various "high priests" make effusive speeches and prayers. The effigy is thrown onto the funeral pyre at the owl's feet. Fireworks explode, and a band strikes up the tune "A Hot Time in the Old Town."[57] At this point, the revelry and hobnobbing of the elite has officially begun.

Sociologist Peter Phillips, who wrote his doctoral dissertation on the Bohemian Club, defines the club as institutionalized race, gender, and class inequality. He describes how these clubs model themselves after the gentlemen's clubs of nineteenth-century England, which became popular as the nation was concentrating on building its empire around the globe. The clubs represented a place where gentlemen could discuss their ideas of expansion and domination away from the distraction, meddling—or consciousness—of women, the underclasses, and nonwhites.

As Phillips describes Bohemian Grove, it is an atmosphere of social interaction and networking. Here, one can sit around a campfire with ex-presidents of the United States and CEOs of Bank of America or Pacific Gas and Electric. You can share a cognac or shoot skeet with secretaries of state and defense. You can enjoy the High Jinx alongside the members of the Council on Foreign Relations. Certain known principles of group dynamics explain the efficacy of the group's community building. Physical proximity is likely to lead to group solidarity. Greater direct interaction leads to friendships, trust, and mutual liking. Groups seen as high in status are more cohesive. The best atmosphere for increasing group cohesiveness is one that is relaxed and cooperative. Social cohesion, in turn, helps to reduce conflicts and reach agreement on big issues.[58] One example of this last point is the Manhattan Project, which produced the first atomic bombs. It was conceived and informally set into motion at the Grove in 1942.[59] This atmosphere serves the purpose of developing social ties and cohesion within the elite social class. These ties "manifest themselves in global trade meetings, party politics, campaign financing, and top-down democracy."[60]

This chapter has been using the concept of networks of power, but such networks have few connections across the lines of social class. For sociologist Bill Domhoff, the Bohemian Club is "evidence for the class cohesiveness that is one prerequisite for class domination."[61] The club becomes an avenue by which the cohesiveness of the elite class is maintained.

Think Tanks, Advisory Boards, and Councils: Creating Policy and Consent

Government officials work primarily to balance the needs and pressures from constituents and primary funders. The system has little room for participatory involvement in redefining major directions of policy or larger shifts of direction. That function is served by other exclusive groups, in and out of government, that are designed specifically to come up with ideas to steer national and global policy.

Council on Foreign Relations and Trilateral Commission

The Chatham House, described as the European predecessor of the Council on Foreign Relations, was founded in 1920, one year before the council. It was noted especially for the "Chatham House Rule," instituted in 1927, which grants complete anonymity to the speakers within its walls for the presumed betterment of international relations. Since its inception in 1921, the CFR has represented the elite who's who in America, with a membership that constitutes U.S. presidents, ambassadors, secretaries of state, Wall Street investors, international bankers, foundation executives, think-tank executives, lobbyist lawyers, Pentagon officials, media owners, senators, university presidents, Supreme Court judges, and corporate entrepreneurs. In their own words, they are "the privileged and preeminent nongovernmental impresario of America's pageant to find its place in the world."[62]

The CFR vision for America's place in the world is market domination. Throughout its history, the CFR has played a major role in shaping foreign policy to benefit American markets. At the end of World War II, members of the CFR, including David Rockefeller, presented the idea for reconstruction of Europe that would become the Marshall Plan. It sought to benefit U.S. corporations directly.[63] Carroll Quigley, professor of history at Georgetown University, stated that the CFR "believes national boundaries should be obliterated and one-world rule established."[64]

On March 12, 2003, just one week before the U.S. invasion of Iraq, CFR's Independent Task Force, chaired by former Defense Secretary and Energy Secretary James Schlesinger and former U.N. Ambassador Thomas Pickering, urged President Bush to "make clear to the Congress, to the American people, and to the people of Iraq that the United States will stay the course" after a war in Iraq.[65] "Stay the course" became the oft-repeated justification to continue the war. James Schlesinger is also currently chairman of MITRE Corporation's Board of Trustees (a defense and intelligence technology company) and a senior advisor at Lehman Brothers. Thomas Pickering is also senior vice president for International Relations at Boeing. Other task force members included a senior executive advisor at Hess Energy Trading and Stanley Fisch and the president of Citigroup International.

With success in Iraq "so clearly tied to American staying power," the task force released another report in June 2003, stating that the "Bush administration should therefore reaffirm its commitment to sustain a large presence of U.S. military forces to ensure stability as long as necessary" and urging him to make a major foreign policy address to explain the importance of "seeing the task through."[66] The report also advised the Bush administration "to improve management and operations in the oil industry . . . and [to] prepare for the next peace stabilization and reconstruction challenge after Iraq."[67]

The CFR is limited to Americans. The Trilateral Commission began at the behest of David Rockefeller in 1973, whose proposal to include Japan in the annual Bilderberg meetings was rejected. With the assistance of then U.S. National Security Advisor Zbigniew Brzezinski, the Trilateral Commission sought to bring the rising economic power—Japan—into political and business cooperation with America and Europe. At the time of its inception in 1973, the Trilateral Commission responded to the oil crisis by extending loans to developing countries. David Rockefeller's Chase Manhattan Bank loaned nearly $52 billion, and the IMF further expanded their loan program to developing nations.[68] The Trilateral Commission comprises political leaders, corporate CEOs, labor leaders, academics, and foundation executives. Many of its American participants are members of the CFR and the Bilderberg Group as well.

Business Advocacy and Lobbying Groups

Although a multitude of advocacy and lobbying groups exist for all types of citizens' needs, not all are equally influential. The National Rifle Association has long been effective in preventing restrictions on gun sales. The American-Israeli Political Action Committee has been highly effective in preventing congressional criticism of Israel or of the extensive military assistance that the United States provides to Israel. But the most effective lobbying efforts come from corporations. The amount of money wielded by some groups creates an uneven playing field and assures a force protecting the interests of the corporate elite.

National Manufacturers Association

The National Manufacturers Association (NAM) is a powerful advocate of a pro-growth, pro-manufacturing agenda. Representing over 100,000 companies, it is the nation's largest industrial trade association. NAM's mission is to "enhance the competitiveness of manufacturers by shaping a legislative and regulatory environment."[69] With over 300 member associations, NAM seeks to be engaged in every congressional district. The NAM "Key Manufacturing Vote" notice alerts lawmakers to votes critical in implementing the NAM agenda. Among the thousands of advocacy groups, *Fortune* magazine ranked NAM among the top ten most influential advocacy groups in the United States.[70] Lobbying supports legislative boosts to the bottom line. The largest corporations, like the largest insurance pension funds, are acquiring capital for investment, often in operations selected by money mangers and remote from their own business activities. Hence bottom-line-driven CEOs may be rewarded for activities that drain from their own operations to support lucrative speculations.[71]

The Business Roundtable

Another powerful advocacy group is the Business Roundtable. What distinguishes this group from other U.S. business associations and advocacy groups is that their membership is composed exclusively of the CEOs of the over 200 companies represented. The group attracts members from all types of American businesses in all regions of the country. The group is "committed to advocating public policies that ensure vigorous economic growth, a dynamic global economy, and the well-trained and productive U.S. workforce essential for future competitiveness."[72] The combined annual revenue of the companies that make up the group is $4.5 trillion.[73]

Two major policy issues for which these groups advocate are energy security and trade liberalization. By their own account, the manufacturing industry consumes roughly one-third of the nation's total energy supply and is therefore "disproportionately" affected by energy availability. Although NAM supports the research and development of all sources of energy production (including renewable sources and the promotion of improved efficiency), their primary goal is to "increase [national] access to domestic sources of reliable energy."[74] In December 2006 NAM achieved a major victory when Congress passed the Gulf of Mexico Security Act, which will open 8.3 million acres in the Gulf to new oil and natural gas production. This is significant because it represents the first increase in domestic energy production in twenty-five years. NAM is also lobbying for Congress to lift the present legislation protecting the Alaska National Wildlife Refuge (ANWR).

NAM opposes federal and state government climate-change mandates that have the potential to "adversely affect U.S. manufacturing competitiveness."[75] In 2004 NAM hosted a conference entitled "Environmental Issues 2004: How to Get Results in an Election Year."[76] The focus of the conference was how to present pro-industry environmental messages to the public and influence the 2004 elections—or elect those policy makers who favor industry over the environment. The keynote speaker at the event was Mike Leavitt, administrator of the U.S. Environmental Protection Agency (EPA), who declared, "We need to do [environmental policy] in a better way that doesn't compromise our economic competitiveness."[77]

In their official policy position on global climate change, NAM states that

> There remains considerable scientific uncertainty and disagreement regarding human impacts on climate . . . [that] in fact, observational data have not confirmed evidence of global warming that can be attributed to human activities. . . . We believe any U. S. climate change policies should be voluntary, cost-effective, compatible with our market economy, flexible, global in scope, and involve all of our trading partners.[78]

Trade liberalization is another major agenda for business advocacy groups. The Business Roundtable was the most instrumental organization in the promotion of the North American Free Trade Agreement (NAFTA).[79] Their strategy included frequent congressional testimonies, regular press releases, and hundreds of lobbying sessions involving CEOs of such influential companies as General Motors, AT&T, and Arthur Anderson & Co. Lobbyists for the closely affiliated National Foreign Trade Council and General Motors lobbied for the NAFTA vote nearly 150 times. U.S. NAFTA members of the Business Roundtable regularly met with President Clinton for briefings with White House officials and worked with the president to select Lee Iacocca as the president's "NAFTA Czar."[80]

With a similar approach, NAM helped win the adoption of the Central American Free Trade Agreement (CAFTA) in 2005. In September of 2005, John Engler, president of NAM, was named vice chairman of the President's Advisory Committee for Trade Policy and Negotiations, the government's senior trade advisory panel. Mr. Engler was also appointed by Secretary of State Condoleezza Rice to serve on the Advisory Committee on Transformational Diplomacy. He also serves on the Deemed Export Advisory Committee.

A close network exists that links lobbyists to nonprofit groups and to government officials.[81] Dreiling argues that these frequent associations within prominent decision-making circles are the result of "the unique structural location afforded inner circle corporate leaders."[82] He describes this powerful vantage point:

> As Useem argued (1984), inner circle corporate actors receive, in addition to numerous other advantages, the political advantages offered by "the stature and resources of the premier business associations" which facilitate not only cohesion, but heightened visibility and access to "government circles . . . and special hearings."[83]

Powerful groups maintain their own public-relations units, but increasingly the lobbying efforts are contracted to another growth industry, professional lobbying firms. They specialize not only in framing the message but more importantly in peddling influence with government officials. The number of registered lobbyists in Washington has more than doubled since 2000 to more than 34,750, whereas the amount that lobbyists charge their new clients has increased by as much as 100 percent. Increases in federal spending, primarily in the defense sector, have led to a belief by contractors that they need inside influence to get large shares of the largesse. The exorbitant starting salaries of corporate lobbyists lure close to half of retiring members of congress.[84]

Patrick J. Griffin, who was President Bill Clinton's top lobbyist and is now in private practice, commented, "They see that they can win things, that there's something to be gained. Washington has become a profit center."[85] Sometimes the practices are illegal. One lobbying firm, the Alexander Strategy group, founded by House Majority Leader Tom Delay's chief of staff, contributed over $376,000 to GOP candidates and fund-raising organizations since 2001, until its association with scandals involving the indictment of Jack Abramoff for money laundering and the resignation of Tom Delay forced it to close down.

The Project for the New American Century

While some think tanks attempt to sculpt the public's views on the effects of smoking or the state of the environment, others focus on shaping foreign policy. The Project for the New American Century (PNAC) was formed in 1997 with the explicit purpose of promoting and planning the American domination of global affairs. In 1998 the group sent a letter to President Clinton advising him to remove Saddam Hussein from power, by reason that his stockpile of weapons of mass destruction posed a threat to the United States, its Middle East allies, and the region's oil resources. They argued that an Iraq war would be justified by Hussein's defiance of U.N. inspections.

In their September 2000 paper entitled "Rebuilding America's Defenses: Strategy, Forces, and Resources for a New Century," PNAC clearly outlines what must be done (by force of arms) in order to create their desired position as sole global superpower. Major themes include a massive increase in the national defense budget; an enlarged and modernized armed forces equipped with the most advanced technologies; and the development and deployment of a global missile defense system. Bush's budget plan in 2003 called for the same exact dollar amount to be spent on defense that was requested by PNAC in their 2000 paper.[86]

In a chilling line often quoted by critics, authors of the 2000 paper propose the perceived need for advanced technologies in the face of a "catastrophic and catalyzing event—like a new Pearl Harbor."[87] Because such an attack on American soil would, they believe, justify a war with Iraq, some critics believe this quote is evidence of U.S. government involvement in the 9/11 terrorist attacks.

PNAC is especially disconcerting not only because they appear to have prophesied 9/11 and the U.S. invasion of Iraq, but because of who they are: Individuals who held the highest positions in the G. W. Bush administration (Vice President Dick Cheney, National Security Council Director Eliot Abrams, Secretary of Defense Donald Rumsfeld, Deputy Secretary of Defense Paul Wolfowitz, Defense Policy Advisory Board chairman Richard Perle, and Undersecretary of Defense Douglas Feith), all with continuing ties to the defense industry. PNAC also included members with ties to the oil industry (Dick Cheney, Jeb Bush); members with ties to the media (Donald Kagan, William Kristol); and members in the defense industry (Bruce Jackson, Vin Weber).[88] The power of this group has been exercised as the "New Paradigm" strategy in the G. W. Bush administration upon advice from David S. Addington, Vice President Cheney's chief of staff and his longtime principal legal adviser. The New Paradigm strategy rests on a reading of the Constitution that few legal scholars share—namely, that the president, as commander-in-chief, has the authority to disregard virtually all previously known legal boundaries, if national security demands it. Under this interpretation, statutes prohibiting torture, secret detention, and warrant-less surveillance have been set aside.[89]

The Defense Policy Board

Whereas some elite planning bodies focus their efforts on legislation that affect their domestic and international corporate interests, others such as the Defense Policy Advisory Board (DPB) focus on the foreign-policy issues that may affect their economic or political interests.[90]

Formed in 1985, the board began its function as a bipartisan advisory body. However, under the G. W. Bush administration, it became overtly involved with making policy decisions, a role it is not mandated to do.[91] Douglas Feith, undersecretary of defense and a former Reagan administration official, chose the thirty members of the DPB for the Bush administration—nine of whom have significant ties to major defense industry contractors including Bechtel, Boeing, TRW, Northrop Grumman, Lockheed Martin, and Booz Allen Hamilton.[92] Four members are registered lobbyists, one of them representing two of the largest military contractors in the country. Members of DPB disclose their business interests annually to the Pentagon, but the disclosures are not available to the public.

In 2003 a controversy ensued around Chairman Richard Perle, a cofounder of PNAC and a vocal advocate for the Iraq war. Considering his numerous corporate dealings, it was apparent that he would profit greatly from the war. At the time, Perle worked for Goldman Sachs, advising clients on investment opportunities in postwar Iraq. He also directed and has major shares in the British Autonomy Corporation, a manufacturer of high-tech eavesdropping technologies, whose major customers are the Department of Homeland Security, the Secret Service, and the National Security Agency. On top of these, Perle's venture-capital company, Trireme, invests in millions of dollars worth of defense products (over half from Boeing). Ironically, none of these positions appeared to pose an ethical conflict; Perle only stepped down from the chair of the Defense Policy Advisory Board after the Pentagon and FBI opposed his attempts to sell his telecommunications company's subsidiaries to a Chinese consortium.[93]

International Groups That Plan and Implement Policy

Quite obviously, the leaders of corporate power are part of an international as well as a domestic network. This network is represented by formal powers invested in continuing organizations, particularly the International Monetary Fund, the World Bank, and the World Trade Association.

The International Monetary Fund

The International Monetary Fund (IMF) emerged from the Bretton Woods conference in 1944. The main focus of the conference was to develop a system that would foster and develop open markets for trade. Industrial nations were encouraged to lower trade barriers and invest capital and were deemed responsible for managing and governing this system; the IMF was created as that governing body. It regulated international exchanges of currency. Voting was proportional to the capital contributed, as Zinn points out, so that American dominance would be assured.[94] The fixed exchange rate system, however, collapsed between 1971 and 1973. Since that time, it has increasingly become more involved in the fiscal counseling of member countries and worked as an advocate for the privatization of state industries.

The IMF Web site describes its mission as "working to foster global monetary cooperation, secure financial stability, facilitate international trade, promote high employment and sustainable economic growth, and reduce poverty."[95] In reality "structural adjustment programs," or IMF-granted loans, have devastated many developing countries' economies. These loans are granted with strict conditions that enforce trade liberalization and encourage direct foreign investment, resource extraction, and the privatization of state entities. Considerable criticism has been raised against the IMF and its policies that undermine national sovereignties and endorse corporate globalization.

Such criticism comes not only from nations devastated by IMF programs (such as Jamaica, Argentina, Ethiopia, and Malawi) who have called for its abolition, but from 2001 Nobel laureate economist Joseph Stiglitz. Stiglitz worked in the Clinton administration as chairman of the Council of Economic Advisors and is a former chief economist for the World Bank. He concluded that institutions such as the IMF and World Bank do not operate in the interest of developing countries. This view is based on his determination that the neoliberal position held by these institutions is basically erroneous.[96]

The World Bank

Like the IMF, the World Bank came into being during the Bretton Woods conference in 1944. Its first loan was approved in 1946 in the amount of $250 million to France for postwar reconstruction.

Composed of five international financial investment and monitoring agencies, the World Bank aims to provide capital and financial advice for the purposes of economic development and the elimination of poverty. The organization's activities focus primarily on financing the building of infrastructure, the development of agriculture and irrigation systems, and the improvement of human services in education and health in developing countries.

Each agency within the World Bank is owned by its member governments. Voting rights are proportional to shareholding; therefore, the organization is effectively controlled by wealthier, developed countries. As put forth at Bretton Woods, the World Bank president is always a U.S. citizen and is nominated by the U.S. government (while the IMF is traditionally headed by a European). One recent bank president, Paul Wolfowitz, former undersecretary of defense, was obliged to resign for ethical violations.

Like the IMF, the World Bank has been criticized by academics and social organizations for imposing economic (free market) policies that support Western interests. In part, this criticism relates to the motives of the World Bank; that is, do they truly intend to assist developing countries, or do they primarily intend to make a profit?

Since its inception, the World Bank has loaned tremendous sums of money to poor countries in need of infrastructure. Frequently, the governments of these countries are corrupt, hording much of the money for themselves, with little left to invest in the proposed development projects. Meanwhile, recipient countries incur an enormous debt that falls on the shoulders of people. Jeffrey Sachs explains that although corrupt governments are often blamed for their country's debts, the failures of these programs often have more to do with a systematic disregard of the related causes or exacerbations of poverty, including poor health-care systems and severely damaged natural environments.[97]

Furthermore, the companies that provide the work (and are paid the money) are invariably large Western corporations (including Bechtel and Halliburton) who intend to make a profit. As noted in chapter 4, World Bank Vice President Ismail Serageldin is the chair of CGIAR (Consultative Group on International Agricultural Research), which advocates agricultural biotechnologies. As a Western entity, the World Bank's philosophy of development is based on Western ideals and principles, which may not only affect the economic sovereignty of non-Western nations but also cultural sovereignty.

The World Trade Organization

The stated goal of the World Trade Organization (WTO) is to increase trade by lowering international trade barriers and by opening trade to international negotiation. It is an international and multilateral organization that creates rules for a system of global trade, and resolves disputes between its member states. The Agreement on Agriculture (AOA) was one of the first WTO rulings to come into effect after the inception of the organization in 1995. The AOA effectively increased subsidies to industrial agriculture, which may be increased without limit. As described in chapter 4, the United States grants 70 percent of its subsidies to 10 percent of its producers. Consequently, this allows major agribusinesses to flood global markets with cheap products, thereby undercutting producers in poor countries. The AOA also mandates market access, or the reduction of tariff barriers, between member states. This creates a problem for small farmers in developing countries—for whom tariff protections were often designed. As a result, small-scale indigenous farmers are forced to compete with subsidized, industrialized agribusinesses.

Apart from the structural violence that free-market policies wield toward less-developed countries, the WTO also favors industrialized nations by turning a blind eye to health, safety, and environmental issues. For example, through the WTO's Production and Processing Methods rule, safety precautions stating where and how something is produced are impermissible. Based on this ruling, lumber from protected forests may be sold indiscriminately, and genetically modified (GM) food products may not be labeled, in spite of their potential danger to human health and the environment.

In 2000 European Union (EU) member nations began labeling some foods containing GM products, demanded regulation, and initiated a five-year moratorium on new GM foods and products. In 2003 the United States, Argentina, Canada, and Egypt filed a claim with the WTO against the EU, charging that they had failed to install a scientific, rules-based review and approval process. Such a process is mandated by the WTO under the Agreement on the Application of Sanitary and Phytosanitary Measures. This agreement, while acknowledging the rights of countries to regulate crops and products for safety, also demands that direct scientific evidence in support of such regulation be presented in a timely manner.

For biotech companies in the United States, the EU's five-year moratorium was time and money lost. CropLife America, the National Corn Growers Association (NCGA), and the U.S. Grains Council welcomed the decision to file the case. According to the NCGA, the moratorium cost U.S. corn exporters $300 million a year.[98] After two and a half years of legal proceedings, in 2006, the WTO quietly announced their ruling that national bans on GM products restrict free trade, and specifically the European Union's five-year moratorium on new GM products posed a barrier to free trade. The evidence produced by some individual EU member states to justify their ban on imports of certain GM plants was judged to lack the required quality of scientific risk assessments showing potential danger. With this ruling, the WTO reaffirmed its position demanding "hard scientific evidence" and deemed that the precautionary principle invoked by the EU was not established as a principle of international law.[99] The case illustrates a long-standing controversy in the field of risk assessment between those, particularly corporations, who demand that a strong demonstration of evidence that damage to humans is caused by the potential hazard and those consumer and public health groups who favor the precautionary principle. Many toxic products, particularly carcinogens, may take years to document. Under the precautionary principle, suspected hazardous substances and those found harmful to animals may not be used until they have demonstrated a long-term record for safety.

The Corporatization of Elections: Taking Power from the People

However removed ordinary people may be from the daily transactions among higher levels of power that control the resources they need, there is still one line of input assured to citizens. They may not have direct access to corporate CEOs or governing boards, but they can hold their elected officials accountable with their votes. That belief enables officials to present the United States as a democracy. For the most powerful, the presence of free elections is an important factor in legitimizing a society in which they happen to be at the top. It is not, however, in their interest that voices from the least powerful, that might challenge their hold on resources, be heard. Hence, the inner network of the corporate elite exercises considerable control over many aspects of the electoral process. They are involved from the backing of candidates, to the accessibility of voting, to the design of electronic voting machines.

The Funding of Candidates

This corporate control of the democratic process begins at the earliest stage: Business elites often solicit candidates from their own ranks, or like-minded celebrities, on the basis of how amenable and how effective the candidate appears to the interests of private business. When candidates for national office are exploring the decision of whether to seek nomination for a major political party, they are mainly assessing how much support they can get from major donors who are, in turn, evaluating what will be the return for their support.

The process works to identify candidates with the greatest potential to bring in big money from wealthy individuals and business corporations. Hillman and Hitt explain, from a management perspective, the "substantial interdependence" between the business world's economic or competitive environment and government.[100] Examples of the impact of government regulation on business include taxation, trade practices, employment regulations, and environmental standards. The authors recall that by the late 1960s the government was conceived by some to be a competitive tool to create the environment most favorable to the business' interests. The communications company MCI utilized this political strategy to create a market opportunity by influencing government officials to deregulate the U.S. long-distance telephone market. As seen in chapter 4, agribusiness now receives huge subsidies from the U.S. government, which forces small family farms—for whom government subsidies were originally intended—out of the competitive market.

Corporate Sponsorship

Proactive approaches to the "corporate political action," described by Hillman and Hitt,[101] include Political Action Committees campaign contributions, lobbying, advocacy advertising, and grassroots mobilization. The ability of corporations to make financial contributions to political candidates is made possible by a series of federal court decisions that interpret the law to view corporations as persons, thus giving corporations many of the same rights that protect individuals.

The idea of corporations as persons began with various challenges to the Fourteenth Amendment to the U.S. Constitution, which grants citizenship to all persons born or naturalized in the United States. In California, in 1882, when big business was epitomized by the railroad industry, the Supreme Court ruled in favor of Southern Pacific Railroad in *San Mateo v. Southern Pacific Railroad.* Corporate lawyers for the railroad giant argued that by taxing the railroad's property differently than the property of natural persons, the state had violated the corporation's rights as secured by the Equal Protection Clause of the Fourteenth Amendment.[102] By interpreting citizens to include corporate entities, the federal courts thereby granted them personhood under the Bill of Rights protections of the First, Fourth, and Fifth Amendments.

In the 1970s court decisions equated political spending with free speech and voided a Massachusetts law prohibiting corporate interference, including funding.[103] It is this precedent that has allowed corporations to finance those candidates and political parties that will perpetuate their interests—specifically, the increased wealth of their business.

Some corporations provide support for both of the major political parties, although typically not equally. One method of enhancing the donation is to invite employees to contribute to the party or candidate of their choice through a voluntary salary deduction. The company then bundles the amounts and dispenses the funds, thereby enhancing the indebtedness of candidates to the company.[104]

Political Action Committees

Political Action Committees (PACs) are private groups that organize to work toward the election of a political candidate and to promote legislation that advances their specific interests. Some PACs work for a specific cause, such as a woman's right to choose whether to abort a pregnancy; some represent an industry as a whole, such as the National Association of Realtors; other PACs represent the specific financial interests of one corporation.

As Coleridge explains, the most sizable contributions come directly from corporations or through corporate-backed PACs. Lobbying groups represent the interests of major industries and major single issues, and contribute substantially to PACs.[105] Between 1998 and 2005 the finance, insurance, and real estate sector spent over $2 billion lobbying for legislation to benefit their business interests.[106]

Corporations and corporate PACs donate to individual campaigns as well as national, state, and local governmental political parties with careful deliberation and in expectation of "commensurate political returns."[107] Considering that many modern corporations are wealthier than most of the world's nations, it appears that the U.S. government has granted them commensurate returns on their political investments.

Campaign donations by corporations have increased dramatically over the last ten years. In 2003 the G. W. Bush campaign raised $577,000 a day, while Senator John Kerry brought in $64,000 a day.[108] Overall, the price of 2004 presidential and congressional elections was $4 billion, up from nearly $3 billion in 2000, $2.2 billion in 1996, and $1.8 billion in 1992.[109]

Some contend that living in a democracy offers an opportunity to have one's voice heard and one's interests addressed by elected officials. Yet the playing field is so uneven that many eligible voters choose not to participate. Rarely is concentration of power a matter that is raised in electoral politics. But on a daily basis, quite apart from elections, corporate spokespersons exert a tremendous influence upon government decisions. Three factors make this happen.

First, entry into national politics requires a large amount of money. Major corporations provide this money, and government officials are indebted to their donors. The Center for Responsive Politics maintains detailed records of the sources and recipients of political contributions in the United States. For example, in the year 2004, the defense sector contributed $16,195,471 (63 percent to Republicans). The oil and gas sector contributed $25,257,689 (89 percent to Republicans). Agribusiness contributed $52,905,694 (80 percent to Republicans). The health sector, including the AMA, hospitals, health insurance companies, and the pharmaceutical industry contributed $234,564,680 (61 percent to Republicans). The real estate industry contributed $338,204,311 (58 percent to Republicans). The disparity, while favoring Republicans, tends to be much smaller when Democrats are in power. Despite the disparity, both major political parties remained deeply beholden to such corporate interests, and smaller parties were left out entirely.

Second, the personnel in major cabinet positions come from, and return to, executive positions in these same corporate sectors, making for a rather limited ruling network. Third, although anyone is free to lobby for their cause, the largest corporate players and their industry societies maintain well-staffed lobbies. Between 1998 and 2005 lobbying firms received large contracts from numerous corporate entities. The U.S. Chamber of Commerce paid $234,564,680 for lobbyists. Others paid more than $75,000,000 for lobbyists: the AMA, the pharmaceutical companies, General Electric, the American Hospital Association, Edison electric, the Business Roundtable, the National Association of Realtors, Northrop Grumman, Phillip Morris, and Blue Cross/Blue Shield. The reasons for inequitable attention to the needs of certain constituencies may be clarified by looking at where the money is.[110]

Although money may either stall or hasten the process, government action is a relatively formal process embedded in the U.S. constitution and affirmed by a history of legislation and precedent derived from adjudication. The real practice of official decision making (as opposed to what is taught in civics classes) centers around lobbying and campaign contributions by moneyed special interests as have been described. What becomes enacted are often policies for which some groups spend lavishly. By contrast, it is difficult for the U.S. government system to enact strong policies that have broad, long-term value for most citizens. Measures dealing with the environment, poverty reduction and third-world development, women's rights, human rights, healthcare for all—matters that make a difference for most people—typically occur in watered-down compromise and then only after the efforts of strong citizen protest. The same is true for local community services. The focus here has been upon federal policy, but cities and towns face similar restrictions as their resources are siphoned through powerful corporate influences to compete in what has been termed a "growth machine."[111]

Campaign Finance Reform

In 2002 legislation introduced by Senators McCain and Feingold was enacted to address campaign finance reform. Major provisions were the prohibition of unlimited soft money contributions to national, state, and local political parties. Although this legislation is viewed as a positive first step in addressing the problem of campaign finance abuse, the bill does not prohibit the unlimited amount of money corporate PACs can spend on advertising in support of candidates or in the promotion of their agendas (they are only required to disclose their contributions). The bill also doubled the amount of hard money that may be contributed by individuals.

Since the enactment of the Bipartisan Campaign Reform Act of 2002, the Federal Election Commissions reported a 27 percent increase in receipts for PACs between the 2002 and 2004 election cycles; contributions to candidates were 13 percent higher.[112]

Wal-Mart was one of the largest corporate donors for the 2004 election campaign; the corporation's PAC contributed over $1.3 million to federal candidates.[113] Contributions for the 2004 campaign were especially high, analysts believe, because Wal-Mart had recently become the target of criticism by unions and community action groups for their unethical employment practices and had billions of dollars riding on U.S. trade policies with China.

Due to the increasing criticism of the Iraq war and some high-profile Republican Party corruption, the 2006 midterm elections predictably favored Democratic candidates. More than one-quarter of corporate businesses increased their contributions to Democratic candidates in that election cycle, in anticipation of the party change in Congress and the Senate. In the 2002 midterm, Wal-Mart donated just $240,000 to Democratic candidates; in the 2006 midterm, they donated $400,000 to Democratic candidates.[114]

Polling Places and Electronic Voting Machines

Where the corporate hand in elections begins with the backing of a political candidate that will serve its legislative purposes, it ends with the physical act of voting itself. The corporate touch is evident in the newly evolved corporate sponsorship programs, where companies "adopt" one or more polling places. These sponsorships are presented to the public in the form of a fundraiser for a local charity. Coleridge describes one such program in Broward County, Florida, where corporations place signs near precinct voting sites while company employees (wearing the corporate logos of their employer) perform the duties of poll workers.

Another more prevalent example of corporations' hands in the voting process are electronic voting machines. In the 2000 presidential election, problems surfaced when voters in Florida, Ohio, and other states touched the screen for one candidate, while their vote was cast for another candidate. According to a federal commission, more than 1 million ballots were ruined in 2004 by faulty voting equipment.[115]

Eager to avoid a scandal like Florida's 2000 election, the federal government passed the Help America Vote Act and granted the Diebold Corporation $3.9 billion to develop and install more than 40,000 electronic voting machines. In July 2003 a team of computer scientists published a review of the machines' software. The report identified hundreds of flaws, from lack of password protection on central databases to a glitch that would allow holders of a "smart card" to vote as many times as they wanted.[116] In 2006, shortly before the midterm elections, whistleblowers asserted that top Diebold corporation officials had ordered workers to install secret files to Georgia's electronic voting machines shortly before the 2002 elections.[117]

Two major issues regard the integrity of electronic voting equipment. The first is the lack of access to company software. When a company's software cannot be viewed by the public, there is no way to account for its accuracy. When one touches the screen for one candidate, there is no way for that person to verify the accuracy of their intended vote. Public access to company software, however, brings up the second issue: computer software systems are vulnerable to tampering and malfunction, as made evident in both the 2002 and 2004 elections. As votes come in from disparate precincts, they are totaled in aggregate databases—databases that may easily be altered.

New Barriers to Voting

The 2002 Help America Vote Act does not, on balance, help voters: New voter registration requirements have made it much harder for new eligible voters to register. Other policies are making it harder for those already registered to vote. Slater, Kyser, and Chasnow argue the new and more stringent requirements "disproportionately impact those citizens who have been traditionally marginalized in the political process: women, low-income people, members of ethnic and racial minorities, youth, people with disabilities and seniors."[118]

New restrictions on voter registration drives, including registration and training requirements, hamper the efforts of large paid and small volunteer programs alike. New registration requirements ask that every program be registered with the state and include the identity of every employee and volunteer in advance of registration activities. State-mandated training programs are infrequently and inconveniently offered. In Delaware, for example, training was offered once a month at one location. These new restrictions have led to a decline in public agency registration of new voters.

A number of states are proposing laws that require photo ID to vote. Americans without photo ID are disproportionately people without resources. For example, in Missouri, where the state legislature is debating a photo ID bill, an estimated 200,000 people of voting age do not have state-issued photo ID. In Georgia, where the legislature is determined to pass the photo ID bill, 300,000 people do not have driver's licenses.[119] Even the right to vote is made difficult for many people. Many choose not to vote, believing that the process is already rigged to exclude their interests. Many accept the dismal display of thirty-second TV ads and public relations guided presentations by candidates as the reality of what it is legitimate to care about.

Social Exclusion

Marilyn Taylor examines our understanding of communities segregated by income.[120] Communities and family ties, she argues, continue to persist, and their networks provide the glue for trust and responsibility—the social capital needed to sustain critical activities in even poor and disadvantaged communities. Yet changing economic, social, and political conditions have also seriously weakened the range of what these local ties can do for people. Their social exclusion is not merely within the threadbare fabric of their personal networks but in the exclusion of their communities from the opportunities and protections offered to their wealthier and more powerful counterparts. The best we can do in nurturing local ties may be to help people cope with gross deprivations, but not to overcome them. That task would require that people have some meaningful, even if infrequent, ties that provide bridges to another type of social capital, the type that might offer opportunities to bring wealth and decision power back to local communities. Locally grown produce, local goods, uncontaminated air, and, particularly in poor countries, local sources of clean water, seeds, and topsoil have, in large measure, been replaced or commoditized. Ironically, Miller points out, that it is the very rich who have locked themselves in gated communities. What keeps the rest of us out of their elite closed enclaves and their secretive societies and meetings is a political process that limits what representative democracy can accomplish.

Chapter 7 will examine the role of the media in shaping a reality suited to the needs of a centralized elite. For now, suffice it to say that although the centralized network of power may have differences among themselves, there is no countervailing power that can restrict many of their policies and activities. Many of these activities employ violence and manipulation. These activities are the subject of chapter 6.

CHAPTER 6

REALPOLITIK: STRATEGIES AND TACTICS FOR WINNING

> The crimes of the United States have been systematic, constant, vicious, remorseless, but very few people have ever talked about them. You have to hand it to America. It has exercised quite a clinical manipulation of power worldwide while masquerading as a force for universal good. It is a brilliant, even witty, highly successful act of hypnosis.
>
> —*Harold Pinter, Nobel Peace Prize acceptance speech December 7, 2005*

Chapter 5 laid out the system of interconnected military and corporate elites whose power dominates decisions that affect the use and distribution of resources. They exercise great, although not absolute, power over decisions about what measures should be taken to protect their wealth and power. As one part of their effort, they have invested heavily in the work of a large number of professional strategists—military planners, economists, and system scientists—who work in and out of government to bring creative ideas to the preservation of the war system and for ways to increase the power, influence, and profits of this elite group. What keeps the powerful in power is the ability to control the flow of large amounts of money. Those who would lay claim to this wealth for other human needs are looked upon as enemies, and a primary goal has been to prevent such a challenge. In this chapter we argue that maintaining and expanding control over resources does more to explain the actions and policies of government than major ideological crusades such as anticommunism or a war on terror. Here we argue that both anticommunism and a war on terror were broad strategies or policy directives contrived by powerful corporate interests, and they serve to fulfill two main purposes: the continuity and the expansion of powerful interests within the military-industrial complex. Communist bureaucracies produced a great deal of violence. Yet, upon closer examination, U.S. global policies such as anticommunism were generated less by the autocratic nature of communist governments following World War II, than by concern over governments that restrained the activities of corporate entrepreneurs. Similarly, the war on terror was aimed less at protecting the security of the United States against a poorly defined group of Muslim fundamentalists who planned violent activities than at protecting corporate interests in the Middle East. We pursue the argument that the war on terror was vastly overblown in comparison to other greater threats to security; yet the promotion of an exaggerated fear was not a mistake but rather a consequence of the way the most powerful networks promote their interests.[1]

Creating the Enemy

Here, we examine the strategies and the tactics used by these powerful networks to achieve their ends. The principal strategy has been to create a fearsome and overarching enemy in the public mind. Hence powerful interests work to vilify an enemy, making it appear self-evident that the adversary is both evil and out to destroy us. This vilification reduces the adversary to a fanatic demon, thus precluding opportunities to see how alike its leaders may be to some of our own more militant leaders or how its people are humans so like ourselves. It makes those who seek peaceful reconciliation appear to be either naïve or unpatriotic and the object of scorn and harassment. I lived as a college student in the McCarthy era, when fears of being labeled sympathetic to communists made it impossible to get American students to sign a petition expressing their support for the Bill of Rights, or to protest the mistreatment of a disabled African American Korean War veteran. I lost a university position when a letter of mine opposing the Vietnam War appeared in the *New York Times*. Many artists, entertainers, scholars, and union leaders suffered far worse harassment. But the major effect was intimidation of those who might speak out against a government that justified its excesses by the fight against communism.

In the Cold War, extreme anticommunism involved calls to start and "prevail" in a nuclear war with the Soviet Union and to harass and deport communist sympathizers. This view vied with the beliefs of moderate, more realistic, bipartisan cold warriors over the best approach to defeat communism. That goal was the accepted consensus. The excesses of the extremists helped to move the center away from any attempts toward reducing weapons or reducing tensions.

With the war on terror, a neoconservative group calls for the destruction of Arabic weapons and culture. The invocation to all-out war was expressed by former Israeli Prime Minister Netanyahu on CNN: "Iran is Germany, and it's 1938. Except that this Nazi regime that is in Iran . . . wants to dominate the world, annihilate the Jews, but also annihilate America."[2] The prime minister has worked closely with members of the Project for a New American Century (PNAC) who pushed the U.S. attack on Iraq and who are now pushing to attack

Iran. A more cautious coalition, which nonetheless supports a war on terror, was recommended by the James Baker–Lee Hamilton Iraq study group. The latter called for maintaining both the control over Middle Eastern oil and the retention of military bases there, but favored a withdrawal of troops from Iraq and greater diplomatic efforts. Plans for a surge of added troops were designed within the Heritage Foundation think tank, where the wife of Vice President Dick Cheney is an official. These replaced the Baker-Hamilton proposals. Plans were also developed to ready the United States for an attack on Iran. The same neoconservative ideologues behind the Iraq war have been using the same tactics—alliances with shady exiles, dubious intelligence on weapons of mass destruction—to push for the bombing of Iran.[3]

Violent and Coercive Tactics

An atmosphere beset with fear from a demonic enemy is recurring now in the war on terror. It provides a cover for a host of violent and coercive tactics to retain governments friendly to the dominant power circles that have been described in chapter 5. These dirty tactics increase the adversary's fears, their animosity, their commitment to armament, and the likelihood of their retaliation.

The list of documented tactics includes *financial gifts, loans, bribes, sale of weapons, trade agreements, and threats.* They include also the *overthrow of governments, media manipulation, the manipulation of elections, covert measures against groups that dissent, legal harassment, destroying habitats, assassinations, campaigns of terror, bombing raids,* and finally *sending in the marines.* More recently, the arsenal of choices actually considered has included the use of weapons of mass destruction and barbaric practices of interrogation. Such an array of activities involves the efforts of many people. Individually they may be kind or cruel, strong believers in the rightness of what they are doing, or just doing the job that was assigned to them. Regardless of their beliefs in the morality or the necessity of coercive or manipulative methods, the ultimate results of these activities are destructive to many people. This has been noted in chapter 1 (dealing with war) and in chapter 3 (dealing with economic globalization). The costs are borne even by those most closely involved in perpetrating these activities.

Nothing in the activities described should be taken to make the United States (or its NATO allies) out to be a demon. There is a heritage in Western civilization that has cultivated the creative use of the intellect and the spirit of adventure. The tradition has introduced universal standards of ethics and opportunities for many to overcome oppressive local conditions. The vitality of striving for excellence, working for the greater good, and of personal freedom is part of our heritage. These positive bases for pride in our country have surely affected the lives of many Americans and have had an impact upon dedicated public service in government at every level. The values, to be discussed in chapter 8, nevertheless have permitted a small network of power brokers to create the pain and injustice that have been described. The people most centrally responsible are not, for the most part, what most would call evil people. The horror of what they do is a product of the system. To say that these are not accidents or mistakes but rather understandable consequences of a distorted process is not to indicate the workings of an omnipotent conspiracy. At the same time, there lies beneath the eyes of the citizenry a high level of planning in a high-stakes game of attaining competitive advantage. Game theory helps us to understand the mindset of the planners.

The Mind-Set of Competitive Games

Game theory is a part of the larger umbrella of decision theory or the science of rational decision making. These theoretical frameworks were developed in business and engineering and have been added to tools of the military planner. Such tools are also commonly used in calculations by corporations of the particular investment strategies they should make to compete most effectively.

Game theory is a classification system, not of material things but rather of situations. In each situation the players are identified, and goals are established. Winning might mean increasing one's profits or destroying one's competition. It might be defined as all-or-none victory versus doing better than one's adversaries. The potential range of permissible moves is spelled out: yes for checking the king in chess, no for overturning the board; yes for bombing raids, no for poisoning the water supply. Mathematics then helps to select the best move. In some games there is a single move that is a best choice regardless of the countermoves of an adversary. In other games one must assign probabilities about what an adversary is likely to do. These estimates are based upon the desirability of different outcomes. They are designed to make a best guess, one that would have the greatest likelihood, in the long run, of coming out ahead. Some conflicts have two parties, others many. Some are characterized by a win-lose definition in which whatever is good for one side is bad for the other to that same degree. Others allow for outcomes in which both parties may come out worse or both may gain.

Applied to war, game theory serves to abstract the particular strategic structure of a conflict. It would be completely irrelevant whether the particular structure is played out on a game board with wooden pieces, on a computer simulation, or on a battlefield strewn with bodies. The magnitude of the payoffs (or losses) is a fact to be considered, as in poker, but the content of the payoff is irrelevant. It is permissible within game theory to consider which country might be coerced into assuring a greater amount of oil for the United States. It would not be permissible within game theory to ask whether more oil is a desirable outcome.[4]

Legitimizing Global Violence

The actual mathematical tools of game theory are not always employed by governments or by corporations. In fact, honest application of the theory might illustrate to the parties that certain conflicts are just too costly and should not be played at all. But the mind-set in which the world and its inhabitants are all instruments in a game to gain competitive advantage is very much a part of the belief system that legitimizes global violence. The theory plays the board as if no particular human existed on the other side. Even on one's own side the sacrifices are not of people but of pawns that will provide gains for one's company or country. In a military occupation where torture is used to find, to punish, and to intimidate resistance, the game has been redefined as one in which the rules permit such abuse. The consequence that being found out might be bad for the side engaging in the practice, and might produce blowback or consequences of retaliation, becomes just one factor in calculating the likelihood of being caught and the ability of the opposition to benefit from exposing the practice.

Externalities: The Acceptability of Risk

Just as the risks of being caught using immoral modes of treating people can be calculated, so also can the loss of lives be entered into the selection of actions. Indeed, we find major corporate decisions taking into account what economists call externalities. Many activities with an intended purpose to profit from developments designed (or justified) to improve or to protect life come with unintended consequences. Dangerous materials used in manufacturing, seriously overcrowded highways, unsafe vehicles or pharmaceuticals, toxic chemical or radioactive waste dumps, and unhealthy fast foods all enter into the cost-benefit analyses. The goal is to produce as cheaply as possible something that will provide the greatest good while keeping certain harmful consequences within the acceptable range. The greatest good is of course dependent upon whose interests are being considered most important. Likewise, the acceptability of risks depends upon who determines what is acceptable. The acceptability may look different for executives of a corporation that produces toxic chemical pesticides used to dust crops than to the parents of a child with leukemia. The model of thought requires that we consider everything—including material products, human lives, timber for construction, and the sound of songbirds—to have a monetary value. The market, like a giant game board, is left to determine what risks will be undertaken. The players with the greatest domination of chips control the directions of the market.

End Goals of Global Games: The Expansion of Markets

Throughout history empires have typically followed the aspirations and military strength of rulers. Trade and resources have long been closely associated with the use of military force.[5] For the U.S. empire, the expansion was primarily a commercial one, dedicated to selling products overseas and dominating foreign markets. Pioneering American firms such as Heinz, Singer, McCormick, Kodak, and Standard Oil shaped the direction of an imperial process by linking the purchase of U.S. consumer goods abroad with "civilization" and "progress." During the late nineteenth and early twentieth centuries, consumerism and commercialism were a driving force, marketing not only products but also racial and gender stereotypes. The messages were apparent in ads for sewing machines, processed food, and agricultural tools. The values of consumerism and commercialism have shaped, and continue to shape, the way the United States is seen. Military force and government action tended to follow, rather than to lead, the expansion of markets.[6]

Ideological Beliefs

The mind-set of those whose decisions govern the paths of empires is important to understand. Surely wealth and power have been acknowledged motivations. But often accompanying such motives is a belief that the particular empire has a virtuous goal of spreading its benefits, as understood by its rulers, to other parts of the world. Powerful elites, successful in their own worlds, encapsulate themselves amongst a network of others who also believe in the virtue and legitimacy of their intentions. Ancient Rome, Qing China, France under Napoleon, imperial Britain, and the United States in the Americas did not simply invade and occupy other peoples' lands out of economic greed. In each case, empire was also driven, at times, by the desire to spread improvement and to export cultural and political practices that were seen as better and more civilized.[7] The contemporary goal of the neoconservative game is often expressed idealistically as the desire to make the world a better place, one with democratic elections and free trade.[8] Such thinking is often used to call upon soldiers and their families for sacrifices, but rarely does it call upon sacrifices from those who profit most from the expanded markets. When such thinking is accompanied by coercive interventionism, it is often the prelude to the fall of the empire.[9] Military historian Caleb Carr notes that empires with strong military forces have almost always taken on the tactics of terrorism, that is, brutal, punitive attacks upon civilians as part of the way they maintained influence. This occurred on the part of Rome, recurred through Middle Eastern and European dynasties, and included the United States in its Civil War and in World War II. He also notes that such brutality to civilians is rarely successful and leads to a decline in the empire.[10]

Sanctions for Force: The Opposition to Communism

The major interest of large corporations is continued growth and expansion. The major threats to that expansion are the aspirations of people and governments who would apply the same resources needed for corporate growth to other purposes. Ideologies of local control, of nationalism, or of communism, each in their own way, are impediments to corporate expansion. In this section we examine the post–World War II unification of European markets, and the ensuing corporate origins of the Cold War.

A "Permanent War Economy"

At the end of World War II, 70 percent of the industrial infrastructure of Europe was destroyed, and the European economy had collapsed. The U.S. economy was booming due as much to a military-industrial complex that made millions for the corporations involved in the war effort as to a backlog in consumer demand. Corporate profits in fact rose from $6.4 billion in 1940 to $10.8 billion in 1944.[11] Charles E. Wilson, the president of General Motors Corporation (and later secretary of defense), was so satisfied with wartime profits that he suggested a continuing alliance between business and the military for a "permanent war economy."[12] Eager to extend this boon in profits, the American business community, as represented by the U.S. Council on Foreign Relations, initiated an investment plan to rebuild Europe.

The Marshall Plan

In 1946 Charles Spofford and David Rockefeller presented a speech to the Council on Foreign Relations entitled "Reconstruction in Western Europe."[13] In 1947, U.S. Secretary of State George Marshall introduced his plan for the economic reconstruction of Europe; Congress enacted the agreement, which came to be known as the Marshall Plan, giving $13 billion in aid to sixteen western European states.[14]

While on the outset the Marshall Plan appears to be an "unprecedented exercise of international generosity (dubbed by Churchill the 'most unsordid act in history')," the less-acknowledged purpose of the plan was to benefit directly the U.S. corporations that promoted it.[15] For example, William Clayton, the undersecretary for economic affairs (who helped prepare the plan) personally benefited $700,000 a year, and his company, Anderson, Clayton & Co., secured $10 million.[16]

The Marshall Plan officially moved American investment capital into Europe. When the plan began, President Truman's secretary of state, Dean Acheson, noted:

> These measures of relief and reconstruction have been only in part suggested by humanitarianism. Your Congress has authorized and your government is carrying out, a policy of relief and reconstruction today chiefly as a matter of national self-interest.[17]

The committee that drafted the Marshall Plan shows the involvement of well-placed advocates of corporate expansion, including Chairman Henry Stimson (former secretary of state and war, Wall Street lawyer, and director of the Council on Foreign Relations); Executive Committee Chairman Robert Patterson (former secretary of war); Executive Committee member Dean Acheson (undersecretary of state and corporate lawyer of Covington & Burling); Winthrop Aldrich (banker and uncle to the Rockefeller brothers); James Carey (CIO secretary-treasurer); Herbert Lehman (Lehman Bros. Investment); Philip Reed

(General Electric executive); Herbert Bayard Swope (former editor and brother of former GE president); and David Dubinsky (labor leader).

The efforts of these American industrial leaders were not in vain. By 1963 American firms in France controlled 40 percent of the petroleum market, 65 percent of films and photographic paper, 65 percent of farm machinery, 65 percent of telecommunications equipment, and 45 percent of synthetic rubber. By 1965 American-controlled investments in Germany were an estimated $2 billion, while the gross capital of all firms quoted on the German stock exchange was only $3.5 billion.[18]

Economic Aid as a Political Tool

To the business elite, Europe represented a vast untapped market for American exports and unlimited investment potential (fronted primarily by U.S. taxpayers); to the U.S. government, economic aid was a political tool. As Secretary of State Averell Harriman explained, "economic assistance is one of the most effective weapons at our disposal to influence European political events in the direction we desire."[19] Indeed, under the terms of the Marshall Plan the strong communist parties of Italy and France were shut out of the cabinets of those countries. From 1952 on, American aid to Europe became increasingly focused on building up military power in noncommunist countries. Over the course of the next ten years, of the $50 billion in aid to ninety countries worldwide, only $5 billion was for nonmilitary economic development.[20]

To U.S. officials, communism was threatening less for ideological reasons, such as violation of individual freedoms, than because communist governments were opposed to the corporate capitalist economic system. The fight against the spread of communism was, in contrast to the way it has typically been described, a fight against the loss of available markets and needed raw materials. The deep fear was that the socialist idea might spread in Europe and in formerly colonized nations, thereby limiting corporate growth.

Creating the Communist Enemy

The American public has been conditioned to react strongly to the term *communist.* It comes with images of the worst excesses of the Stalin era, with wholesale purges and Siberian slave-labor camps. Engraved in the image is the belief that classic Marxist-Leninist predictions of a world revolution found in classic Marxist-Leninist writing are actually the intention of all subsequent actions by communist states.[21] This changes the game to "us" against "them":

> "[T]hem" can mean a peasant in the Philippines, a mural-painter in Nicaragua, a legally-elected prime minister in British Guiana, or a European intellectual, a Cambodian neutralist, an African nationalist—all, somehow, part of the same monolithic conspiracy; each, in some way, a threat to the American Way of Life; no land too small, too poor, or too far away to pose such a threat, the "communist

> threat" . . . it has been largely irrelevant whether the particular targets of intervention—be they individuals, political parties, movements or governments—called themselves "communist" or not. It has mattered little whether they were scholars of dialectical materialism or had never heard of Karl Marx; whether they were atheists or priests; whether a strong and influential Communist Party was in the picture or not; whether the government had come into being through violent revolution or peaceful elections . . . all have been targets, all "communists."[22]

The particular institutional form of socialism in the USSR presented an image in which state ownership of production came to be associated with a totalitarian government and atheism. Marxism, in particular, was viewed as a directly opposing force since the start of the Russian revolution.

In the summer of 1918, when World War I was winding down, approximately 13,000 American troops joined British and other allies inside the newly born Union of Soviet Socialist Republics to support the counterrevolutionary white army of the czar. A young Winston Churchill, then Britain's minister of war, explained the goal was to "strangle at its birth" the Bolshevik state.[23] After two years and heavy casualties, the allies withdrew. Later, as a historian, Churchill wrote:

> Were they the allies at war with Soviet Russia? Certainly not; but they shot Soviet Russians at sight. They stood as invaders on Russian soil. They armed the enemies of the Soviet Government. They blockaded its ports and sunk its battleships. They desired and schemed its downfall. But war—shocking! Interference—shame! It was, they repeated, a matter of indifference to them how Russians settled their own internal affairs.[24]

An anticommunist propaganda campaign had begun even before the military intervention. In 1918 expressions like "Red Peril," "the Bolshevik assault on civilization," and "menace to world by Reds is seen" appeared frequently in the *New York Times*.[25] Historian Frederick Lewis Schuman described the effect of Senate hearings at the time:

> The net result of these hearings . . . was to picture Soviet Russia as a kind of bedlam inhabited by abject slaves completely at the mercy of an organization of homicidal maniacs whose purpose was to destroy all traces of civilization and carry the nation back to barbarism.[26]

Although Russian forces proved an integral part of the allies' win against Nazi Germany in World War II, anticommunist sentiment resurfaced in U.S. foreign policy. Historian Howard Zinn describes the transition between the end of World War II and the Cold War:

> When, right after the war, the American public, war-weary, seemed to favor demobilization and disarmament, the Truman administration (Roosevelt had died in

April 1945) worked to create an atmosphere of crisis and cold war. True, the rivalry with the Soviet Union was real—that country had come out of the war with its economy wrecked and 20 million people dead, but was making an astounding comeback, rebuilding its industry, regaining its military strength. The Truman administration, however, presented the Soviet Union as not just a rival but an immediate threat.[27]

From 1947 to the mid-1960s, an objective of U.S. policy was to instigate the downfall of the Soviet government and other Eastern European regimes. Hundreds of Russian exiles were trained by the CIA and sneaked back into Russia to set up espionage rings, to stir armed political struggle, and to carry out such acts of sabotage as derailing trains, wrecking bridges, damaging arms factories and power plants, and assassinations.[28]

Daniele Ganser of the Center for Security Studies at the Federal Institute of Technology in Zurich, offers substantial evidence for an application in postwar Europe of what has later been called the "Salvador Option." Ganser's book, *NATO's Secret Armies: Operation Gladio and Terrorism in Western Europe*, describes how during the Cold War, U.S. and British intelligence sources worked with European governments to conduct secret attacks in their own countries in order to manipulate the population to reject socialism and communism.[29] The evidence is seen in a document for which the CIA denies authenticity. Ganser cites a revealing portion from one of the NATO field manuals (FM 30-31B) as follows:

> [W]hen the revolutionaries temporarily renounce the use of force . . . US army intelligence must have the means of launching special operations which will convince host country governments and public opinion of the reality of the insurgent danger.[30]

The clear message is that if terrorism by a Communist Party could not be found, the secret armies were prepared to create some. According to Ganser, the secret army was behind waves of terrorist attacks in Italy in the 1970s; it worked with the Franco dictatorship, supporting an estimated 1,000 attacks upon left-wing opponents. In Germany the secret army had standing plans to murder leaders of the Social Democrat Party in the event of a Soviet invasion, and carried out terrorist actions against President de Gaulle and the Algerian peace plan in France. NATO's Prometheus plan was prepared to prevent a communist or a socialist government from coming to power. The plan was used by a group of Greek military officers in a coup that replaced a popularly elected government and established a cruel and dictatorial one. The United States continued support for this reign of the Greek colonels.[31]

Communism in Russia and Eastern Europe has ended. But NATO still provides the cover for five major permanent U.S. military communities: one in Vicenza, Italy, the other four in Germany (Kaiserlautern, Landstuhl/Ramstein, Vilseck/Grafenwoehr, and Ansbach). Per U.S. plans they are all being enlarged.

The United States is also building "forward bases" in the "New Europe" and investing funds in these bases in Romania, Poland, Bulgaria, and other countries. The United States is proposing a so-called missile shield in Poland and the Czech Republic, and opposition to this proposal is building. The increasing integration of the European Union has fulfilled one objective of protecting European nations from engaging in war or even extensive competition with each other, but it has not emerged as a force for peace.[32]

According to U.S. plans, Germany is to remain the logistical-strategic command center for all U.S. military operations in Europe, the Middle East, and Africa. The command center for everything is EUCOM in Stuttgart. Intelligence is mainly in Wiesbaden and Kaiserlautern. The hospital facility is in Landstuhl, and the nuclear bombs are in Ramstein. Therefore, the struggle against the European bases may ultimately become a joint effort of the European and U.S. peace movements.

Ideological Irony

Chomsky highlights the great irony of the Truman administration's ideological problem with communism. Truman reportedly liked and admired Stalin; in a cabinet meeting Truman once remarked that he could "deal with" Stalin, as long as the United States got its way 85 percent of the time. What happened inside the USSR was not his concern. With all of the emphasis and apparent value for "freedom," professed by U.S. leaders, the fascist regime of Mussolini was looked upon with admiration. Roosevelt admired the "Italian gentleman" who had dissolved the country's parliamentary system, blocked the labor movement, and halted domestic socialists and communists.[33]

Preceding the United States entering World War II, major American corporations, with the support of the U.S. government, not only poured money into fascist Italy but also into Nazi Germany; some American corporations reaped the benefit of the overturning of Jewish assets under Hitler's Aryanization program. Between 1929 and 1940 U.S. investment in Germany increased by 48.5 percent, while sharply declining everywhere else in continental Europe.[34]

Tactics to Defeat Communism in the Third World

Anticommunism provided a rationale for a violent foreign policy in the developing world. Secretary of State Henry Kissinger helped President Nixon undermine the Paris peace talks on Vietnam on the eve of the 1968 election. Upon Kissinger's advice, the promise for a new plan to end the unpopular Vietnam War was translated into the bombing of Cambodia and Laos, which killed approximately 1 million civilians. Kissinger was also involved in the assassination of Chilean Chief of Staff General Rene Schneider, whose loyalty blocked the first planned coup against the elected president Allende in Chile. Kissinger's approval and support for Indonesia's invasion of East Timor and the resulting genocide was described previously. In 1971 Kissinger and Nixon supported the

Pakistan military government's genocide in Bangladesh, and then supported a bloody military coup in independent Bangladesh in 1975. In all cases, the actions were justified as efforts to curb the threat of communism.[35]

Creating Governments with the Corporate Agenda

Policies actually undertaken reflect a planning process in which the needs of key players in the global market place are pursued as objectives of the game. Any understanding of the degree of planning that goes into the U.S. corporate and military domination of other nations, owes much to the personal history of John Perkins. His clandestine position, first with the National Security Agency and then transferred to a private company, was predicated upon an ability to make economic forecasts and sell loans to heads of state in undeveloped countries. He supervised a staff that included economists who provided complex models that could be used to exaggerate the benefits to gross national product (GNP) of massive loans. The loans were always for the development of infrastructure, oil drilling and pipelines, dams, electric power grids, and building complexes. The contracts would be awarded to such corporate giants as Bechtel, Halliburton, and Brown and Root. The inducements to foreign leaders included military and police aid and training, lucrative financial benefits, recognition in U.S. diplomatic circles, and even the procurement of personal mistresses. The contracts would make a small group within the accepting country very wealthy.

On the negative side, they would make the particular nation a client state of the United States, dependent upon further loans and adjustments to repay the incurred debts, and unable, therefore, to use the country's resources for a form of development that might provide sustainable productivity for its farmers, education and health care for its children, and protections for its environment. Some populist leaders found the terms unacceptable. Many of the leaders who were more representative of the needs of their own people and who refused the loan terms were removed in coups, assassinations, or plane or helicopter "accidents."[36] If that did not produce a compliant government, the next steps were to foment a violent revolt and finally to send in the bombs and the marines.

Economic Intervention

The major ongoing interventions, occurring without the fanfare of war, are economic. The manipulation of local economies has been part of a worldwide effort to impose what has been labeled the "Washington Consensus." This has been forced on developing countries, via procedures of the U.S. government, the World Bank, the International Monetary Fund, and the World Trade Organization. John Williamson, a well-known British economist, developed its basic tenets in reforms, calling for economic deregulation, privatization, encouragement of foreign investment, unrestricted movement of capital, liberalization of trade policies, and reduction in public expenditures. This program of neoliberalism has been aggressively pushed as primarily a U.S. foreign policy goal. The strategy is focused upon pressuring developing countries that are dependent on aid from major international lending agencies and the United States to implement structural adjustment programs that prescribe the required changes that a specific country must make in order to be considered credit worthy.[37]

Increasingly, official U.S. strategy has been to support governments subservient to U.S. corporate and military interests, to keep them in power through financial indebtedness and military control over their dissenters, and to think of a highly fortified Green Zone with lush accommodations for visiting officials—as if that façade, rather than the people of the country, was the true U.S. ally. This makes sense if one recalls that it is an elite network of diplomatic, financial, and military ties that determine the paths of information and influence. The strategy reflects not only the gamester's mentality and the dehumanization of casualties, but it also reflects the great distance between those few with great power and the rest of us, who are seen as lesser players and whose views are considered irrelevant to the elite-created reality. The more reprehensible tactics may be concealed or, if discovered, may be denied. Where support is needed from voters or from soldiers, it can be handled through persuasion, employment opportunities, and public relations.

Bypassing Legal Constraints

Pressure to create governments willing to play by the rules of neoliberalism has not always been through legal means. Difficult and risky efforts at espionage are the stock trade of highly trained special forces such as the Navy Seals. Other than when used for public-relations value in publicizing successful rescue attempts, the work of the special forces is accountable only to high-level authorities and can act to assassinate individuals and to create mayhem outside of public view.[38] The CIA, in addition to its highly professional role of gathering information, has also played a more clandestine role of subverting governments, destroying buildings and trains, and bribing both officials and crowds of people to gather their support.[39] Recent efforts by the U.S. ambassador to Nicaragua have clearly violated the April 1961 Vienna Convention on Diplomatic Relations, which asserts that representatives or diplomats "have a duty not to interfere in the internal affairs of that state" to which they may be assigned. Despite international law, the United States has rarely felt constrained over intervening in the internal affairs of other countries. The United States has also been able to bypass the legal constraints upon such activity by exerting its influence through private organizations.

The National Endowment for Democracy (NED) was founded in 1983 as a private organization funded completely by government revenue. Its purpose is to influence the direction of elections and policies in foreign countries through its recipient organizations, the National Democratic Institute (NDI) and the International Republican Institute (IRI). Such activities by another government would be illegal in the United States. The NED injects soft money into the domestic elections of foreign countries in favor of one party or the other. In a relatively poor country, a few hundred thousand dollars of assistance can well have a decisive influence. It is particularly Orwellian to call U.S. manipulation of foreign elections "promoting democracy."[40]

Overthrowing Governments

One strategy for the exercise of power is to overthrow governments unwilling to accept domination by American interests. The United States has used military force to overthrow a legitimate government on fourteen occasions, starting with Hawaii toward the end of the nineteenth century.[41] Grandin writes of numerous coup efforts by the United States in Latin America and the continuity of such U.S. responses in the Middle East:

> After World War II, in the name of containing Communism, the United States, mostly through the actions of local allies, executed or encouraged coups in, among other places, Guatemala, Brazil, Chile, Uruguay, and Argentina and patronized a brutal mercenary war in Nicaragua. . . . For 150 years Nicaragua has borne the brunt of more interventions than almost any other country in this hemisphere. . . . Indeed, Reagan's Central American wars can best be understood as a dress rehearsal for what is going on now in the Middle East. It was in these wars where the coalition made up of neoconservatives, Christian evangelicals, free marketers, and nationalists that today stands behind George W. Bush's expansive foreign policy first came together.[42]

Two classic cases for the U.S. exercise of illegitimate force were in Iran and in Guatemala. Both were carried out secretly. A third secret intervention attempt that was thwarted in Venezuela is also described. The case of East Timor is included as one involving clear support of atrocities by an oppressive government. Other cases, such as Panama and Iraq, involved the actual use of massive firepower and an invading U.S. force.

Iran: A Model Removal of a Popular Leader

Popular or democratically elected leaders of countries who have lost favor with the United States have been forcefully removed. This occurred with Mossadegh in Iran[43]; Bosch in the Dominican Republic[44]; Arbenz in Guatemala[45]; and Allende in Chile.[46] Kermit Roosevelt was the CIA agent sent to overthrow the democratically elected Mosadegh in Iran, whose crime had been an attempt to nationalize the Anglo-American Oil Company. The agent began by bribing members of Parliament to denounce him in Parliament. Then religious Mullahs were bribed to denounce him as an atheist enemy of Islam.

Within a few weeks of bribing reporters and editors, Roosevelt had 80 percent of the Teheran press on his payroll. Roosevelt also bribed members of police units and low-ranking military officers to be ready with their units on the crucial day. In his culminating scheme, he hired the leaders of street gangs in

Tehran to help create the impression that the rule of law had totally disintegrated in Iran. At one point, he hired a gang to run through the streets of Tehran beating up any pedestrian they found, breaking shop windows, firing their guns into mosques, and yelling "We love Mossadegh and communism." This would turn any decent citizen against him. Then Roosevelt hired a second mob to attack the first mob, to give people the impression that there was no police presence, and order had completely disintegrated. Within a few weeks, this one agent, operating with a large sum of cash and a network of contacts with various elements of society had taken what was a fairly stable country and thrown it into complete upheaval. The first attempt at a coup failed, but the agent, acting on his own, arranged to give a good day's pay to be part of a mob shouting slogans on the street. None of the participants ever knew they were being paid by the CIA. Roosevelt had been spending $11,000 a week to bribe members of the Iranian Parliament, who then whipped up the crowds. The average annual income in Iran at that time was about $500. At crucial moments, police and military units joined the crowd and started gunfights in front of government buildings, including even the prime minister's house. About 100 people were killed in front of Mossadegh's house. A military leader Roosevelt had bribed arrived with a column of tanks, and Mossadegh was no longer able to retain his position. A general, selected by the CIA, was installed as prime minister. The Shah Pavlevi returned from exile in Rome to become a particularly feared monarch. He, in turn, was eventually overthrown by the religious Mullahs, who have remained suspicious of U.S. intentions ever since. Roosevelt went on to become government relations director and then a vice president for Gulf oil. The CIA director at that time was Alan Dulles, an associate of the law firm providing legal counsel for the Anglo-American Oil Company.[47] Dulles was impressed by this example of regime change in Iran. Ten months later it was attempted in Guatemala, also against a democratically elected leader. This second success led to other attempts from Indonesia to Chile, to Cuba, to Vietnam, to the Congo.

The shah of Iran followed pro-Western policies, particularly restoring control of oil reserves to Anglo-American Oil but with a substantial cut to U.S. companies. The shah relied upon brutal police methods to maintain control. The anti-Western blowback from the religious leaders who overthrew the shah was not what U.S. officials had intended, and the capture of American hostages by Iran helped bring the Reagan administration into power.

Guatemala: Supporting Violent Military Rule

As described in chapter 1, in 1954 a mercenary army organized by the CIA staged the "liberation" of Guatemala. In fact, this was a coup that overthrew the democratically elected President Arbenz and returned Guatemala to military rule.[48] Arbenz was a nationalist and a socialist who had sought to transform oligarchic Guatemalan society through land reform and the development of government-owned enterprises that would compete with the American corporations, which dominated the railroad, electric, and fruit-trade industries. Of these American interests, the United Fruit Company was the most influential. For decades the company was the largest employer, land owner, and exporter in Guatemala. With nearly half of its land expropriated by Arbenz's land reform act, company executives and board members (one of whom was CIA Director Alan Dulles) appealed to the American government. In addition, United Fruit appealed to the public-relations industry, which then painted Arbenz's government and the popular movement that supported it as communist, and therefore a threat to the American people.[49]

To form a new government, the CIA approached Ydigoras Fuentes, who was living in exile in El Salvador. Ydigoras later reported his encounter with the CIA, confirming that they wanted him not only to assist in overthrowing Arbenz but also "to favor the United Fruit Company, to destroy the railroad workers union, and to establish a strong-arm government."[50] Under U.S. guidance, the army organized a powerful military force and a network of counterinsurgency surveillance that would continue for more than thirty years.[51]

As described in chapter 1, over this thirty-six-year period various U.S.-sponsored military regimes killed over 200,000 civilians and wiped out 440 Mayan villages. The United Nations–sponsored Commission for Historical Clarification found that the Guatemalan army had committed nearly 95 percent of the total war crimes, and had carried out over 600 massacres. The commission determined that the Guatemalan army's counterinsurgency campaign legally constituted genocide against the Mayan people.[52] Mass killings of civilian populations have been repeated in Algeria, Nigeria, Chile, South Africa, Colombia, El Salvador, Lebanon, the Philippines, and Palestine, in each case with U.S. government support.[53] The United States has commonly made efforts to create governments that may be no more than a militarized Green Zone, so long as they are subservient to U.S. corporate and military interests.

In 2005 investigative journalists Michael Hersh and John Barry disclosed a Pentagon plan to use the "Salvador Option" in Iraq. This was modeled upon an American counterinsurgency program in the 1980s. The original plan funded nationalist death squads to hunt and kill insurgents. The new plan would evade congressional oversight and deploy secret special forces in both friendly and unfriendly countries to spy, to target terrorists and their sympathizers, and to conduct "hits," all without Congressional oversight. Whether adopted specifically or not, U.S. actions in Iraq did bypass Congressional oversight in the extradition of prisoners to other countries where they would be tortured.[54]

Venezuela: Undermining a Democracy

An attempted coup in Venezuela helps show how corporate oil interests and a fear of national programs to aid the poor led to an attempted coup against a democratically elected president. Venezuela supplies the United States with almost as much oil as Saudi Arabia. The G. W. Bush administration had expressed displeasure with President Hugo Chavez over a number of issues.

Chavez denied the United States access to Venezuelan airspace for U.S. antidrug flights. He was instrumental in oil production cuts that forced a rise in oil prices and then sold oil at discount rates to Cuba. He refused to support the U.S. escalation of the war in neighboring Colombia, where paramilitary groups backed by the U.S. government have killed thousands of civilians each year. Domestically, Chavez levied taxes on the rich and had begun a redistribution of land in Venezuela, where 80 percent of the people live in poverty. A law that Chavez backed almost doubled the royalties that private oil companies, such as Mobil/Exxon and Phillips Petroleum, must pay.[55]

On April 11, 2002, Chavez, the elected president of one of South America's oldest democracies, was ousted in a coup by labor and business groups.[56] President Chavez's replacement, Pedro Carmona, was head of Venezuela's influential business organization Fedecamatras.[57] Just days before the coup, OPEC secretary general Ali Rodriguez phoned Chavez to warn him of information from some Arabic countries, later revealed to be Libya and Iraq. There was a plan to call a new oil embargo against the United States because of its support for Israel, and the Untied States would respond by pushing for a coup against Chavez on April 11. This warning probably saved Chavez's life and explains his swift return.[58] Troops loyal to Chavez hid in the palace, and Chavez supporters surrounded it. Sixty-one hours later, Chavez was back in power.[59]

Nineteen Latin American heads of state denounced the coup as a violation of democratic principles. The Bush administration remained silent, making the United States the only member of the Organization of American States that favored Chavez's downfall.[60] Senator Christopher Dodd noted, "To stand silent [during] the illegal ouster of a government is deeply troubling and will have profound implications for hemispheric democracy."[61]

On April 19, 2002, Bush told reporters that Chavez must "embrace those institutions which are fundamental to democracy, including freedom of press and freedom for the . . . opposition to speak out.[62] However, prior to the coup, U.S. officials met with Carmona and other coup leaders. Others close to the Bush administration were also associated with the coup. Cuban-born Gustavo Cisneros, a friend of the Bush family, is the owner of Venezuela's largest media group and one of the richest men in Latin America. He was inside the presidential palace at the time of the coup and was called twice by Otto Reich, the Cuban-born U.S. assistant secretary of state for Western Hemisphere affairs.[63] Wayne Madsen, a former U.S. Navy intelligence officer, revealed that the United States had been planning to overthrow President Chavez since June 2001. The U.S. Navy, he claimed, was in the area jamming communications to the Venezuelan military. Venezuelan National Assembly member, Roger Rondon, accused U.S. Ambassador to Venezuela Charles Shapiro and two U.S. embassy military attaches of involvement in the coup. "We saw [Shapiro] leaving Miraflores palace, all smiles and embraces, with the dictator Pedro Carmona Estange. . . . Shapiro's participation in the coup d'etat in Venezuela is evident."[64]

President Chavez supported Rondon's statement when he told Newsnight of the *BBC*, "I have written proof of the time of the entries and exits of two United States military officers into the headquarters of the coup plotters—their names, whom they met with, what they said—proof on video and on still photographs."[65] At the night of the attempted coup, IRI President George A. Folsom praised the uprising against Venezuela's democratically elected president, "Last night, led by every sector of civil society, the Venezuelan people rose up to defend democracy in their country." It was later revealed that the NED provided U.S. government funds through the IRI to those organizations that initiated the violent revolt in the streets against Venezuela's legal leaders. More than a dozen civilians were killed and hundreds were injured in this attempted coup.

Two of the major military backers of the short-lived transitional government in Venezuela received training at the U.S. Army School of the Americas (SOA) in Georgia. The school graduates include at least eleven Latin American dictators, for example, Panamanian dictator Manuel Noriega, who was overthrown by a violent invasion after displeasing the elder President Bush.[66] Former Congressman Joseph Kennedy stated, "The U.S. Army School of the Americas . . . is a school that has run more dictators than any other school in the history of the world."[67]

Eastern Europe: Supporting Mafia Regimes

British Helsinki Human Rights Group director Christine Stone has observed that the NED has targeted the nations of Eastern Europe after the end of the Cold War. Many of the problems that now exist have resulted from ill-conceived foreign-policy decisions made by the Europeans and their more powerful American allies in the Balkans and Eastern Europe, in particular. This has involved promoting and supporting patently mafia regimes, which, when established, are difficult to control. Among government officials who have successfully been assisted into power through IRI assistance are Skender Gjinushi, who until 1990 had been a member of Stalinist Politburo in Albania. In 1997 Gjinushi helped to organize the downfall of the Democratic Party movement and the death of 2,000 Albanians. President Stoyanov of Bulgaria thanks the IRI for Bulgaria's rapid progress, in which he elevated a teacher of Marxism-Leninism to the post of prime minister and the person in charge of reform. In Slovakia the NED funded several initiatives aimed at defeating the freely elected government of Prime Minister Vladimir Meciar, who had been persecuted by the previous communist regime. The IRI claimed credit for changing the nature of the campaign, without mentioning that their successful candidate was previously an official of the oppressive communist government in the former Czechoslovakia. Each of these leaders showed indebtedness to the U.S. government by supporting the widely opposed U.S.-British attack on Iraq. Still others have permitted the torture of prisoners sent by the United States to secret prisons.[68]

Dick Marty, a Swiss lawyer working on behalf of the Council of Europe, the continent's official human-rights organization, found evidence that the CIA was maintaining secret prisons and interrogation centers in Poland and Romania. Marty also cited evidence to support the claim that at least seven other European nations colluded with the CIA to capture and secretly detain terrorist suspects, including several who were ultimately cleared of any wrongdoing.[69]

While democracy may have been shortchanged in the reconstruction of Eastern Europe, the counties have become havens for privatization, accompanied by large-scale unemployment and human trafficking. The institutions set up by the United States and its allies have not brought democracy to the former eastern bloc countries. As with so much international policy making, these institutions and doctrines appear to be little more than tokenism designed to disguise what often appears to be arbitrary and brutal rule of the international community. Younge points out a disturbing conclusion:

> America supports democracy when democracy supports America. But when there is no democracy, dictatorships will do just as well—and at times even better. The sticking point is not whether citizens of all nations have the right to choose their leaders, but whether leaders, freely elected or not, of any nation have the right to choose a course which runs against whatever the U.S. perceives its interests to be at a given moment.[70]

East Timor: Conspiring and Aiding Violent Suppression

Like Iran, Indonesia is another oil-rich country in which U.S. military aid created an oppressive government and turned a blind eye to its abuses. Major abuses occurred in the Indonesian rule over East Timor. Approximately 800,000 people live in East Timor. It is half of an island off the eastern end of the Indonesian archipelago. In 1975, after 400 years of colonial rule, the Revolutionary Front for an Independent East Timor declared independence from Portugal. Nine days later, Indonesia's President Suharto met with U.S. President Ford and Secretary of State Kissinger. In the meeting, Suharto described the problem in East Timor and his desire to take rapid action. Kissinger and Ford discussed the use of U.S. arms and the technical and legal problems involved. Within hours after their meeting, the United States authorized an invasion of East Timor by Indonesian troops.[71] The National Security Archive declassified a secret State Department telegram detailing the Suharto, Ford, and Kissinger meeting.[72] Kissinger in a Department of State telegram observed:

> It depends on how we construe it; whether it is in self-defense or is a foreign operation. It is important that whatever you do succeeds quickly. We would be able to influence the reaction in America if whatever happens, happens after we return.

> This way there would be less chance of people talking in an unauthorized way. The President will be back on Monday at 2:00 p.m. Jakarta time. We understand your problem and the need to move quickly but I am only saying that it would be better if it were done after we returned.[73]

U.S. military and political support was essential for the invasion of East Timor. Over 200,000 East Timorese died from bombings, napalm, and famine. Years after the invasion, successive Democratic and Republican administrations funneled hundreds of millions of dollars of economic and military aid to Indonesia and protected it from serious political challenge to its illegal occupation of East Timor. Disregard for international law must be an element of a theory of violent conflict.

After twenty-four years of occupation, 80 percent of East Timorese adults voted in a U.N.-supervised referendum on August 30, 1999, for independence from Indonesia. Within hours of the election, pro-Indonesian militias hunted down supporters, massacred them, burned down villages, and raped the village women. It was not until one week after this rampage that President Clinton made the decision to end U.S. support for the Indonesian military. Stapleton Roy, Washington's ambassador to Jakarta, explained why it had taken a U.S. president so long to reach this decision: "The dilemma is that Indonesia matters and East Timor doesn't."[74] Roy now heads Kissinger Associates, the consulting firm of the former secretary of state who was instrumental in condoning the invasion of East Timor in 1975.[75]

On May 20, 2002, East Timor became the first new nation of the twenty-first century. But the period of brutal devastation has left its effects. The nation has a mortality rate of 200 children per 1,000 under the age of five. Malaria and tuberculosis are endemic. Of the 2,400 villages, over 50 percent have no wells or piped water.[76] The hope is that the organically grown coffee that had previously been purchased by Starbucks can reap $50,000 annually. However, the main economic prospect is oil. It is estimated that when recently discovered oil fields are fully productive commercially, the industry will earn $3,000,000 annually and up to $28 billion in revenue over the next forty years.[77]

East Timor laid claim to the entire Greater Sunrise gas field in the Timor Sea. Its prime minister, Mari Alkatir, who was obliged to resign, looked upon Australia's claim to 80 percent of this huge gas reserve as a clear violation of current international law.[78] If this dispute is resolved legally, there is a possibility that East Timor can become a self-sustaining nation. This will not be an easy task. In April 2002 Secretary of State Powell wrote a warning to the incoming government to give a written promise not to prosecute any U.S. citizens for crimes against humanity under the procedures of the newly established International Criminal Court. Otherwise, the U.S. Congress would find it difficult to go on giving aid. East Timor quickly gave in. Its new leaders were aware that Washington has long been willing to sacrifice their population and their popular government to promote U.S. interests.[79]

The case of East Timor provides a basis for the skepticism with which U.S. policy is viewed in much of the world. It also gives reason to doubt America's professed opposition to the use of violence against civilians.[80]

Iraq and the Middle East: Preemptive Military Action

Plans for the U.S.-initiated war in Iraq were reminiscent of plans for the Vietnam War in certain ways. The enemy in Vietnam was an assumedly unified communism, which had to be stopped lest all of Southeast Asia fall. The history of Vietnamese nationalism, after years of fighting off Chinese, Japanese, and French occupations, was ignored by the elite strategists. Iraq's history of 100 years of petro-imperialism was also ignored. In 1897 England' government assumed a protectorate over Kuwait, which was carved out of Iraq. As oil was gaining importance, England and Germany warred over the Berlin-Baghdad railroad, with Britain invading the entire region of Turkish Mesopotania, eventually overcoming German-led Kurdish troops. The secret 1916 Sykes-Picot Agreement arranged for a French and British split over the oil-rich area, although the British later claimed the greatest share. Turkey, in 1922, fought to regain the area of Mosol but was defeated. Reneging on promises of self-determination, the British, from 1919 to 1958, relied on aerial bombing to crush Iraqi resistance. In 1941 Iraq was the battleground for war between England and Germany (with Italy and the puppet Vichey government of conquered France). The first half of the twentieth century was a story of France, Britain, Germany, and the United States repeatedly overthrowing governments in Iraq and Iran in a struggle for domination over oil.[81] In 1959 the United States attempted a coup of Iraq Prime Minister Abdul Qarim Qasim in response to his nationalist intentions regarding the profits from oil. The history casts doubt upon the public rationale provided for an invasion of Iraq in 2003.

Heavy-handed involvement by the United States appeared in 1973, when Secretary of Defense Schlessinger sought British support for a joint airborne attack. To address the threat of OPEC control, the plan promoted by Secretary of State Kissinger called for seizing Saudi oil fields and installations. In 1983 President Reagan initiated a diplomatic opening to Iraq. Iraq was in the third year of a war of attrition against neighboring Iran. By 1982 the tide had turned to favor the larger Iran. The Reagan administration sent Donald Rumsfeld as an emissary to Hussein. Rumsfeld helped to arrange support for the Iraqi strongman, even after learning that Iraq had begun to use chemical weapons against Iran, the first sustained use of poison gas since a 1925 treaty banning chemical weapons.

After the Rumsfeld mission the United States offered Hussein financial credits, making Iraq the third-largest recipient of U.S. assistance. It normalized diplomatic relations and began providing Iraq with battlefield intelligence that was used to target Iranian troops. And when Iraq turned its chemical weapons on the Kurds in 1988, killing 5,000 in the town of Halabja, the Reagan administration sought to obscure responsibility.[82]

On Aug. 25, 1988—five days after the Iran-Iraq War ended—Iraq attacked forty-eight Kurdish villages more than 100 miles from Iran. The next year, President George H. W. Bush's administration doubled U.S. financial credits for Iraq. A week before Hussein invaded Kuwait, the administration opposed legislation that would have conditioned U.S. assistance to Iraq on a commitment not to use chemical weapons and to stop the genocide against the Kurds. At the time, Dick Cheney was secretary of defense and a member of the National Security Council that reviewed and supported Iraq policy. By all accounts, he supported the administration's appeasement policy. The Iraqi misdeeds were ignored by the administration and by the mainstream press, that is, until the United States had determined that Iraq was to be demonized in preparation for a U.S. attack. That Rumsfeld, subsequently secretary of defense, and Cheney, subsequently vice president, should be among those citing Iraq's brutal use of chemical weapons as a reason for war seems paradoxical. Yet it shows the internalized worldview of the strategic gamester. Iraq was supported as a balance to the power of Iran and a possible helper in the Middle East peace process. Hussein seriously miscalculated by invading Kuwait in response to its role in lowering oil prices. But the individuals who appeased this cruel ruler were the same who later accused opponents of the Iraq war of appeasing a Hitler-like monster. Informed observers see the neoconservative planned invasion of Iraq to have been based upon an ideological belief that the United States is the dominant military power; that it can privatize its resources and its reconstruction to the benefit of corporate investors; that it can take over and change regimes in other countries without attempting to understand either their history, their values, or their culture, and without paying serious attention to the human consequences on the ground.[83] The righteous cause outweighed the obstacles and the need to hear other voices. One former CIA agent, Pelletiere, cites major deception by U.S. officials leading to both the 1991 and the 2003 invasions of Iraq, comparing them to the "big lie" that Germany used to defend its launching of World War II.[84]

The modern history of clashes between the United States and the Middle East goes back to U.S. efforts to train the radical Mujahdin, predecessors of the Taliban, in Afghanistan to fight against the Soviet Union.[85] It includes the CIA-organized overthrow of a popular Iranian leader, the brutal rule of the pro-Western shah of Iran, and the revolt of the fundamentalist mullahs led by the Ayatollah Khomeini. The U.S. support for Iraq to wage a war with chemical weapons against Iran (until Iraq's ill-advised invasion of Kuwait) is yet another fact of recent history.[86] In 1990 George Bush, Sr. gave Saudi King Fahd a written promise that he would remove U.S. troops after the Gulf War. However, U.S. troops, warplanes, and other military hardware remained in the Gulf Arab monarchies thereafter. The continued presence of U.S. troops in Saudi Arabia is claimed to have so enraged Osama bin Laden that he orchestrated the horrific 9/11 attack on the United States.[87] On January 20, 2002, Secretary of State Colin Powell stated that the U.S. military presence in Saudi Arabia would end when the world had turned into "the kind of place we dreamed of."[88] Powell explained that the American troops on Saudi Arabian soil "serve a useful purpose there as a deterrent to Saddam Hussein, but beyond that a symbol of American presence and influence. We've always wanted to maintain a presence in that part of the world, for a variety of reasons."[89]

There are two related answers to why this is true. First, Iraq's rich oil reserves were relatively untapped. The other answer is seen in the history of map making. In 1914 the *Petroleum Review* of London printed its map of Mesopotamian oil and asphalt fields and the route of the Berlin-Baghdad railroad. Since 1930 two types of maps have evolved. The first indicated the nations, mostly new, that have been created. The second type cut the entire region into squares, each one with the initials of the petroleum corporate giant laying claim to the area. Maps prepared for Vice President Cheney's National Energy Policy Group in 2001 and the National Security Council were later revealed under a federal court order. These detailed Iraq's oil fields, pipelines, and refineries, as well as a list of "foreign suitors for Iraqi oilfield contracts." That list included sixty firms from thirty countries—including Russia, France, China, and India—all of whom were ready to negotiate contracts with Iraq, much to the dismay of U.S.-based oil companies. Fadel Gheit, a New York–based oil analyst wrote, "think of Iraq as a military base with a very large oil reserve underneath. . . . You can't ask for better than that."[90]

Iraq was considered first on the U.S. list of targets for a new national security doctrine of preemptive action against states considered hostile. The United States would become a law unto itself, creating new rules regarding international engagement without agreement by other nations. The current plan, as outlined in the National Security Strategy, has a suggested budget of $379 billion. It makes explicit the objective of a major expansion of U.S. military presence on a global basis (beyond troops already present in approximately 130 countries), for constabulary or policing functions. It discusses the development of the "robust nuclear earth penetrator" for combat use, the use of American power to remove by force foreign leaders seen as threats, and the reliance upon American political leadership rather than that of the United Nations.[91] However, the threat from Iraq was not specific, not clearly established, and not shown to be imminent. The invasion, therefore, went beyond provisions of international law for anticipatory self-defense. A unilateral attack on Iraq was outside the framework of global law that the United States initially helped create.[92] The display of military power, the securing of oil reserves, and the hope to assure a government friendly to U.S. corporate interests have been noted as other motives for a war against Iraq:

> Contrary to propaganda orchestrated from Washington and London, the coming attack has nothing to do with Saddam Hussein's "weapons of mass destruction," if these exist at all. The reason is that America wants a more compliant thug to run the world's greatest source of oil.[93]

Viewed from the angle of global oil prices, there is a striking symmetry underlying the two U.S.-led wars against Iraq. The first, in 1990, was started by Saddam Hussein because he considered the price of oil too low; the second, in 2003 was started by George W. Bush because he considered price of oil too high. Writing in opposition to the 2003 Iraq war, eminent international relations scholars Stephen Walt and John Mearsheimer pointed out that Saddam's decision to invade Kuwait in 1990 was primarily an attempt to deal with Iraq's continued economic vulnerability following the Iran-Iraq War. Kuwait exacerbated Iraq's problems by refusing to loan Iraq $10 billion and to write off debts Iraq had incurred during the Iran-Iraq War. Kuwait overproduced the quotas set by OPEC, which drove down world oil prices and reduced Iraqi oil profits.[94]

Conversely, a key objective of the 2003 Iraq war can be inferred from an economic vision for postwar Iraq propounded by Ariel Cohen and Gerald O'Driscoll, Jr., writing for the Washington DC–based conservative Heritage think tank. They note:

> An unencumbered flow of Iraqi oil would be likely to provide a more constant supply of oil to the global market, which would dampen price fluctuations, ensuring stable oil prices in the world market in a price range lower than the current $25 to $30 a barrel. Eventually, this will be a win-win game: Iraq will emerge with a more viable oil industry, while the world will benefit from a more stable and abundant oil supply.[95]

The opposite turned out to be true. Iraq's oil industry was destroyed. Between $5 billion and $10 billion would be needed to return capacity to prewar levels, and an additional $15 billion–$25 billion to raise output 5-million barrels per day, leaving it still short of the 7- to 8-million barrels per day eventually envisaged by Cohen and O'Driscoll.[96] Limited supply during this time led to U.S. oil companies enjoying record profits.

Likewise, U.S. corporations enjoyed a tremendous windfall from mismanaged and unsuccessful reconstruction efforts. One hundred fifty corporations received up to $50 billion in contracts. Military planning for the invasion and its aftermath are now widely recognized as seriously bungled.[97] Nonetheless, stunning successes of corporations in penetrating Iraq have been recorded. As Antonia Juhasz points out in her book *The Bush Agenda: Invading the World, One Economy at a Time*, the contracts were meticulously planned by the consulting company BearingPoint, Inc, which received a $250 million contract to rewrite the entire economy of Iraq.[98] This was part of an attempt to implement the neoliberal economic policies of the Washington Consensus. The BearingPoint Web site proclaims their ability to deliver "Sustainable success. Not just a single event but a series of successful outcomes." The people of Iraq, many of whom were still lacking regular electricity, running water, and sewage services three years after the reconstruction began, might differ from BearingPoint on the definition of success. One clear conclusion is that the neoliberal economic agenda and consulting firms like BearingPoint that help implement it are an integral component of the machinery of modern warfare.

In January 2007, within days of George W. Bush's announcement of his plan to increase the number of U.S. troops in Iraq by 20,000, with over 3,000 American soldiers and more than 600,000 Iraqi citizens dead, it became public knowledge that the U.S. and U.K. governments were radically redrawing Iraq's oil industry and opening the doors to the third-largest oil reserves in the world, allowing the first large-scale operation of foreign oil companies in the country since the industry was nationalized in 1972.[99] With this legislation came production-sharing agreements (PSAs) between the Iraqi government and oil industry giants Exxon Mobil, Shell, and British Petroleum; in exchange for investing in and maintaining the infrastructure and operation of the wells, pipelines, and refineries, Western corporations will receive up to 75 percent of Iraqi oil profits for the next thirty years.[100]

Lando reminds us of the U.S. president's repeated citing of the threat to freedom in Iraq if the U.S. withdrew:

> But that lofty cause was nothing but political window dressing. Indeed allowing the people of Iraq a real choice in their future had always been a *threat* to the U.S. and other great powers, not a goal. What counted was which local leaders would gain control of the region and its resources and how amenable they would be to great power interests. Not if they were freely elected.[101]

In its fifth year since invading Iraq, U.S. officials relate only to a heavily fortified Green Zone and to a government serving at the behest of the occupiers as if that represented Iraq. The terms offered to that government of surrendering the oil reserves, permitting permanent U.S. bases, and crushing or containing those who resist, suggest the limited understanding of why the opposition to bombing and military occupation cannot be managed by any government.[102]

Preemptive attack is military aggression. The beliefs and institutions that condone such activity require a theory that includes identification of the inner network of military decision makers, of their ability to create enemies, and of the mechanisms that facilitate multinational corporate expansion. This case also illustrates the need for a theory that explains why violence is itself cyclical rather than a means to ending violence.

The Vulcans Expand the Agenda

World history reveals many cases of brutal imperial expansion. The United States has a long history of supporting corporate and military interests through the use of military force, particularly in what was considered the U.S. sphere of influence. But toward the end of the twentieth century, a new and more far-reaching agenda was introduced. Until this time the elite centers of power were balanced by several directives. Corporations wanted few constraints and little accountability for the risks undertaken in their activities. But many corporate leaders also held a profound commitment to some of the ideals of freedom and of the constitutional guarantees that got their families to such privileged status. Powerful religious leaders sanctioned the interventions into other countries for their missionary goals, but some also pressured for humane treatment of the victimized people. Military elites competed for allocations and for weapon systems for their own branch and sometimes promoted conflict. Yet some within the upper military echelons felt a responsibility for the loss of their soldiers and were cautious about unnecessary wars. These centers of power long dominated political decision making, and their success is found in the enduring gross inequality described earlier. But a more recent center of power—the Vulcans—has been redefining the options of the United States for military intervention and control.

The Vulcans is the name coined by George W. Bush's original foreign-policy team to refer to themselves, in honor of the Roman god of fire, the forge, and metalwork. James Mann's book *Rise of the Vulcans* focuses on six individuals—Cheney, Rumsfeld, Powell, Armitage, Wolfowitz, and Rice—and although the team included a wide variety of worldviews, they were united by their belief in the primary importance of using American power proactively to shape the world. They were a military generation, their wellspring being the Pentagon.[103]

Powell and Armitage questioned the increasingly overt disdain for the international community shown by the group and gradually moved out of the inner circle. Others such as Perle, Adelson, Abrams, and Feith retained a powerful insider status. In historical context, the more hawkish of the Vulcans represented a new mix in U.S. policy circles. They combined dispassionate realism with an idealistic belief about America's role in the world. It was important not just that America *possess* vast power, but that it *use* it. They envisaged an "unchallengeable America, a United States whose military power was so awesome that it no longer needed to make compromises or accommodations (unless it chose to do so)."[104] Such a public stance by the United States contributes to the aspirations of other nations, particularly those threatened by an existing nuclear power such as the United States, to develop nuclear weapons of their own. With this comes the added threat of nongovernment groups attaining such weapons and using them.[105]

The Vulcans are so convinced of their infallibility that alternative voices are shunned. The belief that American know-how and power can forcefully impose control over people, without even the need to listen to their own culture, is not new. But the scale of this operation and the degree in which it was turned over to contractors, selected for allegiance to the administration, was remarkable. Shortly after the fall of Baghdad, General Garner, who was prepared to return the reconstruction effort to Iraqis, was unexpectedly dismissed and replaced by Paul Bremer of Kissinger Associates. This led to a dramatic turnover in the leadership managing the war. Over the objections of the military and the CIA, Bremer dissolved the Iraqi government and its military. Bremer then closed state-run industries, leaving the country impossible to run. Known experts were replaced with Bush loyalists to plan for rebuilding. A White House advisor to the Pentagon vetted all appointees for loyalty. People were asked whether they voted for Bush, opposed abortion, and favored the death penalty. A twenty-four-year-old loyalist with no experience or relevant education decided that the Baghdad stock exchange needed to be automated (it had been using blackboards) and could be done in four months. An extremely qualified public-health physician in charge of healthcare rehabilitation was replaced by a politically connected social worker without relevant experience, who focused on an antismoking campaign, built 150 new community medical clinics, and updated Iraq's formulary. The actual needs were for providing clean water, hospital generators, properly equipping emergency rooms, and ending shortages of medicines (26 of 32 drugs used for chronic diseases were unavailable, and 40 percent of 900 drugs deemed essential were out of stock in Iraq's hospitals).

Anything that could be outsourced was. Iraqi unemployment jumped to 40 percent, while private guards, flown in, made more than $1,000 per day. Custer-Battles, a firm with few employees that lacked both experience and working capital, was given a large contract to provide security at Baghdad airport. Funds were used to provide working capital to front companies to fraudulently boost profits to 162 percent. One year after Bremer left, auditors had concluded that as much as $8.8 billion of $20 billion Iraqi oil funds could not be accounted for.

Those running the show lived in what has been called the "Emerald City," the walled enclosure, which kept them totally disconnected with the world outside. Everything they had was flown in from Kuwait—food, consumer goods, and bottled water. The world outside the wall meant nothing to idealists, political appointees, and those who selected numbers they could use to justify the contracts they sought.

During the period of the Cold War, the threat of nuclear attack provided an excuse for military buildup but also a source of caution, lest a particular military incursion escalate into a nuclear war. An anticommunist agenda, pursued with a fanatical fervor by Secretary of State John Foster Dulles, permitted a number of proxy wars and secretive interventions in poor countries of the undeveloped world. But with the possibility of smaller conflicts escalating into a nuclear war, critics were asking whether the use of war as a tactic for resolving disputes had become an oxymoron. Nuclear weapons and delivery systems were considered useful in most policy circles, but only as a deterrent.

This period of standoff had its critics. In contrast to the relatively circumspect, cautious policies of containment and détente practiced during the Cold War, and the emphasis on economic interdependence fostered during the Clinton era, in the post–Cold War era the Vulcans saw an opportunity to assert military power without constraints. Wolfowitz, who had been charged with drafting a new military strategy for the Pentagon after the collapse of the Soviet Union, remarked that "we've never done it right in the past."[106] He charged that America had demobilized too quickly after the previous world wars and now needed instead to consolidate and expand its power. Their goal is to usher in a new era in which the United States would use coercion as the primary tool of foreign policy, a forward strategy of confronting and preempting any attempt at challenge from rising powers, rogue states, or nonstate actors below. It would "build up its military power to such an extent that it would be fruitless and financially crippling for any other country to hope to compete with it."[107] In such a world, the potential for the deployment of violence is virtually unlimited.

One of the more frightening manifestations of this may be seen in Joint Publication 3-12: "Doctrine for Joint Nuclear Operations" (JP 3-12), by the Joint Chiefs of Staff, regarding policy on the use of nuclear weapons. The report indicates that the United States shall reserve the right for first use of nuclear weapons against circumstances deliberately left ambiguous in order to keep adversaries wary of U.S. intentions. In the disembodied language common in military planning that does not use the words "massive killing with nuclear bombs," the document refers to "cautions in use of nuclear weapons within a theater."[108] This requires that nuclear and conventional plans be integrated to the greatest extent possible and that careful consideration be given to the potential impact of nuclear effects on friendly forces. A follow-up document, JP 3-12.1, "Joint Tactics, Techniques, and Procedures for Theater Nuclear Planning," was designed to provide theater planners the nuclear-weapons data necessary to determine troop safety information such as minimum safe distances, collateral damage distances, and least separation distances.[109]

The detached view of first use of nuclear weapons is particularly worrisome with ideological true-believers at the helm. The power motivations of the Vulcans appear insatiable, and their grasp of history and of diverse cultures appears faulty. Their key belief in the use of force has led to a foreign policy predicated upon threats, and contributing to a state of unending war to preserve absolute subservience. In such a plan, only the increased likelihood of nuclear war or a collapse of the environment would lead to an alternative outcome, and the prevention of these disasters is not part of the plan. The willingness of the Vulcans to launch a war on terror of such significant cost and consequence that its end may never occur is becoming an enduring image for the twenty-first century. If there is any positive outcome that can come from the bloodshed created by the Vulcans and their supporters, it may be that their actions have raised public consciousness about the extensive power of nonelected officials to shape a nation's destiny for questionable reasons.

Concentrating Power in the Executive

Immediately following the attack of September 11, a guiding principle for the world's most powerful nation became the search for enemies at home and abroad. Ron Suskind's *The One Percent Doctrine* describes the secret playbook, designed largely by Dick Cheney, that has been the driving force for wars in Afghanistan and Iraq and for the global search for jihadists.[110] The book's title comes from a policy expressed by Dick Cheney that even if the evidence suggested only a 1 percent chance of a subsequent attack, the consequences could be so devastating that any such instance required comprehensive and unrestricted action. The result of this could be predicted. The government squandered lives, resources, and human rights chasing shadows and overreacting to what little terrorist activity it did detect.

Suskind's investigation distinguishes the notable persons who appeared to explain the "war on terror" to the public—including the president and vice president, George Tenet of the CIA, and then National Security Advisor Condoleeza Rice—from a group of less visible underlings, who were left with directives to produce results but with little supervision from above. Their work was to improvise plans to defeat this new kind of terrorist enemy.[111]

Liberal democracies have evolved elaborate checks and balances to ensure that while the executive is sufficiently empowered to move decisively in critical situations, he or she is also constrained from acting unaccountably and abusing power. Writing in the *Political Science Quarterly* in 2005, Montgomery observed that after 9/11

> The Bush-Cheney White House moved with more alacrity than had perhaps any administration since World War II to orchestrate an even greater concentration of executive power in the White House and to expand the mantle of secrecy surrounding executive branch actions." [These developments] signal an unraveling of much of the post-Watergate legislation that Congress passed to curb the enormous abuse of power by the executive branch under former President Nixon. The full extent of this concentration of power . . . and its ramifications, however, remain to be seen.[112]

What has been seen to date, however, is alarming. Amid the large, active antiwar demonstrations in the United States and throughout the world, and in defiance of the United Nations and most of its NATO allies, the United States, along with Great Britain, went to war against Iraq. The practices used to sustain that ill-conceived war have included the use of torture, arrests, and detention without charge in a network of secret prisons, as well as the privatization of military operations to avoid international standards of military conduct. These practices have involved challenges to anyone who leaks information about these practices, while at the same time U.S. officials leak classified information when it might be to used to threaten those who have opposed their policies. Finally, they involve the manipulation of information.

Paradoxically, one key tactic in preserving the ability to make war has been to reduce the influence of professional military voices at the highest decision-making levels. Cheney, Wolfowitz, and Rumsfeld learned an important lesson from the first Gulf War, in which Powell was outspoken about his doubts as to whether military action to liberate Kuwait was in America's best interests.

> Rumsfeld took care not to let anyone in the military acquire as much power as Powell had once wielded. When Rumsfeld appeared at press conferences with the chairman of the Joint Chiefs of Staff, the defense secretary usually dominated the podium and let the chairman stand quietly alongside or behind him. It was a

> reversal of the way the Cheney-Powell briefings had been conducted. In 2002 and 2003, as a new military crisis brewed with Iraq, the civilians of the George W. Bush administration, from the president on down, suddenly began to appear in public holding a book by a scholar named Eliot A. Cohen. The book, titled *Supreme Command*, argued that in time of war civilian leaders should make the key decisions on military strategy and should not show too much deference to their generals.[113]

That the tactic permitted Rumsfeld to continue to hold his job despite widespread criticism for a series of catastrophic military blunders—and even to seriously contemplate striking Iran—is testimony to its effectiveness. The strategy served to circumvent the natural cautiousness of generals (who must deal directly with those being put in harm's way) and to empower civilian officials whose inclinations for a grand power game are less hampered by personal experience with wartime deaths.

Legal scholars fear that Bush has abrogated to himself much of the law-making role intended for Congress, as well as the Constitution-interpreting role of the courts. Phillip Cooper, a Portland State University law professor, noted that the Bush administration has been involved in a carefully thought-out process of expanding presidential power at the expense of the other branches of government.[114]

The Matter of Torture

When an authority has power to execute policies without need for accountability, then excessive means are likely to occur. The Abu Ghraib scandal has exposed the sordid underbelly of the war on terrorism and modern warfare in general. The shocking revelation that grisly torture practices had long been widespread and routine within the U.S. military and intelligence agencies provided a nasty wake-up call to the publics of liberal democracies.[115] Ideally, such governments owe their legitimacy to their adherence to laws and treaties enacted by representatives of the people. Many citizens of professed democracies assumed their governments were above the medieval practices thought to be the exclusive domain of tyrants and dictators.

However, as Darius Rejali explains in his book *Torture and Democracy*, the demand for and practice of such covert violence is actually greater in democracies than in dictatorships.[116] The greater openness of democratic societies forces the practitioners of torture to cover their tracks more effectively. While the political position of dictators bent on imposing a reign of terror is actually strengthened by leaving evidence of their gruesome practices in plain public view, democratic leaders who subscribe to the practice are driven underground. The result is increasingly sophisticated strategies of concealment or, when that fails, legal strategies of justification.

An example of such concealment is the practice of *extraordinary rendition*, an American practice in which an American extrajudicial procedure involves sending suspects to countries other than the United States for imprisonment and interrogation. According to former CIA Case Officer Bob Baer, "If you want a serious interrogation, you send a prisoner to Jordan. If you want them to be tortured, you send them to Syria. If you want someone to disappear—never to see them again—you send them to Egypt."[117] The purpose of torture is sometimes misconstrued as the extraction of accurate information to assist in future military operations. For example, in the case of a "clicking time bomb," it is argued that torture is justified to elicit vital information that could save the lives of millions. However, the rationale does not meet the test of credibility. Torture is widely known to be ineffective in such instances because the victims will say whatever their captors want to stop the pain.[118] This raises the question of whether the prolonged misery inflicted on detainees in Abu Ghraib and Guantanomo Bay is instead aimed at deterring recruitment of new militants by demonstrating that jihadists will be denied the benefits of martyrdom, or perhaps as an excuse for sadistic revenge against an enemy who has been demonized.

A more compelling explanation, however, can be seen in the need to justify the harsh treatments that accompany any unpopular military occupation. Walter Schrepel reminds us of the following actions by the French military in Algiers:

- Created a counterrevolutionary form of warfare designed to fight against colonial insurrections. The model modified some of the traditional constraints that had applied to international wars.
- Imposed an alien Christian and European political order on a rebellious Islamic people.
- Protected the seizure and control of the limited arable land.
- Engaged in mass killings of civilians. Furthermore, the major elite force, the paras showed greater loyalty and camaraderie to their fellow officers than to the needs and policies of the French government.
- Reacted to acts of terror with extensive acts of terror themselves.
- Often operated without moral restraint, conducted indiscriminate arrests, and justified torture in interrogation.
- Violated the laws of war and fundamental standards of morality.
- Court-martialed the lone whistleblower among their ranks.[119]

Schrepel argued that the Algerian case showed a need to professionalize the training of military personnel to prevent military behavior that clearly violates ethical standards of warfare. But perhaps the problem is deeper. *Battle of Algiers* is Gillo Pontecorvo's famed 1965 film about the National Liberation Front's attempt to liberate Algeria from French colonial rule. In one of the film's key scenes, Colonel Mathieu, based on real-life French commander General Jacques Massus, is being grilled by journalists about allegations that French paratroopers are torturing Algerian prisoners. Mathieu neither denies the abuse nor claims that those responsible will be punished. Instead, he flips the tables on the scandalized reporters, most of whom work for newspapers that overwhelmingly supported France's continued occupation of Algeria. Torture "isn't the problem," he says calmly. "The problem is the FLN wants to throw us out of Algeria and we want to stay. It's my turn to ask a question. Should France stay in Algeria? If your answer is still yes, then you must accept all the consequences."[120]

Military occupations, like any governments, have two mechanisms to rule. One is by consensus, the other by coercion. Lacking consent, the current U.S.-Iraqi regime relies heavily on fear, including the most terrifying tactics of them all: disappearances, indefinite detention without charge, and torture.[121] Cruel and abusive treatment or torture has a long-time association with war and with the punishment of resisters. U.S. participation in such practices is extensive.[122] In addition, we have seen increased reliance upon mercenaries.

Mercenaries: Privatizing the Military

The use of mercenaries has a long tradition in the history of warfare, dating back at least to the Peloponnesian War.[123] Debate has raged ever since that time over whether and how to regulate them.[124] Although tacitly accepted until the end of the nineteenth century, since then there has been growing international consensus against their use. This culminated with the ratification by twenty-two countries, in October 2001, of the "International Convention Against the Recruitment, Use, Financing and Training of Mercenaries."[125] A 2005 report by U.N. Special Rapporteur Enrique Bernales Ballesteros noted that mercenarism "affects the self-determination of peoples and serves foreign interests that pose a threat to life and to the natural resources, political stability and territorial integrity of the affected countries."[126] However, although countries such as Angola, Libya, Saudi Arabia, Democratic Republic of Congo, and Uzbekistan are signatories, the United States is not. Among Western democracies, only Italy and Germany have signed (though Germany has not ratified). When the world's most powerful states routinely ignore, or in the case of the United States even specifically attack such conventions, their enforcement remains problematic.

Despite widespread international condemnation, the use of mercenaries has recently grown rather than diminished, owing to a transformation in image. Mercenarism is now presented in a more sanitized form under the auspices of publicly traded private military corporations.[127] This more respectable façade makes them increasingly difficult to target under international law. In effect, there is now a serious gap between the spirit of international law, which clearly disfavors mercenary activity, and the letter of the law, which is yet to be amended to cope with private security contractors. Further, to the extent existing law and conventions do constrain the United States, the United States appears to have made a "concerted effort . . . to extricate itself from its obligations."[128] It has attempted to argue that international customs and conventions it has signed "create no obligations of compliance."[129]

Private security firms constitute "a new means of disguised efforts by their home states to influence conflicts in which the home states are technically neutral."[130] There has been both an increase in the availability of individuals with military experience and expertise since the end of the Cold War, and an expansion of the market for such security contractors. For example, in early 2004 the United States was employing roughly 20,000 private military contractors in Iraq, many of whom may be providing interrogation support. An example is Blackwater Security Consulting, which provides mobile security teams composed of former special-operations and intelligence personnel.[131]

In April of 2006, Hofsteller, the mother of a security worker hired by Blackwater enterprises, filed suit against the company for the death of her son in Iraq. The company was able to use its large contract with the Department of Defense to rehire former special-forces soldiers at salaries significantly higher than those paid to actual U.S. soldiers. The four men were killed in an ambush prior to the U.S. attack on Fallujah. Hofsteller's son was told that his job would be the personal protection of U.S. envoy Paul Bremer. However, on his mission the men were sent out without time to prepare, and in unarmored vehicles, with smaller teams than were known to be needed for security from attack. Blackwater's skimping on safety resulted in enormous profits. The U.S. military carries no legal liability for its contractors, so accountability was left to a nonexistent Iraqi judiciary system.[132]

The strategy of the moneyed elite has consistently been to justify the expansion of their power and influence. Within the grand design has been the need to create fear by finding overarching enemies such as communism or terrorism. Once the enemy is identified, the goal becomes to magnify the threats, combat defiant governments, bolster compliant ones, and identify these corporate and military interests as national interests. The clearly amoral and sometimes clandestine tactics, whether successful to their intended objectives or not, are the real news affecting our lives deeply and preventing any efforts to move toward equality or to slow the pace of empire. As historian Edward Said has explained, "Every single empire, in its official discourse has said that it is not like all the others, that its circumstances are special, that it has a mission to enlighten, civilize, bring order and democracy and that it uses force only as a last resort."[133] At this time in history there are a remarkable number of allegations charging government complicity in the deaths of Martin Luther King, Jr., in the high-level government involvement through the CIA, in drug trafficking, and in the bombings that occurred on 9/11. Of these, the drug trafficking revealed in the Iran-contra scandal is perhaps the best documented.[134] But all of these have been dismissed or trivialized, and few have had the quality of official investigation needed to reveal the entire truth. At this time we do know enough about the dehumanized mind-set that goes into the selection of tactics to win the game pursued by the centers of power. We should at least be wary of the dismissals from official sources of the allegations. One may reasonably ask why the evidence of practices that offend human sensibilities and bypass law does not produce widespread public outrage. One answer lies in systematic efforts at disinformation, to be examined in the next chapter.

Chapter 7

Disinformation

The majority of politicians, on the evidence available to us, are interested not in truth but in power and in the maintenance of that power. To maintain that power it is essential that people remain in ignorance, that they live in ignorance of the truth, even the truth of their own lives. What surrounds us therefore is a vast tapestry of lies, upon which we feed.

—*Harold Pinter, Nobel Lecture: "Art, Truth and Politics," 2005*

"Who controls the past," ran the Party slogan, "controls the future: who controls the present controls the past." It was quite simple. All that was needed was an unending series of victories over your own memory. "Reality control," they called it; in Newspeak, "doublethink."

—*George Orwell, 1984*

Governments constantly choose between telling lies and fighting wars, with the end result always being the same. One will always lead to the other.

—*Thomas Jefferson (1743–1826), 3rd U.S. President*

Those who can make you believe in absurdities can make you commit atrocities.

—*Voltaire*

The preceding chapters have described structural violence within industry and agriculture. The chapters have documented a multibillion-dollar defense industry and past military conflicts and coups for corporate gain. They have described a system of power that serves the largest corporate players, much to the detriment of many of the world's people. Since there are relatively few beneficiaries and many casualties of this system, one might expect there would be major voices of dissent. But there is little information circulating about power and influence. Opposing voices are heard, but focused discontent is discouraged by a flow of information that makes the system difficult to penetrate.

One answer to why there is so little outrage is that the media obfuscate issues of power and perpetuate beliefs that protect the broad interests of a powerful elite. Few people are present to watch a major financial deal that sets up a no-bid government contract for military supplies or for a natural gas pipeline. Few people witness directly the corporate and government decision makers in agreements that assure the destruction of an essential rainforest, or that perpetuate the routine loss of life from inadequate food and water, or that cause us to go to war. For most people, our knowledge about events beyond our immediate experience comes from the media. What is presented molds our views of the world. In studying the media we observe that the power to dominate resources comes also with a power to dominate ideas through control over the public discussion of issues. There are two primary methods to stifle dissent: public relations and military force. Force was illustrated in chapter 6. Here, the focus is cast upon public relations that have come to replace meaningful remedial action. This chapter describes how information is molded to support certain policies and attitudes, minimize exposure of exploitative power, and prevent widespread circulation of divergent views.

The information we typically get is always selected and filtered. It is sometimes exaggerated, sometimes trivialized, often used to demonize, and consistently used to affirm underlying values that favor those with power. The media contribute to co-opting our attention with trivia and with the lives of celebrities while important things that affect our lives, such as corporate welfare, voter fraud, carcinogenic contaminants, infant mortality, government involvement in the sale of narcotics, and the contribution of transnational corporations to the despair of poverty are often hidden. The message of social protesters in the major media is reduced to sound bites.

Private companies, nongovernmental organizations, and government agencies alike pay millions to public relations firms that specialize in (according to the Web site of one group) "achieving information superiority in order to impact public opinion and outcomes."[1] One of the largest and most successful companies in the area of image management is the Edelman Company.[2] Between fiscal years 2003 and 2005, the U.S. government paid an annual average of $78.8 million to private public relations firms.[3] In the five years following September 11, 2001, the Pentagon alone paid a single private public relations firm more than $56 million.[4] Furthermore, through corporate mergers over the last few decades, the media are now controlled by five megacorporations.[5] Newspapers and television stations, amusement parks, jet engine manufacturers, and nuclear power plants may all be owned by the same parent company. As business enterprises, the corporate media are legally bound to put the interests of shareholders above everything else, including the public good.

Mainstream media may be viewed as a threat to a democratic system because they do not represent or promote the interests of all people but instead serve the interests of a small, very powerful minority. Media historian Robert McChesney maintains that the core problem with the media today is that people in power are dictating what information is legitimate and newsworthy.[6] This chapter outlines the ways in which information is restricted and modified to advance the agenda of a network of powerful interests.

The chapter begins with a review of the origins of propaganda during World War I. The topic then moves to describe a period of struggle between the muckrakers and big business, and the controversy over journalistic integrity. The chapter describes who owns and therefore controls what is presented as well as the influence of big business upon media content. One section illustrates distortion in the presentation of two issues, hurricane Katrina and global warming. The next topic focuses on how current political and economic interests have used the media to justify the U.S. war on terror and to deflect the public attention from such domestic issues as health care, educational funding, environmental protection, and the long-term human costs of war. A final section examines a long-term distortion of American history.

World War I and Propaganda

Propaganda originated not in totalitarian regimes but rather in more democratic societies.[7] The very first coordinated propaganda effort was put forth by Britain's Ministry of Information, during World War I, with the explicit goal of convincing American intellectuals of the need to go to war with Germany. Sir Gilbert Parker, in charge of a secret propaganda bureau within the United States, began by creating a mailing list of 200,000 opinion leaders whose names were drawn from *Who's Who in America*.[8] These intellectuals received countless pamphlets, speeches, interviews, and films illustrating German atrocities. The appeal to these selected individuals played on the elitist sentiment that it was the responsibility of the intellectual community to determine what was best for the general population.

The most influential document was a report prepared by Lord James Bryce. The Bryce Report compiled over a thousand depositions taken from Belgian refugees. The report did not convince all opinion leaders. Will Irwin, American muckraker and U.S. war correspondent, noted there was no cross-examination of witnesses and was suspicious of Bryce's heroic tone. But the document seemed to "sustain the Allied claim that theirs was a contest of good versus evil."[9] Notably, in the 1930s the document was discredited altogether, years after the United States had been drawn into the war.

The business community, represented by the League to Enforce Peace, advocated for war and was soon followed by the progressive community, which promoted the idea that U.S. participation in the war was an opportunity to advance democracy on a worldwide scale. The American people, however, were not interested in going to war; in 1916 they elected Woodrow Wilson, on an antiwar platform with the slogan "Peace without Victory."[10] Wilson was soon convinced of the need for war by the intellectual and business communities. Faced with the task of changing public opinion in favor of war, he supported the formation of the first (and only) major state propaganda agency in U.S. history.

The Committee on Public Information

The Committee on Public Information, headed by journalist George Creel, had a monumental task. It had to convince the American people to enter a war that had been going on for three years and thousands of miles away, without any direct threat to U.S. soil. Creel sent out over 70 million copies of various pamphlets about American ideals and the purposes of war across the United States, and millions more abroad. He hired 75,000 speakers (called the "Four Minute Men") to perform concise but influential patriotic speeches, which reached over 400 million people. Speaking at movie houses, churches, and grange halls, the presentations covered conscription, the Red Cross, income tax, and food conservation. Poster art was created by the committee's division of pictorial publicity. In the words of the division's director, these colorful posters, displayed everywhere, were designed to "appeal to the heart."[11] Images invoked fear, with accompanying text calling for the purchase of war bonds. Other images idealized U.S. soldiers. Hollywood did its part by creating a multitude of anti-German films, including *The Beast of Berlin* and *The Little American.* The National School Service Bulletin was provided to public schools; the National Board for Historic Service took over *History Teachers Magazine.* At Stanford University, lectures on foreign policy leading up to the war came to be entitled "The German Ideal of World Domination."[12]

The committee's efforts were highly successful. At the end of the war, Creel proudly and openly described the entire operation in his book *How We Advertised America: The First Telling of the Amazing Story of the Committee on Public Information That Carried the Gospel of Americanism to Every Corner of the Globe.*[13] The committee was dissolved at the end of the war, considered unfit for service during peacetime.

Creel was not solely responsible for the success of the Committee on Public Information. Another influential figure, Edward Bernays, pioneer of the public relations industry, wrote a number of books including *Propaganda, Crystallizing Public Opinion,* and *Engineering Consent.*[14] The success of the committee, he explained, showed that it is possible to "regiment the public mind every bit as much as an army regiments their bodies."[15] This was an undertaking that could only be performed by the intelligent minority to influence an unsophisticated majority. Bernays described this intelligent minority as "the invisible government . . . concentrated in the hands of a few because of the expense of manipulating the social machinery which controls the opinions and habits of the masses."[16] After the war, Bernays went on to launch an advertising campaign marketing cigarettes to women. Playing on the burgeoning women's movement, he hired models to march in New York's Easter parade in 1929 wearing banners reading "Torch of Liberty," while smoking Lucky Strike cigarettes. The company was an immediate success.[17]

A highly respected journalist, Walter Lippman, was another member of the committee. He was a strong proponent of the war at its onset, believing it to be an opportunity to spread democracy around the globe. Lippman was of the mindset that the intellectual classes had a responsibility to make such decisions for the less-astute classes, or masses, of society. With propaganda, a "revolution in the art of democracy," as he described, the public could be made to believe and support choices made without their knowledge or participation. He called this the "manufacture of consent."[18]

Unlike Creel and Bernays, Lippman later expressed misgivings and questioned whether the Committee's means of molding public opinion were congruent with democratic ideals. As a serious journalist, he was troubled by the fact that the committee had not reported factual information but rather "news and argument which put America in the best possible light and sustained the fighting morale."[19] Based on the success of their information campaign, leaders now viewed public opinion as critical. Looking into the future, Lippman saw that in the interest of democracy, the news (on which public opinion was formed) must be protected from propaganda. The word *propaganda*, it should be noted, only became a pejorative term after it became associated with Hitler in World War II, who developed his own nationalistic propaganda campaign inspired by the success of the Allied program. But the manipulation of information available to the public is testimony not only to an elite perception that the public cannot be trusted to make informed judgments but also to the need to conceal truths that might prove embarrassing to those with power.

For centuries most of the world was ruled by kings or emperors who were unseen by all but a few of their royal followers. They were granted a mystical or divine status by those whom they ruled. Such divine status permitted rulers to tithe farmers, raise armies, and construct palaces or monuments with indentured labor. The concept that masses of ordinary people had either the right or the wisdom to partake in broader decisions had evolved only in smaller entities, such as the Iroquois tribes, oceans away from the empires of Europe and Asia. It was not until the beginning of roads and of village literacy that some criers were able to transmit rudiments of information that helped in the decline of the monarchies. With the rise of a merchant class able both to travel and to read, issues of participation in decision making came to the fore. If people's voices could make a difference, then the question of what information they had was a matter of power. An elitist belief held that most people were too dumb and too disinterested about larger issues to take a reasonable part in decisions. They had to be fed with information prepared for them. But some journalists spoke out against abusive power.

The Muckrakers and Big Business

In the 1930s, a fight ensued over journalism's integrity. That integrity was founded upon work of the muckrakers, who exposed powerful institutions and their use of the media to inform public opinion. Before that, in 1905–1906, Ray

Stannard Baker published a series of articles on the railroad industry. What began as an exposé on excessive rates for shipping customers and secret rebates for those in power (such as Rockefeller), the series ended by zeroing in on the railroad corporations' practice of hiring press agents to inform public opinion. Baker discovered the heads of all the major railroad lines had joined forces and hired a publicity firm, launching a campaign against railroad regulation. Recognizing the power of newspapers in forming opinion, publicity agents prepared news-style articles and forwarded them to newspaper editors. When these agents found editors to be disagreeable, they played upon commercial interests of business and industry leaders in that city to convince editors not to favor regulation. Railroad interests prevailed in court by hiring witnesses to provide congressional testimony.

Will Irwin is credited with exposing the newspaper business. In a fifteen-part series that began in 1911, Irwin described how editorials had become less fashionable, and a plethora of new and cheaply produced papers depended on sensationalistic news to sell their papers. Irwin explained the power plays that occurred between journalist and editor, and between editor and contributor. The old system of direct subsidies to newspapers from political parties and businesses had dissolved, with the new advertising system in its place.[20] Irwin noted that editors were careful not to offend their advertisers. Still worse, editors and publishers who identified with the wealthy class assimilated their views. As one progressive editor concluded,

> The future of America is safe as long as the American people have the ballot and can obtain information and facts on which to base an intelligent opinion. When, however, the steel trust, the railroads, the packers, the coal barons and the industrial plutocrats can pervert public opinion to suit their purposes then we are treading on dangerous ground.[21]

I. F. Stone wrote a detailed report on labor relations in the agricultural industry. Migrant workers were trying to organize and obtain protection under new labor legislation of the 1930s. Stone's article explained how California farm organizations had come together to form the Associated Farmers group in an attempt to block the efforts of labor groups. Stone documented countless contributions of major corporations to Associated Farmers and showed how the association's publication discounted labor organizing as subversive communist activity. Playing on this pervasive fear, hundreds of farmers were deputized by local sheriffs, enabling them to wield more power over strikers and labor organizers. Stone recounted to the National Labor Relations Board evidence of Associated Farmers using violent means to discourage workers from organizing.[22]

The pervasive fear of and fervor against communism perhaps best exemplifies the collusion of interests between government and corporate power. Indeed, as shown in the previous chapter, economic interests in foreign countries were frequently behind the U.S. "defense" against the media image of encroachment of communism all over the world. With the Cold War behind us, the rallying cry against communism has shifted to a rallying cry for democracy and free markets, and against an amorphous force called terrorism. The media are essential to the task of making such goals appear both good and inevitable. The next section outlines how corporations use media to shape public opinion and advance their own interests.

Media Monopolies and the Effect on Journalism

The corporate mergers that took place throughout the 1980s and 1990s have resulted in today's handful of megacorporations. In 1983 fifty corporations dominated the media industry. At that time the greatest merger was valued at $340 million. In 2000 the merger between AOL and Time Warner was valued at $350 billion. In 2004 only five media corporations dominated the U.S. industry: Time Warner, Disney (ABC), Murdoch's News Corporation (Fox), Bertelsmann of Germany, and Viacom (CBS). General Electric's NBC is a close sixth.[23] Since 1995, the number of companies that own commercial TV stations has declined by 40 percent. Viacom owns CBS; General Electric owns NBC; Disney owns ABC; and News Corp. owns Fox Broadcasting, which in turn runs Fox News Channel. News Corp. also owns the *New York Post*, the publisher HarperCollins, and the film production company Twentieth-Century Fox. The effect of mergers is not limited to U.S. audiences. Viacom owns stations in Canada; NBC owns Telemundo, the Spanish-language network; Murdoch's companies own the DirecTV sector in Central and South America, British Sky Broadcasting, and START TV in Asia.[24] These corporations also have a vertical integration beyond their media enterprises, controlling production and distribution of media-related products. This means companies are able to cross-promote and sell products across market sectors. In 1994 Disney's animated film *The Lion King* generated $1 billion in profit—and produced 186 items of merchandise, which they manufactured and sold, in part, through the theme parks that Disney also owns. This merchandising potential translates to a fourfold increase in profit beyond the box office.[25] Public media are not free from the corporate interest, because underwriting permits an opportunity both for subtle oversight and for tax-deductible image promotion. For example, Archer Daniels Midland, one of the three largest agribusiness conglomerates, joined AT&T, the giant of telecommunications, in underwriting the *Lehrer NewsHour*.

The power held by the giant media corporations results in a strong bias, imposed from the top, on what passes for news. Robert Greenwald's documentary film *Outfoxed* examines the impact on society when a broad consolidation of media is controlled by one person, in this case Rupert Murdoch of Fox News. The film provides an in-depth look at Fox News and the dangers of ever-enlarging corporations taking control of the public's right to know. The documentary presents evidence by former Fox News reporters, producers, bookers, and writers who describe what working for Fox News is like. Former Fox employees talk about how they were forced to push a "right-wing" point of view or risk their jobs. Some chose to remain anonymous for fear of losing their current livelihoods. One employee observed, "There's no sense of integrity as far as having a line that can't be crossed." In August 2006 Serene Sabbagh and Jomana Karadsheh, two producers working for Fox News in Amman, Jordan, resigned in protest. Their action speaks to the integrity and courage of journalists working under coercive pressure. Their resignation letter stated, "We can no longer work with a news organization that claims to be fair and balanced when you are so far from that. Not only are you an instrument of the Bush White House, and Israeli propaganda, you are war mongers with no sense of decency, nor professionalism."[26]

In 2005 MySpace, a highly used social networking Web site, was bought by Rupert Murdoch's News Corp., owner of Fox News. As if to illustrate how media consolidation can curtail open communication, MySpace refused to accept an advertisement by the public interest group Common Cause informing people about proposed new Federal Communications Commission (FCC) regulations that would permit even greater consolidation. Members of Common Cause had already sent tens of thousands of messages to the FCC, but in this final week before the deadline, Common Cause wanted to advertise on high-traffic Web sites to recruit new activists. MySpace told them that they "won't allow that to be shown."[27]

Many of the same advertisers who support the major media also support a group of talk-show hosts, typically conservative, who daily demonstrate that bullying, humiliation, and the "big lie" are attractive to large audiences. These commentators confound news with sarcastic and offensive comedy and partisan advocacy, making a strong appeal to people ready to accept scapegoats. The values tapped here are discussed in chapter 8.

Interlocking directorates further complicate the interests of media companies. An interlock occurs when the same individual sits on the board of directors of more than one corporation. In this case, a board member of a media corporation is also a board member of a bank, an investment company, an oil company, a pharmaceutical company, and a technology company. This is only illegal, however, if the corporations involved would form a complete monopoly if they merged. According to an article in *Columbia Journalism Review,* in 2003 Murdoch's News Corporation, Disney, Viacom, and Time Warner had forty-five interlocking directors.[28] Network analysis (described in chapter 5) can offer a tool for precise plotting of the interlocks among the media giants and between these megacorporations and other sectors of the corporate world and government agencies. Some of the financial ties suggest the power for a monopoly over information.

Although classic capitalist philosophy predicts that competition in the free market leads to greater diversity and better quality of products, the opposite has proven true when there are only a few big players. With too much at stake in an all-or-nothing rivalry, the five media conglomerates compete only on a superficial level. Instead, their interests are better served by joining with one another.

This joining of forces is accomplished by shared investment of media products; the big five media conglomerates share over 100 joint business ventures.[29] Media corporations may appear to be competing in ratings. A closer look at content, however, undermines this argument. Highly duplicative content—such as the current myriad of reality television programs—allows for only fractional losses compared to consistent gain. In television, for example, 30 percent profit is considered low. A 60 percent profit margin (considered good) is consistently reached by successful broadcasters.[30]

The big five media conglomerates have come together most openly in one of the nation's most powerful lobbying groups, the National Association of Broadcasters (NAB). In the year 2000 NAB spent $5.7 million on lobbying for laws and regulations to increase corporate power.[31] This figure does not include campaign contributions for that same year, in which 64 percent of NAB contributions went to Republican campaigns. On their own, the parent companies of the big five spent nearly $27 million on lobbying firms in the year 2000 alone.[32] It is ironic that when politicians hail the urgent need to defend our democratic traditions, their words are communicated by giant media corporations, which are essentially authoritarian structures of power. There is no pretence of democracy in a corporation. Power flow is strictly top-down, and there is little employee input and no public input in decision making.

Lack of Government Regulation

Government bodies created to protect consumers from overt corporate domination have become, in Robert McChesney's words, "toothless organizations." The landmark Telecommunications Act in 1996 resulted in the massive deregulation of media corporations. According to the *Wall Street Journal*, this legislation was initiated by "Gingrich-class" Republicans in 1994, who "asked the industry what it wanted and almost literally gave them the law they asked for."[33] Proponents of this legislation, operating by the ideology of the free market, argue that competition will result in better products and prices for the consumer—and therefore, in effect, the market will regulate itself. But the Telecommunications Act legislation has resulted instead in the monolithic cartel of media mega corporations. In the words of Rupert Murdoch, "We can join forces now, or we can kill each other and then join forces."[34]

The media sector most dramatically transformed by this ruling has been radio broadcasting. Between 1996 and 1999, half of the nation's 11,000 radio stations changed hands, and there were over 1,000 mergers.[35] In each of forty-three different cities, a third of the radio stations are owned by a single company, despite an existing law stating that no company can own more than eight in any market. Clear Channel, the nation's largest radio broadcasting company, owns over 1,200 radio stations. In Mansfield, Ohio, Clear Channel owns eleven of the seventeen radio stations; in Corvallis, Oregon, seven out of thirteen.[36] Clear Channel, home of right-wing propagandist Rush Limbaugh, reaches an estimated 20 million listeners daily.[37]

Consolidation of ownership of radio stations in local areas has permitted Clear Channel to reduce local personnel and coverage of local events and replace them with broadcasts from a remote central location. Ownership of stations by minorities has declined, as has the ability to respond to local emergencies. When a train derailment in Minot, North Dakota, released tons of toxic chemicals into a residential area, the panicked residents who called for help were told to turn to radio and cable TV, but no help was available. Centralized corporate ownership of local media outlets has transformed American cultural and political life into world of empty television news stations, preprogrammed radio shows, and copycat newspapers.[38]

Perhaps the most worrisome concern with media concentration lies in its inducement of what Bill Moyers has called a plantation mentality.[39] People can live under horrendous conditions, even slavery, and believe that the system is unchangeable. If they hear only the voices selected by more powerful others, then their own voice is silenced. They lose the potential to engage in dialogues with others like themselves in which they may come to see that the reality they assume is a social construction prepared by others, that such social constructions can be remade, and that, collectively, ordinary people hold the potential power for change.[40]

The FCC, created in 1934, recognized that airwaves belong to the public and that leases require some responsibility. The FCC was to ensure that radio broadcasters would continue public-service programs in an environment increasingly controlled by advertising. However, regulatory protection of the airwaves has been minimal, and government organizations and enactments originally created to protect the public interest now protect the interests of big business. When Viacom merged with CBS, the resulting conglomerate was in clear violation of the rule that no company can control stations that reach more than 35 percent of the total audience. The FCC responded by offering the emergent corporation a temporary waiver.[41] Major media conglomerates have been able to influence the FCC. Local news entities produced by independently owned outlets provide Americans a valuable tool in the public debate of issues. While the FCC was fighting to relax rules that would prevent further media consolidation, the agency was charged with suppressing the release of two federally funded studies showing negative effects of consolidation, including the reduction of local news coverage. The information was eventually leaked to the office of Senator Barbara Boxer. The FCC, however, has not become a proponent of corporate interests on its own accord. McChesney describes the FCC as the classic "captive" regulatory agency. For example, in 1994 the FCC proposed an investigation into Rupert Murdoch's broadcast empire. After being threatened by Representative Jack Fields, on the House committee and a friend of Murdoch, they dropped the investigation.[42]

This media entanglement with politicians (supposedly its regulators) and corporate interests is bound together by lobbyists. In exchange for government deregulation, the corporate media return the favor to their friends in government with enormous sums of money, thereby essentially giving them a "cut" from their unrestricted profits. Lobbying expenditures rose significantly, 74 percent in the years between 1998 and 2003, while the FCC was considering additional relaxing of ownership regulations. In 2001 Clear Channel spent only $12,000 on lobbying, but in 2003—the year of the FCC vote—it spent $2.28 million, an increase of 19,000 percent in two years.[43] In an interview with *Fortune* magazine in 2003, Clear Channel CEO Lowry Mays described the philosophy of his company: "We're not in the business of providing news and information. We're not in the business of providing well-researched music. We're simply in the business of selling our customers products."[44]

The cable, telephone, and Internet industries use several tools to gain a competitive advantage in telecommunications reform legislation. Some of these lobbying tools are easy to spot—campaign contributions, television ads that run only inside the Beltway, and meetings with influential members of Congress. Other tactics are more deceptive.

Using Fake Groups and Fake News

One of the tactics popularized because of its extensive use by the missile industry is increasingly used by telecommunications companies. Dubbed "Astroturf lobbying" by former U.S. Senator Lloyd Bentsen, the practice involves creating front groups that try to pass as grassroots citizen groups but that are actually corporate-sponsored efforts to put fake grassroots pressure on Congress. Astroturf campaigns generally claim to represent huge numbers of citizens, but in reality their public support is minimal or nonexistent.[45] Common Cause researchers found nine such telecommunications front groups and Astroturf organizations: Consumers for Cable Choice, Freedom Works, Progress and Freedom Foundation, American Legislative Exchange Council, New Millennium Research Council, Frontiers of Freedom, Keep It Local NJ, Alliance, and MyWireless.org. Behind these innocuous names, the groups get their funding from the telecommunications industry giants, sometimes working directly from their offices, rarely indicating the sources of their funds, and never mentioning the financial windfalls to the media giants from consolidation following the deregulation they advocate. In addition to fake groups, we find fake news reports, a problem that is particularly important for television.[46]

In recent years the number of media formats and outlets for information have grown dramatically. However, television has remained the major news source in the United States. According to a January 2006 Harris Poll, more than three-quarters of U.S. adults rely on local TV news, and more than 70 percent turn to network TV or cable news on a near-daily basis. The quality and integrity of television reporting has, therefore, a significant impact on what the public learns about consumer products, health services, and, most important, government policies.

Public-relations firms have a keen desire to reach this audience with the messages of their corporate and government clients and have a way to make the very biased messages of their clients appear as an impartial reporting of the news. To add an appearance of credibility to clients' messages, the public relations industry uses video news releases (VNRs). VNRs are prepackaged "news" segments and additional footage created by broadcast public-relations firms, or by publicists within corporations or government agencies. The VNRs are provided free to TV stations and are designed to fit seamlessly into newscasts. Although the TV stations know the source of this information, they do not identify it in the broadcast. In the absence of strong disclosure requirements, viewers have no way of knowing when the news segment they have just seen was bought and paid for by the very subjects of that "report."

The Center for Media and Democracy (CMD) conducted a ten-month study of selected VNRs and their use by television stations. They tracked thirty-six VNRs issued by three broadcast public-relations firms. Their results show that the television newscasts—on which most Americans rely—frequently air VNRs without disclosure to viewers, without conducting their own reporting, and even without checking the facts in claims made in the VNRs. VNRs are overwhelmingly produced for corporations. They are part of larger public-relations campaigns to sell products, to brighten corporate images, or to promote policies or actions beneficial to the corporation.[47]

The Effect on Journalism

Corporations are, by design, money-producing entities. They are legally bound to put the interest of their stockholders as their first priority, even above the public good. The ramifications of their decisions are considered outside the realm of their responsibility. When corporations own media, news becomes a product to sell, and the public audience is the consumer.

Advertisers (often owned by the same parent company as the media outlet) and media board members (interlocked with other industries) decide what is newsworthy. They promote their products and present a favorable corporate image to the public. A survey by FAIR (Fairness and Accuracy in Reporting) found that 75 percent of investigative journalists and editors surveyed in television news admitted that advertisers had "tried to influence the content" of news stories; 59 percent felt pressure from within their own stations to produce news stories to please advertisers.[48] In this environment the actual activity of many dedicated professional journalists reflects a difficult road of access to government sources, resources for other source materials, knowledge of the acceptable range of what can be said, and cautions about crossing that line.[49] McChesney describes how unlike the current situation is from the days of the muckracker journalists, who exposed corporate greed to protect the public:

> The corporate media system has none of the inherent interest in politics or journalism. . . . Its commercialized news fare, if anything, tends to promote depolitization, and all evidence suggests that its fundamental political positions, such as they are, are closely linked to political and business elites.[50]

Consider, for example, the influence that General Electric, the world's largest company by market share, has over its media company NBC. GE is one of the world's top-three producers of jet engines, supplying Boeing and Lockheed Martin. GE has also designed ninety-one nuclear power plants in eleven countries. GE director Sam Nunn was the senator of Georgia for twenty-seven years and sits on the board of Chevron/Texaco.[51] The power held by such giant media corporations results in a strong bias, imposed from the top, on what passes for news. Journalism ceases to exist in an environment where the news is becoming a public-relations mouthpiece for the corporate and political interests. The media then becomes a tool to disseminate propaganda for the interests that control and finance them.

Some have held out hope for the Internet and broadband as a way to decentralize control over information. Chester warns that the country's powerful communications companies have other plans that threaten freedom in the new digital world.[52] Assisted by a host of hired political operatives and probusiness policy makers, major cable, TV, and Internet providers are using their political connections to gain greater control over the Internet and other digital communication channels. Bill Moyers notes the promise of digital communications but also the dangers:

> The Internet, cell phones and digital cameras that can transmit images over the Internet makes possible a nation of storytellers, every citizen a Tom Paine. Let the man in the big house on Pennsylvania Avenue think that over, and the woman of the House on Capitol Hill. And the media moguls . . . no longer own the copyright to America's story. It's not a top-down story anymore. Other folks are going to write this story from the ground up. And the truth will be out that the media plantation, like the cotton plantation of old, is not divinely sanctioned. It's not the product of natural forces. The media system we have been living under for a long time now was created behind closed doors where the power brokers met to divvy up the spoils. [Consolidation has added the danger that] . . . we are being shadowed online by a slew of software digital gumshoes, working for Madison Avenue. Our movements in cyberspace are closely tracked and analyzed, and interactive advertising infiltrates our consciousness to promote the brand washing of America. . . . Do we really want television sets that monitor what we watch? Or an Internet that knows what sites we visit and report back to advertising companies? Do we really want a media system designed mainly for Madison Avenue?[53]

Political and Economic Agendas: The Modern-Day Manufacture of Consent

Recall the philosophy of Edward Bernays that the "the very essence of the democratic process" was that intelligent minorities of society can—and should—direct the population through the "engineering of consent."[54] Bernays and especially Lippman, who coined the phrase "manufacture of consent," identified themselves as progressive democratic intellectuals. The idea of a small elite controlling and manipulating "the bewildered herd" (as Lippman referred to the general public) was not their original idea. That idea has been promoted throughout Western history. Important here is the belief that the public cannot be trusted to think for themselves. If they do, it will only cause trouble, so they must be herded. During the Reagan presidency, a high level of concern emerged when it was revealed that the CIA was bypassing congressional laws by supporting the contras to overthrow the government of Nicaragua. A scam known as the Iran-contra affair allowed the CIA to fund this operation by permitting the aerial dropping of cocaine into the United States and returning with arms routed from Iran. Although this was eventually uncovered, the administration set up a public diplomacy office directed by Otto Reich. Its task, like that of other government ministries before it, was perception management. Its job was to present information in ways that would preclude knowledge of such activities from reaching the public (and in this case a Congress) who could not be trusted to support policies being used.

The techniques for managing public images are straightforward. Linguist Geoffrey Nunberg addresses a self-fulfilling practice of repeating ignorant slogans until they become part of the culture, in his book *Talking Right: How Conservatives Turned Liberalism into a Tax-Raising, Latte-Drinking, Sushi-Eating, Volvo-Driving, New York Times-Reading, Body-Piercing, Hollywood-Loving, Left-Wing Freak Show.*[55] Another linguist, George Lakoff, has described in detail the art of framing issues in ways that are palatable to people and substituting stereotypical buzzwords for actual understanding. Lakoff also elaborates upon a theme by Eric Fromm, arguing that large numbers of people who reflect family backgrounds of a strong authoritarian father are seeking a leader who offers simple, all-or-none solutions.[56]

Propaganda plays on simple but powerful images and slogans. A concise message is repeated over and over until it is accepted and integrated seamlessly into our thinking (and may remain long after the message has been discredited). Fear provides the leverage, the motivating force behind propaganda. When we feel threatened, we are most likely to stand behind leaders who take on the role of protector.

Psychologists Pratkanis and Aronson suggest four strategies of successful propaganda: (1) Create an environment or climate in which the actual message will be believed ("pre-persuasion"); (2) Refer to a credible source, a public figure, or a likable and/or authoritative speaker; (3) Present a simple and clear message; (4) For this message to take hold, fear must be evoked and projected upon some target group.[57]

Keywords and phrases, repeated incessantly, act as word-encoded symbols that contain our national history and identity—peace, democracy, defending freedom, God bless America, growth, and prosperity. But the symbols often have a dark side that is not acknowledged. Consider, as Michael Parenti does, the real meaning behind the keywords we are exposed to every day:

> "Peace" means global U.S. military domination. . . . "Prosperity" means subsidizing the expansion of U.S. corporate interests abroad. . . . And "democracy" . . . means a

system in which political decisions are made by the transnational and publicly unaccountable corporate interests and their government allies.[58]

In Parenti's view, an absence of military violence because those facing gross degradation are too frightened to fight back, could be described in the media as a time of peace and stability; increases in gross national product are used to signify prosperity, even if the actual number living in poverty is increasing and the true beneficiaries are subsidized transnational corporations; and democracies can be said to exist even when wealth determines who has access to be heard and death squads intimidate voters. Chapter 2 looked at the media role in promoting enemy images prior to military violence. This section highlights examples of the propaganda campaign put forth by the G. W. Bush administration's war on terror, with the assistance of corporate media who have their own economic agenda in mind.

The Defense Department's Media Contracts

Although the first organized propaganda campaign was designed to create American support against Germany in World War I, it was the Vietnam War that prompted the U S. government—or more accurately, the Pentagon—to attempt more direct control over the media. The United States had followed China, Japan, and France in efforts to dominate Vietnam. The war was swept by a crusade of anticommunism and an unwillingness to consider the possibility that the U.S. war in Vietnam was an ill-conceived effort to bury the forces of Vietnamese nationalism. Many military officials believed that reporting on the slaughter of Vietnamese women and children, the mental and physical breakdown of American soldiers, and the suspicion of the government's political policy was responsible for American defeat. Images of Vietnamese children screaming, their skin burning with napalm, were seared into American consciousness. For many in power, the disaster of the Vietnam War was not the loss of life but rather the interference of the public in what leaders had determined to be a policy addressing U.S. interests. The perceived need to mobilize both domestic and global opinion in response to a threat of terrorism was later addressed by a report of the Defense Science Board Task Force on Strategic Communication.

The G. W. Bush administration led a comprehensive and sophisticated propaganda campaign, first by contracts with public relations firms and second by appointing marketing experts to its official staff. In February 2006 the nonpartisan Government Accountability Office (GAO) released a 160-page report on recent media contracts by seven federal departments. Diane Farsetta points out that the findings were based on the self-reporting of federal departments.[59] They do not include the public-relations activities of government employees, and the products generated under such contracts (the "deliverables") are undefined. However, the report gives some indication of the amount of government spending on public relations and the sharp increases sustained over the last several years. For example, between fiscal years 2003 and 2005, the Bush administration's reported spending on private public-relations firms averaged \$78.8 million per year, a figure more than twice that of Clinton's second term (1997–2000) of \$32 million per year.[60] The partisan 2005 House Committee on Government Reform report stated that the Defense Department, Army, and Navy together spent \$10.8 million on public relations from 2001 through 2004. By contrast, the more objective GAO reported that the Pentagon alone spent \$1.1 billion in media contracts over thirty months.[61] Why was this money spent? It was needed to convince the world of the good intentions of U.S. policy. In the president's words,

> One month after the 9-11 attack President G. W. Bush asked "How do I respond when I see that in some Islamic countries there is vitriolic hatred for America? . . . I'll tell you how I respond: I'm amazed. I'm amazed that there's such misunderstanding of what our country is about that people would hate us. I am—like most Americans, I just can't believe it because I know how good we are."[62]

A more independent and informed media might have asked the president how he would feel about a government that had supported tyrants and undermined governments in this country, but, given the influence of media ownership, those able to reach the president were not inclined to do so. A tremendous effort was initiated by the Pentagon to use psychological operations, information warfare, and cutting-edge media to convince those who might otherwise not recognize the goodness of the United States.

The Rendon Group

One of the largest recipients of Pentagon contracts is the Rendon Group. Headed by John Rendon, self-described "information warrior" and "perception manager," the Rendon Group has worked for clients in seventy-eight countries, including the Colombian army, the government of Indonesia, and Monsanto Chemical Company.

Rendon's work with the U.S. government began in the 1970s as an election campaign consultant to Democratic Party politicians, including Jimmy Carter. Head of his own firm in 1989, Rendon was contracted by the CIA to campaign for the U.S.-installed government of Panama after the ousting of Manuel Noriega. Following his success there, Rendon orchestrated opposition to Saddam Hussein during the occupation of Kuwait. In broadcasts all over the world, hundreds of Kuwaitis were seen waving American flags just as U.S. troops rolled into town.[63]

Immediately thereafter, Rendon worked for the CIA to run a covert anti-Saddam campaign in Iraq, encouraging Iraqi army officers to defect. Rendon worked with the Iraqi National Congress (INC), even giving them their name. As evidenced by Pentagon documents, between 2000 and 2004, the Rendon

Group received thirty-five contracts with the Department of Defense, totaling between $50 and $100 million.[64]

In the task of creating the INC, Rendon helped the CIA install Ahmed Chalabi as head of the organization. Chalabi is reported to have received $350,000 a month, channeled from the CIA, through the Rendon Group. In December 2001, nearly ten years after the inception of the INC, al-Haideri was brought forward by the INC as an eyewitness to Saddam Hussein's possession of weapons of mass destruction (WMDs). Judith Miller, journalist for the *New York Times*, was granted worldwide exclusive print rights for an interview with the defector. In a correspondence with her bureau chief in Baghdad, Miller described how, for a decade, Chalabi had been one of her key sources on stories of WMDs. Paul Moran was the other journalist chosen to interview al-Haideri and granted worldwide broadcast rights for the story. Moran had not only worked for the INC but also the Rendon Group for many years, even before the organization of the INC.[65] Although al-Haideri failed a lie detector test, Bush administration officials brought him back to Iraq to point out the location of the weapons. Even after none were found and al-Haideri was discredited, his testimony was still cited in President Bush's State of the Union address—as evidence of Iraq's WMDs.[66] Judith Miller's articles in the *New York Times* were cited repeatedly. In May 2004 the *New York Times* ran an editorial to apologize for five articles, written between 2001 and 2003, that described accounts of biological, chemical, and nuclear weapons in Iraq. The editorial stated

> In some cases, information that was controversial then, and seems questionable now, was insufficiently qualified or allowed to stand unchallenged. . . . Looking back, we wish we had been more aggressive in reexamining the claims as new evidence emerged—or failed to emerge.[67]

The Lincoln Group

Rendon is not the only media contractor for the Pentagon. Formed in 2003 and based in Washington DC, the Lincoln Group states that their "expertise lies in providing insight to our clients in the markets they wish to reach and the ability to influence their target audience."[68]

In November 2005, the *Los Angeles Times* reported that the Lincoln Group had covertly helped the Pentagon place "dozens" of pro–United States stories, written by the U.S. military, in Iraqi news outlets. Designed to mask any connection with the U.S. military, the Lincoln Group assisted in the translation and placement of the stories, while their Iraqi staff, posing as freelance reporters or advertising executives, delivered stories to Baghdad media outlets. The effort was directed by the U.S. military's Information Operations Task Force in Baghdad, which had reportedly purchased an Iraqi newspaper and had taken control of a radio station in order to "channel pro-American messages to the Iraqi public."[69]

In response to the report, Department of Defense spokesman Bryan Whitman said "this article raises some questions as to whether or not some of the practices that are described in there are consistent with the principles of this department. . . . And that's what we're going to take a look at."[70]

Voice of America noted that although the official communications principles state information will be "timely and accurate," they "do not include any prohibition against paying to place stories in the newspapers."[71] The inspector general, the Pentagon's internal watchdog, did conduct a review of three Lincoln Group contracts. In one instance it found that a military contracting office did not maintain enough documentation to verify expenditures under the program. Hence the inspector could not determine whether the contract was awarded properly or if the payments were appropriate. The Department of Defense report shows that the Pentagon cannot account for millions paid to the Lincoln Group for their propaganda program and that basic contracting rules were not followed. Nevertheless, an unclassified summary of results of the inspector general's probe concluded "that the Multi-National Force-Iraq and Multi-National Corps-Iraq complied with applicable laws and regulations in their use of a contractor to conduct Psychological Operations and their use of newspapers as a way to disseminate information."[72]

Official Manipulation: The Office of Strategic Influence

In September of 2004 the Defense Science Board, an advisory committee to the Department of Defense, released its report, "Strategic Communication."[73] The report states that policy must be determined not by public opinion but by "interests," although opinion and the need to influence it must be considered an important factor. The report assumed as self-evident that the United States is engaged in a war of ideas with Islamic terrorists and that, despite immense amounts of money spent to disseminate our message, we had grown complacent by the past successful ways of marketing brand name products and political candidates. We were thus losing out to a tiny and more agile insurgent voice. Building an insurgent global strategic culture that borrows from the most effective private-sector marketing and political campaign techniques would be at the core of rebuilding and reinventing the way the U.S. listens, engages, and communicates with the world.

In *Weapons of Mass Deception: The Uses of Propaganda in Bush's War on Iraq*, Rampton and Stauber show us a shocking world where marketers, "information warriors," and "perception managers" can sell an entire war to consumers.[74] The principle behind the practice had been explained before in 1945. At the Nurenburg trials of Nazi war criminals Hermann Goering, a minister of information, was asked how the Nazis were able to convince so many of the German people to support the war they initiated. He replied,

> Why of course the people don't want war. . . . But after all it is the leaders of the country who determine the policy, and it is always a simple matter to drag the

> people along, whether it is a democracy, or a fascist dictatorship, or a parliament, or a communist dictatorship. . . . Voice or no voice, the people can always be brought to the bidding of the leaders. That is easy. All you have to do is to tell them they are being attacked, and denounce the pacifists for lack of patriotism and exposing the country to danger.[75]

Missing entirely from the Department of Defense report was the matter of what the opposing voices had to say. There are eloquent and well-reasoned attempts by scholars of Islamic history to explain why the U.S. government is distrusted and disliked. However, neither scholarly explanations nor the words of the adversary were taken into consideration. The name bin Laden appears in the report, but the words of the demonized adversary Osama bin Laden are dutifully concealed:

> The White House policy, which strove to open war fronts to give business to their various corporations—in armament, oil, and construction . . . also helped accomplish these astonishing achievements for Al Qaeda. It appeared to some analysts and diplomats that we and the White House play as one team to score a goal against the United States of America, even though our intentions differ.[76]

The Office of Strategic Influence (OSI) was established shortly after the September 11, 2001, terrorist attacks in response to concerns that the United States was losing public support overseas for its war on terror. The Pentagon's official announcement of the OSI declared its goal as "to provide news items, possibly even false ones, to foreign media organizations as part of a new effort to influence public sentiment and policy makers."[77] This statement led to an immediate outcry by both public and congressional leaders. Addressing the Defense Writers Group, Undersecretary of Defense for Policy Douglas Feith explained, "We're going to preserve our credibility and we're going to preserve the purity of the statements that defense officials make to the public. . . . We're also going to preserve our option to mislead the enemy about our operations. And those are not inconsistent."[78]

So locked into the assumptions of a conflict in which we, the good side, are opposed by them, the evil side, the administration could not comprehend why its massive propaganda campaign did not win friends for the United States. The image created by saturation bombing, invasion, occupation, destruction of homes, torture, depleted uranium, killing hundreds of thousands of people, and daily humiliation of civilians of all ages was visible to most Iraqis. Only within the fortified Green Zone in which U.S. officials and visitors could be protected and treated to comfort was it possible to ignore the extent of the military debacle. The inept contractors, who failed to include Iraqis in plans for rebuilding the destroyed electric power stations and health care system, added to a visible reality that could not be spun to indicate good intentions. For unlike those who have the luxury to be engaged by trivial pursuits and to accept official mythologies, the direct victims of oppressive actions are not so easily deceived.

Official Manipulation: The Office of Special Plans

Initiated by Paul Wolfowitz, deputy secretary of defense, and put into action shortly after September 11, 2001, the Office of Special Plans (OSP) produced intelligence reviews to shape public opinion and American policy toward Iraq. The members and supporters of OSP are many of the same founders of the conservative ideology expressed in the Project for a New American Century and its spin-off, Committee for the Liberation of Iraq.

Unsatisfied by the intelligence generated by the CIA and DIA (the Defense Department's intelligence agency), the OSP was created to find evidence of what Wolfowitz, Rumsfeld, and others believed (i.e., wanted everyone else to believe) to be true—that Saddam Hussein had ties to al Qaeda, and that Iraq had an arsenal of chemical, biological, and nuclear weapons.[79] With access to an enormous amount of raw intelligence from the CIA (much of which sifted through and discredited by the CIA directorate of operations), various pieces of information were picked up by the OSP.[80] Combined with intelligence from their own sources—specifically, Chalabi and the INC—the OSP synthesized intelligence to support the ideas that Saddam had chemical, biological, and nuclear weapons and links to al Qaeda.

Intelligence experts point out that most of the OSP staff was not trained in intelligence. Pushing for action against Afghanistan immediately after 9/11, with less than ten full-time staff and mountains of intelligence documents to sort through, the office hired over 100 temporary consultants. Most of these lawyers, congressional staffers, and various conservative think-tank ideologues, were off the books, thus allowing the department to hire individuals without specifying their job description.[81] As defense analyst John Pike described it, such contracts "are basically a way they could pack the room with their little friends."[82]

Intelligence experts have criticized the OSP's reliance on defectors as sources of intelligence. In 1991 Shulsky (the only OSP member trained in intelligence) coauthored a textbook about intelligence and the use of defectors. Despite their importance, he wrote, "it is difficult to be certain they are genuine. . . . The conflicting information provided by several major Soviet defectors to the United States . . . has never been completely sorted out."[83]

One defector informant, Colonel Saddam Kamel, supplied information that Bush and Cheney used to convince the public of the failure of the U.N. inspections. Kamel, along with his brother General Hussein Kamel, the man in charge of Iraq's weapons program, defected to Jordan in 1995, bringing with them detailed information about Iraq's efforts to produce nuclear weapons. Based on Kamel's testimony, Bush described the dramatic picture of thousands of liters of anthrax and stockpiles of biological weapons. Cheney stated that Kamel's testimony proved that "we often learned more as the result of defections than we learned from the inspection regime itself."[84] What is most interesting about the Kamel interview is what was left out from the OSP accounts. In the full record of Hussein Kamel's interview with U.N. inspectors, he notes that Iraq's stockpile of chemical and biological weapons—made before the first Gulf War—had been destroyed.

The International Atomic Energy Commission officially informed the United States that the claims of Saddam Hussein possessing nuclear weapons were untrue. The National Security Council described OSP evidence of Iraq's chemical, biological, and nuclear weapons program and Iraq's link to al Qaeda as "a classic case of rumit—rumor-intelligence plugged into various speeches and accepted as gospel."[85]

The Media's Failure to Examine Questions about the Events of 9/11

The harsh fact is that all of what actually took place on 9/11, or what was known by U.S. officials prior to the event, has not been made available to the public, to Congress, or to the media. A group called Scholars for 9/11 Truth has called for immediate release of the full Pentagon surveillance tape and for videotapes seized by FBI agents, minutes after the Pentagon was hit. They asked for release of the complete inventory of plane wreckage and debris from the four flights or any other aircraft that crashed or was destroyed on the day of the attack and for a catalog of photographs and videotapes taken of any items from the planes, as well as results of all tests and examinations conducted concerning any of these items. The request also mentioned 6,899 photographs and 6,977 segments of video footage held by National Institute of Standards and Technology; tape recordings of interviews by air traffic controllers, at least some of which were deliberately destroyed while in the possession of representatives of the government; a complete accounting of "terror drills" that were being conducted that morning, which may have been used to mask the attack; the cockpit voice recorders and other black boxes, three of four of which are reported to have survived the Twin Towers' collapse. Professor James Fetzer, cofounder of the scholars group, noted that the Security and Exchange Commission possesses knowledge of "put options" on American and United Airlines, which are suggestive of advanced knowledge that the attacks would take place. Secretary of Transportation Norman Mineta gave important testimony to the 9/11 Commission, which it chose not to include in its report. In addition, the Secret Service conducted itself in a manner suggesting that it knew there was no serious threat to the president, even following the attacks in New York, while the commander-in-chief ignored the unfolding drama. Fetzer notes,

> We are inclined to believe that these events were orchestrated by the Bush administration in order to instill fear in the American people. The use of violence and threats of violence to manipulate a populace based on fear is the definition of terrorism.[86]

The concerns raised, whether fully substantiated are not, are serious enough to merit investigation. The major media did not do this.

Historical Examples of Media Manipulation and the Justification for War

Media manipulation is not new. William Mandell reports of efforts supported by Columbia University and the *New York Times* revoking a Pulitzer Prize and suppressing even mention of Professor Walter Duranty. Duranty had won the O. Henry Prize for best short story of the year and had won the Pulitzer Prize for journalism more than fifteen years earlier for his coverage of the Soviet Union for the *New York Times* from 1920 to the mid-1940s. He was falsely charged with denying the starvation in the Ukraine, but his real offense was an opposition to the growing hysteria of the Cold War.[87]

The deception carried out by the media to justify an attack upon Iraq was not a new phenomenon. In 2001 Robert J. Hanyok, a historian with the National Security Agency (NSA), wrote an article for internal publication. Although it dealt with an event that occurred in 1964, the paper was classified "top secret" and released only following a freedom of information request by other historians. Hanyok's paper showed that the agency's intelligence officers "deliberately skewed" the evidence that was passed on to policy makers and the public. They falsely suggested that American destroyers had been attacked by North Vietnamese ships on August 4, 1964.[88] Following the report that an attack had occurred, President Johnson ordered air strikes on North Vietnam, and Congress passed a broad resolution authorizing military action. Ignoring the evidence that Vietnamese nationalism had been fighting against Chinese, Japanese, and French colonizers for half a century, the NSA pushed its dominos theory upon public and Congress. If the puppet governments of South Vietnam fell to the communists all of Southeast Asia would follow. With media an unquestioning partner, the purported attack began the major escalation of a war that killed more than 58,000 U.S. soldiers and 2 million Vietnamese.

Many stories dutifully carried in mainstream media lead to major consequences long before they have been found to be untrue. Sometimes the lure of capturing a new story makes journalists vulnerable to being set up. A CIA plan to overthrow the democratically elected President Arbenz in Guatemala in 1954 was preceded by a report of a Guatemalan security threat. The publisher of the *New York Times* was persuaded by a United Fruit agent to send a reporter to Guatemala who "dutifully wrote a series of alarming reports about "'Reds' in the country."[89] Starting in the 1950s and extending into the 1980s, a series of reports appeared of "missile gaps," showing calculations that supported missile superiority on the part of the Soviet Union. The reports were exposed as fraudulent, but with a time lag that permitted their use to justify large contracts for a responsive U.S. buildup.[90]

Often, media are relied upon to carry the message that it is one's own side that is offering peace while the adversary's refusal necessitates an escalation of the war. In 1965, U.S. bombing of Vietnam was greatly increased. This led to widespread protests within the United States, and the Johnson administration responded with reports that it was offering pauses in the bombing to provide opportunity for unrestricted talks with the North Vietnamese. The *New York Times* reported this with a comment that the responsibility for the war was now entirely in the hands of the Hanoi government. The ploy, dubious at the time, was later discredited with evidence that the secret offer was actually one requiring complete surrender.[91]

The media again have taken the bait with offers to talk with Iran about its security without first suspending efforts at regime change. By the start of 2007 such efforts already included a series of aggressive moves designed to achieve that outcome, including subsidizing internal dissidents within Iran, encouraging cross-border attacks from Iraq by Iranian expatriate terrorists, collecting data on Iranian targets by spy drones and on-the-ground incursions, and threatening to attack. The United States rejected a European Union effort to negotiate a deal with Iran by refusing to agree to security guarantees to Iran. Yet media replayed the Iranian refusal to accept U.S. demands to give up its nuclear facilities before talks can begin. The U.S. proposal was apparently intended to fail and to push the argument for sanctions against Iran, a path followed previously against Iraq.

The media's role in movement toward war seems clear. The suggested threat from abroad must be accepted as the real purpose of the activity. They must ignore the military provocations and transgressions from the U.S. side and must insist upon removing the target country's right to self-defense. Media must then demonize the enemy of the moment—Qaddafi, Castro, Noriega, Milosevic, Khomeini, or Hussein—and ignore U.S. violations of international treaties or U.N. resolutions. There are exceptions, but in the lead-up to war media serve less as a provider of factual information and more as the propaganda arm for officials seeking war.[92]

Strategic Media: Embedded Journalism

Coverage of the Iraq war introduced a new phenomenon of embedded reporters. U.S. General Tommy Franks called the press, once referred to as the fourth estate, the "fourth front."[93] Franks pulled together a team of media and public-relations specialists to put the fourth front into action in the field. Heading his team was public-relations professional Victoria Clarke. Clarke, who became a Pentagon official, wrote up extensive contracts with major media networks and news organizations, securing the Department of Defense's control of media. Proudly describing her work at the Pentagon to an audience at the Radio and Television Museum, Clarke stated,

> We took the same kind of planning and training and discipline that you put into military operations and put it into this aspect of the military operations. And Rumsfeld and Myers, being enlightened guys, had included people like me in the war plan from the very earliest stages.[94]

Clarke oversaw this Pentagon media program, which embedded journalists with U.S. troops in the field. Journalists remained with the same battalion throughout their assignments, thus getting to know the soldiers in a very personal way. They heard about their families and about their fears. They lived with the soldiers and were, in fact, dependent on the soldiers for their protection. The situation is antithetical to one of the standard rules of journalistic ethics, that journalists should not accept anything of value from the sources they are covering. The Pentagon developed a training course for embedded journalists at the outset of their assignments. The course was presented as survival training in which journalists were instructed about chemical warfare—enhancing the fraudulent idea that the Iraqis were engaging in chemical and biological warfare.

Strategic Media: The Pentagon's Doha Media Center

The multimillion-dollar press center at General Tommy Franks' Central Command headquarters in Doha, Qatar, constructed by a Hollywood set designer, was erected months before the U.S. invasion of Iraq. Far from the frontline, the environment of the media center was calm and comfortably air-conditioned. Here at least 700 journalists were gathered and sequestered for daily news briefings provided by the Pentagon. *New York* magazine correspondent Michael Wolff described such briefings as "a TV-ready war update spoon-fed to hundreds of journalists by the U.S. military."[95] A typical press briefing begins by viewing Pentagon-produced videos, which show, for example, the efficacy of precision bombing, or show smiling Iraqi children greeting American soldiers. Next, Pentagon officials brief journalists on such things as "terrorist"—meaning Iraqi—activity. When one reporter noted that the term *terrorist* refers to individuals who use violence against civilians and not soldiers, Franks declined to comment.[96]

Journalist and media critic Robert Young Pelton characterized the Doha media center as the fire-hose phenomenon:

> If you can give the media more content than they can handle and, as far away from the battlefield as possible, they will focus their energies where the source of that fire-hose is. So, Doha is the center of the fire-hose. And the idea is, you simply have press conferences every day, and every once in awhile you throw a little tidbit—you hand out videotapes, free coffee, whatever. So that if you leave, you're gonna miss the story that everybody else is covering. . . . Fire-hose coverage and fire-hose delivery blocks out all the secondary sources.[97]

When the war in Iraq went badly, the administration began to offer less information to reporters, and the media helped remove attention from the tragedies of the Iraq war.[98]

Media Complicity: Spinning the War on Terror

In March 2003 then chairman of the FCC Michael Powell (son of Colin Powell) assessed the media's coverage of the U.S. invasion and occupation of Iraq. He described how it was "thrilling to see the power of the media."[99] Media analysts, however, recognize the Iraq war as the lowest point in American journalism. In their book *Tragedy and Farce: How the American Media Sell Wars, Spin Elections, and Destroy Democracy*, Nichols and McChesney describe how the decline of quality in journalism is not related to inept or corrupt journalists, but rather is due to the massive corporate ownership of the media. As noted earlier, under corporate ownership, the media become a product and the audience becomes a consumer: What is newsworthy is what will increase market share or reflect favorably on objectives that favor corporate advertisers. But how do corporate values and political agendas affect the practice of journalism?

One way such values and agendas affect journalism is through selection of content. In 2003 the Council for Excellence in Government published a study that found over the preceding twenty years, coverage of the federal government dropped by 31 percent on television news shows, 12 percent in national newspapers, and 39 percent in regional newspapers.[100] The amount of international coverage in U.S. newspapers and on TV news devoted to foreign affairs dropped by 70 to 80 percent in the 1980s and 1990s.[101] Based on news coverage in 2005, Michael Jackson's trial, Martha Stewart's conviction terms, and Natalie Holloway's disappearance appeared more interesting to the American public than the coverage of United States engaging in torture. This is not because of an overwhelming demand for this type of news; as Nichols and McChesney explain, this kind of journalism is supply driven. Covering the mishaps and romantic escapades of celebrities is more conducive to the consumer environment. It is also much less expensive for media companies to produce. It is entertaining, politically insignificant, and offers the "illusion of controversy."[102]

Meanwhile, issues that may actually have a major impact on the public or may inform public opinion slip by uncovered and unnoticed. The Downing Street Memo, minutes of a July 2002 British security meeting, described how Bush wanted to forcibly remove Saddam and was fixing intelligence and facts in order to justify doing so. The memo barely made it into U.S. print. Mainstream U.S. media kept quiet on the leaked document, which first appeared in the London *Sunday Times* on May 1, 2005. But the *Times* article circulated widely on the Internet, with bloggers wondering why the article was not being covered in U.S. media. At the first Bush press conference after the memo was leaked, not one of the nearly twenty reporters called upon asked Bush to respond to the memo.[103]

After mounting pressure from various media watchdog groups (such as FAIR), a handful of major media outlets finally reported on the memo; it didn't make the front page of a major U.S. newspaper until it was picked up by the *Chicago Tribune* on May 17, more than two weeks after the story broke. In an article about the British electoral campaign on May 20, the *New York Times* finally commented on the memo in a one-column story that did not mention manipulation of intelligence until the eighth paragraph. In response to a deluge of letters and emails, the *New York Times'* editor explained how his Washington bureau chief had characterized the memo simply as the interpretation of British intelligence and not proof that Bush and his administration were distorting intelligence to support their push for war.[104]

A *Washington Post* article by Dana Milbank (which ran on page 18) referred to media activists calling for attention to the story as "wing nuts"; *Los Angeles Times* editorial page editor Michael Kinsley characterized activists as "paranoid." In most U.S. articles, discussion of the content of the Downing Street Memo was downplayed as proving what was already known to be true—contributing to ample, already established evidence—or by dismissing it completely as old news. FAIR reporters Hollar and Hart describe how such arguments are revealing:

> By acknowledging the "ample evidence" that indicates a secret, publicly denied Bush administration decision to invade Iraq, but then dismissing it as old news, journalists manage to avoid saying that the Bush administration lied to the American public—something they are exceedingly reluctant to do.[105]

Eliminating Journalists

The images from the siege on Fallujah came almost exclusively from reporters embedded with U.S. troops. This is because Arab journalists who had covered April's siege from the civilian perspective had effectively been eliminated. Al-Jazeera had no cameras on the ground because it has been banned from reporting in Iraq indefinitely. Al-Arabiya did have an unembedded reporter, Abdel Kader Al-Saadi, in Fallujah, but U.S. forces arrested him and held him for the length of the siege. Al-Saadi's detention has been condemned by Reporters Without Borders and the International Federation of Journalists.

This was not the first time journalists in Iraq faced intimidation. When U.S. forces invaded Baghdad in April 2003, central command urged all unembedded journalists to leave the city. Some insisted on staying, and at least three paid with their lives. On April 8, a U.S. aircraft bombed Al-Jazeera's Baghdad offices, killing reporter Tareq Ayyoub. Al-Jazeera has documentation proving it gave the coordinates of its location to U.S. forces. On the same day, a U.S. tank fired on the Palestine hotel, killing José Couso of the Spanish network Telecinco and Taras Protsiuk of Reuters. Three U.S. soldiers faced a criminal lawsuit from Couso's family, which alleged that U.S. forces were well aware that journalists were in the Palestine hotel and that they committed a war crime.[106]

A major document completely dismissed by major U. S. news media was the results of a scientific study published by the *Lancet*, the journal of the British Medical Society. This study investigated the number and causes of civilian Iraqi deaths as a result of the invasion of Iraq. Conducting door-to-door surveys in thirty-three Iraqi neighborhoods (amounting to 8,000 interviews), researchers found that, compared with the preinvasion period, Iraqi civilian deaths increased by 95 percent as a result of the U.S. and U.K. invasion. By conservative estimates, they believe that 100,000 Iraqi civilians had died since March 2003.[107] The findings showed the humanitarian cost to be extraordinary. Violence accounted for most of the deaths, and most violent deaths were related to air strikes. More than half of the deaths caused by the occupying forces were of women and children. The point here deals with how facts were treated.

In the United States, major media news ignored or buried the story, while the article made headlines around Europe. Many U.S. news articles took a dismissive tone, casting doubt on the quality of research, despite the fact that previous mortality statistics of conflicts published by Les Roberts, of Johns Hopkins University, have been utilized by the U.S. State Department and the United Nations.[108]

Attempting to discredit the study, the *Washington Post* printed an article that quoted Human Rights Watch senior military analyst Marc E. Garlasco as saying, "these numbers seem to be inflated." In a subsequent interview, however, Garlasco stated that at the time of the *Post* interview, he had not even read the report, and had told the journalist he was therefore unqualified to comment on it.[109] David R. Meddings, a medical officer with the Department of Injuries and Violence Prevention at the World Health Organization, points out why the study was so important: "If you can put accurate information out [on civilian casualties], it shifts the burden of proof onto militaries to substantiate why what they're doing is worth this humanitarian cost."[110]

A subsequent study by a team of epidemiologists revealed a far greater number of civilian casualties resulting from the invasion of Iraq. The study, also published in the *Lancet*, was conducted between May and July 2006. It made use of a national cross-sectional cluster sample survey of mortality in Iraq. Information on deaths was obtained from forty households in each of fifty different randomly selected areas. By comparing deaths since the invasion with the forty-month period preceding it, the study estimated that, as of July 2006, there had been 654,965 excess Iraqi deaths as a consequence of the war, corresponding to 25 percent of the population in the study area. Of postinvasion deaths, 601,027 were due to violence, the most common cause being gunfire.[111] This study also received little attention.

General Tommy Franks is widely quoted in media as saying, "We don't do body counts." The Geneva Conventions have clear guidance about the responsibilities of occupying armies to the civilian population they control. In particular, Convention IV, Article 27 states that protected persons "shall be at all times humanely treated, and shall be protected especially against acts of violence." It is difficult to understand how a military force could monitor the extent to which civilians are protected against violence without systematically counting those killed or, at least, looking at the kinds of casualties they induced. Civility and enlightened self-interest demand a reevaluation of the consequences of weaponry used by coalition forces in populated areas.[112] War is savage. The Geneva Conventions limits its scope. Media neglect permits violations.

Spinning the Story

Another way corporate values and political agendas affect the practice of journalism is by "spinning" the story, wherein the facts and dynamics in the story are twisted—even fabricated—to lead to a specific interpretation. The Jessica Lynch story illustrates spin by Pentagon media specialists. Two weeks into the war, after coverage of the war had taken a less enthusiastic turn—including Al-Jazeera's footage of dead American soldiers—the media found the story it needed. Private Jessica Lynch, a blond nineteen-year-old from West Virginia, had been captured in an Iraqi ambush and taken to Saddam Hospital in Nasiriya. From central command's Doha media center, reporters learned that in a daring middle-of-the-night operation, U.S. Army Special Forces had rescued Jessica from the Nasiriya hospital. As *Time* magazine described, the story "buoyed a nation wondering what had happened to the short, neat liberation of Iraq."[113]

In the days following her rescue, different versions of the story began to circulate regarding how she was captured and what happened during her capture. A front-page story in the *Washington Post* cited unnamed U.S. officials that described Lynch with gunshot and stab wounds. The official was quoted as saying, "She was fighting to the death . . . She did not want to be taken alive."[114] Many similar reports focused on the fierce battle Lynch was engaged in with Iraqi soldiers; some claiming that she had been abused or denied basic care by the Iraqis that tended to her. Other reports described an Iraqi lawyer who risked his life to tell U.S. troops where Lynch was after witnessing her being interrogated and slapped in the Nasiriya hospital.

An eyewitness account published in the *London Times* reported a very different story. Lynch's rescue by U.S. special forces "was not the heroic Hollywood story told by the U.S. military, but a staged operation that terrified patients and victimized the doctors who had struggled to save her life."[115] Doctors told the British reporters that the Americans had met no resistance, as Iraqi forces had left the city the day before the operation and Lynch herself denied any mistreatment.

Spin was clear in the presentation of who to blame in the Abu Ghraib prison scandal. As evidence of the abuse of Iraqi prisoners at Abu Ghraib was revealed, the U.S. government—including Defense Secretary Rumsfeld and President Bush—repeatedly attributed the blame to "a few bad apples," an isolated case of a few rogue soldiers not following the chain of command. As the graphic photographs depicting physical and sexual abuse and humiliation circulated around the globe, causing a worldwide public uproar, politically conservative media hammered the notion of "a few bad apples" into the minds of their audiences. At Fox News, right-wing political pundits (under contract to deliver opinions prepared for them) echoed this idea with little discussion. Even more extreme was the commentary by right-wing radio host Rush Limbaugh, with weekly broadcasts to 20 million listeners, who trivialized the actions of the abusers as "blowing off steam."

> This is no different than what happens at the Skull and Bones initiation. . . . And we're going to ruin people's lives over it and we're going to hamper our military effort, and then we are going to really hammer them because they had a good time. . . . I'm talking about people having a good time. These people, you ever heard of emotional release? You heard of the need to blow off some steam?[116]

In their characterization of "a few bad apples," or just "blowing off steam," such media interpretations and reiterations show a disrespect of humanity but also demonstrate a flagrant disregard for journalistic integrity. In this case, proper investigation into prisoner abuse would have lead to the acknowledgment of the widespread, systematic, and orchestrated covert program of prisoner abuse put into action by the Bush administration in its war on terror.

Such an investigation was conducted by Pulitzer-Prize winning journalist Seymour Hersh, in a series of reports on Abu Ghraib for the *New Yorker*. Unlike Bush and Rumsfeld's dismissal of accounts of abuse as the responsibility of a few young soldiers, the fifty-three-page report by Major General Antonio Taguba, obtained by the *New Yorker*, revealed "the collective wrongdoing and failure of Army leadership at the highest levels."[117] From Taguba's comprehensive study as well as accounts from intelligence and Pentagon officials, Hersh uncovers the real story behind Abu Ghraib, which began just weeks after 9/11 with the Pentagon's formation of a covert, special-action program designed to generate intelligence on al Qaeda. Known inside the intelligence community by such code words as Copper Green, the operation encouraged physical coercion and sexual humiliation of Iraqi prisoners.[118] Working under these explicit guidelines, the interrogators at Abu Ghraib—consisting of civilian-clad military intelligence officers as well as "interrogation specialists" from private defense contractors—used military dogs to frighten and attack detainees, forced them to perform humiliating sexual acts, beat and sodomized detainees, and poured phosphoric chemicals onto their skin.[119]

Taguba's report of Abu Ghraib shows how army regulations and the agreements of Geneva Convention were routinely violated, and how the day-to-day management of prisoners was put into the hands of Army military intelligence and civilian contract employees.

Furthermore, the majority of detainees at Abu Ghraib—amounting to several thousand people, including women and teens—were civilians who had been picked up in military sweeps and at highway checkpoints.[120] Like the prisoners at Guantanamo, many remained in custody month after month, without the right to appeal or have their cases reviewed. In its February 2004 report to Coalition forces, the International Committee of the Red Cross (ICRC) reported that military intelligence officers told the ICRC that 70 to 90 percent of those in custody in Iraq the previous year had been arrested by mistake.[121]

Human Rights Watch describes Abu Ghraib as "Guantanamo meets Afghanistan." Outlining the Bush administration's policy to evade international law, Human Rights Watch points to Rumfeld's description of the first detainees to arrive at Guantanamo on January 11, 2002, as "unlawful combatants," thus precluding them from protection as prisoners of war under the Geneva Convention. Also during this time, the Justice Department, as made evident in a series of legal memoranda, was supporting the circumvention of international law by arguing that the Geneva Convention did not apply to detainees from Afghanistan war.[122] In a memo to President Bush, Attorney General Alberto

Gonzales endorsed the Justice Department's (and Rumsfeld's) interpretation and encouraged the president to declare the Taliban and al Qaeda as outside the coverage of the Geneva Convention, thereby adding flexibility in the U.S. war against terrorism.[123]

After the first reports of stress-and-duress tactics against detainees began to circulate in late 2002, Human Rights Watch asked President Bush to investigate and condemn the allegations of torture and inhumane treatment. In response, Department of Defense General Counsel William Haynes stated, "United States policy condemns torture," but failed to acknowledge the legal obligation to refrain from cruel, inhumane, and degrading treatment.[124] Haynes later appointed a working group, headed by Air Force General Counsel Mary Walker, which included senior civilian and uniformed lawyers from each military branch and which consulted the Justice Department, the Joint Chiefs of Staff, the DIA, and other intelligence agencies. In a classified memo, the lawyers argued that the president was not bound by the laws banning torture—that the president had the authority as commander-in-chief of the armed forces to approve almost any physical or psychological actions during interrogation, including torture, in order to obtain "intelligence vital to the protection of untold thousands of American citizens."[125]

Journalism Matters: The Effect of Propaganda

A research study by the Program on International Policy Attitudes (PIPA) illustrates the influence of false information presented by news sources on public perception. The study, which examined the results of seven nationwide polls, conducted between January and September 2003, found that (1) misperceptions held about Iraq were related to support of the war, and that (2) the variance of misperception corresponded with news source.[126]

In-depth analysis revealed that 48 percent incorrectly believed that evidence of links between Iraq and al Qaeda had been demonstrated; 22 percent believed that WMDs had been found in Iraq; and 25 percent believed that world public opinion supported the U.S. invasion of Iraq.[127] Such misperceptions were to be found "highly related" to support for the war: Of respondents who held none of the three misconceptions, only 23 percent supported the war; but of those respondents who believed all three misperceptions, 86 percent were in favor of war.

Furthermore, the study found that the frequency of Americans' misperceptions varied widely according to their source of news. Respondents who watched Fox News held the most misperceptions, with 80 percent of viewers holding one or more misperceptions, followed by CBS, with 70 percent of viewers holding one or more misperceptions. ABC and NBC tied with 55 percent of viewers holding one or more of the three misperceptions. Respondents who follow print sources for their news held slightly fewer misperceptions, with 47 percent having one or more misconceptions. Of the NPR/PBS news audience, 23 percent held one or more misconceptions. Variations in misperceptions are not a result of demographics; the same variations were found when comparing within demographic subgroups of each audience.[128]

Authors of the PIPA study concluded the following:

> While it would seem that misperceptions are derived from a failure to pay attention to the news, in fact, overall, those who pay greater attention to the news are no less likely to have misperceptions. Among those who primarily watch Fox, those who pay more attention are more likely to have misperceptions. Only those who mostly get their news from print media have fewer misperceptions as they pay more attention.[129]

In other evidence of the effect of disinformation, a September 2003 *Washington Post* poll found that 69 percent of Americans thought it was at least "somewhat likely" that Saddam Hussein was personally involved in 9/11.[130] According to a CBS News poll in November of 2003, 46 percent of correspondents said that the war in Iraq is a major part of the "war on terrorism," while 14 percent called it a minor part, and 35 percent saw them as two separate matters.[131] Because the events are distant and their effect upon the viewer is not an immediate one, it is only necessary to create the illusion that the facts are complex, that the experts are divided, in order to sow a latent public belief in something that is not true. This was done on the harmful effects of tobacco, the inadequacy of government response to hurricane Katrina, and the dangers of global warming.[132]

News on the Home Front: Domestic and Environmental Issues

It has been said that when the guns boom the truth dies. War provides an optimal climate for disinformation. But the major media also contribute to a bias in what passes for news on a number of issues that deal with corporate power, distribution of resources, and the promulgation of scapegoats. Many of these are, at least in part, domestic issues. The reporting of the inadequate response to effects of hurricane Katrina shows media involvement in the search for scapegoats.

On August 29, 2005, Katrina, the sixth strongest hurricane ever recorded, hit the Gulf coast of the United States, leaving its mark over 100 miles from the center of the storm and causing $75 billion in damages. New Orleans incurred the most dramatic damage: 80 percent of the city was flooded due to the inadequate levee system; nearly 2,000 people were killed directly by the storm. The slow pace of official response left many reporters to see for themselves the information that they might otherwise have gotten in filtered releases from official sources. Many Americans were reportedly shocked by the abject poverty of the city's mostly black residents. Relief from government agencies such as the Federal Emergency Management Agency (FEMA) was poorly executed and coordinated; basic supplies did not reach those who needed them for, in some cases, several days.

Some questions and criticisms of government relief efforts were initially raised by the mainstream corporate media. But what soon became evident in corporate media's coverage of the aftermath of the hurricane was a shift in blame to the victims themselves. For example, *New York Times* columnist David Brooks reasoned, "Most of the ambitious and organized people abandoned the inner-city areas of New Orleans long ago."[133] In the Ft. Lauderdale *Sun-Sentinel*, Fox New pundit Bill O'Reilly had these words of advice for those "suffering" in New Orleans:

> Connect the dots and wise up. Educate yourself, work hard and be honest. . . . If you don't . . . the odds are that you will be desperately standing on a symbolic rooftop someday yourself. And trust me, help will not be quick in coming.[134]

O'Reilly followed up these comments with the notion that outside assistance should not be offered: "The white American taxpayers are saying, 'How much more do we have to give here?'"[135]

Most racial stereotypes involved wild descriptions of New Orleans as a city under siege of looters, murderers, and rapists. Although later investigations showed that there was no more violence after Katrina than in any typical week in New Orleans, media focused attention on the violence that was, apparently, hampering relief efforts. Wolf Blitzer on CNN had this report:

> People with guns are opening fire, including on ambulances leaving hospitals. . . . There are many, many people who are stranded, they can't get out of their homes, they can't walk anyplace, A, because it's too flooded; B, because it's disease-ridden, many of those waters; and C, because it's getting very ugly and violent in many parts of New Orleans.[136]

In his report for the *Cincinnati Post*, Allen Breed described a similar scene, where "naked babies wail for food as men get drunk on stolen liquor" and a crowd whose "almost feral intensity" prevented delivery of water to victims by helicopter.[137] The *Washington Post* equated looting with the damage from the flood itself: "the city grew more desperate as thousands fled on foot, hundreds of residents clambered onto rooftops to escape floodwaters, and looters plundered abandoned stores for food, liquor, and guns."[138]

Later reports revealed that follow-up reporting had discredited the most extreme reports of pedophilic rape, murder at the Superdome, and gang members wreaking havoc on the city.[139] A Knight Ridder report put to rest the unverified reports of snipers shooting at ambulances and other emergency vehicles, reporting that "more than a month later, representatives from the Air Force, Coast Guard, Department of Homeland Security and Louisiana Air National Guard say they have yet to confirm a single incident of gunfire at helicopters."[140]

The media's portrayal of victims, after several days without clean water, food, dry clothes or shoes, was frequently associated with the color of their skin. Blacks who desperately attempted to procure food, water, and clothing were portrayed as "looters," while whites were "finding" provisions.[141] Most portrayals of blacks described them as selfish at best, if not antisocial and criminal; whites on the other hand, were represented as grateful, generous, and enterprising. Kris Axtman in the *Christian Science Monitor* described the white communities of suburban New Orleans as having "no shortage of enthusiasm and heart," in spite of the example of one such community showing their compassion by sending those trying to flee the city away by bus and even firing warning shots.[142]

One of the major myths of global capitalism is that discipline and hard work pay off in wealth and security for anyone. People buy this myth when the poor are hidden from view and when their poverty can be blamed upon low intelligence, low motivation, poor education, or flaws in character. The evidence against this theory is extensive. Yet the corporate media help to perpetuate this as a major tenet of modern society. The myth conceals a more flagrant cause of poverty, the ability of wealthy corporations to polarize the distribution of income in the global economy.

Hiding Scientific Warnings of Danger

Media play a role in the exposure of scientific findings to the public. Some scientific findings have critical importance for our lives. We can respond to them only if they are well covered. The case of global warming is an important one. Truth is not always easy to assess. Certain orders of monks have committed themselves to a lifetime of mental discipline to remove the vestiges of self-interest from their inquiries into the meaning of life. In contemporary society we rely on science to provide objective tests of certain ideas. Because these ideas have great potential to affect our lives, people need access to what scientists have found without concern for whether the findings might offend people in power. The Union of Concerned Scientists conducted a survey of 460 scientists from the National Oceanic and Atmospheric Administration (NOAA) that gave evidence of political pressure on scientists. Among the findings, 53 percent of the scientists who responded said they knew of cases in which "commercial interests have inappropriately induced the reversal or withdrawal of scientific conclusions or decisions through political intervention." And 58 percent knew of cases in which "high-level U.S. Department of Commerce administrators and appointees have inappropriately altered NOAA Fisheries' determinations."[143] Such findings were similar to those of an earlier survey of 1,400 biologists with the U.S. Fish and Wildlife Service.

In 2002 the Environmental Protection Agency removed a part on global warming from an annual report on pollution, after the White House had heavily edited the section. This fits a pattern of censorship. In March, Rick S. Piltz resigned his position as a senior associate at the U.S. Climate Change Science Program, citing pervasive politicization of science by the Bush administration. He sent a fourteen-page memo to officials who deal with climate change at ten government agencies in which he detailed how the White House was interfering with the scientific mission of the program. Piltz included a flagrant example of a national assessment study on potential effects of climate change, produced by more than 100 expert scientists, that was deleted before it could reach either Congress or the public. He wrote:

> I believe the overarching problem is that the administration . . . does not want and has acted to impede forthright communication of the state of climate science and its implications for society. . . . [The administration had] . . . decided early on to essentially send the National Assessment into a black hole.[144]

New York Times reporter Andrew C. Revkin documented the charge by Piltz. The documents Revkin found showed that a White House official edited climate science reports to discount the human impact on warming. Philip A. Cooney, then chief of the White House Council on Environmental Quality, and a former official with the American Petroleum Institute, made dozens of changes. For example, in a 2002 draft of a summary of government climate-change research called "Our Changing Planet," Cooney struck out a paragraph on shrinking glaciers and snow pack. In margin notes, he claimed the paragraph was "straying from research strategy into speculative findings/musings."[145]

In June 2005 Michael Mann, director of Pennsylvania State University Earth System Science Center, one of the leading researchers on global warming, and two of his research colleagues received letters from representative Joe Barton (R-TX), chair of the House Energy and Commerce committee. The letter demanded computer data and funding sources for Mann's work. The congressional investigation was to focus upon the famous "hockey stick" graph that shows the twentieth century to be the warmest in 1,000 years. The probe was intended to investigate "methodological flaws" in Mann's work that were alleged by two nonscientists in the *Wall Street Journal.* The action by Barton was considered by several colleagues in his own Republican Party to be an intimidation of scientists who publish scientific findings that are distasteful politically. Such intimidation threatens the relationship between science and public. Good scientists welcome responsible criticism of the validity of their findings. But government interference in their work on behalf of corporate clients can remove the value of objective information. Barton had received nearly $200,000 in campaign contributions from oil and gas companies in his most recent run for office.[146] On Democracy Now!, January 8, 2007, Amy Goodman interviewed a director of the environmental group Greenpeace. They had been audited after they and two other groups filed a lawsuit on the withholding of information on global warming. The audit of Greenpeace records found nothing. The audit was paid for by Exxon-Mobil, raising suspicions of a lapse between the lines of government and business in efforts to retaliate against those who opt for a free flow of information.

In living systems, from the one-celled organism to the nation state, we understand that as conditions change survival depends upon a capacity to adapt. Systems that continue to go in a certain direction without the ability to use corrective feedback are highly vulnerable. Democracy is, ideally, an experiment in which some large social systems obtain feedback from their citizens on how their policies are addressing the needs of these citizens, thus permitting changes in direction. Similarly, science is a way in which understanding of how things are related can be put to a test of their validity. In a complex world such knowledge can be essential in decisions about the benefits and the risks of different technologies and of different choices of behavior. Science tells us the probable outcomes of certain choices. It does not tell us what questions to study or what studies to fund. It does not tell us to use the knowledge to promote life or to destroy it. It does not tell people what to do with vexing problems about their health or about environmental issues such as global warming. Nor does science provide ultimate answers, but only the best, necessarily imperfect, information available. Policy makers can consider this before making their decisions.

Elected officials who wish either to protect the energy industry from regulations to control emissions or to reduce oil dependence have the right to favor the free market over regulatory controls. On issues of policy the final call is with officials who have been elected. The biases reflected in judgments of elected officials that do not coincide with the needs of their constituents often reflect the inordinate strength of ties between these government officials and wealthy donors such as oil companies. But interference with the findings removes the ability of people to make informed choices and damages the capacity of the society to correct its course.

Stressing particular findings to suit one's own interests is a common problem in the fair use of scientific knowledge, and abusing science for political ends did not start with the G. W. Bush administration. The G.W. Bush White House and some of its supporters in Congress have, however, gone beyond their legitimate policy-making roles to interfere with the free exercise of scientific inquiry. They have censored scientific information and the scientists themselves for political reasons. Citizens whose taxes funded research have every right to hear what it has yielded. Then they can use an accurate picture of what science has found to help make up their minds. Media manipulation and censorship are marks of an elite that does not trust ordinary people to hear information that might prove inconvenient or embarrassing. For them, the ubiquity of poverty, the dangers of global warming, and the costs of war require a great deal of disinformation. Media that do not challenge the excesses of power are a necessary part of a violent world.

The degree of danger from any government that considers itself beyond the need to answer to other voices was seen in 2002 when *Wall Street Journal* reporter Ron Suskind met with the White House to discuss a recent story he had written that was critical of the administration. What a senior White

House aide told Suskind captures the essence of a frightening propaganda machine:

> The aide said that guys like me were "in what we call the reality-based community," which he defined as people who "believe that solutions emerge from your judicious study of discernible reality." I nodded and murmured something about enlightenment principles and empiricism. He cut me off. "That's not the way the world really works anymore," he continued. "We're an empire now, and when we act, we create our own reality. And while you're studying that reality—judiciously, as you will—we'll act again, creating other new realities, which you can study too, and that's how things will sort out. We're history's actors . . . and you, all of you, will be left to just study what we do."[147]

Such beliefs reflect an arrogant denial of our human and community capacities to learn. Psychologists would refer to such beliefs as delusional megalomania. To have people who think that way in positions with the power to determine what information others will receive is dangerous. To lack access to information because of corporate-dominated and centralized media is to permit such danger.

Chapter 8

Values and Habits That Maintain a Violent System

Countering prior physicalist views, the new principles of causality affirm that subjective human values are today the most strategically powerful driving force governing the course of events in the civilized world—and the key to our global predicament and its solution.

—*Roger Sperry, Nobel Prize winner in Physiology of Medicine*

We must rapidly begin the shift from a thing-oriented society to a person-oriented society. When machines and computers, profit motives and property rights, are considered more important than people, the giant triplets of racism, extreme materialism, and militarism are incapable of being conquered.

—*Martin Luther King, Jr.*

The thesis posed so far in this book is that military and economic violence in the global era is a reflection of the increasing concentration of wealth and power among a few dominant players and the exclusion of others.[1] These powerful players live in a world of selective information that reduces legitimacy from any who would contest their power. This final chapter examines the widely held beliefs among ordinary people that help to preserve the powerful elite and its increasing threat to freedom.

When a U.S. president or a secretary of state visits a university campus or public forum, major security precautions are taken. The sites are carefully screened not only for physical safety but from the wrath of people who have objections to government policy. Their official route is often barricaded to deny access to any protesters. When they hold a news conference, they speak to journalists whose jobs are dependent upon their words and who they know on a first-name basis. When they visit another country, they meet selected leaders with protesters often removed from the areas. When they mention another country by name, they are referring to its ruling policy makers and not its people. Hence, they may speak of allies for their policies even among countries where most of the people would be deeply opposed to those same policies. Whether that country is mired in poverty, destroyed by an earthquake, or torn by war, the officials are accommodated lavishly in highly protected Green Zones. Their hosts are typically important figures in a global network of corporate and military elites. The host governments' sources of information and their sources of money derive from their close contacts with a centralized elite group.

The network of dominating corporate interests has become a smaller group of more tightly interlocked mega-corporations and grown more distant from ordinary people. They nurture their connections with governments that set the rules by which they compete, with the militaries that enforce such rules, and with the media who help to make their activities appear inevitable and even laudable. Their normal activities permit people to struggle for small gains but also perpetuate the violence of war and of poverty. We can construct from what has been described so far, a theory of what perpetuates a world of recurring violence.

An elite group of military and corporate officials have sufficient power to act without fear of any countervailing power.[2] A global economy pushes natural and human resources and the flow of capital away from local communities and toward multinational conglomerates.[3] People displaced from prior sources of livelihood experience destitution and humiliation and sometimes fight back with either violent or nonviolent activities.[4] Powerful strategists, serving the elite, are organized to respond to these challenges with propaganda and military action.[5] Enemies are created by the government with the help of the mainstream media.[6] Suppression of enemies by force or disenfranchisement leads to a cycle of violence.[7] Still missing from this theory is a description of what beliefs and institutions condone the activities just described. Why do the beliefs of many support the interests of a few?

Selling the Image of Being for the People

However powerful the central institutions may be, they are obliged to retain a measure of support from ordinary people that is sufficient to keep them in power. To retain such support, they strive to control the media and to minimize a vast gap between the aims of their own networks and the concerns of ordinary people. They, with the help of public-relations experts, often project an image of opposition to powerful interests and deep concern for the unrealized hopes of ordinary people, who know them only by their media images. Corporations are able to polish their image with well-publicized efforts to combat poverty, fight disease, and support the arts. Noble and useful as these activities may be, the efforts serve also a diversionary purpose. Take, for example, the sponsorship of Breast Cancer Awareness week designed to encourage mammograms and early detection. The actions advocated do not include advocacy of controls on the cancer-causing residues in toxic industrial wastes or in chemical pesticides. The sponsors gain publicity for their public concern with women's health. One sponsor has been General Electric, which makes the mammography equipment. Another has been AstraZeneca, the pharmaceutical company that makes Tomoxafin, which is the widely used treatment for breast cancer. The sponsors benefit by substantial tax reductions for their charitable giving. The Bill and Melinda Gates Foundation has given generously to the global treatment of AIDS and to its prevention. Approximately 5 percent of corporate profits support the foundation, enough to reduce income taxes of the donors to zero. The other 95 percent is judiciously invested in corporations selected for their return on investment. Some of these are companies whose activities create massive poverty in third-world countries. Some are in the pharmaceutical companies that have blocked cheap access to their AIDS treatment drugs.[8] But the net effect of polishing the corporate image is to convince people that large corporations are ordinary good citizens rather than the amoral growth machines that they have become. Always they are aided by well-paid experts.

As Macy and Brown[9] point out, the power elite, who benefit most from the global economy, also benefit by encouraging us to rely on "experts." Experts are sought from two sources, both well able to fund their work. First are experts who see no detrimental relationship between products of the industrial growth society—such as smoke, climate change, radiation, pesticides, and impacts to human health and the environment. Second are experts who study responses to the tragedy of these occurrences. Least well funded, and therefore less well heard, are a third group who question why such distressing affronts occur so consistently. Because we may be unable to explain our feelings of distress, it is easier to let our subconscious repress them, while letting ourselves believe the "experts." And they provide a collective endorsement of the idea that the problems are theirs to resolve and not ours.

Electoral Games

Nowhere is the distorted image that the government and corporate elite work for the interests of ordinary people more clearly marketed than in election campaigns. Electioneering has been taken from the hands of the politicians and turned over to experts—advertising people and strategists. While some such firms lean to one party, most are professionals who sell their service to whoever pays. Their personal opinions do not count; their business is to sell the product. The main goal of an advertising expert in planning a campaign is not to explain the program of the party but to attract voters. Avnery describes the process:

> Election propaganda is like a gown. It should emphasize the attractive features of its owner and hide the less attractive ones. The difference is that the advertising expert can invent limbs that do not exist and cut off limbs that do, according to the

> demands of the market. One of the major headaches of the propagandists is that their candidates may speak up [and] expose their real views, thus spoiling the show.[10]

Hence election propaganda says little about the real aims of the leaders and their parties. Much of the content of the broadcasts can be assumed to be fraudulent and irrelevant to the monetary deals that are paying for TV spots and expecting a return. A company distributing such a mendacious prospectus on the stock exchange might well be indicted.

Although the message does not reflect the true positions of the candidates, it does reflect an aspect of public opinion. These are not the opinions that people might express if given the opportunity to consider the implications of major issues that affect their lives. It is the surface public opinion as it appears to experts, who conduct daily polls and listen to test groups. The candidates have already been selected by their ability to raise money from corporate interests. The views they project are a combination of what the strategists can sell to voters and the wishes of the donors. Despite differences, the hidden promise candidates make is that they will not reshuffle the centers of wealth and power. The prosperous few will remain so, and others will remain in need.[11]

The advocacy of personal tax savings and of a raise in the minimum wage to $7.25 per hour (over two years) are hailed as signs of caring for people, while the continuing deals with corporate funders are carefully hidden by public-relations specialists. We are taught to expect the most modest gains as solutions to problems that will continue without changes in the corporation-friendly lifestyles that comfort us. Al Gore's excellent warning on global warming is followed by suggestions to use energy-efficient cars and light bulbs but not proposals to address the radical changes in lifestyle that must be part of the solution. George Monbiot, author of *Heat: How to Stop the Planet from Burning* wrote this:

> We wish our governments to pretend to act. We get the moral satisfaction of saying what we know to be right, without the discomfort of doing it. My fear is that the political parties in most rich nations have already recognized this. They know that we want tough targets, but that we also want those targets to be missed. They know that we will grumble about their failure to curb climate change, but that we will not take to the streets. They know that nobody ever rioted for austerity.[12]

The election process provides legitimacy for an underlying belief system, to be described in detail. Yet elections are grossly unfair because of their dependence upon wealthy contributors. Money is as important for determining which people and what issues are placed upon the public agenda as it is for the outcomes on particular issues.[13] The wealth represents the same interests that propel corporate globalization.[14] The institutional practices that sustain gross inequality are made legal by a legislative process unduly influenced by corporate lobbyists.[15] The centrality of corporate involvement introduces an undemocratic element in the policy process. "The power of corporate management is, in the political sense, irresponsible power and so answerable ultimately only to itself."[16] The mainstream media, described in chapter 7, serve to manufacture sufficient consent to allow this inequality and to justify the means needed to control those who do not fit into this system.[17] Among such controls we find the depiction of dissenters as violent or as insignificant, and increased imprisonment of those who fail.[18] Other controlling factors are the inducement to insatiable consumption[19] and the accelerated pace of life, involving longer working hours and less time for civic participation.[20]

The Public's Role in Protecting Centralized Power

We all play a part in the acceptance of the corporate image. Spokespersons for concentrated interests are helped in their efforts by a set of widely shared values and beliefs that extend far beyond the holders of great power. They are psychological and cultural beliefs and values to which most of us subscribe.

Most cultures define a set of preferred beliefs and practices commonly accepted as given. Some are images of the *ideal culture*, those likely to be found in the myths and folklore that are taught to children and are readily identified images of the way things ought to be. Often these beliefs are not entirely explicit. By contrast, the *real culture* is about the internalized, often latent, assumptions of what is acceptable in our actual behavior. All cultures appear to give a special value to those who are identified as participants among the collectivity of its believers and practitioners. Some languages refer to those within one's own cultural group by the same term that is used to designate humans. This prejudicial favoring of one's own group is of only academic importance in cultural settings that have no aspirations to proselytize or to subjugate their neighbors. For cultural settings that have more hegemonic aspirations, the latent assumptions may determine whether outsiders are to be converted, conquered, enslaved, or annihilated. The outlook toward outsiders is therefore essential to the understanding of aggressive societal policies. Similarly, most cultural collectivities attach high value to the ecological settings considered their own, some making little distinction between self, community, and ecological niche.[21] Others may still have a pride in a place they identify as their own and yet consider the natural world something for those within their own group or country to exploit.[22]

What are these latent beliefs that define the dominant paradigm of Western culture? Who holds them? Who benefits from them? And who ascribes to them simply as the givens of the world they know? Much has been written about the dominant paradigm, particularly as it deals with a nonsustainable or exploitative orientation to the natural world. Starting with beliefs about the self, the Western view can be culturally identified as (1) maintaining an individual-centered worldview, (2) holding a belief in control over nature, (3) viewing the self with fixed and strong boundaries, (4) believing in progress and growth, (5) believing in a dichotomy between subject and object, (6) maintaining a linear perspective on time, (7) oriented around self-interests, (8) holding a functional belief in materialism, and (9) holding a moral code oriented toward the idea of self-fulfillment.[23] These overlap with beliefs about the world beyond the self.

These central beliefs and values of modern society focus upon development and competitive success for people, corporations, and nations.[24] Such beliefs are deeply embedded in Western culture, not as a set of popular views, but as a set of assumptive propositions. These propositions are deemed to be true by elite sectors that benefit most from them and are deemed inevitable by others, mainly because of the powerful institutions that promote them. They are, by such criteria, the dominant Western worldview. The propositions encompass ownership of resources, inequality, legitimacy of power, amorality and force, and inevitability.[25]

The dominant Western worldview is a constellation of beliefs and values that include the following:

- All people have the freedom to pursue and compete for success, typically defined as the expansion of wealth.
- Private property is to be favored by law over either unowned nature or public property.
- Freedom to speak includes the unlimited right to use wealth to influence both opinion and policy.
- Problems can be met with technical solutions.[26]
- Corporations shall have the protection by law afforded to citizens.
- Corporate investors are the creators of wealth and of jobs.
- Efficacy is more important than ethical principle in the attainment and protection of wealth.
- Disparities in wealth of any magnitude are natural and acceptable.
- Poverty is to be explained by deficiencies in the poor.
- Military force is justified to protect corporate interests (often defined as national interests).
- Limited parliamentary democracy (mandating elections while allowing wealth to be used for persuasion) is the much-preferred form of government.
- The resources of the world exist for the use or exploitation by those best able to take advantage of its gifts.
- Those who do not accept these views or the policies that flow from them pose a danger and must be either trivialized or eliminated.
- Psychocultural values of power, masculine domination, acquisition, and development support a worldview with hegemonic intensity and little tolerance for alternatives.[27]
- All these beliefs and values define the path to progress. They should be, and inevitably will be, universal.[28]

The belief in the moral rightness of competitive individualism works to the advantage of those who are deemed successful. Their success is attributed to their own personal attributes and efforts; the poverty of others viewed as their own fault. The core values listed blend seamlessly into a conservative agenda with a catchy message, expressed by conservative strategist Grover Norquist, "You can spend your money better than the government can." The agenda has three basic themes. The first theme is that people rely upon individual initiative (their own or the charity of others) for health, education, financial security, and a safe environment. Hence, governments have no role in their well-being other than guarding the border, policing within the borders, and national defense. Second, people elect the government, particularly a president, with complete authority. The third theme is that free markets are the natural way to assure that needs are met.[29]

The professed left-center goals depart from the stark and harsh reality that would be imposed upon ordinary people by the conservative agenda. This alternative agenda leaves some attention to the government role as a steward of the commons. It recognizes that healthcare is not available to everyone in a free market, that commercial media do not on their own serve the public's diverse needs, and that the environment is devastated to the danger point by unrestrained corporate initiatives. This rather timid alternative voice does see a broader role for government, particularly in areas where quick profits cannot be made. Note, however, that neither the core values of the dominant pattern nor the rights of mega-corporations to continue exploiting, nor the assumption of a vast military to secure these advantages are questioned in either view.

Why Are These Core Values Supported by Ordinary People?

Such core values clearly work toward the interests of powerful elites who promote them as dogma. Why then do so many of us accept this version of reality? In fact, the promise of success and the good life as the reward for hard work has been a mythology for large numbers of people. Many poor and middle-class people are convinced of the gospel of wealth but find the American dream to be more symbol than reality.[30] Some particular discourses about the real world become all-powerful within societies. Such representations are adopted and perpetuated while others are discarded. The possibilities seem infinite, but only some attain dominance.

What appears real is in fact socially constructed. However accepted ideologies may be promoted, their success depends, in part, on the tapping of fantasies shared with other members of a society. Sharing permits people to project their fantasies and wishes into reality. The content of the beliefs, however, suggest a latent meaning. It is to be free, in the libertarian sense of having no restrictions, while at the same time believing that the marketplace of all such self-serving efforts is ordained to provide the ultimate good.

Theology professor Harvey Cox finds that the themes on the financial pages of the *Wall Street Journal* are remarkably similar to religious themes found in the book of Genesis. The god in the business pages is the Market. Because it is the ultimate right path, it can tolerate no other economic arrangements, and what suffering has occurred must be explained either as the failure of other attempts that deviated from the Market or as the bitter price that must be paid to enter the kingdom. Like other gods, the Market is assigned magical qualities of omnipotence. Cox says that omnipotence is "the capacity to define what is real . . . the power to make something out of nothing and nothing out of something." The Market is moving toward omnipotence.[31] It has the power to change all created things into commodities. In fact, a number of markets—automakers, airlines, the country of Argentina—have verged on collapse and required resuscitation by massive infusions of government dollars. But adversity, in these instances, as in any orthodox religion, is interpreted to strengthen the case. Some economists note that the largest centers of corporate activities in oil, agribusiness, transportation, chemicals, and electronic equipment are not the examples of free trade they purport to be but rather are buoyed up by extensive subsidies.[32]

What was considered sacred is now transformed into what can be sold. This can be tribal homelands, ancient forests, homes of poor people in gentrifying cities, or even shrines, churches, or graveyards. Anything can be purchased if the price is right. The human body, once considered the sacred temple of the spirit, can be sold for parts. Kidneys, bone marrow, sperm, eggs, livers, and hearts are now available as commodities for purchase. When everything, including human beings, carries a price tag, then nothing has inherent value. The Market is ever-present and moving into personal areas of life. Dating, family life, marital relations, care of older parents, once considered beyond the reach of the Market are increasingly dominated by monetary transactions. Even the innermost spiritual part of ourselves is on the shelf. Where inner peace once required a strong sense of connection to the land and to the community, it is now for sale in trips to a pristine wilderness. Ecstasy, spiritual connection, and self-realization are all advertised to be found in a weekend workshop or in a tropical resort.[33]

One distinguishing feature of the Market from major religions that have preceded it is the belief that there is never enough. Each year, $36 billion is spent to urge Americans to buy unhealthy foods high in salt, sugar, and fat. A corporate CEO who allows concerns of health or the environment ahead of short-term profits may be acting illicitly in the eyes of stockholders. Corporations must expand, people must be insatiable as consumers, and those at the bottom must grasp at the work available to them.[34] These values reward the wealthy and powerful elites. They also speak to the most important need for change. Chapter 6 discussed the framework of game theory. One of the greatest errors made by our centers of power is to play all games as if they were purely competitive contests in which one's own success and the success of the other players is not possible. The most important contests, however, call for an optimum calculation of what is good for the commons, for all parties. To beat one's competitors by permitting global warming or contaminating the environment, or to increase profits by creating desperate conditions for people who may go on to become terrorists—these are examples of playing the wrong game.

But the dominant paradigm is widely accepted, and one must ask what value these beliefs have for the rest of the people who hold them. The symbolic order may have been pressed upon people by elite opinion molders, but they were not imposed upon blank slates. Why, we must ask, have we permitted the construction of such a world? Are there psychological origins that underlie the societies that human beings have constructed?

Lakoff and Johnson developed a theory of cognition that is a reflection of deeply embedded characteristics of the person. Metaphoric meanings are not merely abstract aspects of the rich language of poets but rather a form of deep, perhaps bodily, attachment to certain beliefs and images that guide much of our thought and action. Often they reflect early familial expectations about egalitarian or authoritarian sources for determining what is right. Words like motherland, fatherland, homeland, obedience, safety, and body politic, according to this theory, cannot be detached from the organism that produces them.[35] The importance of this is that in order to effect change in the world order, we may need to change not only our conditioned beliefs about the inevitability of the existing order, but also the patterns by which we raise children so that the latent metaphors they bring to understanding the world will have more space for compassion, caring, connection, and justice. That is a part of major cultural change.

The beliefs described are part of a cultural paradigm, latently acknowledged by many and forcefully pursued by a few.[36] These beliefs make possible a model of development that is pushed by multinational corporations. It is a system of beliefs equated, in the minds of its defenders, with progress, as the description of an inevitable progression of all nations and peoples into a global economy of ever-expanding productivity. This dominant paradigm of Western thought has been contrasted to a new paradigm, more supportive of the need to preserve the environment.

Actual population surveys tend to show few adherents to the dominant paradigm,[37] but its presence as a latent force seems clear. The dominant worldview stands in some contradiction to opinion polls that have consistently and increasingly found people to favor the protection of their environment,[38] the elimination of nuclear weapons,[39] and the belief that corporations and government entities have too much power to determine policy decisions that should be in the hands of local citizens.[40]

The power of the core beliefs, however, does not reside in their popularity. Rather it resides in the assumption, widely supported in the media, that they describe a historically inevitable path while providing advantages over life in countries that live by different assumptions.[41]

The decline in real wages in the United States since the 1970s, the decline in secure union jobs with benefits, and the current reductions in funds for education, hospitals and health care, libraries, and parks—all are viewed, if viewed at all, as an inexorable and necessary consequence of the need to be competitive in a global economy. Why should unskilled workers expect a living wage when their labor can be replaced more cheaply by workers from China or India? Why should those who earn more than $6 million per year have their taxes reduced while increasing numbers of people lack funds for education or for adequate nutrition? The expectations of a better life, for those who are not wealthy, are transformed into the competitive message to work harder for the leftovers and to push ahead of some others who will remain more destitute than oneself. If being poor is a personal failure despite one's efforts, then someone must be blamed, and corporate media provide scapegoats that remove the corporate market from responsibility. The occasional leaks of corporate scandals or political bribes vanish from the media when elections turn on efforts to find scapegoats—homosexuals, immigrants, street criminals, or terrorists. As elections pass without producing deep changes in the concentration of power, the inevitability of the dominant power of an unrestrained market gets reinforced. Hence voters most in need of change withdraw from the political process.

Interests Served by the Dominant Paradigm

The value placed upon open competition affects the way people view their own worth. But departures from this value are permitted when benefits accrue to the largest corporations. If all the airlines were engaged in unrestricted competition, they would have no choice but to engage in price wars. This sort of competition occurred in the nineteenth-century railroads. Bankruptcy became commonplace until J. P. Morgan began to organize railroads into large cartels to prevent competition. According to economist Michael Perelman, no really competitive industry today is very profitable. Profits are highest in industries protected by intellectual property rights or by the influence necessary to garner government contracts.[42] Nowhere is this clearer than in the defense industries. Among the ten top contractors—General Electric, General Dynamics, United Technologies, Newport News, Northrop Grumman, and the Carlyle Group—all had most of their business through no-bid contracts. These corporations thrive on the presence of disasters such as floods, droughts, and wars. While large corporations, under colonialism, exploited the raw materials and the wealth of poor countries, the game has shifted to privatizing and pillaging of governments. The corporate domination of governments and of monetary policies assures what Naomi Klein has called the rise of disaster capitalism. They have moved the economy to a new stage in which ordinary services for health care, education, water, transportation, law enforcement, and even for the military are increasingly privatized. They create incentives for war and for turmoil, while economic incentives for a world at peace have been constricted. Record oil-company profits are only possible because oil companies escape the costs, which are passed onto taxpayers, of global warming, oil exploration, environmental destruction, and wars to guarantee the oil. In Iraq, a major task of the U.S. occupation was to hire private security to protect U.S. administrators as they handed off the oil reserves and the basic services to a group of well-connected contractors.[43]

The professed dominant values negate the reality of people in different classes with different interests. It was James Madison who observed, long before Karl Marx was born, that there exists an inevitable conflict in society between those who have property and those who do not. More than 100 years ago, historian Charles Beard wrote that the U.S. constitution represented the interests of the slaveholders, the merchants, and the bondholders, not those of working people or of slaves.[44] The idea that the CEO of Halliburton, Lockheed-Martin, or Exxon-Mobil has the same interests as the workers of their companies, or of soldiers who fight the wars that enrich them, or even of their own household servants, is a myth. It is perpetuated by the repetition of such terms as "national interest" and "national security." We are continually reminded that we are one nation that has been blessed by God.

American Greatness and Exceptionalism

Americans are taught in school that ours is a special land of equal opportunity. It is considered morally superior to all others and therefore justified in spreading our form of democracy and enterprise to all parts of the world. This moral superiority is not based on our actions as a nation. To be honest, we must face our long history of ethnic cleansing, in which millions of Native Americans were driven off their land by means of massacres and forced evacuations. We were built upon a history of slavery, segregation, and racism that is still with us. We were conquerors in the Caribbean and in the Pacific and initiators of shameful wars against small countries, for example, Vietnam, Grenada, Panama, Afghanistan, and Iraq. We used the most destructive weapons known against civilian populations in Hiroshima and Nagasaki.[45]

Neither can a sense of moral superiority be honestly based upon how well people in the United States live. The World Health Organization in 2000 ranked countries on overall health performance. The United States, although it spends more per capita for health care than any other nation, was thirty-seventh on the list. One of five children in the world's richest country is born in poverty. More than forty countries, including Cuba, have better records on infant mortality. And as a clear sign of social pathology, the United States leads the world in the number of people in prison—more than 2 million.

The September 7, 2005, United Nations Human Development Report accuses the rich countries of having "an overdeveloped military strategy and an under-developed strategy for human security." Among the report's striking findings is that when it comes to inequality, poverty, and mortality rates, the United States has little to justify a perception of success. The U.S. child poverty rate exceeds 20 percent, like Mexico. The child (under age five) mortality rate has been rising since year 2000, while the infant mortality rate is the same as Malaysia. Such facts are psychologically dissonant with the emotionally appealing myths of moral superiority. With corporate domination of the global economy, the domestic agenda in the United States suffers. One State Department official noted that it is too hard for politicians to deliver at home in health care, jobs, schools, or homelessness. It is easier to appear to be doing something in a war that no one sees directly.[46]

In *The American Dream vs. the Gospel of Wealth,* Garfinkle asks why

> The richest nation in the world has to borrow hundreds of billions of dollars to pay its bill. When its middle class citizens sit on a mountain of debt to maintain their living standards, when the nation's economy has difficulty producing secure jobs, or enough jobs of any kind, something is amiss.[47]

The historic vision of the American dream is not really of equality or even of care for all its members. Rather it is that continuing economic growth and political stability can be achieved by supporting income growth and economic security of middle-class families, without restricting the ability of successful businessmen to gain wealth. The view is now being altered by a recently ascending view that providing maximum financial rewards to the most successful is the way to maintain high economic growth. Not raised in the public dialogue is whether pursuit of unlimited wealth is something that might be replaced by assurances of security and dignity to everyone.[48]

Historian Howard Zinn helps us to explain why we are so ready to accept the mythical version of U.S. greatness.[49] We, and our major sources of information, lack historical perspective. We accept presidential decrees about foreign threats as true since we do not retain, in our cultural memory, the deceptions that have occurred in the past. President Polk, for example, lied about the reason for going to war with Mexico in 1846. He said it was because Mexico "shed American blood upon the American soil." In actuality, Polk, and the slave-owning aristocracy, coveted half of Mexico in order to create more slave states to resist the abolition movement.

In 1898 President McKinley justified invading Cuba to liberate the Cubans from Spanish rule. In fact, McKinley, whose presidency reflected the emerging corporate monopolies, wanted Spain out of Cuba so that the island could be open to United Fruit and other American corporations. McKinley also claimed that the reason for our war in the Philippines was only to "civilize" the Filipinos, although what was actually wanted was a military and corporate foothold in the Pacific, even at the cost of killing hundreds of thousands of Filipinos. President Woodrow Wilson—characterized in history books as an idealist—deceived the public about the reasons for entering World War I, calling it a war to "make the world safe for democracy." In reality it was a war to make the world safe for the Western imperial powers. President Truman lied when he said the atomic bomb was dropped on Hiroshima because it was "a military target."

Three presidents deceived the people about Vietnam: Kennedy about the extent of early U.S. involvement, Johnson about the Gulf of Tonkin incident used to convince Congress for support, and Nixon about the secret bombing of Cambodia. President Reagan deceived the public by claiming Grenada was invaded because it posed a threat to the United States and again by denying his support for the contras' attempt to overthrow the government of Nicaragua. The elder President Bush claimed that the invasion of Panama, leading to the death of thousands of ordinary citizens, was because of drug trafficking rather than as an excuse to prevent Panama from negotiating with other nations regarding work on the canal zone. It would be hard to believe that the first President Bush's concern over the autonomy of Kuwait was not a subterfuge for intentions to assert U.S. military power in the oil-rich Middle East.

Given the overwhelming record of falsehoods told to justify wars, how could anyone listening to the younger Bush believe him as he laid out the reasons for invading Iraq? However, without a memory of past presidential misrepresentation to justify war, there was little likelihood that most Americans would distrust the claims of weapons of mass destruction that were used to justify the Iraq war.[50]

In addition, Zinn observes, thought processes are constrained by an inability to think outside the boundaries of nationalism. We are penned in by the arrogant idea that this country is the center of the universe, exceptionally virtuous, admirable, and superior. In Germany in 1930s, the Nazis proclaimed the doctrine of "Deutschland uber alles." The professed Aryan superiority was reinforced by a glorification of the military in parades and by Riefenstahl's propaganda films.

Some conditions in the United States today are markedly different, but we do rejoice in the July 4th holiday with flags, food, and fireworks. We are rallied to the defense of the homeland and give "the troops" a nearly messianic status. The actual meaning of Independence Day (autonomy and the overthrow of colonial rule) is barely noted. Neither are the brilliant concepts of governments responsible to the people and people's rights as guaranteed by the Constitution. Rather it is a glorification of the state and its inherent superiority.[51] This view projected in the United States is one that makes the great diversity of the world's cultures appear irrelevant to the tasks of peace and sustainable development. That diverse cultural knowledge is vital to changes needed to preserve the species. Yet these diverse cultures are being gutted by military and economic expansion. Today, this arrogant posture is expressed by the adage, "We don't need to understand them; they need to understand us. After all, we are the world's sole superpower!" It is rooted historically in a belief in Manifest Destiny for white Americans as they displaced and decimated the native peoples of North America. Earlier in our history a congressman noted, "We must march from ocean to ocean. . . . It is the destiny of the white race."[52]

It is not so much that those who live in the heartland of Western society believe that the ways their society works are entirely preferable. Rather the dominant beliefs are sufficiently in the background as to remain typically unexamined. And for many, they are not necessarily right; they just are. But the significance of these beliefs and patterned behaviors is that they perpetuate not only a way of life but also a social structure. It is a structure that provides legitimacy for the great disparities found in access to resources deemed good and necessary for an acceptable quality of life. Surely the central beliefs of all cultures contribute to the legitimacy of their most powerful players, and the divine power of the chief is not primarily a Western concept. However, since Western institutions are establishing themselves in all corners of the world, beliefs and actions that sustain the power of these institutions are a critical pillar upholding serious domination of people and disparagement of their cultural strengths. The corporate culture that has taken hold poses dangers particularly because its amoral form invites both domination and tolerance for totalitarian states that condone violence.

Mander argues that corporate forms and the laws governing corporations determine the behavior of people who work in corporations. The large corporation is like a machine that spreads around the world. It turns people into consumers and converts natural resources into wealth. The ideology of corporations includes styles of acceptable behavior, ways of organizing people to work on a project, and values that legitimize, but also conceal, the extent of corporate power. These have come to be identified with the American way of life. Such corporate culture has sanctioned a corporate invasion of most of the world.

> *Corporate culture* has become the virtual definition of American life, to be defended at all costs, even militarily. Now that global trade agreements have removed most obstacles to corporate invasion of all the countries of the world, and with the power of U.S. media globally dominant, U.S. corporate culture will soon be ubiquitous.[53]

Why We Allow Concentrated Corporate Power

Although there have been radical changes in the operation of large corporations from the early 1900s to the present time, opposition to the corporate takeover of resources and communities has a long history that may be important in understanding how such expansion may be controlled. The opposition was not only from well-educated socialist and communitarian scholars but from ordinary citizens organizing for their rights.

Antimonopolist critique of the new industrial economy had broadly supported rural and populist beginnings. Well into the nineteenth century, corporate charters remained a privilege rather than a right. The diffusion of ownership to shareholders, and the limitations on liability they guaranteed, could only be granted to the degree they served the public interest. The large size that mass production required, however, led to intensive organizations of capital and management, and in the 1890s the Supreme Court granted legal personhood to corporations. With this ruling, expected return on investment had become a new category of property for a new type of citizen with eternal life and, therefore, no inheritance taxes.

Opposition came in the form of brutally suppressed strikes in industrial areas and in waves of agrarian revolt in the South and West. Industrial giants were widely viewed as evil economic cabals relying upon adulterated money and shady dealing. The muckraking journalists described in chapter 7 helped to call forth congressional hearings.

The capital-generating potential of the corporation ultimately proved sufficient to trump the efforts of indebted homesteaders, farm cooperatives, and unorganized workers. Yet despite the gradual loss of appeal of these protests in the press and in government, and the surge of support for corporations as a necessary evil in World War I production, the populist opposition to remote, "greedy" capitalists, who would take away their property and their communities, has remained. It remains in part because people who put in a solid day's work can no longer afford to buy a house, send their children to college, or even get sick. Under the guise of "freeing the market," conservative and corporate forces have been waging a covert war against the middle class, dismantling policies such as Social Security, Medicare, the minimum wage, and fair labor laws—the safeguards that encourage economic opportunity and citizen engagement. The result is an economic system designed to enrich the super-rich, and diminish the clout of the middle class.[54]

A look at Wal-Mart helps us to understand the shift toward a society of working, yet powerless, poor serving immensely wealthy corporations under horrendous conditions.

The Humble Origins of Wal-Mart

The period from 1914 until 1973 has been characterized as one of mass production, and consumption, of durable goods. The Ford-inspired revolution, including the regimentation of work and of time and the creation of consumer desire, ushered in an age of modernity. In that time power-sharing occurred on the part of big business, big government, and big labor. The era included social conformity through bureaucratic institutions, nuclear families, and a homogenizing nationalism, all of which were challenged by the turbulent protests of the late 1960s. The period since 1973, however, has relied increasingly on production and consumption for "niche" consumers of more disposable items. This was accompanied by a retreat from the government regulation and social safety nets that had sought to protect people in the face of cycles of boom and recession. The shift emphasized flexible labor markets and work arrangements, and a dramatic acceleration of credit and circulating capital. The changed social and cultural emphasis was upon differences. Behind this shift we find a surprising history of some progressive forces with a willingness to write off the conservative yet populist groups of small-town farmers, small businessmen, and churchgoers; to focus upon their backwardness and the prejudices of their ideologies. Progressives missed the fact that these people were resisting not only the chain stores but also the loss of community and of self-reliance they saw being inflicted upon them. Now the big-box stores have taken over.[55]

Wal-Mart is the world's largest retailer, with 1.8 million employees and a net annual income of $12.178 billion. As of January 2007 it ran, in the United States,

2,257 super centers (187,000 square feet), 112 neighborhood markets (42,000 square feet) and 579 warehouse clubs. Wal-Mart International operations include 2,700 stores in fourteen countries outside the United States. Its sales on a single day reportedly topped the gross domestic products (GDPs) of thirty-six nations. If Wal-Mart were an independent country, it would rank as China's sixth largest export market, and its economy would rank thirtieth in the world (following Saudi Arabia). Its origins in the small north Arkansas town of Bentonville seem odd, and its story helps to explain the values of the American heartland. It is a town, like many in rural America, that fought against the intrusion of chain stores in the 1930s. The anti–chain store movement was something far greater than a call for protectionism by local merchants.

The Ozarks, including northern Arkansas, were ethnically homogenous, 95 percent white as recently as 1996 and typically old-stock Anglo-Saxons with traditional Republican values of thrift, sufficiency, and hard work; many are retirees. Its recreational focus is upon hunting, fishing, and country-western music. In some parts, a diversified farm economy of small farmers produced livestock, fruit, and grain. With limited capital they could still make ends meet, and the area avoided the pattern of massive plantations of the South and the massive labor-exploiting commodity farms made possible in other areas by a flow of migrant workers, subsidies, and technology. The viability of this economy relied upon unneeded adults moving away and on the acceptability of low consumption levels. They lagged in farm machinery, electricity, phones, cars, and running water. The Ozarks were at the economic bottom of the United States in the 1930s.[56]

Earlier, in the 1870s, railroads began to penetrate the area, which permitted outside capital for clear-cutting the forest reserves that had previously supplemented diets through game hunting. Unrestrained lead mining further harmed the soil, and families on marginal farms became a source of inexpensive labor as they struggled to keep up their decreasingly viable farm identity. By the late 1940s, the small-farm independence had ended. Chemical fertilizers and herbicides, automatic tomato pickers, domination of single-crop hybrids, and mechanization all made farming so capital-intensive that only farms of vastly increased acreage could last.

There was, until fairly recently with Tyson's massive poultry farms, little foreign immigration. But the rural image, widely marketed, did attract younger retiring whites, most of whom were office workers from the Midwest drawn by the promoted image of outdoor living. Many of them later lost everything in unsuccessful efforts to plant fruit orchards. But the lure of the independent farm community was a magnetic pull when the Great Depression showed the vulnerability of depending upon bureaucratic enterprises. They sought the image of a past in which Anglo-Saxon pioneers (rather than slaves or dark-skinned immigrant laborers) made good on the land. They knew little of the history in which Columbus and Cortez had helped lay claim for Spain to all of California and the Southwest, north to Kansas and east to Georgia. These men had little appreciation for indigenous people or those swept from Eastern Europe into the melting pot. The white pioneer farmers were their image of Americans. Amidst a sinking economy in the late 1970s, only the most ideologically or traditionally committed could hang on to their failing small-scale farms. These farmers supplied many of Wal-Mart's early managers as well as hourly employees, paid at very low wages.[57]

Through the early twentieth century, the wholesome image of nature and of farms provided an antidote to the image of crowded factories and cities. The image contributed to federal funding to sustain farmers through the Homestead Act. Independent retailers in the big cities had no such glamour and gradually lost out to the larger and more efficient department stores. Small-town merchants, meanwhile, attempted to use the small farm allure to make their case against chain stores. The intrusion of catalogue stores was made successful by an extension of parcel post services in 1912, shifting costs of the business to taxpayers. Still, at the time of the stock market crash, there were more than 400 local anti-chain organizations, supported by local radio and newspapers, the Farmers' Alliance, and even by the Ku Klux Klan. The chain-store menace drew most opposition in the Midwest and South, and many pieces of legislation came close to eliminating them. Progressive forces such as the *Nation* magazine, however, came out in favor of the more efficient chain retailers to provide the modern route to consumer choice at lower costs. Two labor unions also helped to defend the chain stores. The argument had a scientific ring as an evolutionary product of natural selection, which would favor laissez-faire capitalism.[58]

The competing fundamentalist position, which went on trial in the 1925 Scopes trial, argued for a divine special status in humans and in the preservation of their independent ways. Opposition was strongest in areas that had suffered most from the expansion of northern railroads, eastern banks, and industrial monopolies that extracted wealth of the countryside in a semicolonial relationship. The Klan in Clarke County, Georgia, called the chain owners a "Little Group of Kings in Wall Street" and warned that Jewish and Catholic immigrants were using the chain to pauperize native-born white Protestants.

The fundamentalist message was tied to the image of manhood in the pioneer homesteader. Chain stores, in contrast, would be owned by distant stockholders and managed "scientifically." The factory efficiency of Taylorism (work broken down into repetitive segments) would standardize work creating a nation of clerks. Folks feared the dehumanizing northern factories that had swallowed the immigrant populations. Working for the boss would turn boys into the yes-men later characterized as "the man in the grey flannel suit." Wal-Mart came to being in the heartland of fierce antimonopoly capitalism. It had to overcome opposition to faceless and remote ownership and the threat to white rural masculinity.

Historically, rural Americans had personalized their hostility toward the corporate robber barons of the northeast. The new tycoons of the Sun Belt were able to put a human face on the boss as everyman. Northwest Arkansas produced many examples, including Ozark chicken king John Tyson, whose son and grandson dressed in the khaki uniforms of their employees. The multibillionaire captains of such industries showed off their egalitarian and modest-consumption lives. The region's trucking empires were led by poorly educated men in overalls who did not take on trophy wives or yachts but instead turned their original spouses into family business partners. Mrs. Helen Walton's family money, for example, bankrolled the original discount stores, and her degree in economics was a solid asset in the Walton's enterprises. They stressed their entrepreneurial family image. They kept family names and avoided such words as "General" or "International." Secrecy was presented as an aversion to sharing family discussions in public. By insisting that they never forgot where they came from, they humanized the image of some of the world's biggest corporate fortunes. Sam Walton was not actually a rags-to-riches story, since his grandfather and father had benefited from federal handouts for homesteading after Native Americans had been driven out. The family made their money on land speculation and foreclosing mortgages on farmers during the depression rather than on actual farming. But a millionaire with a job was itself impressive, and both major presidential candidates in 1992 honored Sam Walton at his death. His paternalistic image included a wish to bring respect to his employees by using a family tradition rather than a managerial one. Managers were male and paid more than women, who were clerks. A romanticized book (and movie) called *Where the Heart Is* highlighted the personal touch of allowing a poor pregnant woman to hide in a Wal-Mart store, where she kept track of all the goods she borrowed. Sam Walton visits her and her newborn in the hospital, forgives her debt, and promises her a job. The image of honesty and low prices was carefully cultivated. Salespeople gave away nothing in fake inducements. At the headquarters, visitors and employees could help themselves to coffee with an honor system box into which they put fifteen cents. Everything proclaimed the image of a sober, thrifty, church-going white patriarch, and his early store and pick-up truck are preserved for visitors.

In its developing years Wal-Mart courted Wall Street investors such as Warren Buffet with home-style barbeques, laid-back hunting and fishing excursions, and joyfully playing up the contrast between hillbilly Arkansas and high-tech big business. Bethany Moreton[59] argues that founder Sam Walton was completely about planned innovation, and the folksy image is essentially part of Wal-Mart's sales plan. The homey Sam Walton was an ad for Wal-Mart to local customers, and in the financial markets as well.

Part-time hourly work permitted women to adjust to children's school needs. In the early days in-store baby showers and craft fairs provided an alternative to hard work in chicken processing or on their husbands' failing farms. Despite receiving less than minimum wage, many women recalled working at Wal-Mart as a wonderful experience. Their attachment defies the business-model assumptions of economics in which every person is an isolated, profit maximizing, rights-demanding, and self-interested individual. The men who were paid more and moved around more as managers also derived nonmaterial gains. They were real men, the bosses of a host of underlings as on the family farm, and they got to organize the flood of "guy" activities, which included selling guns and fishing tackle with regular store displays of trophies. The family model helped in a critical transition to the service economy of the new capitalism. No longer did workers of successful corporations expect success in fighting to elevate their status. The maquiladoras—young women of Honduras or Guatemala—embroidering designs in sweatshops for the discount stores are, like some of the current workers of Wal-Mart, expected to work off the clock, without affordable healthcare, subjected to age and sex discrimination, and dismissed for talking about a union. Wal-Mart has hired former CIA and FBI agents to spy upon and intimidate such activities.[60]

Wal-Mart strives to protect its image with monthly expenditures in the millions to public-relations firms rather than to provide higher wages and affordable health care for its employees. Local businesses that once offered jobs and returned taxes to local communities have been forced out of existence by discount competitors. And Wal-Mart has gone beyond its country-store image and moved into financial services and high-fashion merchandise, as their high-tech management scouts the world for expansion and their political contributions oil their efforts to grow. In the 1980s Wal-Mart boasted about its commitment to American-made products. In 2007 they were getting most of their products from suppliers in seventy different countries and paying lobbyists to oppose any requirement to label beef products for their country of origin.[61] But the structural violence inflicted by Wal-Mart and the big box retailers is only part of the story.

Divine Politics and Signs of Fascism

The rugged individual and family model values that propelled Wal-Mart reflect the larger phenomenon of a Christian fundamentalism that some see dangerously reminiscent of the Christian church and the Nazi party in Germany. One manifestation is seen in the debate over the use of God in the Pledge of Allegiance in Schools. The apparently small issue is symbolic of a change in what the schools are becoming with regard to teaching citizenship. Some fundamentalists have viewed education of children as a way to shape their allegiance to the authorities of the state and the church. With the help of lobbyists in educational technology, they have pressed for disciplined schools with measurable outcomes in particular subjects as measured by standardized multiple-choice tests. Priorities are fixed upon obtaining marketable skills rather than upon problem solving, free expression, tolerance for diverse views, challenging authority, and peaceful methods for resolving differences. A sympathetic Attorney General Ashcroft suggested that criticism of the president at times of war should not be allowed. Others see such an agenda as training rather than education—training more suitable to shaping the behavior of a laboratory rat or a follower of an authoritarian ruler. True democracy, they hold, requires a broad understanding of humanities, of different cultural heritages, and of the value, in fact the imperative, of questioning authority.[62]

James Luther Adams, a professor of ethics at Harvard Divinity School who barely escaped from the Nazi Gestapo to the United States, issued a warning letter. Adams recalled the fascist message in Germany finding biblical support for labeling opponents—homosexuals, Jews, and non-Aryans—as satanic demons who had to be crushed. His analysis was that the great universities and the major media of the United States were, like those in Germany in the 1930s, self-absorbed and would be easily compromised by their close relationship with government and corporations. If they could be given a slice of the pie (e.g., research contracts, access to higher circles) they would prove to be complacent and would not deal with the most fundamental moral questions that unrestrained government and corporate power would present. We would lack the spine to fight if the cost was to our prestige and comfort.[63]

A sign of this willingness to tolerate what happens to others is seen in the absence of challenge to planning for detention camps in the United States. Early in 2006 Halliburton subsidiary KBR (Kellog, Brown, and Root) received a $385 million contract from the Department of Homeland Security to provide "temporary detention and processing capabilities." The contract was to prepare for "an emergency influx of immigrants, or to support the rapid development of new programs" in the event of other emergencies, such as "a natural disaster." The absence of details left the door open to cost overruns, such as have occurred with KBR in Iraq. A Homeland Security spokesperson has responded that this is a "contingency contract," and conceivably no centers might be built. Contracts are, however, already making the interdiction of immigrants a profitable industry.[64] So far few U.S. citizens have expressed concern that detention centers could be used to detain American citizens if the president were to declare martial law.

Daniel Ellsberg, a former military analyst who in 1971 released the Pentagon Papers, (the U.S. military's account of its activities in Vietnam), gave this warning:

> Almost certainly this is preparation for a roundup after the next 9/11 for Mid-Easterners, Muslims and possibly dissenters. They've already done this on a smaller scale, with the "special registration" detentions of immigrant men from Muslim countries, and with Guantanamo.[65]

The history of detention facilities or camps in the United States goes back to the confinement of Japanese Americans during World War II and to fears in the 1970s of a national uprising by black militants. An executive order for continuity of government was drafted by FEMA in 1982. It called for "suspension of the Constitution" and "declaration of martial law." In 1985 President Reagan signed a series of National Security Decision Directives that authorized continued planning for continuity by a private parallel government.

In April 2002 Defense Department officials implemented a plan for domestic U.S. military operations by creating a new U.S. Northern Command (CINC-NORTHCOM) for the continental United States. In response to Hurricane Katrina in September 2005, according to the *Washington Post*, White House senior adviser Karl Rove told the governor of Louisiana, Kathleen Blanco, that she should explore legal options to impose martial law "or as close as we can get." The White House ultimately failed to compel Governor Blanco to yield control of the state National Guard, but she did grant authority for FEMA assistance, which arrived in the form, not of emergency rescue operations, but of Blackwater security forces sent to protect property from looting. Much of the media had already portrayed the Katrina hurricane victims as looters, rapists, and snipers.[66] The picture of scapegoating a group for coercive treatment is made easier by the Christian Coalition's damnation of minorities and foreigners. The security contractors arrive quickly at the scene with preset plans. And a wave of farm workers and other immigrants, whose failed local economies have driven them to the United States to find work, become the excuse for an industry of cruel detention and removal of people.[67] The militant's hostility to those who differ with them has also been seen in attacks upon environmentalists.[68]

Since 1994 and the enforcement of NAFTA, the United States has spent billions militarizing the border. Missions called Operation Gatekeeper, Blockade, Safeguard, Hold-the-Line, Triple Strike, and Rio Grande have all failed to slow immigration, and the vigilantes have failed as well. The reason is that the policies are targeting immigration, the symptom, rather than the disease. The disease is a corporate model, global economic system. It is the source of incredible misery, exploitation, and wealth disparity throughout the world and is forcing people to immigrate in search of work.[69]

A frequently raised fear of terrorists has allowed for legislation and enforcement of rules highly destructive to immigrant families. As U.S. agribusiness companies unload cheap corn and wheat, they destroy small Mexican and Guatemalan farms and drive people to migrate north, many without legal permits, to find work. Their stories reflect a long history of people forced to cross borders to find work to keep their families fed. But they, rather than white-collar criminals, are the ones who have been labeled illegal and dehumanized. Armed vigilante groups have appeared to assist their removal, and fences are being built to restrict their entry. In a program called Operation Return to Sender, the Federal Immigration and Customs Enforcement (ICE) has arrested and detained thousands of immigrants in raids across the country.[70]

In the New Bedford factory in Massachusetts, ICE agents came with warrants for a few people, but they detained and arrested many more. Those arrested were mainly working mothers, who were shipped without warning to a distant detention center in Georgia, separating them from their children. Dissatisfied white folk looking for scapegoats support the corporations that would do away with the system of family reunification, a system under which people get permanent residence visas to come to the United States to reunite their families.

Legislation is being crafted to assure the flow of low-wage guest workers (but not their families) who agree to the terms of a company ready to hire them.

The media-enhanced public dialogue on immigration comes in the wake of destroyed and impoverished economies obliging immigration to wealthy countries in hope of finding income for their families to survive. Immigration rates from the southern hemisphere have risen sharply since NAFTA.[71]

Current proposals would extend guest-worker programs to allow people to come to the United States only when they are offered a job or being recruited by a big corporation. Such programs do away with the system of family reunification, under which people get permanent residence visas to reunite their families in the United States.

Beneath the media coverage lies the reality of the guest-worker program as a form of indentured servitude. The exploitation begins with unregulated private companies that recruit Mexicans, Central Americans, Thais, and Indonesians, who borrow money to pay high fees in order to be taken to a job in the United States. These workers arrive with great debt and families to support. They are given temporary work and not provided with housing, healthcare, or adequate sanitation. Their visas, passports, and social security cards are taken from them so they cannot leave when the hiring company wants them to remain. Complaints about wages or conditions result in being blacklisted so they cannot find work, as well as receiving threats of deportation and threats of harm to their families back in the their country of origin.[72]

The seriousness of mistreatment of minority populations may be seen in Britt's[73] analysis of common themes in seven different fascist regimes: Nazi Germany, Fascist Italy, Franco's Spain, Salazar's Portugal, Papadopoulos's Greece, Pinochet's Chile, and Suharto's Indonesia were found to have fourteen common threads:

1. Powerful and continuing expressions of nationalism
2. Disdain for the importance of human rights
3. Identification of enemies/scapegoats as a unifying cause
4. The supremacy of the military/avid militarism
5. Rampant sexism
6. A controlled mass media
7. Obsession with national security
8. Religion and ruling elite tied together
9. Power of corporations protected
10. Power of labor suppressed or eliminated
11. Disdain and suppression of intellectuals and the arts
12. Obsession with crime and punishment
13. Rampant cronyism and corruption
14. Fraudulent elections

At this time, the power brokers of the Christian Coalition have moved closer to the centers of power. They are inspired by a Reconstructionist movement, which amended the teachings that the messiah would return, unaided, during the "Rapture," and escort the true believers to heaven. The more militant message was for a Christian society that was unforgiving and violent. Such crimes as adultery, witchcraft, blasphemy, and homosexuality should receive the death penalty. The world was to be subdued and ruled by a Christian United States. The new twist was that select preachers would lead the way to the development of a Christian country with dominion over the world. Dr. Tony Evans, minister of a Dallas church and the founder of Promise Keepers, called on believers, often during emotional gatherings at football stadiums, to commit to Christ and exercise power as agents of Christ.[74]

Gary North, who founded the Institute for Christian Economics wrote

> We must use the doctrine of religious liberty to gain independence for Christian schools until we train up a generation of people who know that there is no religious neutrality, no neutral law, no neutral education, and no neutral civil government. Then they will get busy in constructing a Bible-based social, political and religious order, which finally denies the religious liberty of the enemies of God.[75]

Portions of the Christian bible, selected from the apostle Paul and the gospel of John, divide the world into good and evil. Taken out of a larger biblical context, they provide an apocalyptic view and permission for violence. Secular humanists are considered the vilest targets. The message of peace, forgiveness, and embracing one's enemies is ignored. The march toward global war, even nuclear war, is not to be feared but welcomed as the harbinger of the second coming.

Faith-based initiatives now provide support for religious indoctrination in schools and human services. Science and law are being attacked. Christian fundamentalists now hold a majority of seats in 36 percent of all Republican Party state committees, or eighteen of fifty states, along with large minorities in 81 percent of the rest of the states. Forty-five senators and 186 members of the House of Representatives earned between 80 percent and 100 percent approval ratings from the three most influential Christian Right advocacy groups—Christian Coalition, Eagle Forum, and Family Resource Council.[76]

The success of Wal-Mart is related to the rise of extremist fundamentalism. Zoghby poll data show a correlation between how often consumers shop at Wal-Mart and how conservative they are. In the 2004 U.S. election, 76 percent of voters who shopped at Wal-Mart once a week voted for George W. Bush, while only 23 percent voted for John Kerry. By contrast 80 percent of voters who never shopped there voted for Kerry, with 18 percent voting for Bush. African American and Hispanic voters who shop there are described as "significantly more conservative" than their non–Wal-Mart shopping peers. When measured against other similar retailers in the United States, frequent Wal-Mart shoppers were rated the most politically conservative. This correlates roughly with the geographic locality of Wal-Mart stores: Most of them are in rural areas, whose residents tend to be more conservative than suburban residents.[77] The gap in traditional independence and local community that Wal-Mart pretended to fill is real. It is still present and is a recruiting tool for right-wing preachers and politicians.

The image of Christ as warrior is appealing to many within the radical Christian movement. The loss of manufacturing jobs, lack of affordable health care, negligible opportunities for education, and poor job security have left many millions of Americans locked out. This ideology is attractive because it offers them the hope of power and revenge. It sanctifies their rage. It stokes the paranoia about the outside world maintained through bizarre conspiracy theories, many contained in evangelist Pat Robertson's *The New World Order.*[78] The book is a xenophobic attack against the United Nations and many other international organizations. Blaming foreigners plays well to a working class that has been abandoned by the larger society. The current war on immigrants, who have been driven from their homes by corporate takeover of their lands in Mexico and the Caribbean, is an example. A complex of military, prison groups, gun-sellers, and construction contractors benefit from this misplaced anger of locals whose own serious needs have been neglected.[79] This disregard has been crucial to the success of the Christian evangelical movement. The power of the Christian right can only be limited by reintegrating the working class into society through job creation, access to good education and health care, and, perhaps most important, an attention to their needs for community. Revolutionary movements may be led by scholars, priests, or generals, but they are built on the support of an angry, disenfranchised laboring class. Neither the Christian fundamentalists nor the Islamic fundamentalists are exceptions.[80]

Powerful corporate elites have found ways to mobilize the leaders of evangelical groups. Whatever their politics or extreme beliefs, they have managed to organize working people around caring and nurturing church activities and a belief in some greater purpose than senseless competition and consumption. Among these working people are millions who have no use for ideological extremism and who devote parts of their life to making the world a better place. Laura Flanders reminds us not only of how extensive these activist efforts are but also of the fact that a political system, built upon protecting the interests of wealth, typically ignores local activists, contributing to a sense of fatalism.[81]

A Western Worldview—in Service to Whom

Fundamentalist views exceed the dominant paradigm to which most of us give passive consent. Most Westerners would not ascribe to the core values or the extremist ideologies as descriptions of their own values. But few would fail to recognize the power that these assumptive beliefs have in framing the limits of what may change and what will remain the same. The paradigm to which most in the Western world tacitly acquiesce is in fact the deeply held value system of a small elite network within its political, economic, and military sectors, a network that is the prime beneficiary of the institutions supported by these beliefs. They have found a way to partner with the dispossessed of Middle America. Writing in the *New York Times* in 1944, Vice President Henry Wallace described these power-aggrandizing corporatists:

> They claim to be super-patriots, but they would destroy every liberty guaranteed by the Constitution. They demand free enterprise, but are the spokesmen for monopoly and vested interest. Their final objective toward which all their deceit is directed is to capture political power so that, using the power of the state and the power of the market simultaneously, they may keep the common man in eternal subjection.[82]

A Summary and Somewhat Hopeful Prognosis

The power described in this book has shown itself to be vulnerable. A massive public outcry ended both official racial segregation and a costly war in Vietnam. A president who used illicit ways to retain power was obliged to resign. International protesters confronted the World Bank and the World Trade Organization wherever these bodies met, and some military intelligence agency voices joined the opposition to military expansion in the Middle East. The colonized South and Central America has thwarted complete U.S. domination by voting for leaders calling for an end to exploitation. The military outposts of the empire have grown unable to dominate even the "secure" zones of Iraq and Afghanistan. The plans for one-party domination of U.S. politics and imperial domination of the world have faced serious setbacks. The isolation of the Vulcans among the power elite, throughout the administration of the second President Bush, led to their assumptions of invulnerability and impunity. Yet they could not cover up all of the scandals and the greed that had become commonplace. The dream of an American empire appeared to fall victim to its cronyism and self-serving efforts to impose its own truth.[83] But the power base that Henry Wallace warned of, the networks described in this book, have not been shaken from their central hold on policy.

That is sad for several reasons. The most cogent is that the institutions of governance, military force, and business, upheld by these core beliefs, lack some of the wisdom from other cultural settings that may be needed to address the most critical challenges of contemporary civilization. We have not found ways to live in harmony with our environs and are destroying what is needed to maintain life. We have not been able to convert our families, our neighborhoods, or our workplaces into mutually supportive communities.[84] We have not figured a role for the wisdom of elders in the fast-changing world that directs us more than we control it. The cross-cultural psychologist and the anthropologist know many examples of cultures in which the ecology is treated as sacred and preserved. Like the natural surroundings, the tribe also becomes a source of one's belonging and identity. We know of cultures in which the wisdom gained in a lifetime is respected and not automatically deprecated by the know-how of the moment. We even know of societies that lived free of war. These are neither matters of nostalgia nor a belief in some romanticized image of the past. They are rather recognition of the dangerous limits to our imagination imposed by the core beliefs that sustain Western power. As this power develops and expands in creative ways, it also desecrates the environment, generates poverty, and creates enemies. The dominant paradigm shelters institutions that have come to dominate people and environments the world over.

The latent beliefs of one's own culture are often the most difficult to notice. Increasingly, the broad cultural force underlying what has been called Western civilization has been vying for a degree of global hegemony that is unprecedented. Within the United States, the clear message to diverse cultural enclaves of successive waves of immigrants is that assimilation into the beliefs and practices, deemed as given, is essential to maintaining a satisfactory life and livelihood. While advances in global communication create opportunities to see people in cultural settings different from one's own, the appreciation of these differences has focused largely upon their commercial value and the mainstream has tended to look upon them as undeveloped, both economically and psychologically.

The world is rapidly dividing itself into imperial powers, on one hand, and dissidents, the impoverished, and terrorists on the other. It behooves the international social scientist to bring to our attention the blinders, the dangers, and the arrogance of a cultural pattern that now contributes to the demise of other cultures. Attention to other cultures could provide an essential diversity of options for actions and beliefs that have much to teach if we are to continue the experiment of life on this planet. Conversely, loyalty to a failing form of governance may be the most unpatriotic behavior imaginable. Mark Twain wrote,

> [M]y kind of loyalty was loyalty to one's country, not to its institutions or its office-holders . . . institutions are extraneous, they are its mere clothing, and clothing can wear out, become ragged, cease to be comfortable, cease to protect the body from winter, disease, and death. To be loyal to rags, to worship rags, to die for rags—that is a loyalty of unreason, . . . it belongs to monarchy, was invented by monarchy, let monarchy keep it. I was from Connecticut, whose constitution declares "that all political power is inherent in the people, and all free governments are founded on their authority and instituted for their benefit; and that they have at all times an undeniable and indefeasible right to alter their form of government in such a manner as they may think expedient." Under that gospel, the citizen who thinks he sees that the commonwealth's political clothes are worn out, and yet holds his peace and does not agitate for a new suit, is disloyal; he is a traitor. (from *A Connecticut Yankee in King Arthur's Court*)

The challenge to contemporary patriots is to take from the promises of a democratic heritage the task of hearing all voices, of reinventing loyalty to the entire human family and to the ecology that sustains it. The obstacles have been described. We can now move on to the question of whether wonderful projects, large and small, for peace, justice, and sustainability hold any hope for changing the colossus. There are reasons to believe this can happen and that the process has begun. The power of beneficiaries of violence is waning. The world's only superpower is being challenged by the power of Asian nations and by the upsurge of the progressive Latin American unity. The United Nations is accomplishing more than most people know. Blueprints for a peaceful and just world exist. The economic system is greening by popular demand. Amazing examples of involved communities developing their own projects, entrepreneurs, and links to communities all around the world are occurring. Most important, a surge in local grassroots involvement in projects large and small is creating a new type of social movement, not dependent upon adherence to some creed or following a leader, but more like a groundswell of humanity toward creating a caring society and preserving a planet suitable for our long-term viability. But that is a story being written by people outside of the main circles of power and the topic for another book.

Notes

Chapter 1

1. Peace Pledge Union, (2005), "War and Peace," http://www.ppu.org.uk/war/facts/ (site now discontinued).

2. Grossman, Z., (2001), "A Century of U.S. Military Interventions: From Wounded Knee to Afghanistan," http://zmag.org/CrisesCurEvts/interventions.htm (accessed June 6, 2007; revised September 20, 2001).

3. Ferraro, K. J., (2005),"The Culture of Social Problems: Observations of the Third Reich, the Cold War, and Vietnam," *Social Problems* 52 (1): 1–14.

4. Englehart, T., (2005), "Bases, Bases Everywhere: It's a Pentagon World and Welcome to It," *Common Dreams*, http://www.commondreams.org/views05/0602-28.htm.

5. War Resisters League, (2007), "Where Your Income Tax Money Really Goes," http://www.warresisters.org/piechart.htm (accessed June 6, 2007); Brauer, Jurgen, and Nicholas Anglewitz, (2005), Two Thirds on Defense. *Live Journal 6/13/05*, http://www.mparent7777TwoThirds%20On%20Defense.html (accessed December 5, 2006); Piven, F. F., (2004), *The War at Home: The Domestic Costs of Bush's Militarism* (New York: New Press; W.W. Norton).

6. Hagen, K., and I. Beckerton, (2007), *The Unintended Consequences of War* (Chicago: University of Chicago Press).

7. Fergusen, Niall, (2006), *The War of the Worlds: Twentieth-Century Conflict and the Descent of the West* (New York: Penguin Books).

8. Pilisuk, M., (2007), "Disarmament and Survival," in *Peace and Conflict Studies Handbook*, ed. Charles Webel and Johan Galtung, 94–105 (London: Routledge).

9. Cordesman, Anthony H., (2002), *Terrorism, Asymmetric Warfare, and Weapons of Mass Destruction: Defending the U.S. Homeland* (Westport, CT: Praeger); Grossman (2001).

10. Ibid.

11. Klare, M. T., (2004), *Blood and Oil: The Dangers and Consequences of America's Growing Petroleum Dependency* (New York: Metropolitan Books/Henry Holt & Co.).

12. Schell, J., (2004), *The Unconquerable World: Power, Nonviolence, and the Will of the People* (New York: Holt).

13. Shanker, T., (2005), "Weapons Sales Worldwide Rise to Highest Level Since 2000," *New York Times,* November 30, 2005, http://www.nytimes.com/2005/08/30/politics/30weapons.html.

14. Greider, W., (1998), *Fortress America: The American Military and the Consequences of Peace* (New York: Public Affairs); Renner, M., (1998), "Curbing the Proliferation of Small Arms," in *State of the World 1998,* ed. L. R. Brown, C. Flavin, and H. French, 131–148 (New York: Norton).

15. Bertell, R., (2004), Health and Environmental Costs of Militarism, presented in Barcelona, Thursday, June 24.

16. Barnaby, W., (1999), *The Plague Makers: The Secret World of Biological Warfare* (London: Vision); Wright, Susan, (2003), "Rethinking the Biological Warfare Problem," *Gene Watch* 16 (February 2).

17. Bertell (2004).

18. Reynolds, Paul, (2005), White Phosphorus: Weapon on the Edge, World Affairs correspondent, BBC News Web site, November 16.

19. President John F. Kennedy, September 25, 1961.

20. McNamara, R. S., (2005), "Apocalypse Soon," *Foreign Policy Magazine,* May/June, http://www.foreignpolicy.com/story/cms.php?story_id=2829 (accessed September 15, 2005).

21. Macy, J. R., (1983), *Despair and Personal Power in the Nuclear Age* (Philadelphia: New Society).

22. Meade, C., and R. Molander, (2005), "Analyzing the Economic Impacts of a Catastrophic Terrorist Attack on the Port of Long Beach, RAND Corporation, presented at Society for Risk Analysis Annual Meeting, W11.2, http://birenheide.com/sra/2005AM/program/singlesession.php3?sessid=W11, http://www.ci.olympia.wa.us/council/Corresp/NPTreportTJJohnsonMay2005.pdf.

23. McNamara, (2005).

24. Kennan, G. F., (1983), *Nuclear Delusion: Soviet American Relations in the Nuclear Age* (New York: Pantheon).

25. Scientists Committee for Radiation Information, (1962), "The Effects of a Twenty-Megaton Bomb," *New University Thought,* Spring, 24–32.

26. Roche, D., (2002), "Rethinking the Unthinkable," *Globe and Mail,* print edition, March 12, A19.

27. Renner, M., (1990), "Converting to a Peaceful Economy," in *State of the World 1990,* ed. L. R. Brown, 154–172 (New York: W.W. Norton).

28. Wessells, Micheal, (1995), "Social-Psychological Determinants of Nuclear Proliferation: A Dual Process Analysis," *Peace and Conflict: Journal of Peace Psychology* 1: 49–96.

29. Center for Defense Information. (1996). "Nuclear Leakage: A Threat without a Military Solution," *Defense Monitor* XXV (6): 1–7.

30. Cobain, I., and E. MacAskill, (2005), "MI5 Unmasks Covert Arms Programmes," *Guardian,* October 8, http://www.guardian.co.uk/nuclear/article/0,2763,1587752,00.html; Cirincione, Jon B., J. B. Wolfsthal, and Miriam Rajkumar, (2005), *Deadly Arsenals: Nuclear, Biological and Chemical Threats,* Revised Edition (Washington, DC: Carnegie Endowment for International Peace).

31. Langewiesche, Wm., (2007), *The Atomic Bazaar: The Rise of the Nuclear Poor* (New York: Farrar. Strauss & Giroux).

32. Krieger, D. (2007) "Nuclear Disarmament," in *Handbook of Peace and Conflict Studies*, ed. Charles Webel and Johan Galtung, 106–122 (London: Routledge).

33. Hitchens, C., (2002) *The Trial of Henry Kissinger.* London: Verso Press.

34. Gusterson, H., (1991), "Rituals of Renewal among Nuclear Weapons Scientists," American Association for the Advancement of Science (Washington DC).

35. Schwartz, S. I., ed., (1998), *Atomic Audit: The Costs and Consequences of U.S. Nuclear Weapons Since 1940* (Washington DC: Brookings Institution Press).

36. Roche (2002).

37. Natural Resources Defense Council (2001), *The U.S. Nuclear War Plan: A Time for Change*, last revised June15, 2001.

38. Ibid.

39. Cobain and MacAskill (2005).

40. Krippner, S., and T. M. McIntyre, eds., (2003), *The Psychological Impact of War Trauma on Civilians, an International Perspective* (Westport, CT: Praeger).

41. Roth-Douquet, Kathy, and Frank Schaeffer, (2006), *AWOL: The Unexcused Absence of America's Upper Classes from Military Service—and How It Hurts Our Country* (New York: Harper Collins); Ricks, Thomas E., (1997), *Making the Corps* (New York: Scribner); Bacevich, Andrew J., (2005), *The New American Militarism: How Americans Are Seduced by War* (New York: Oxford University Press).

42. Robichaud, C., (2005), "Focusing on the Wrong Number," *Century Foundation*, October 28, http://www.tcf.org/list.asp?type=NC&pubid=1125.

43. Ibid.

44. Grohols, J., (2005), Facts About PTSD from National Center for PTSD, November 26, 2000, http://www.google.com/search?hl=en&q=National+Center+for+PTSD+&btnG (accessed March 12, 2007); American Psychiatric Association, (1994), Diagnostic and Statistical Manual of Mental Disorders (DSM-IV), 4th edition; Pilisuk, M., (1975), "The Legacy of the Vietnam Veteran," in "Soldiers In and After Vietnam," ed. D. Mantell and M. Pilisuk, *Journal of Social Issues* 31 (4): 3–12.

45. Kulka, R. A., ed., (1988), *Contractual Report of Findings from the National Vietnam Veterans Readjustment Study* (Research Triangle Park, NC: Research Triangle Institute).

46. Kulka, R. A., ed., (1990), *Trauma and the Vietnam War Generation: Report of Findings from the National Vietnam Veterans Readjustment Study* (New York: Brunner/Mazel).

47. Ibid

48. Ibid.

49. National Center for Post-Traumatic Stress Disorder, (1991a), "The Legacy of Psychological Trauma from the Vietnam War for American Indian Military Personnel," National Center for PTSD fact sheet, http://www.ncptsd.va.gov/ncmain/ncdocs/fact_shts/fs_native_vets.html?opm=1&rr=rr40&srt=d&echorr=true.

50. National Center for Post-Traumatic Stress Disorder, (1991b), "The Legacy of Psychological Trauma of the Vietnam War for Native Hawaiian and Americans of Japanese Ancestry Military Personnel," National Center for PTSD fact sheet, http://www.ncptsd.va.gov/ncmain/ncdocs/fact_shts/fs_hawaiian_vets.html?opm=1&rr=rr41&srt=d&echorr=true.

51. National Gulf War Resource Center (2002).

52. Weaver, A., and R. McGovern, (2007), "Troops Return to Painful Wait for Needed Help," *The Baltimore Sun*, February 4.

53. Persian Gulf Veterans Coordinating Board, (1995), "Unexplained Illnesses among Desert Storm Veterans: A Search for Causes, Treatment, and Cooperation," *Archives of Internal Medicine* 155: 262–268.

54. Price, J. L., (2004), "Effects of the Persian Gulf War on U.S. Veterans," National Center for PTSD Fact Sheet, http://www.ncptsd.va.gov/facts/veterans/fs_gulf_war_illness.html (updated December 15, 2004).

55. Fukuda, K., R. Nisenbaum, G. Stewart, W. W. Thompson, L. Robin, and R. M. Washko, (1998), "Chronic Multisymptom Illness Affecting Air Force Veterans of the Gulf War," *JAMA* 280: 981–988.

56. Hoge, C. W., C. A. Castro, S. C. Messer, D. McGurk, D. I. Cotting, and R. L. Koffman, (2004), "Combat Duty in Iraq and Afghanistan, Mental Health Problems, and Barriers to Care," *New England Journal of Medicine* 351: 13–22.

57. "Posttraumatic Stress Disorder and Acute Stress Disorder," (2000), in *Diagnostic and Statistical Manual of Mental Disorders DSM-IV-TR*, 4th edition, 463–472 (Washington, DC: American Psychiatric Association).

58. Ibid.

59. Krippner and McIntyre, (2003).

60. Associated Press, (2005), "More Troops Developing Latent Mental Disorders," Associated Press Online, July 28, http://www.msnbc.msn.com/id/8743574/.

61. Coleman, P., (2006), *Flashback: Posttraumatic Stress Disorder, Suicide, and the Lessons of War* (Boston: Beacon Press); Henderson, K., (2006), *While They're at War: The True Story of American Families on the Homefront* (Boston: Houghton Mifflin).

62. Benedict, H., (2007), "The Private War of Women Soldiers," *Salon*, March 7, http://www.salon.com/news/feature/2007/03/07/women_in_military/index.html (accessed March 12, 2007); Nikolic-Ristanovic, V., (1996), "War and Violence against Women," in *The Gendered New World Order*, ed. J. Turpin and L. A. Lorentzen, 195–210 (New York: Routledge).

63. Henderson, (2006).

64. Bloch, E., (1993), "Psychologists in Croatia Work to Ease Trauma among Young War Victims," *Psychology International* 4 (3): 1–7.

65. McIntyre, T. M., and M. Ventura, (2003), "Children of War: Psychological Seququelae of War Trauma in Angolan Adolescents," in *The Psychological Impact of War Trauma on Civilians*, ed. S. Krippner and T. M. McIntyre, 19–24 (Westport, CT: Praeger).

66. Friedman, M., and J. Jarenson, (1994), "The Applicability of the Post-traumatic Stress Disorder Concept to Refugees," in *Amidst Peril and Pain*, ed. A. J. Marsella, T. Bornemann, S. Ekblad, and J. Orley, 327–339 (Washington, DC: American Psychological Association).

67. Machel, G., (2001), *The Impact of War on Children* (Cape Town: David Philip).

68. Wessells (1995).

69. Ibid.

70. Ibid.

71. Peace Pledge Union (2005).

72. CNN, (1999), "Peace Activists Say 90 Civilian Casualties in 20th Century," *CNN.com*, August 6, http://www.cnn.com.

73. Kimmel, P., and C. E. Stout, eds., (2006), *Collateral Damage: The Psychological Consequences of America's War on Terror* (Westport, CT: Praeger).

74. Human Rights Watch, (2003a), "Off Target: The Conduct of the War and Civilian Casualties in Iraq," www.hrw.org/reports/2003/usa1203/4.htm.

75. Human Rights Watch, (2003b), "U.K. Military Practices Linked to Iraqi Civilian Casualties," press release, December 12, http:www.hrw.org/press/2003/12/uk-iraq-press.htm.

76. Human Rights Watch, (2003c), "Background on the Crisis in Iraq," http://www.hrw.org/reports/2003/usa1203/4.htm#_ftnref79, and http://www.hrw.org/campaigns/iraq/ (accessed March 10, 2006).

77. Barash, David P., and Charles P. Webel, (2002), *Peace and Conflict Studies* (London: Sage Publications).

78. Kleff (1993).

79. O'Neill (1993).

80. Nunberg, G., (2001), "Terrorism: The History of a Very Frightening Word," *San Francisco Chronicle*, October 28, C5.

81. Bastien, B., J. W. Kremer, J. Rivers-Norten, and P. Vickers, (1999), "The Genocide of the Native-Americans," *ReVision* 22 (1): 13–20.

82. Chang, Jung, and Jon Halliday, (2005), *Mao: The Unknown Story* (NewYork: Knopf).

83. Koufa, K., (2001), "Terrorism and Human Rights," *United Nations Economic and Social Council. Commission on Human Rights. Sub-Commission on the Promotion and Protection of Human Rights*, June 27, 43, 45, 46.

84. Amnesty International, (1993), *Getting Away with Murder: Political Killings and "Disappearances" in the 1990s*, (New York: Amnesty International Publications).

85. Centro Internacional para Investigaciones en Derechos Humanos (CIIDH) and Grupo de Apoyo Mutuo (GAM), (1999), *En Pie de Lucha: Organizacion y Represion en la Universidad de San Carlos*, Guatemala *1944–1996*, in *State Violence in Guatemala, 1960–1996: A Quantitative Reflection*, ed. P. Ball, P. Kobrack, and H. F. Spirer (Washington, DC: American Association for the Advancement of Science).

86. Melville, T., and M. Melville, (1971), *Guatemala: The Politics of Land Ownership* (New York: Free Press).

87. Jonas, S., (1991), *The Battle for Guatemala: Rebels, Death Squads and U.S. Power* (Boulder: Westview Press).

88. Black (1984).

89. Aguilera Peralta, G., and J. R. Imery, (1981), *Dialectica del tierra in Guatemala* (San Jose: EDUCA).

90. Blanck, E., and R. M. Castillo, (1998), "El palacio de las intrigas," *Cronica*.

91. Americas Watch, (1982), *Human Rights in Guatemala: No Neutrals Allowed* (New York: Americas Watch).

92. Amnesty International, (1989), *Guatemala: Human Rights Violations under Civilian Governments*. (London: Amnesty International).

93. Amnesty International, (1982), *Guatemala: Massive Extrajudicial Executions in Rural Areas under the Government of General Efrain Rios Montt* (London: Amnesty International); Nairn, A. (1983), "Guatemala Bleeds," *New Republic*, April 11; Falla, R., (1983), *Masacre de la Finca San Francisco, Huehuetenango, Guatemala* (Copenhagen: International Work Group for Indigenous Affairs).

94. Ball, Kobrack, and Spirer (1999).

95. Schirmer, J., (1998), *The Guatemalan Military Project: A Violence Called Democracy* (Philadelphia: University of Pennsylvania Press).

96. Giraldo, J., (1996), *Colombia: The Genocidal Democracy* (Monroe, ME: Common Courage Press).

97. Amnesty International (1993).

98. Giraldo (1996).

99. Wilson, S., (2001), "Paramilitary Troops Massacre Villagers in Colombia," *Washington Post*, October 12, A29.

100. Hawk, D., (1989), "The Photographic Record," in *Cambodia 1975–1978: Rendezvous with* Death, ed. K. D. Jackson (Princeton: Princeton University Press); Quinn, K. M., (1989), "Explaining the Terror," in *Cambodia 1975–1978: Rendezvous with Death*, ed. K. D. Jackson, 215–240 (Princeton: Princeton University Press); Foreman, C., (2003), "An Asian Youth as Offender: The Legacy of the Khmer Rouge," in *The Psychological Impact of War Trauma on Civilians*, ed. S. Krippner and T. M. McIntyre, 95–106 (Westport, CT: Praeger).

101. O'Kane, R. H. T., (1996), "Terror as Government and Its Causes, Cambodia, April 1975–January 1979," *Terror, Force, and States: The Path from Modernity* (Cheltenham, UK: Edward Elgar).

102. United Nations High Commissioner for Refugees, (2004), "Trends in Unaccompanied and Separated Minors in Industrialized Countries (2001–2003)," Geneva, http://www.UNHCR CH/Statistics (accessed July 10, 2007).

103. United Nations High Commissioner for Refugees, (2005), "204 Global Refugee Trends: Overview of Refugees, New Arrivals, Durable Solutions, Asylum Seekers, Stateless and Other Persons of Concern to UNHCR," June 17, http://www.UNHCR.CH/Statistics (accessed July 10, 2007).

104. International Campaign to Ban Landmines, (2005a), http://www.icbl.org/treaty (accessed September 11, 2005).

105. International Campaign to Ban Landmines (2005a); Landmine Monitor Report, (2003), "Toward a Mine-Free World," August, http://www.icbl.org/lm/2003/ (accessed May 16, 2005).

106. International Campaign to Ban Landmines (2005a); International Campaign to Ban Landmines, (2005b), http://www.icbl.org/problem/what (accessed September 11, 2005).

107. Ibid.

108. International Campaign to Ban Landmines (2005b).

109. Markusen, A., and J. Yukden, (1992), *Dismantling the War Economy* (New York: Basic Books).

110. Sivard, L., (1996), *World Military and Social Expenditures* (Washington, DC: World Priorities); Woodward, C., (2005), "Nixon Blanched at 'Horror Option,'" Associated Press, *San Francisco Chronicle*, November 25, A12.

111. Gabel, M., (1997), "What the World Wants and How to Pay for It," What the World Wants Project, World Game Institute.

112. Fischetti, M., (2001), "Drowning New Orleans," *Scientific American*, October.

113. McQuaid, J., (2005), "The Drowning of New Orleans: Hurricane Devastation Was Predicted," Democracy Now*!*, September 1, http://www.democracynow.org/search.pl?query=mcQuaid.

114. Boly, W., (1990), "Downwind," *Health*, July/August, 58–69; Schneider, K., (1990a), "U.S. Admits: A Plant Released Harmful Radiation in the 50s," *San Francisco Chronicle*, July 12, A1, A14 (from the *New York Times*); Schneider, K., (1990b), "Thousands Exposed to Radiation in '40s," *San Francisco Chronicle*, July, A2 (from the *New York Times*).

115. Glendinning, C., (1990), *When Technology Wounds: The Human Consequences of Progress* (New York: William Morrow & Co.); Gould, J. M., E. J. Sternglass, J. J. Mangano, and Wm. McDonald, (1996), *The Enemy Within: The High Cost of Living Near Nuclear Reactors: Breast Cancer, AIDS, Low Birth Weights, and Other Radiation-Induced Immune*

Deficiency Effects (New York: Four Walls Eight Windows Press); Vyner, H., (1988), *Invisible Trauma: The Psychosocial Effects of Invisible Environmental Contaminants* (Lexington, MA: Heath &Co).

116. Boly (1990).

117. *Tri-City Herald* (2005), "Construction Workers Sent Home Early from Hanford Plant Site,"Associated Press, September 23, 2005.

118. DeFrank N. M., J. M. Gholke, E. A. Gribble, E. M. Faustman, (2005), "Value of Information Approaches to Evaluate Models of Low Dose Radiation Effects on Neurons in the Developing Brain" Society for Risk Analysis Annual Meeting, http://birenheide.com/sra/2005AM/program/singlesession.php3?sessid=M4; Gofman, John W., (1996), *Preventing Breast Cancer: The Story of a Major, Proven, Preventable Cause of This Disease*, ed. Egan O'Connor (San Francisco, CA: C.N.R. Book Division, Committee for Nuclear Responsibility, Inc.); Gofman, John W., and Arthur R. Tamplin, (1971), *Poisoned Power: The Case Against Nuclear Power Plants* (Emmaus, PA: Rodale Press).

119. Physicians for Social Responsibility, (2004), "Cancer and the Environment," Cancer_ and_ the _ envir#11D668.pdf (accessed March 13, 2007).

120. Gofman and Tamplin (1971); Gould, J. M., and B. A. Goldman, (1993), *Deadly Deceit: Low-Level Radiation High-Level Cover-Up* (New York: Four Walls Eight Windows Press).

121. Government Accountability Project, (2006), Systemic Injustice: Hanford's Workers' Compensation Program Review of Conditions and Prescription for Remedies, August 2006, Government Accountability Project Nuclear Oversight Program, Washington, DC, http://www.whistleblower.org.

122. Miller, R. D., (2006), "The Energy Employees Occupational Illness Compensation Program: Are We Fulfilling the Promise We Made to These Veterans of the Cold War When We Created the Program?" testimony by Richard D. Miller, Government Accountability Project, Committee on Judiciary, U.S. House of Representatives, March 1.

123. Fergusen (2006).

124. DuBoff, R., (2001), "Rogue Nation," *Znet Daily Commentaries*, December 21, http://www.zmag.org/roguenation.htm (accessed June 6, 2005).

125. Barnaby (1999).

126. Ibid.

127. Ibid.

128. Ibid.

129. Berrigan, F., (2001), "U.S. 'Supplier of Choice' for Weapons Sale," *Common Dreams*, http://www.commondreams.org/views01/0821-02.htm (accessed July 13, 2002).

130. McSherry, J. P., (2005), *Predatory States: Operation Condor and Covert War in Latin America* (Lanham, MD: Rowman & Littlefield Publishers).

Chapter 2

1. Tuchman, B. W., (1984), *The March of Folly: From Troy to Vietnam* (New York: Random House).

2. Hagen, K., and I. Beckerton, (2007), *The Unintended Consequences of War* (Chicago: University of Chicago Press).

3. Sorenson, R. E., (1978), "Cooperation and Freedom among the Fore of New Guinea," in *Learning Non-Aggression*, ed. Ashley Montage (New York: Oxford).

4. Fabbro, D., (1990), "Equality in Peaceful Societies" in *Making War/Making Peace: The Social Foundations of Violent Conflict*, ed. F. M. Cancian and J. W. Gibson, 127–142 (Belmont, CA: Wadsworth Pub.Co).

5. Lorenz, K., (1966), *On Aggression* (New York: Bantam), 234; Lewontin, R., (1991), *Biology as Ideology: The Doctrine of DNA* (New York: Harper Collins); Goodall, J., (1986), *The Chimpanzees of Gombe; Patterns of Behavior* (Cambridge: Harvard University Press).

6. Langer S., (1942), *Philosophy in a New Key: A Study in the Symbolism of Reason, Rite, and Art* (Cambridge: Harvard University Press).

7. Kelly, G. A., (1963), *A Theory of Personality: The Psychology of Personal Constructs* (New York: W. W. Norton).

8. Keen, S., (2004), *Faces of the Enemy: Reflections of the Hostile Imagination* (San Francisco: Harper & Row).

9. Kelman, H., (1973), "Violence without Moral Restraint," *Journal of Social Issues* 29 (4): 25–61.

10. Ross, M. H., (1990), "Childrearing and War in Different Cultures," in *Making War/Making Peace: The Social Foundations of Violent Conflict*, ed. Francesca M. Cancian and James William Gibson, 55–63 (Belmont, CA: Wadsworth Pub. Co.).

11. Bohart, A. C., R. Elliott, L. Greenberg, and J. C. Watson, (2002), "Empathy," in *Psychotherapy Relationships That* Work, ed. J. R. Norcross et al. (New York: Oxford University Press).

12. Arendt, H., (2004), *The Origins of Totalitarianism* (New York: Scho Press).

13. Zimbardo, P. G., (2004), "A Situationist Perspective on the Psychology of Evil," in *The Social Psychology of Good and Evil: Understanding Our Capacity for Kindness and Cruelty*, ed. A. Miller (New York: Guilford).

14. Lee, M., P. G. Zimbardo, and M. Berthof, (1977), "Shy Murderers," *Psychology Today* 11 (November): 69 ff.

15. Milgram, S., (1974), *Obedience to Authority* (New York: Harper & Row).

16. Bandura, A., B. Underwood, and M. E. Fromson, (1975), "Disinhibition of Aggression through Diffusion of Responsibility and Dehumanization of Victims," *Journal of Personality and Social Psychology* 9: 253–269.

17. Zimbardo (2004).

18. Watson, J. R. I., (1973), "Investigation into De-individuation Using a Cross-Cultural Survey Technique," *Journal of Personality and Social Psychology* 25: 342–345.

19. Wallis, J., (2006), "Christmas in the Trenches," *Sojourners*, http://www.beliefnet.com/blogs/godspolitics/2006/12/jim-wallis-christmas-in-trenches.html (accessed December 27, 2006).

20. Zimbardo (2004).

21. Bandura, A., (1988), "Mechanisms of Moral Disengagement," in *Origins of Terrorism: Psychologies, Ideologies, Theologies, States of Mind*, ed. W. Reich, 161–191 (New York: Cambridge University).

22. Coles, R., (1983), "The Needs for Scapegoats Causes War," in *War and Human Nature*, ed. D. L. Bender and B. Leone, 60 (St. Paul, MN: Greenhaven Press).

23. Lifton, R. J., (1967), *Death in Life: Survivors of Hiroshima* (New York: Simon & Schuster).

24. Netzer, O., (2005), "The Real Causes of War Discovered," Interactivist Info Exchange, August 13 http://info.interactivist.net/article.pl?sid=05/08/13/2232239.

25. Eisenhart, R. W., (1975), "'You Can't Hack It Little Girl': A Discussion of the Covert Psychological Agenda of Modern Combat Training" *Journal of Social Issues* 31 (4): 13–23.

26. Gilmore, I. and T. Smith, (2006), "If You Start Looking at Them as Humans, Then How Are You Gonna Kill Them?" *Guardian, March* 29, http://www.guardian.co.uk/Iraq/Story/0,,1741942,00.html.

27. Brooks, R., (2006), "Why Good People Kill: Iraq Murders Reveal the Warping Power of Conformity and Dehumanization," *Los Angeles Times,* June 9.

28. Merari, A., (1990), "The Readiness to Kill and Die: Suicidal Terrorism in the Middle East," in *Origins of Terrorism: Psychological Theologies, States of Mind,* ed. W. Reich (New York: Cambridge University Press).

29. Lorenz (1966).

30. Netzer (2005).

31. Bourke, J., (1996), *Dismembering the Male: Men's Bodies, Britain and the Great War* (Chicago: University of Chicago Press), 336.

32. Macy, J. R., and M. Y. Brown, (1998), *Coming Back to Life: Practices to Reconnect Our Lives, Our World* (Gabriola Island, BC, Canada: New Society Publishers).

33. Bstan-'dzin-rgya-mtsho, Dalai Lama, (1999), 204–205.

34. LeShan, L., (2002), *The Psychology of War: Comprehending Its Mystique and Its Madness* (New York: Helios Press).

35. Ibid.

36. Koenigsberg, R. A., (2005), "The Soldier as Sacrificial Victim: Awakening from the Nightmare of History," http://home.earthlink.net/~libraryofsocialscience/soldier_nightmare.htm (accessed November 8, 2005).

37. Andreas, J., (2004), *Addicted to War—Why the U.S. Can't Kick Militarism* (Oakland, CA: AK Press).

38. Kagen, D., G. Schmidt, and T. Donelly, (2000), "Rebuilding America's Defenses: Strategy, Forces and Resources for a New Century," Project for a New American Century, September (Washington DC).

39. Peterson, Evan Augustine III, (2005), "Of Militarism, Fascism, War and National Consciousness," NFPNZ essay, February 6, http://nuclearfree.lynx.co.nz/of.htm.

40. Ekirch A. A., Jr., (1999), *Militarism and Antimilitarism: The Oxford Companion to American Military History* (Oxford: Oxford University Press), 2, 438.

41. LeShan (2002).

42. Koenigsberg (2005).

43. Fromm, E., (1964), *Escape from Freedom* (New York: Holt Rinehart and Winston).

44. Holthouse, D., (2006), "Extremism and the Military: A Timeline," Southern Poverty Law Center, http://www.splcenter.org/intel/news/item.jsp?aid=66 (accessed July 13, 2006).

45. Hedges, C., (2003), *War Is a Force That Gives Us Meaning* (Woodston, Peterborough, UK: Anchor).

46. Broyles, Wm. Jr., (1990), "Why Men Love War: Socialization and Masculinity," in *Making War/Making Peace: The Social Foundations of Violent Conflict,* ed. Francesca M. Cancian and J. W. Gibson, 29–37 (Belmont, CA: Wadsworth Pub. Co).

47. Ensign, T., (2005), *The America's Military Today* (New York: New Press).

48. Jamail, D., (2005), Dahr Jamail's Iraq dispatches, http://dahrjam.

49. Fitzsimmons, A., (2004), "Mourning People on Santa Monica Beach: Arlington West," Veterans for Peace, July 18, http://www.veteransforpeace.org/.

50. Jamail (2005).

51. Cortwright, D., (1975), *Soldiers in Revolt: GI Resistance during the Vietnam War* (Chicago: Haymarket Books).

52. James, W., (1995/1910), "The Moral Equivalent of War," *Peace and Conflict: Journal of Peace Psychology* 1: 17–26.

53. Ehrenreich, B., (1997), *Blood Rites: Origins and History of the Passions of War* (New York: Henry Holt), 238.

54. Bstan-'dzin-rgya-mtsho, Dalai Lama (1999).

55. Elshtain, J. B., (1987), *Women and War* (New York: Basic Books); Nikolic-Ristanovic., V., (1999), *Women, Violence and War: Victimization of Refugees in the Balkans* (Budapest: Central European University Press); Brownmiller, S., (1975), *Against Our Will: Men, Women and Rape* (NewYork: Ballantine Books).

56. Morgan, R., (2001), *The Demon Lover: The Roots of Terrorism* (New York: Washington Square Press).

57. McKay, S., (1998), "The Effects of Armed Conflict on Girls and Women," *Peace and Conflict: Journal of Peace Psychology* 2:93–107; Morgan, R., (2006), "Rape, Murder, and the American GI," Women's Media Center, August 17.

58. Machel, G., (2001), *The Impact of War on Children* (Cape Town: David Philip).

59. Wessells, M. G., (1998), "Children, Armed Conflict and Peace," *Journal of Peace Research* 35: 635–646.

60. Bstan-'dzin-rgya-mtsho, Dalai Lama (1999), 204–205.

61. Cohn, C., (1987), "Sex and Death in the Rational World of the Defense Intellectuals," *Journal of Women in Culture and Society* 12: 687–718.

62. Frank, J., (1982), *Sanity and Survival in the Nuclear Age: Psychological Aspects of War and Peace* (New York: Random House).

63. Cohn (1987).

64. Ibid.

65. Gusterson, H., (1991), "Rituals of Renewal among Nuclear Weapons Scientists," American Association for the Advancement of Science (Washington DC); Gusterson, H., (1998), Nuclear Rites: A Weapons Laboratory at the End of the Cold War (Berkeley: University of California Press); Cohn (1987); Pilisuk, M., (1999), "Addictive Rewards in Nuclear Weapons Development," *Peace Review: A Transnational Journal* 11(4): 597–602; Caldicott, H., (2002), *The New Nuclear Danger: George W. Bush's Military-Industrial Complex* (New York: New Press).

66. Niebuhr, R., (1952), *The Irony of American History* (New York: Scribners), 84.

67. Stouffer, S. A., (1949), *Studies in Social Psychology in World War II: The American Soldier* (Princeton: Princeton University Press); Merton, K., and P. Lazersfeld, (1950), *The American Soldier*, vol. 2 (Glencoe IL: Free Press).

68. Reiber, R. W., and R. J. Kelly, (1991), "Substance and Shadow: Images of the Enemy," in *The Psychology of War and Peace: The Image of the Enemy*, ed. R. W. Reiber, 3–39 (New York: Plenum).

69. Bronfenbrenner, U., (1961), "The Mirror Image in Soviet-American Relations: A Social Psychologist's Report," *Journal of Social Issues* 17 (3): 45–56.

70. Carroll, J., (2005), "The Day after the Fireworks," CD/BG essay, July 5, http://www.commondreams.org/views05/0705-24.htm.

71. Friedman, M., (1984), "The Nuclear Threat and the Hidden Human Image," *Journal of Humanistic Psychology* 24 (3): 65–76.

72. Rogers, C., (1984), "Notes on Rollo May," in *American Politics and Humanistic Psychology*, ed. T. Greening, 11–12 (San Francisco: Saybrook Publishing Company).

73. May, R., (1984), "The Problem of Evil: An Open Letter to Carl Rogers," in *American Politics and Humanistic Psychology*, ed. T. Greening, 12–23 (San Francisco: Saybrook Publishing Company).

74. Freud, S., (1949), "Why War?" *Collected Papers*, vol. 4 (London: Hogarth Press).

Chapter 3

1. Wallis, J., (1992), "Violence, Poverty and Separation," *Public Welfare* 50, no. 4 (Fall): 14–15.

2. Galtung, J., (1996), *Peace by Peaceful Means: Peace and Conflict, Development and Civilization* (London: Sage Press); Christie, D., (1996), "Peacebuilding: The Human Needs Approach Locally and Globally," Division 48 (Peace Psychology) Presidential Address, 104th Annual Convention of the American Psychological Association, August 1996; Christie, D., (1997), "Reducing Direct and Structural Violence: The Human Needs Theory," *Peace and Conflict: Journal of Peace Psychology* 3: 315–332; Pilisuk, M., (2001), "Globalism and Structural Violence," in *Peace, Conflict, and Violence: Peace Psychology for the 21st Century 2001*, ed. D. Christie, R. Wagner, and D. Winter (Englewood, NJ: Prentice Hall).

3. Galtung (1996).

4. Langer, S., (1942), *Philosophy in a New Key: A Study in the Symbolism of Reason, Rite and Art* (Cambridge: Harvard University Press).

5. Marrow, A. J., (1977), *The Practical Theorist: The Life and Work of Kurt Lewin* (New York: Teachers College Press).

6. Arendt, H., (2004), *The Origins of Totalitarianism* (New York: Schocken Books).

7. Staub, E., (2001), "Genocide and Mass Killing: Their Roots and Prevention," in *Peace, Conflict, and Violence: Peace Psychology for the 21st Century 2001*, ed. D. Christie, R. Wagner, and D. Winter, 76–86 (Englewood, NJ: Prentice Hall).

8. Syme, S. L., and L. Berkman, (1976), "Social Class, Susceptibility and Illness," *American Journal of Epidemiology* 104 (1): 1–8; Browne, A., and S. S. Bassuk, (1997), "Intimate Violence in the Lives of Homeless and Poor Housed Women," *American Journal of Orthopsychiatry* 67 (2): 261–275; Syme, S. L., (1989), "Control and Health: An Epidemiological Perspective, in *Stress Personal Control and Health*, ed. A. Steptoe and A. Appels (New York: Wiley and Sons).

9. Berkman, L., and S. L. Syme, (1979), "Social Networks, Host Resistance and Mortality: A Nine-Year Follow-Up Study of Alameda County Residents," *American Journal of Epidemiology* 109 (2): 186–204; House, J. S., K. R. Landis, and D. Umberson, (1988), "Social Relationships and Health," *Science* 241: 540–545; Pilisuk, M., and S. H. Parks, (1986), *The Healing Web: Social Networks and Human Survival* (Hanover, NH: University Press of New England).

10. Syme (1989).

11. Goff, F., and M. Locker, (1971), "The Violence of Domination: U.S. Power and the Dominican Republic," in *The Triple Revolution Emerging: Social Problems in Depth*, ed. R. Perrucci and M. Pilisuk (Boston: Little Brown); Pilisuk, M., (1972), *International Conflict and Social Policy* (Englewod, NJ: Prentice Hall).

12. Rainforest Action Network, (1986), "Coca Cola to Convert 50,000 Acres of Rainforest to Frozen Orange Juice," *Rainforest Action Network Alert*. May, 3; Rainforest Action Network, (1987), "Belize Update," *Rainforest Action Network Alert*, February, no. 11.

13. Blanding, M., (2005), "Coke: The New Nike," *The Nation,* http://www.thenation.com/doc.mhtml?i=20050411&s=blanding (accessed May 6, 2005); Lederman, Doug, (2005), "Inside Higher Ed 'Coke: The New Nike,'" *Campaign to Stop Killer Coke,* http://www.corporatecampaign.org/killer-coke/who.htm (accessed May 6, 2005).

14. Rainforest Action Network (1986), 1.

15. Litterer, Juliet, (1997), "ICE Case Studies: Belize Logging Conflict," *Inventory of Conflict and Environment* http://www.american.edu/ted/ice/belize.htm (accessed April 29, 2005).

16. Weiss, L., (1997), "Nigerians Risk All for Their Forests," http://www.earthisland.org/journal/f96-24.html.

17. Emerich, T., (2001), "PTSD and Child Abuse among Salvadoran Refugees: The After-Effects of War," unpublished doctoral dissertation Saybrook Graduate School, San Francisco; Tan, G., M. Ray, and R. Cate, (1991), "Migrant Farm Child Abuse and Neglect within an Ecosystem Framework," *Family Relations* 40, no. 1 (January): 84–92.

18. Gelles, R., (1976), "Demythologizing Child Abuse," *Family Coordinator* 25:135–141; Gil, D., (1971), "Violence against Children," *Journal of Marriage and the Family* 33: 639–648; Gil, D., (1975), "Unraveling Child Abuse," *American Journal of Orthopsychiatry* 45: 336–346; Steinberg, L. D., R. Catalano, and D. Dooley, (1981), "Economic Antecedents of Child Abuse and Neglect," *Human Development* 52: 975–985; Tan, Ray, and Cate (1991).

19. SOAWATCH, (2004), "What Is the SOA?" http://www.soaw.org/type.php?type=8.

20. Ching Yoon Louie, M., (2001), *Sweatshop Warriors: Immigrant Women Workers Take On the Global Factory* (Boston: South End Press).

21. Bissel, T., (1997), "Campaign for Labor Rights," Nike Packet, parts 1–7, personal correspondence, April 24.

22. Canadian Auto Workers, (1997), "Indonesian Fight of Human Rights," Canadian Auto Workers Web site, http://www.caw.ca/news/videonews/archives/indonesian_fight_of_human_rights.asp (accessed May 5, 2005); Australian-Asian Union Support Group, (2000), "Solidarity Speaking Tour: The Fight for Union Rights in Indonesia," media release, May 10, http://intranet.usc.edu.au/wacana/isn/pakpahan_visit.html (accessed March 26, 2006).

23. Rhodes, M., (1997a), Nike Workers Strike! analysis, resources, personal correspondence, May 1, 11:46.

24. Mokhiber, R., (2003), "Politics of Chemistry 101," *Multinational Monitor* 24 (10), http://www.multinationalmonitor.org/mm2003/03october/front.html (accessed May 6, 2005).

25. Rhodes, M., (1997c), Day 1 Nike worker tour, personal correspondence, May 6.

26. Elich, G., (2006), *Strange Liberators: Militarism, Mayhem, and the Pursuit of Profit* (Valparaiso, IN: Lumina Press).

27. Rhodes (1997c).

28. PR Newswire Associates, (1997), McDonald's Happy Meals Promotion, March 19.

29. Hacker, A., (1997), *Money: Who Has How Much and Why?* (New York: Scribner); Rhodes, M., (1997b), Disney and McDonald's linked to $.06/hour sweatshop in Vietnam, personal correspondence, May 1, 16:48; Rhodes (1997c).

30. Technology, Entertainment, Design (TED), (nd), "Nike Shoes and Child Labor in Pakistan," http://www.american.edu/TED/nike.htm#r1; Schanberg, Sydney H. (1996) "On the Playgrounds of America, Every Kid's Goal Is to Score: In Pakistan, Where

Children Stitch Soccer Balls for Six Cents an Hour, the Goal Is to Survive," *Life* (June): 38–48.

31. Moore, M., (1994), *TV Nation*, NBC Television, August 2.

32. Meadows, D., (1992), "Corporate Run Schools Are a Threat to Our Way of Life," *Valley News*, October 3, 22.

33. Farmer, P., (1999), *Infections and Inequalities: The Modern Plagues* (Berkeley: University of California Press).

34. Barry, K., (1995), *Prostitution of Sexuality* (New York: New York University Press); Rosenfeld, S., (1997), "Women Suffer Brutal Captivity," *San Francisco Examiner*, April 6, A1, A16.

35. World Bank, (2005), "Philippines Country Brief," *World Bank*, http://www.worldbank.org.ph (accessed April 30, 2005).

36. Ignacio, A., E. de la Cruz, J. Emmanuel, and H. Toribio, (2004), *The Forbidden Book: The Philippine American War in Political Cartoons* (San Francisco: T'Boli Publishing and Distribution).

37. Augustine, E., (2007), "The Philippines, the World Bank and the Race to the Bottom," in *A Game as Old as Empire: The Secret World of Economic Hit Men and the Web of Global Corruption*, ed. S. Hiatt, 175–193 (San Francisco: Berrett-Koehler); Erlbaum, M., (2005), "*The Forbidden Book*—A Book Review," *Socialism and Democracy Journal* #37 19, no. 1 (Spring), http://www.sdonline.org/index2.htm.

38. International Solidarity Mission (ISM), (2005), Report Back and Discussion on the Continuing Human Rights Violations in the Philippines, UTLA Headquarters (Los Angeles, CA), Friday, October 21.

39. Barnet, R. J., and J. Cavanaugh, (1994b), "The Sound of Money," *Sojourners*, January 12; Barnet, R. J., and J. Cavanaugh, (1994a), *Global Dreams: Imperial Corporations and the New World Order* (New York: Simon and Schuster).

40. Mander, J., and E. Goldsmith, (1996), *The Case against the Global Economy* (San Francisco: Sierra Club Books).

41. Comas-Diaz, L., and M. A. Jansen, (1995), "Global Conflict and Violence against women. *Peace and Conflict: Journal of Peace Psychology* 1 (4): 315–331; Pilisuk, M., (2001), "Globalism and Structural Violence," in *Peace, Conflict, and Violence: Peace Psychology for the 21st Century 2001*, ed. D. Christie, R. Wagner, and D. Winter (Englewood, NJ: Prentice Hall).

42. International Labour Organization, (2005), "Facts on Child Labour," http://www.ilo.org/public/english/bureau/inf/fact/index.html (accessed December 16, 2005); King, G., (2004), *Woman, Child for Sale: The New Slave Trade in the 21st Century*(New York: Penguin Group); Hochschild, A. R., and B. Ehrenriech, (2004), *Global Woman: Nannies, Maids, and Sex Workers in the New Economy* (New York: Owl Books/Harpers); Kyle, D., and R. Koslowsky, (2001), *Global Human Smuggling: Comparative Perspectives* (Baltimore: John Hopkins University Press); McGill, C., (2003), *Human Traffic Sex, Slaves and Immigration* (London: Vision Paperbacks); Parrenas, R. C., (2001), *Servants of Globalization: Women, Migration and Domestic Work* (Palo Alto, CA: Stanford University Press).

43. Batstone, David B., (2007), *Not for Sale: The Return of the Global Slave Trade—and How We Can Fight It* (New York: Harper).

44. Simmons, J., P. Farmer, and B. Schoepf, (1995), "A Global Perspective," in *Women, Poverty and AIDS: Sex, Drugs and Structural Violence*, ed. P. Farmer, M. Connors, and J. Simmons (Monroe, ME: Common Courage Press).

45. Simmons, Farmer, and Schoepf (1995), 42–43.

46. Simmons, Farmer, and Schoepf (1995), 23.

47. Connors, M., (1995), "Unraveling the Epidemic among Poor Women in the US," in *Women, Poverty and AIDS: Sex, Drugs and Structural Violence*, ed. P. Farmer, M. Connors, and J. Simmons, 98 (Monroe, ME: Common Courage Press).

48. Connors (1995); Daily, J., P. Farmer, J. Rhatigan, J. Katz, and J. Furin, (1995), "Women and HIV Infection—a Different Disease? in *Women, Poverty and AIDS: Sex, Drugs and Structural Violence*, ed. P. Farmer, M. Connors, and J. Simmons (Monroe, ME: Common Courage Press).

49. Connors (1995).

50. Gardner, W., and K. Preator, (1996), "Children of Seropositive Mothers in the U.S. AIDS Epidemic," *Journal of Social Issues* 52 (3): 177–195.

51. Ellwood, D., (1996), "Welfare Reform in Name Only," *New York Times*, July 22, A15.

52. Martinez, R., Jr., (1996), "Latinos and Lethal Violence: The Impact of Poverty and Inequality," *Social Problems* 43, no. 2 (May): 131–143.

53. Mexican Action Network on Free Trade (Réseau Mexicain d'Action Sur le Libre-Échange), (n.d.), "NAFTA and the Mexican Economy," Development GAP, fact sheet, http://www.developmentgap.org (accessed June 9, 2000). This fact sheet is excerpted from Espejismo y realidad: el TLCAN tres años después, Análisis y propuesta desde la sociedad civil, by the Mexican Action Network on Free Trade (RMALC). The full report is available for US$10 from RMALC, tel/fax (525) 355-1177, email rmalc@laneta.apc.org. Translated by the Development GAP.

54. Farmer, P., (2005), *Pathologies of Power: Health, Human Rights, and the New War on the Poor* (Berkeley: University of California Press).

55. Maquila Solidarity Network, (2005), "Asia-Latina Women's Exchange: Mapping the Impacts of the Quota Phase-Out on Workers' Lives," October, http://www.maquilasolidarity.org/resources/post_mfa/AWID%20exchange/index.htm (accessed March 28, 2006).

56. Argetsinger, A., (2005), "Immigration Opponents to Patrol U.S. Border," *Washington Post*, March 31, A03.

57. CNN, (1997), "Criminal Warrants Sought in Texas Standoff," *CNN.com*, April 28, http://www.cnn.com/US/9704/28/texas.militia (accessed April 29, 2005).

58. Ivins, M., (1997), "So Much for Putting People First," *Houston Chronicle Interactive*, April 14.

59. Ibid.

60. Hartmann, Thom, and Mark Crispin Miller, (2006), *Screwed: The Undeclared War against the Middle Class—and What We Can Do About It* (San Francisco: Barret Koehler); Reich, R., (1997), *Locked in the Cabinet* (New York: Alfred A. Knopf).

61. Gomes, L., (2003), *The Economics and Ideology of Free Trade: An Historical Review* (Cheltenham, UK: Edward Elgar).

62. National Security Council, (2006), "The National Security Strategy," Whitehouse, Washington, DC, March, http://www.whitehouse.gov/nsc/nss/2006/ (accessed June 6, 2006).

63. Galtung (1996).

64. Barnet, R. J., and J. Cavanaugh, (1994a).; Makhijani, A., (1992), *From Global Capitalism to Economic Justice: An Inquiry into the Elimination of Systematic Poverty, Violence and Environmental Destruction in the World Economy* (New York: Apex Press).

65. Korten, D. C., (2001), *When Corporations Rule the World* (West Hartford, CT: Kumerian Press Inc. & San Francisco: Berrett-Koehler Publishers).

66. Chatterjee, P., (1992), "World Bank Failures Soar to 37.5% of Completed Projects in 1991," *Third World Economics*, December 16–31, 2; Straus, S., (1997), "Eritrea a Do-It-Yourself Nation," *San Francisco Chronicle*, June 11, C2, C16.

67. Easterly, W., (2002), *The Elusive Quest for Growth: Economists' Adventures and Misadventures* (Cambridge: MIT Press).

68. Bello, W., (1994), *Dark Victory: The United States, Structural Adjustment, and Global Poverty* (London: Pluto).

69. Korten (2001); Pilisuk, M., (1998), "The Hidden Structure of Contemporary Violence," *Peace and Conflict: Journal of Peace Psychology* 4 (3): 197–216.

70. Bales, K., (2000), *Disposable People: New Slavery in the Global Economy* (Berkeley: University of California Press); Batstone (2007).

71. Bales, K., (2005), *Understanding Global Slavery: A Reader* (Berkeley: University of California Press); Batstone (2007); International Labour Organization (2005).

72. *BBC News*, (2006), "Forbes Reports Billionaire Boom," http://news.bbc.co.uk/2/hi/business/4791848.stm.

73. Korten (2001); Reich (1997).

74. Leiss, W., and C. Chociolko, (1994), *Risk and Responsibility* (Buffalo, NY: McGill-Queens University Press); Leach, W., (1993), *Land of Desire: Merchant's Power and the Rise of the New American Culture* (New York: Pantheon), xiii.

75. Parenti (1995); Renner, M., (1991), "Assessing the Military's War on the Environment," in *State of the World: 1991*, ed. L. R. Brown, et al., 139 (New York: W. W. Norton).

76. Renner (1991), 119.

77. Santos, Ricco Alejandro M., (2003), *Crime of Empire: A Case against Globalization and Third World Poverty as a World System* (Sidelakes Press and Literary Agency).

78. Farmer (2005), 18.

79. Fisher, R., (1993), "Grassroots Organizing Worldwide," in *Mobilizing the Community: Local Politics in a Global Era*, ed. R. Fisher and J. Kling (Thousand Oaks, CA: Sage Publishers); Fisher, R., (1994), *Let the People Decide: Neighborhood Organizing in America*, revised edition (Boston: Twayne); Singer, P., (2002), *One World: The Ethics of Globalization* (New Haven, CT: Yale University Press).

Chapter 4

1. Institute for Food and Development Policy, (2001), *The Global Banquet: Politics of Food*, film, Maryknoll Productions.

2. Goering, P., H. Norberg-Hodge, and J. Page, (1998), "Industrial Agriculture in Context, *IFG News*, 3: 4–5.

3. Corporate Accountability International (formerly Infact), (2000), Challenging corporate abuse, building grassroots power since 1997, http://www.infact.org (accessed December 23, 2001 on Infact Web site).

4. Manning, R., (2001), "Hunger Speaks," *Forum for Applied Research and Public Policy* 16: 48–53.

5. Pimentel, D., and M. Pimentel, (1999), "Population Growth, Environmental Resources and the Global Availability of Food," *Social Research* 66: 417–428.

6. Murphy, S., (2001), "The Global Food Basket," *Forum for Applied Research and Public Policy* 16: 36–42.

7. Watson, Paul, (2006), "Some Say India Deal Ignores Another Energy Need: Food," *Los Angeles Times*, March 7.

8. Lang, Tim, and Michael Heasman, (2004), *Food Wars: The Global Battle for Mouths, Minds and Markets* (New York: Earthscan Publications).

9. Food Research and Action Center, (2005), "Hunger and Food Insecurity in the United States," http://www.frac.org/html/hunger_in_the_us/hunger_index.html (accessed November 6, 2005).

10. Nord, M., S. Andrews, and Carlson, (2005), "Household Food Security in the United States, 2004," http://www.ers.usda.gov/Publications/err11/ (accessed November 6, 2005).

11. Food Research and Action Center (2005).

12. America's Second Harvest, (2001), "Hunger Study 2001 Fact Sheet," http://www.secondharvest.org/learn_about_hunger/hunger_study_2001_Fact_sheet.html (accessed November 6, 2005).

13. Alaimo, K., R. R. Briefel, E. A. Frongillo, and C. M. Olson, (1988), "Food, Insufficiency Exists in the United States: Results from the Third National Health and Nutrition Examination Survey (NHANES III)," *American Journal of Public Health* 88 (3): 419–425; Lamison-White, T., (1997), "Poverty in the United States: 1996," Current Population Report, Series P60-198 (Washington, DC: U.S. Government Printing Office).

14. Food Research and Action Center (2005).

15. Bellamy, C., ed., (1997), *The State of the World's Children, 1996*, UNICEF (Oxford: Oxford University Press).

16. Manning (2001), 2.

17. Ibid.

18. Reid, T. R., (1998), "Feeding the Planet," *National Geographic* 194: 56–74.

19. Elliott, I., (2001), "Pulling a Fast One," *Ecologist* 31: 36–37.

20. Fraser, D., (2001), "The 'New Perception' of Animal Agriculture: Legless Cows, Featherless Chickens, and a Need for Genuine Analysis," *Journal of Animal Science* 79: 634–641.

21. Friedman, T. L., (1999), "A Manifesto for the Fast World," in *Globalization*, ed. K. Sjursen, 5 (New York: H. W. Wilson Company).

22. Murphy (2001), 1.

23. Barber, B. R., (2000), "Challenge to the Common Good in the Age of Globalism," *Social* Education 64: 8–13.

24. Hayward, M., (1999), "Globalized Mergers and Acquisitions: The Dangers of a Monoculture," *Competitiveness Review* 9: i–iv; Barnet, R. J., and J. Cavanaugh, (1994a), *Global Dreams: Imperial Corporations and the New World Order* (New York: Simon and Schuster).

25. Chang, S. J., and D. Ha, (2001), "Corporate Governance in the Twenty-First Century: New Managerial Concepts for Supernational Corporations," *American Business Review* 19: 32–44.

26. Bello, W., (1998), "The End of a 'Miracle': Speculation, Foreign Capital Dependence and the Collapse of the Southeast Asian Economies," *Multinational Monitor* 19: 10–16.

27. Korten, D., (1998), *Globalizing Civil Society: Reclaiming Our Right to Power* (New York: Seven Stories Press).

28. Specter, M., (1998), "Contraband Women: A Special Report: Traffickers' New Cargo: Naïve Slavic Women," *New York Times* January 11, Sunday, http://archives.nytimes.com/archives/search/.

29. Murphy (2001), 40.

30. Hayward (1999).

31. Murphy (2001).

32. MacCannell, E. D., and J. White, (1984), "Social Costs of Large-Scale Agriculture: The Prospects of Land Reform in California," in *Land Reform American Style*, ed. C. C. Giesler and F. J. Popper, 35–54 (Totawa, NJ: Rowman and Allenheld).

33. Hayward (1999).

34. Pimentel and Pimentel (1999).

35. Murphy (2001).

36. Barber (2000), 8

37. Biotechnology Industry Organization, (2005), "Biotechnology Industry Facts," http://www.bio.org/speeches/pubs/er/statistics.asp (accessed November 3, 2005).

38. Ibid.

39. Kesan, J. P., (2000), "Intellectual Property Protection and Agricultural Biotechnology," *American Behavior Scientist*, 44: 464–503.

40. James, C., (2004), "Executive Summary Preview: Global Status of Commercialized Biotech/GM Crops: 2004," International Service for the Acquisition of Agri-biotech Applications (ISAAA). Those developing countries were China, India, Argentina, Brazil, and South Africa. Countries that grow 50,000 hectares or more of biotech crops are classified as biotech mega-countries. ISAAA found that in 2004 there were fourteen mega-countries, up from ten in 2003, with Paraguay, Spain, Mexico, and the Philippines joining the mega-country list (along with the United States, Argentina, Canada, Brazil, China, India, South Africa, Uruguay, Australia, and Romania).

41. Ibid.

42. Grain, (2005), "Field Trials and Commercial Releases of Bt Cotton around the World," http://www.grain.org/research/btcotton.cfm?id=306 (accessed December 6, 2005).

43. Consultative Group on International Agricultural Research, (2004), "Who We Are: The CGIAR Mission," http://www.cgiar.org/who/index.html and http://www.cgiar.org/publications/secretariat.html (both accessed December 6, 2005).

44. Corporate Watch, (2005), "UK: Patents on Flowers: Profits to Blossom," http://www.corpwatch.org/article.php?id=11874retrived 6/5/07.

45. Kesan (2000).

46. Murphy (2001).

47. Kesan (2000).

48. Brush, S. B., (1999), "Bioprospecting the Public Domain," *Cultural Anthropology* 14: 535–555.

49. Kloppenburg, J., (1994), "Scientific Poaching and Global Biodiversity," *Elmwood Quarterly* 10 (2 & 3): 7–11.

50. Teitel, M., (1994a), "Ownership of the Seed of Life," *Elmwood Quarterly* 10 (2 & 3): 2–6; Teitel, M., (1994b), "Selling Cells," *Elmwood Quarterly* 10 (2 & 3): 12–14.

51. Brush (1999).

52. Padron, M. S., and M. G. Uranga, (2001), "Protection of Biotechnological Inventions: A Burden Too Heavy for the Patent System," *Journal of Economic Issues* 35: 315–322.

53. Corporate Watch (2005).

54. Stumo, M., (2000), "Down on the Farm," *Multinational Monitor* 21: 17–22.

55. Hayward (1999), 1.

56. Murphy (2001).

57. Teitel (1994b).

58. Stumo (2000).

59. Johnson, D., (2000), "Solving Water Scarcity," *Journal of Family and Consumer Sciences* 92:17.

60. Khor, M., (1997), "Communities Countering the Negative Consequences of Aquaculture," http://www.earthisland.org/map/w95-nwbriefs.html.

61. Barlow, M., (1999), "The Global Water Crisis and the Commodification of the World's Water Supply," http://www.ifg.org/bgsummary.html (accessed December 23, 2001); Johnson (2000).

62. Shiva, V., (2000), "Monsanto's Expanding Monopolies," http://www.purefood.org/Monsanto/waterfish.cfm (accessed December 23, 2001).

63. Grusky, S., (2001), "Privatization Tidal Wave: IMF/World Bank Water Policies and the Price Paid by the Poor," *Multinational Monitor* 22: 14–19.

64. Barlow (1999).

65. COHA (Council on Hemispheric Affairs), (2006), "Washington's Faltering Anti-Drug Strategy in Colombia, and Bogotá's Evaporating Extradition Policy," Thursday, April 13; Shultz, (2001), "Update: World Bank and Multinational Corporations Seek to Privatize Water," http://www.projectcensored.org/stories/2001/1.html (accessed December 23, 2001).

66. Goldman Environmental Prize, (2001), http://www.goldmanprize.org/recipients/recipients.html (accessed December 23, 2001); Shultz, J., (2000a), "Bolivians Take to the Streets over the Price of Water," http://www.inthesetimes.com/issue/24/10/shultz2410.html (accessed December 23, 2001); Shultz, J., (2000b), "Water Fall Out: Bolivians Battle Globalization," http://www.inthesetimes.com/issue/24/12/shultz2412.html (accessed December 23, 2001); Shultz, J., (2005)., "Launching the Final Battle in Bolivia's Water War," http://www.democracyctr.org/blog/2005_11_01_democracyctr_archive.html (accessed December 8, 2005).

67. Shultz, J., (2007), "Bolivia Pulls Out of World Bank Trade Court," http://www.democracyctr.org/blog/2007/05/bolivia-pulls-out-of-world-bank-trade.html (accessed May 17, 2007).

68. Chaterjee, P., (2000), "The Earth Wrecker," http://www.sfbg.com/News/34/35/bech1.html (accessed December 23, 2001).

69. Democracy Center, (2006), "Bechtel vs. Bolivia," http://www.democracyctr.org/bechtel/bechtel-vs-bolivia.htm (accessed March 12, 2007); Schultz, J., (2006), "Bechtel to Drop World Bank Trade Case over Water Revolt," Democracy Center, January 17, http://www.democracyctr.org/blog2006/01/bechtel-to-drop-world-bank-trade-case.html.

70. Richards, J. F., (1981), "The Indian Empire and Peasant Production of Opium in the Nineteenth Century," *Modern Asian Studies,* 15 (1): 59–62.

71. Adams, M., (2007), "The Secret History of Big Pharma's Role in Creating and Marketing Heroin, LSD, Meth, Ecstasy and Speed," *News Target,* Tuesday, April 03, http://www.newstarget.com/021768.html (accessed April 7, 2007).

72. Parenti, M., (1995), *Democracy for the Few,* sixth edition (New York: St. Martin's Press).

73. Fratepietro, S., (2001), "Plan Columbia: The Hidden Front in the U.S. Drug War," *Humanist,* 61: 18–21.

74. Ibid.

75. Ibid.

76. Cray, C., (2000), "The U-wa-Oxy Standoff," *Multinational Monitor,* 21: 7–8.

77. Mokhiber, R., and R. Weissman, (1997), "Beat the Devil: The 10 Worst Corporations in 1997," *Multinational Monitor* 18: 9–18.

78. Reinsborough, P., (2001), "Colombia's U'Wa People: The Real Price of Oil," *NACLA Report on the Americas* 34: 44.

79. Soltani, A., P. Reinsborough, and J. Carwil, (2001), "Colombia's U'wa Tribe and Supporters Celebrate Oxy's Failure to Find Oil," *Amazon Watch*, July 31, http://www.amazonwatch.org/newsroom/newsreleases01/jul31_uwa.html (accessed October 21, 2001).

80. Fratepietro (2001).

81. Dudley, S., (2000), "The Colombia Quagmire," *The American Prospect* 11: 32–37.

82. Fratepietro (2001).

83. Ibid.

84. Goodman, A., (2007), "Chiquita's Slipping Appeal," *Truthdig* http://www.truthdig.com/report/item/20070320_chiquitas_slipping_appeal/ (accessed March 26, 2007).

85. Giraldo, J., (1996), *Colombia: The Genocidal Democracy* (Monroe, ME: Common Courage Press).

86. Human Rights Watch, (2005), "Displaced and Discarded: The Plight of Internally Displaced Persons in Bogota and Cartagena," http://www.hrw.org/english/docs/2005/10/14/colomb11864_txt.htm (accessed December 13, 2005).

87. Ibid.

88. COHA (2006).

89. Fratepietro (2001).

90. Dudley (2000).

91. Ibid.

92. Adams, P., (2005), "The Beginning of the End to a Coherent U.S. Drug Strategy," Council on Hemispheric Affairs, http://www.coha.org/NEW_PRESS_RELEASES/_2005/05.82 (accessed December 29, 2005).

93. Giraldo (1996).

94. Calle, F., (2000), "The Children's Movement for Peace in Colombia," *Social Justice* 27: 158–159.

95. "Afghanistan: A History of Turbulence," (2001), *MSNBC*, http://www.msnbc.com/news/6555554146.asp (accessed November 20, 2001).

96. World Bank, (2001), "World Development Indicators," CD-ROM version, International Bank for Reconstruction and Development, from University of California at Berkeley Library Network.

97. Makhmalbaf, M., (2001), "Limbs of No Body," *Iranian*, Opinion section, http://www.iranian.com/Opinion/2001/June/Afghan/index.html (accessed November 15, 2001).

98. MacDonald, S. B., (1992), "Afghanistan's Drug Trade," *Society* 29: 61–66.

99. Makhmalbaf (2001).

100. Shen, F., (2001), "Hard Lives: People of Afghanistan Face War and Poverty," *Washington Post*, October 3, C16.

101. Ford, N., and A. Davis, (2001), "Chaos in Afghanistan: Famine, Aid and Bombs," *Lancet* 358: 1543–1544.

102. Goodhand, J., (2005), "Frontiers and Wars: The Opium Economy in Afghanistan," *Journal of Agrarian Change* 5 (2): 191–216.

103. Mendenhall, P., (2001), "Afghanistan's Cash Crop," *MSNBC*, http://www.msnbc.com/news/564809.asp (accessed November 15, 2001).

104. Golden, T., (2001), "A War on Terror Meets a War on Drugs," *New York Times*, November 25, http:www.nytimes.com (accessed November 26, 2001); Goodhand, J., (2000), "From Holy War to Opium War? A Case Study of the Opium Economy in North Eastern Afghanistan," *Central Asian Study* 19: 265–280.

105. Scheer, R., (2001), "Bush's Faustian Deal with the Taliban," *Los Angeles Times*, May 23, 22.

106. Mendenhall (2001).

107. Golden (2001).

108. Weiner, T., (2001), "With Taliban Gone, Opium Farmers Return to Their Cash Crop," *New York Times*, November 26, 1.

109. LaVine, S., and D. Pearl, (2001), "As the Taliban Recede, Opium Blooms Again—Until Afghanistan Gets a New Government, Growers Are Planting," *Wall Street Journal*, A15.

110. Weiner (2001).

111. LaVine and Pearl (2001).

112. North, A., (2005), "Losing the War on Afghan Drugs," *BBC News*, Lashkar Gah, Helmand, December 4, http://news.bbc.co.uk/2/hi/south_asia/4493596.stm.

113. Rubin, B. R., and O. Zakhilwal, (2005), "A War on Drugs, or a War on Farmers?" *Wall Street Journal* (Eastern Edition), A.20.

114. Ibid.

115. Goodhand (2005); Rubin and Zakhilwal (2005).

116. North (2005).

117. Ford and Davis (2001).

118. Perry, A., (2001), "Hunger and Despair in the Camps," *Time* 158 (December 3): 33.

119. Perry (2001).

120. Makhmalbaf (2001), 1

121. Marlay, R., and B. Ulmer, (2001), "Report on Human Rights in Burma: Background and Current Status," *Journal of Third World Studies* 18: 113–128.

122. Coday, D., (2001), "Burma," *National Catholic Reporter* 37: 12.

123. McCarthy, S., (2000), "Ten Year of Chaos in Burma: Foreign Investment and Economic Liberalization under the SLORC-SPCD, 1988 to 1998," *Pacific Affairs*, 73: 233–262.

124. Coday (2001).

125. Marlay and Ulmer (2001).

126. Lewis-Horne, (2000), "School for Rape: The Burmese Military and Sexual Violence," review *School for Rape: The Burmese Military and Sexual Violence, Violence Against Women*, 6: 1174–1178.

127. Bruno, K., and J. Valette, (2001), "Cheney & Halliburton: Go Where the Oil Is," *Multinational Monitor* 22: 22–25.

128. McCarthy (2000).

129. Bruno and Valette (2001).

130. McCarthy (2000).

131. Hopey, D., (2000), "An Inextricable Link: Human and Environmental Rights," *Pittsburgh Post-Gazette*, A-6.

132. "Battered Economy Sees Kyat on the Ropes," (2001), *South China Morning Post*, October 12, http://www.scmp.com, http://www.ibiblio.org/obl/docs3/BEW-2006-01.pdf.

133. Warr, P. G., (2000), "The Failure of Myanmar's Agricultural Policies," *Southeast Asian Affairs*, 219–237.

134. Ibid.

135. Matthews, B., (2001), "Myanmar: Beyond the Reach of International Relief?" *Southeast Asian Affairs*, 229–248.

136. Warr (2000).

137. Marlay and Ulmer (2001).

138. Ibid.

139. Chelala, C., and C. Beyrer (1999), "Drug Use and HIV/AIDS in Burma," *Lancet* 354: 1119.

140. Coday (2001).

141. Vicary, A., (2006), "Employment and Poverty in Mae Hong Son Province Thailand: Burmese Refugees in the Labour Market," *Burmese Economic Watch* (1): 47–87.

142. Teitel (1994a).

143. Makhijani, A., (1992), *From Global Capitalism to Economic Justice: An Inquiry into the Elimination of Systematic Poverty, Violence and Environmental Destruction in the World Economy. The Council of International and Public Affairs* (New York: Apex Press).

144. Goldsmith, E., (1997), "Can the Environment Survive the Global Economy?" *Ecologist*, 27 (6): 47.

Chapter 5

1. Mann, M., (1993), *The Sources of Social Power: The Rise of Classes and Nation-States, 1760–1914*, vol. 2 (New York: Cambridge University Press); Mills, C. W., (1956), *The Power Elite* (New York: Oxford University Press).

2. Hartmann, T., (2004), *Unequal Protection: The Rise of Corporate Dominance and the Theft of Human Rights* (New York: St. Martin's Press).

3. Useem, Michael, (1984), *The Inner Circle: Large Corporations and the Rise of Business Political Activity in the U.S. and U.K.* (New York: Oxford University Press).

4. Mann (1996), 1.

5. Domhoff, W. G., (2005), "The Four Networks Theory of Power: A Theoretical Home for Power Structure Research," http://sociology.ucsc.edu/whorulesamerica/theory/four_networks.html (accessed September 21, 2006).

6. Dwight Eisenhower, quoted in Kampfner, J., (2003), "The Pentagon Basks in Triumph," *New Statesman*, 23 (April 28).

7. Shah, A., (2006), "High Military Expenditure in Some Places," http://www.globalissues.org/Geopolitics/ArmsTrade/Spending.asp (accessed March 7, 2006).

8. Ibid.

9. Center for Arms control and Non-Proliferation, (2006), "Highlights of the FY'06 Budget Request February 7, 2005," http://www.armscontrolcenter.org/archives/001658.php.

10. Bilmes, L., and J. Stiglitz, (2006), "War's Stunning Price Tag," *Los Angeles Times*, January 17, http://www.latimes.com/news/opinion/commentary/la-oe-bilmes17jan17,0,7038018.story?coll=la-news-comment-opinions (accessed March 7, 2006).

11. Huber, P., (2003), "The Palm Pilot-JDAM Complex," *Forbes* 171 (10): 88.

12. Moss, M., (2005), "Struggle for Iraq: Troop Shields; Pentagon Study Links Fatalities to Body Armor," *New York Times*, A1.

13. Schwartz, A., and J. Watson, (2004), "The Law and Economics of Costly Contracting," *Journal of Law, Economics, and Organization* 20 (1): 2–31.

14. Ibid.

15. Center for Public Integrity, (2005), "Post-War Contractors Ranked by Total Contract Value in Iraq and Afghanistan from 2002 through July 1, 2004," http://www.publicintegrity.org/wow/resources.aspx?act=total (accessed March 7, 2006).

16. Cowles, D., (2005), "2 BR, 1.5 BATH, All the Defense Contracts You Can Handle," *New Republic*, 8.

17. Makison, L., (2006), "Outsourcing the Pentagon: Who Benefits from the Politics and Economics of National Security?" http://usgovinfo.about.com/od/thepoliticalsystem/a/aboutpacs.htm (accessed August 12, 2006).

18. Ibid.

19. Adler, M., (2006), "Sometimes, Government Is the Answer," *Los Angeles Times*, March 4, http://www.latimes.com/news/opinion/commentary/la-oe-adler4mar04,0,515451.story?coll=la-news-comment-opinions (accessed March 7, 2006).

20. Ibid.

21. Ireland, Doug, (2004), "The Cheney Connection: Tracing the Halliburton Money Trail to Nigeria," *Los Angeles Times*, June 17, http://www.laweekly.com/news/news/the-cheney-connection/1601/ (accessed June 10, 2007).

22. Washington Technology, (2005), "Top 100 Federal Prime Contractors—2005," http://www.washingtontechnology.com/top-100/2005/82.html (accessed March 7, 2006).

23. Heuners, quoted in St. Clair, J., (2005), *Grand Theft Pentagon* (Monroe, ME: Common Courage Press), 43.

24. Zepezauer, M., and A. Naiman, (1996), *Take the Rich Off Welfare* (Tucson: Odonian Press).

25. Caldicott, H., (2002/2004), *The New Nuclear Danger: George W. Bush's Military-Industrial Complex* (New York: The New Press), xxx.

26. Bechtel, (2006), September, http://en.wikipedia.org/wiki/Bechtel (accessed December 12, 2006).

27. Caldicott (2002/2004).

28. Peterson, L., (2006), "The Windfalls of War: Bechtel Group, Inc.," Center for Public Integrity, http://www.publicintegrity.org/wow/bio.aspx?act=pro&ddlC=6 (accessed September 21, 2006).

29. Ibid.

30. Caldicott (2002/2004).

31. Ismail, M. A., (2006), "Investing in War: The Carlyle Group Profits from Government and Conflict," Center for Public Integrity, http://www.publicintegrity.org/pns/report.aspx?aid=424 (accessed September 22, 2006).

32. Ibid.

33. Caldicott (2002/2004).

34. Global Policy Forum, (2006), "Hurricane Halliburton: Conflict Climate Change and Catastrophe," http://www.globalpolicy.org/security/issues/iraq/contractindex.htm (accessed May 19, 2007).

35. Caldicott (2002/2004).

36. St. Clair (2005).

37. Ibid.

38. Ibid.

39. Caldicott (2002/2004).

40. Ibid.

41. Anonymous bonesman, quoted in Robbins, A., (2002), *Secrets of the Tomb: Skull and Bones, the Ivy League, and the Hidden Paths of Power* (Boston: Little Brown).

42. Kenneth Guenther, quoted in Robbins (2002).

43. Schweizer, P., and R. Schweizer, (2004), *The Bushes: Portrait of a Dynasty* (New York: Doubleday).

44. Robbins (2002).

45. Ibid.

46. Peters, M., (2001), "The Bilderberg Group and the Project of European Unification," http://www.xs4all.nl/~ac/global/achtergrond/bilderberg.htm (accessed August 12, 2006).

47. Ibid.

48. Ibid.

49. Mendez, A., (n.d.), "An Uncommon View of the Birth of an Uncommon Market," http://www.bilderberg.org/bildhist.htm#Mendez (accessed August 12, 2006).

50. Sourcewatch, (2006e), "Council on Foreign Relations," http://www.sourcewatch.org/index.php?title=Council_on_Foreign_Relations (accessed September 24, 2006).

51. Ross, R. G., Sr., (2004), *Who's Who of the Elite* (United States: RIE).

52. Pitt, W., (2003), "The Project for the New American Century," http://www.informationclearinghouse.info/article1665.htm (accessed March 8, 2006).

53. Van der Zee, J., (1974), *The Greatest Men's Party on Earth: Inside the Bohemian Grove* (New York: Harcourt Brace Jovanovich); Domhoff, G. W., (2005c), "Social Cohesion and the Bohemian Grove: The Power Elite at Summer Camp," *Who Rules America?* http://sociology.ucsc.edu/whorulesamerica/power/bohemian_grove.html (accessed September 24, 2006).

54. Domhoff (2005c).

55. Phillips, P., (1994), "A Relative Advantage: Sociology of the San Francisco Bohemian Club," doctoral dissertation, Sonoma State University, http://libweb.sonoma.edu/regional/faculty/phillips/bohemianindex.html (accessed August 12, 2006).

56. Domhoff (2005c).

57. Ibid.

58. Ibid.

59. Cockburn, A., (2001), "Meet the Secret Rulers of the World: The Truth about the Bohemian Grove," *Counterpunch*, June 19, http://www.counterpunch.org/bohemian.html; Domhoff, G. William, (1974), *The Bohemian Grove and Other Retreats: A Study in Ruling-Class Cohesiveness* (New York: Harper, Colophon Books).

60. Phillips (1994).

61. Domhoff (2005c).

62. Council on Foreign Relations, (2006), "History of CFR," http://www.cfr.org/about/history/ (accessed September 24, 2006).

63. Peters (2001).

64. Sourcewatch (2006e).

65. Council on Foreign Relations, (2003a), "Iraq: The Day After," task force report, March, http://www.cfr.org/publication/5682/president_bush_should_stay_the_course_in_postwar_iraq_to_ensure_battlefield_victory_is_not_lost_says_council_task_force.html?breadcrumb=default (accessed October 4, 2006).

66. Council on Foreign Relations, (2003b), "Iraq: The Day After—Chairs' Update," task force report, June, http://www.cfr.org/publication/6075/iraq.html?breadcrumb=default (accessed October 4, 2006).

67. Ibid.; Council on Foreign Relations (2003a).

68. Ross (2004).

69. NAM, (2007a), "About Us," http://www.nam.org/s_nam/sec.asp?CID=4&DID=2 (accessed April 24, 2007).

70. NAM, (2007b), "Bottom Line Policy Achievements for Manufacturers," http://www.nam.org/s_nam/doc1.asp?CID=24&DID=201889 (accessed April 24, 2007); NAM, (2007c), "Official Policy Positions: Global Climate Change," http://www.nam.org/s_nam/sec.asp?TRACKID=&SID=1&VID=1&CID=43&DID=41&RTID=0&CIDQS=&Taxonomy=False&specialSearch=False (accessed May 2, 2007); NAM, (2007d), "Talking Points for Manufacturers: Energy Security for American Competitiveness," http://www.nam.org/s_nam/doc1.asp?CID=202556&DID=238282 (accessed May 2, 2007).

71. Useem (1984).

72. Business Roundtable, (2007), "About Business Roundtable," http://www.businessroundtable.org:80/aboutUs/index.aspx (accessed April 24, 2007).

73. Ibid.

74. NAM (2007d).

75. NAM (2007c).

76. Griscom, A., (2004), "Industry Flaks Learn How to Snooker the Public with Their Not-So-Friendly Messages," *Grist*, Jan 1, http://www.grist.org/news/muck/2004/01/21/spin/index.html (accessed April 24, 2007).

77. Leavitt, quoted in Griscom (2004).

78. NAM (2007c).

79. Dreiling, M. C., (2000), "The Class Embeddedness of Corporate Political Action: Leadership in Defense of the NAFTA," *Social Problems*, no. 47, 1, 21–48.

80. Ibid.

81. Domhoff, G. W., (2005b), "The Corporate Community, Nonprofit Organizations, and Federal Advisory Committees: A Study in Linkages," *Who Rules America?* http://sociology.ucsc.edu/whorulesamerica/power.fac.html (accessed September 24, 2006).

82. Dreiling (2000), 39.

83. Ibid, 39.

84. Bimbaum, J. H., (2005), "Hill a Steppingstone to K Street for Some: More Ex-Lawmakers Who Join Private Sector Are Becoming Lobbyists, Study Says," *Washington Post*, Wednesday, July 27, A19; Public Citizen, (2005). "Congressional Revolving Doors: The Journey from Congress to K Street. Public Citizen Investigative Report." http://www.lobbyinginfo.org.

85. Birnbaum, J. H., (2005), "The Road to Riches Is Called K Street," *Washington Post*, June 22, A01.

86. Pitt (2003).

87. Project for the New American Century, (2000), "Rebuilding America's Defenses: Strategy, Forces, and Resources for the New Century," 51.

88. Sourcewatch, (2006b), "Project for the New American Century," http://www.sourcewatch.org/index.php?title=Project_for_the_New_American_Century#PNAC_Documents (accessed March 8, 2006); Caldicott (2002/2004); Pitt (2003).

89. Mayer, J., (2006), "The Hidden Power: The Legal Mind behind the White House's War on Terror, *New Yorker*, July 3; Sourcewatch (2006b).

90. Sourcewatch, (2006d), "Defense Policy Board Advisory Committee," http://www.sourcewatch.org/index.php?title=Defense_Policy_Board (accessed September 30, 2006).

91. Caldicott (2002/2004).

92. Sourcewatch (2006d).

93. Caldicott (2002/2004).

94. Zinn, Howard, (1990), *A People's History of the United States* (New York: Harper Perennial).

95. International Monetary Fund, (2007), International Monetary Fund Web page, http://www.imf.org (accessed June 15, 2007).

96. Stiglitz, J., (2002), *Globalization and Its Discontents* (New York: W. W. Norton & Co).

97. Sachs, J., (2005), *The End of Poverty* (London: Penguin Books).

98. Jones, P. B. C., (2003), "US Files SOS with WTO: End EU's GM Moratorium ASAP," Information Systems for Biotechnology News Report, August, http://www.isb.vt.edu/news/2003/artspdf/aug0306.pdf (accessed January 11, 2007).

99. Oxford Analytica, (2006), "WTO: EU Food Ban Violated Agreement," *Forbes*, http://www.forbes.com/business/2006/10/11/genetically-modified-food-biz-cx_1012oxford.html (accessed January 10, 2007).

100. Hillman, A., and M. Hitt, (1999), "Corporate Political Strategy Formulation: A Model of Approach, Participation, and Strategy Decisions," *Academy of Management Review*, 24 (4): 825–842.

101. Ibid.

102. Grossman, Lindzey, and Brannen, (n.d.), "Model Brief on Corporate Personhood," Program on Corporations, Law, and Democracy, http://www.poclad.org/ModelLegalBrief.cfm (accessed November 15, 2006).

103. Zepernick, M., (2004), "The Impact of Corporations on the Commons," address at the Harvard Divinity School's Theological Opportunities Program, http://www.poclad.org/articles/zepernick02.html (accessed November 13, 2006).

104. Center for Responsive Politics, (2005), "Campaign Finance Reform: What's the Issue?" http://usgovinfo.about.com/gi/dynamic/offsite.htm?zi=1/XJ&sdn=usgovinfo&zu=http%3A%2F%2Fwww.opensecrets.org%2F (accessed November 15, 2006).

105. Coleridge, (2004), "Closing the Circle: The Corporatization of Elections," Free Press, http://www.freepress.org/departments/display/19/2004/875 (accessed November 2, 2006).

106. Center for Responsive Politics (2005).

107. Coleridge (2004).

108. Knott, A., (2004), "Who Gives the Most Money: Financial Corporations and Law Firms Dominate Career Patrons List," Center for Public Integrity, http://www.publicintegrity.org/bop2004/report.aspx?aid=168 (accessed November 2, 2006).

109. Center for Responsive Politics (2005).

110. Detailed information may be found on the Web site of the Center for Responsive Politics, http//www.opensecrets.org/industries/indu.asp?ino=F01.

111. Logan, J. R., and H. Molotch, (1987), *Urban Fortunes: The Political Economy of Place* (Berkeley: University of California Press); Molotch, H., (1999), "Growth Machine Links: Up, Down, and Across," in *The Urban Growth Machine: Critical Perspectives, Two Decades Later*, ed. A. Jonas and D. Wilson 247–265 (Albany: State University of New York Press).

112. Longley, R., (2006), "Political Action Committees," http://usgovinfo.about.com/od/thepoliticalsystem/a/aboutpacs.htm (accessed November 13, 2006).

113. Alden, E., and N. Buckley, (2004), "Wal-Mart Becomes Largest Corporate Political Investor," *Financial Times*, February 24, http://reclaimdemocracy.org/articles_2004/walmart_largest_political_donor_investor.html (accessed November 14, 2006).

114. Cummings, (2006), "Business Owners Hedge Their Bets: Many Increase Their Donations to Democrats, Evening War Chests in Final Days," *Wall Street Journal* (Eastern Edition), A4.

115. Coleridge (2004).

116. Berkman Center for Internet and Society, (2004), "Diebold v. the Bloggers," *Berkman Briefings*, Harvard Law School, http://cyber.law.harvard.edu/briefings/dvb (accessed November 13, 2006).

117. Cardinale, M., (2006), "Diebold Added Secret Patch to Georgia e-Voting Systems in 2002, Whistleblowers Say," *Atlanta Progressive News*, September 28, http://www.atlantaprogressivenews.com/news/0091.html (accessed November 2, 2006).

118. Slater, M., L. Kyser, and J. Chasnow, (2006), "New Barriers to Voting: Eroding the Right to Vote," *National Voter* 55 (3): 7, http://findarticles.com/p/articles/mi_m0MLB/is_3_55/ai_n16689802 (accessed November 15, 2006).

119. Ibid.

120. Taylor, M., (2004), "Community Issues and Social Networks," in *Social Networks and Social Exclusion: Sociological and Policy Perspectives*, ed. Chris Phillipson, Graham Allan, and David Morgan, 205–218 (Hauts England: Ashgate Publishers).

Chapter 6

1. Mueller, J., (2006), *Overblown: How Politicians and the Terrorism Industry Inflate National Security Threats, and Why We Believe Them* (New York: Free Press).

2. Netanyahu, B., (2006), interview with Glenn Beck, CNN Headline News, November 17.

3. Unger, C., (2007), "From the Wonderful Folks Who Brought You Iraq," *Vanity Fair*, March.

4. Rapaport, A., (1964), *Strategy and Conscience* (New York: Harper and Row).

5. Gerace, M. P., (2004), *Military Power, Conflict, and Trade: Military Power, International Commerce and Great Power Rivalry* (London: Frank Cass).

6. Domosh, M., (2006), *American Commodies in an Age of Empire* (London: Routeledge Publishers).

7. Colley, L., (2005), "The US Is Now Rediscovering the Pitfalls of Aspirational Imperialism," *Guardian*, December 17.

8. D'Souza, D., (2000), *The Virtue of Prosperity: Finding Values in an Age of Techno-Affluence* (New York: Touchstone).

9. Colley (2005).

10. Carr, C., (2002), *The Lessons of Terror: A History of Warfare Against Civilians: Why It Has Always Failed and Why It Will Fall Again* (New York: Random House).

11. Zinn, H., (1980), *A People's History of the United States* (New York: HarperCollins).

12. Ibid.

13. Ibid.

14. Peters, M., (2001), "The Bilderberg Group and the Project of European Unification," http://www.xs4all.nl/~ac/global/achtergrond/bilderberg.htm (accessed August 17, 2006).

15. Ibid.

16. Fleming, D. F., (1961), *The Cold War and Its Origins 1917–1960* (New York: Doubleday).

17. Peters (2001).

18. Zinn (1980).

19. Mendez, A., (2006), "An Uncommon View of the Birth of an Uncommon Market," http://www.bilderberg.org/bildhist.htm#Mendez (accessed August 17, 2006).
20. Zinn (1980).
21. Ibid.
22. Parenti, M., (1969), *The Anti-Communist Impulse* (New York: Random House), 35.
23. Jardine, M., (2001), "Days of Infamy and Memory," *In These Times 4* (10).
24. Churchill, W., (1951), *The Second World War Vol. 4: The Hinge of Fate* (London: Cassell & Co.), 428.
25. Churchill, W. (1929). *The World Crisis: The Aftermath.* New York: Scribners.
26. Shuman, F. L., (1928), *American Policy Toward Russia Since 1917* (London: Martin Lawrence).
27. Zinn (1980), 417.
28. Blum, W., (2004), *Killing Hope: US Military and CIA Interventions Since World War II* (Monroe, ME: Common Courage Press).
29. Ganser, D., (2005), *NATO's Secret Armies: Operation Gladio and Terrorism in Western Europe* (London: Frank Cass Verlog); Rajiva, L., (2005), "The Pentagon's 'NATO Option,' http://www.commondreams.org/views05/0210-22.htm (accessed February 10, 2006).
30. Ganser (2005).
31. Ibid.
32. Øberg, J., (2006), "Does the European Union Promote Peace?" Transnational Foundation for Peace and Future Research, Lund, Sweden, October 6.
33. Chomsky, N., (2003), *Hegemony of Survival: America's Quest for Global Dominance* (New York: Holt).
34. Zinn (1980).
35. Hitchens, C., (2001), *The Trial of Henry Kissinger* (London: Verso Press).
36. Perkins, J., (2006), *Confessions of an Economic Hitman* (New York: Plume); Hiatt, S., ed., (2007), *A Game as Old as Empire: The Secret World of Economic Hit Men and the Web of Global Corruption* (San Francisco: Berrett-Koehler).
37. COHA (Council on Hemispheric Affairs), (2006), "Report on Nicaragua: How the United States Continues to Manipulate Nicaragua's Economic and Political Future," http://www.coha.org/2006/06/22/how-the-united-states-continues-to-manipulate-nicaraguas-economic-and-polical-future.
38. Robinson, L., (2004), *Masters of Chaos: The Secret History of Special Forces* (Public Affairs Press).
39. Prados, J., (2006), *Safe for Democracy: The Secret Wars of the CIA* (Chicago: Ivan R. Dee).
40. Paul, R., (2003), "National Endowment for Democracy: Paying to Make Enemies of America," http://www.antiwar.com/paul/paul79.html.
41. Kinzer, S., (2006), *Overthrow: America's Century of Regime Change from Hawaii to Iraq* (New York: Times Books).
42. Grandin, G., (2006), *Empire's Workshop: Latin America, the United States, and the Rise of the New Imperialism* (New York: Metropolitan Books).
43. Tulley, A., (1962), *CIA: The Inside Story* (New York: William Morrow); Kinzer, S., (2003), *All the Shah's Men: An American Coup and the Roots of Middle East Terror* (Hoboken, NJ: Wiley & Sons).
44. Goff, F., and M. Locker, (1971), "The Violence of Domination: U. S. Power and the Dominican Republic," in *The Triple Revolution Emerging*, ed. R. Perrucci and M. Pilisuk (Boston: Little, Brown).

45. Pilisuk, M., (1972), *International Conflict and Social Policy* (Englewood Cliffs, NJ: Prentice Hall).

46. Leggett, J., (1978), *Allende, His Exit, and Our Times* (New Brunswick, NJ: Cooperative Press).

47. Wise, D., and T. Ross, (1964), *The Invisible Government* (New York: Random House).

48. Ibid.

49. Schlesinger, S., and S. Kinzer, (1999), *Bitter Fruit: The Story of the American Coup in Guatemala* (Cambridge: Harvard University).

50. Wise and Ross (1964).

51. Amnesty International, (1989), *Guatemala: Human Rights Violations Under Civilian Governments* (London: Amnesty International).

52. Guatemalan Commission for Historical Clarification, (n.d.), "Guatemala: Memory of Silence," report of the Commission for Historical Clarification Conclusions and Recommendations, http://shr.aaas.org/guatemala/ceh/report/english/toc.html.

53. Black, G., (1988), *The Good Neighbor* (New York: Pantheon); Amnesty International, (1996), "Amnesty International Report 1996," http://web.amnesty.org/library/index/engPOL100011999.

54. Hirsh, M., and J. Barry, (2005), "The Salvador Option," *Newsweek*, January 14.

55. Busby, H., M. Turck, and C. Mitchell, (2002), "U.S. Works Closely with Coup Leaders," http://www.americas.org/News/Features/200205_Venezuela_Coup/20020501_US_Role.htm (site discontinued).

56. Cancache, D., (2002), "From Bullets to Ballots: The Emergence of Popular Support for Hugo Chavez," *Latin American Politics and Society* 44: 69–90.

57. Birns, L., and A. Volberding, (2002), "U.S. Is the Primary Loser in Failed Venezuelan Coup," *Newsday*, April 21, http://www.ratical.org/ratville/CAH/linkscopy/USprimaryL.html.

58. Palast, G., (2002), "OPEC Chief Warned Chavez about Coup," *Guardian*, May 13, http://www.guardian.co.uk/venezuela/story/0,,858072,00.html.

59. Robinson, G., (2002), "If You Leave Us, We Will Die," *Dissent* 49: 87–99.

60. Cooper, M., (2002), "The Coup That Wasn't," *Nation*, May.

61. Ibid.

62. Anderson, N., (2002), "Venezuelan President Must Embrace Democracy, Bush Says: The U. S. Government Seeks to Manage Fallout from the Failed Coup as Regional Leaders Debate What Happened and Why," *Los Angeles Times*, April 19.

63. "Tales from a Failed Coup," (2002), *Economist*, April 25.

64. Campbell, D., (2002), "American Navy 'Helped Venezuelan Coup,' *Guardian*, April 29, http://www.guardian.co.uk/international/story/0,3604,706802,00.html.

65. Palast (2002).

66. Wilpert, G., (2002), "Coup in Venezuela: An Eyewitness Account," April, http://www.commondreams.org/views02/0412-08.htm.

67. Nelson-Pallmeyer, J., (1997), *School of Assassins* (New York: Orbis Books), quoted in David Mericle, *Impact Press*, http://www.impactpress.com/articles/aprmay99/soa4599.html.

68. Almond, M., (2002), "Nightmare at Camp Bondsteel: Djakova, Kosovo," *New Statesman*, February 18.

69. Marty, D., (2006), "Alleged Secret Detentions and Unlawful Interstate Transfers Involving Council of Europe Member States," Council of Europe Committee on Legal Affairs and Human Rights (AS/Jur, 16 Part II); Whitlock, C., (2006), "European Probe

Finds Signs of CIA-Run Secret Prisons," *Washington Post*, June 8, http://projects.washingtonpost.com/staff/email/craig+whitlock/.

70. Younge, G., (2002), "The Good Dictators," *Guardian*, April 29, http://www.guardian.co.uk/Columnists/Column/0,5673,706931,00.html.

71. Trowbridge, E., (2002), "Back Road Reckoning," *Dissent* 49: 101–113.

72. Hitchens, C., (2002), "Kissinger's Green Light to Suharto," *Nation*, February, http://www.thenation.com/doc/20020218/hitchens.

73. Burr, W., and M. L. Evans, eds., (2001), National Security Archive Electronic Briefing, Book No. 62, http://www.gwu.edu/~nsarchiv/NSAEBB/NSAEBB62.

74. Jardine (2001).

75. Ibid.

76. Da Silva, W. (2002), "Letter from East Timor," *Nation*, July, 22–24.

77. Trowbridge (2002).

78. Hill, H., (2006), "Why Do Australians Want Mari Alkatiri Out of the Prime Ministership of East Timor?" May 6, http://samanddaniel.blogspot.com/2006/05/why-do-australians-want-mari-alkatiri.html.

79. Steele, J., (2002), "East Timor Is Independent So Long as It Does as It's Told," *Guardian*, May 23, http://www.guardian.co.uk/comment/story/0,,720552,00.html.

80. Robinson (2002).

81. Pelletiere, S. C., (2004), *Iraq and the International Oil System: Why America Went to War in the Gulf* (Washington, DC: Maisonneuve Press); Phillips, K., (2006), *American Theocracy: The Peril and Politics of Radical Religion, Oil, and Borrowed Money in the 21st* Century (New York: Penguin Books).

82. Galbraith, P. W., (2006a), *The End of Iraq: How American Incompetence Created a War without End* (New York: Simon and Shuster); Galbraith, P. W., (2006b), "The True Iraq Appeasers," *Boston Globe*, August 31, http://www.boston.com/news/globe/editorial_opinion/oped/articles/2006/08/31/the_true_iraq_appeasers/.

83. Galbraith (2006a).; Ricks, T. E., (2006), *Fiasco: The American Military Adventure in Iraq* (New York: Penguin Press).

84. Pelletiere (2004).

85. Lohbeck, K., (1993), "Holy War, Unholy Victory: Eyewitness to the CIA's Secret War in Afghanistan," (Washington, DC: Regnery Gateway).

86. Pilisuk, M., and A. Wong, (2002), "State Terrorism: When the Perpetrator Is a Government," in *Psychology and Terrorism*, ed. C. Stout (Westport: CT: Praeger); Coll, S., (2001), *Ghost Wars: The Secret History of the CIA, Afghanistan, and Bin Laden, from the* Soviet *Invasion to September 10, 2001.* (New York: Penguin).

87. Hiro, D., (2002), "Saudis: US Go Home?" *Nation*, March, http://www.thenation.com/doc/20020311/hiro.

88. Knowlton, B., (2002), "Saudis Haven't Requested Pullout, U. S. Officials Say," *International Herald* Tribune, January 21, http://www.iht.com/articles/2002/01/21/diplo_ed3_php.

89. Ibid.

90. Roberts, P., (2004), *The End of Oil: On the Edge of a Perilous New World* (Boston: Houghton Mifflin); Phillips (2006).

91. Bookman, J., (n.d.), "The President's Real Goal in Iraq," http://www.thirdworldtraveler.com/Iraq/Presidents_Real_Goal_Iraq.html.

92. Galston, W. A., (2002), "Why a First Strike Will Surely Backfire," *Washington Post*, June 16, http://www.washingtonpost.com/ac2/wp-dyn/A54644-2002Jun14?language=printer.

93. Pilger, J., (2002), "The Great Charade," *Observer*, July 14, http://observer.guardian.co.uk/worldview/story/0,,754972,00.html.

94. Mearsheimer, J. J., and S. M. Walt, (2003), "An Unnecessary War," *Foreign Policy*, January/February, http://www.foreignpolicy.com/users/login.php?story_id=169&URL=http://www.foreignpolicy.com/story/cms.php?story_id=169.

95. Cohen, A., and G. P. O'Driscoll, Jr., (2003), "Achieving Economic Reform and Growth in Iraq," Web Memo #236, Heritage Foundation, http://www.heritage.org/research/middleeast/wm236.cfm.

96. Barnes, J., and A. Meyers Jaffe, (2006), "The Persian Gulf and the Geopolitics of Oil," *Survival* 48 (1), 152.

97. Diamond, L. J., (2005), *Squandered Victory: The American Occupation and the Bungled Effort to Bring Democracy to Iraq* (New York: Times Books).

98. Juhasz, A., (2006), *The* Bush *Agenda: Invading the World, One Economy at a Time* (New York: Regan Books, HarperCollins).

99. Floyd, C., (2007), "Claiming the Prize: Escalation Aimed at Securing Iraqi Oil," *Information Clearing House*, January 12, http://www.alternet.org/waroniraq/46602/.

100. Fortson, D., (2007), "Iraq Posed to End Drought for Thirsting Oil Giants," *Independent*, May 22, http://news.independent.co.uk/business/news/article2132467.ece.

101. Lando, B., (2007), *Web of Deceit: The History of Western Complicity in Iraq, from Churchill to Kennedy to George W. Bush* (New York: Other Press), 267.

102. Chandrasekaran, R., (2006), *Imperial Life in the Emerald City: Inside Iraq's Green Zone* (New York: Random House).

103. Mann, J., (2004), *Rise of the Vulcans: The History of Bush's War Cabinet* (New York: Viking), xiii.

104. Mann (2004).

105. Ibid.

106. Ibid, 198.

107. Ibid, 363.

108. Joint Chiefs of Staff, (2005), *Doctrine for Joint Nuclear Operations Joint* (Publication 3-12), March 15, (Washington DC: Joint Chiefs of Staff).

109. Ibid.

110. Suskind, R., (2006), *The One Percent Doctrine* (Parsipanny, NJ: Simon and Schuster).

111. Ibid.

112. Montgomery, B., (2005), "Congressional Oversight: Vice President Richard B. Cheney's Executive Branch Triumph," *Political Science Quarterly* 120: 615–616.

113. Mann (2004), 196–197.

114. Cooper, P. J., (2002), *By Order of the President: The Use and Abuse of Executive Direct Action*. Lawrence: University Press of Kansas.

115. McCoy, A., (2006), *A Question of Torture: CIA Interrogation, from the Cold War to the War on Terror* (New York: Metropolitan Books, Henry Holt and Company).

116. Rejali, D., (in press), *Torture and* Democracy (Princeton, NJ: Princeton University Press).

117. Rajiva, L., (2005), "The Torture-Go-Round," *Counterpunch*, December 5, http://www.counterpunch.org/rajiva12052005.html.

118. Department of the Army, (1987), "Intelligence Interrogation," Army Field Manual 34-52, http://www.globalsecurity.org/intell/library/policy/army/fm/fm34-52/.

119. Schrepel, W., (2005), "Paras and Centurions: Lessons Learned from the Battle of Algiers," *Peace and Conflict: Journal of Peace Psychology* 11 (1): 71–90.

120. Klein, N., (2005), "Torture's Part of the Territory," *Los Angeles Times*, June 7, B13.

121. Ibid.; Pilisuk, M., (2005), "Unprofessional Warriors: Lessons Small and Large," *Peace and Conflict: Journal of Peace Psychology* 11 (1): 95–100.

122. McCoy (2006); Packer, G., (2005), *The Assassin's Gate: America in Iraq* (New York: Farrar, Straus, and Giroux).

123. Strassler, R. B., ed., (1996), *The Landmark Thucydides: A Comprehensive Guide to the Peloponnesian War* (New York: Free Press).

124. Milliard, T., (2003), "Overcoming Post-Colonial Myopia: A Call to Recognize and Regulate Private Military Corporations," *Military Law Review* 176: 1–95.

125. Thomson, J. E., (1990), "State Practices, International Norms, and the Decline of Mercenarism," *International Studies Quarterly* 34 (1): 23–47; Coleman, J. R., (2004), "Constraining Modern Mercenarism," *Hastings Law Journal* 55: 1493–1138.

126. Coleman (2004).

127. Ibid.

128. Ibid, 1519.

129. Ibid, 1519.

130. Zarate, J. C., (1998), "The Emergence of a New Dog of War: Private International Security Companies, International Law, and the New World Disorder," *Stanford Journal of International Law*, 75, 82.

131. Coleman (2004).

132. Scahill, J., (2007), *Blackwater: The Rise of the World's Most Powerful Mercenary Army* (New York: Nation Press).

133. Edward Said, quoted in Engdahl, W., (2004), *A Century of War: Anglo-American Oil Politics and the New World Order* (London: Pluto Press), 270.

134. Schou, N., (2006), *Kill the Messenger: How the CIA's Crack-Cocaine Controversy Destroyed Journalist Gary Webb* (New York: Nation Books); Scott, P. D., and J. Marshall, (1991), *Cocaine Politics: Drugs, Armies, and the CIA in Central America* (Berkeley: University of California Press); Webb, G., (2001), "The New Rules for the New Millennium," in *The Disinformation Guide to Media Distortion, Historical Whitewashes, and Cultural Myths*, ed. R. Kick, 38–39 (New York: Disinformation Company).

Chapter 7

1. The Rendon Group, (2005), "The Rendon Group, http://www.therendongroup.com, http://www.sourcewatch.org/index.php?title=Edelman.

2. Sourcewatch, (2007), "Daniel J. Edelman, Inc.," http://www.sourcewatch.org/index.php?title=Edelman.

3. Farsetta, D., (2006), "The Devil Is in the Lack of Details: The Defense Department's Media Contracts," PR Watch, http://www.prwatch.org/node/4481.

4. McChesney, R., (2004), *The Problem of the Media: U. S. Communication Politics in the 21st Century* (New York: Monthly Review Press); Hedges, S. J., (2005), "Firm Helps U.S. Mold News Abroad," *Chicago Tribune*, November 14, http://www.mediachannel.org/blog/node/1860.

5. Bagdikian, B., (2004), *The New Media Monopoly* (Boston: Beacon Press).

6. McChesney (2004).

7. Chomsky, N., (2002), *Media Control: The Spectacular Achievements of Propaganda*, second edition (New York: Seven Stories Press).

8. Sproule, J. M., (1997), *Propaganda and Democracy: The American Experience of Media and Mass Persuasion* (Cambridge: Harvard University Press).

9. Ibid, 8.

10. Chomsky (2002).

11. Sproule (1997), 10.

12. Ibid., 11.

13. Snow, N., (1998), *Propaganda, Inc.: Selling America's Culture to the World* (New York: Seven Stories Press).

14. Bernays, E., (1928), *Propaganda* (New York: H. Liveright); Bernays, E., (1934), *Crystallizing Public Opinion* (New York: Liveright); Bernays, E., (1955), *The Engineering of Consent* (Norman: University of Oklahoma Press).

15. Edward Bernays, quoted in Chomsky, N., (2001), "What Makes the Mainstream Media Mainstream," in *The Disinformation Guide to Media Distortion, Historical White-washes, and Cultural Myths*, ed. R. Kick, 24 (New York: Disinformation Company).

16. Edward Bernays, quoted in Snow (1998), 18.

17. Snow (1998).

18. Chomsky (2001).

19. Sproule (1997), 18.

20. Sproule (1997).

21. William Evjue, quoted in McChesney, R., (1999), *Rich Media, Poor Democracy: Communication Politics in Dubious Times* (Chicago: University of Illinois Press).

22. Sproule (1997).

23. Bagdikian (2004).

24. Shah, A., (2006), "Media Manipulation," http://www.globalissues.org/HumanRights/Media/Manipulation.asp?p=1.

25. McChesney (1999).

26. "Fox News Producer Resigns over Middle East Coverage," (2006), Democracy Now! August 16, http://www.democracynow.org/article.pl?sid=06/08/16/148232.

27. Iype, D. H., (2007), "MySpace Refused Our Ad," Common Cause, May, http://www.commonblog.com/story/2007/1/10/103219/774.

28. Moore, A., (2003), "Interlocking Directorates and Megamedia. Columbia Journalism Review," March/April, http://cjrarchives.org/issues/2003/2/lists-moore.asp.

29. Bagdikian (2004).

30. Ibid.

31. Lynch, A., (2005), "U.S.: The Media Lobby," *AlterNet*, March, http://www.corpwatch.org/print_article.php?id=11947.

32. Ibid.

33. Bagdikian (2004), 138.

34. Rupert Murdoch, quoted in McChesney (1999), 74.

35. McChesney (1999).

36. Moyers, B., (2003), "U.S. Media Gets Bigger," *Now* with Bill Moyers on PBS, October 10, http://www.corpwatch.org/print_article.php?id=7836.

37. Bagdikian (2004).

38. Klinenberg, E., (2007), *Fighting for Air: The Battle to Control America's Media* (New York: Henry Holt & Co.).

39. Moyers, B., (2007), "Digital Destiny," address to the National Conference on Media Reform in Memphis,TN, on Pacifica Radio, *Democracy Now*, January 16.

40. Freire, P., (1968), *Pedagogy of the Oppressed* (New York: Seabury Press).

41. Moyers (2003).

42. Bagdikian (2004).

43. Lynch (2005).

44. Lowry Mays, quoted in Lynch (2005).

45. Common Cause, (2006), "Wolves in Sheep's Clothing: Telecom Industry Front Groups and Astroturf,", http://www.commoncause.org/site/pp.asp?c=dkLNK1MQIwG&b=1499059; Center for Strategic and International Studies and the Massachusetts Institute of Technology, (2004), "Astroturf: Interest Group Lobbying and Corporate Strategy," *Journal of Economics & Management Strategy,* Winter, 563.

46. Farsetta, D., and D. Price, (2006), "Fake TV News: Widespread and Undisclosed," Center for Media and Democracy PR Watch, http://www.prwatch.org/fakenews/exec summary.

47. Ibid.

48. Soley, L., (1997), "The Power of the Press Has a Price," *Extra!* July/August, http://www.fair.org/index.php?page=1387.

49. Borjesson, K., ed., (2005), *Feet to the Fire: The Media After 9/11, Top Journalists Speak Out* (New York: Prometheus Books).

50. McChesney (1999), 271.

51. Corpwatch, (n.d.), "General Electric," http://www.corpwatch.org/print_article.php?list=type&type=16.

52. Chester, J., (2007), *Digital Destiny: New Media and the Future of Democracy* (New York: New Press).

53. Moyers (2007).

54. Edward Bernays, quoted in Chomsky, N., (2005), *Imperial Ambitions: Conversations on the Post 9/11 World* (New York: Metropolitan Books), 20.

55. Nunberg, G., (2006), *Talking Right: How Conservatives Turned Liberalism into a Tax-Raising, Latte-Drinking, Sushi-Eating, Volvo-Driving,* New York Times-*Reading, Body-Piercing, Hollywood-Loving, Left-Wing Freak Show* (New York: Public Affairs).

56. Lakoff, G., (2002), *Moral Politics: How Liberals and Conservatives Think* (Chicago: University of Chicago Press); Fromm, E., (1964), *Escape from Freedom* (New York: Holt, Rinehart, and Winston).

57. Pratkanis and Aronson, quoted in McKay, F., (2006), "Propaganda: America's Psychological Warriors," *Seattle Times,* February 19, http://seattletimes.nwsource.com/html/opinion/2002812441_sundayfloyd19.html.

58. Michael Parenti, quoted in Snow (1998), 10.

59. Farsetta (2006).

60. Ibid.

61. Ibid.

62. *Boston Globe,* October 12, 2001, 28. Report analyzed in Blum, William, (2005), "The Anti-Empire Report: Some Things You Need to Know before the World Ends," June 13, http://members.aol.com/bblum6/aer22.htm.

63. Billings, E., (2002), "Hearts and Minds: The Rendon Group's Top-Secret Spin Machine for the Pentagon Is Big Business," Washington Business Forward, http://72.14.253.104/search?q=cache:xUJGAujdlyAJ:www.bizforward.com/wdc/issues/2002; Sourcewatch, (2007b), "Rendon Group," http://www.sourcewatch.org/index.php?title=Rendon_Group.

64. Bamford, J., (2005), "The Man Who Sold the War: Meet John Rendon, Bush's General in the Propaganda War," *Rolling Stone,* November, http://www.rollingstone.com/politics/story/8798997/the_man_who_sold_the_war/.

65. Ibid.

66. Ibid.

67. *New York Times*, quoted in Chaterjee, P., (2006), "Information Warriors: Rendon Group Wins Hearts and Minds in Business, Politics, and War," http://www.corpwatch.org/print_article.php?id=11486.

68. Lincoln Group, (n.d.), "Lincoln Group," http://www.lincolngroup.com.

69. Mazzetti, M., and B. Daragahi, (2005), "The Conflict in Iraq: U.S. Military Covertly Pays to Run Stories in Iraqi Press," *Los Angeles Times*, November 30, http://www.latimes.com/news/nationworld/world/la-fg-infowar30nov30,0,5638790.story?page=1&coll=la-home-headlines; Berkowitz, B., (2006), "Lincoln Group: Unethical Weapon of Mass Deception," Working for Change, http://www.workingforchange.com/printitem.cfm?itemid=2127; Sourcewatch, (2006), "Planting Fake News in Iraq," http://www.sourcewatch.org/index.php?title=Lincoln_Group#Planting_Fake_News_in_Iraq.

70. Brian Whitman, quoted in Pessin, A., (2005), "Defense Department Checking Allegations US Military Paid to Place 'News' Articles in Iraqi Press, http://www.voanews.com/english/archive/2005-11/2005-11-30-voa77.cfm?CFID=87111056&CFTOKEN=46551917.

71. Pessin (2005).

72. Roberts, K., (2006), "Iraq Propaganda Program Legal: Pentagon Report," Reuters, October 19, http://freepress.net/news/18536.

73. Department of Defense, (2004), Report of the Defense Science Board Task Force on Strategic Communication.

74. Rampton, S., and J. Stauber, (2003), *Weapons of Mass Deception: The Uses of Propaganda in Bush's War on Iraq* (New York: Tarcher/Penguin).

75. Goering, Hermann, interview with reporter during the Nuremburg trials, http://www.metafilter.com/30279/Shocking-They-were-lied-to.

76. Lawrence, B., ed., (2006), *Messages to the World: The Statements of Osama bin Laden* (New York: Verso Press).

77. Sourcewatch, (2006), "Office of Strategic Influence," http://www.sourcewatch.org/index.php?title=Office_of_Strategic_Influence.

78. Douglas Feith, quoted in Allen, M., (2002), "White House Angered at Plan for Pentagon Disinformation," *Washington Post*, February 25, http://www.washingtonpost.com/ac2/wp-dyn?pagename=article&contentId=A61716-2002Feb24¬Found=true.

79. Hersh, S., (2003), "Selective Intelligence," *New Yorker*, http://www.newyorker.com/archive/2003/05/12/030512fa_fact?currentPage=1.

80. Dreyfuss, R., and J. Vest, (2004), "The Lie Factory," *Mother Jones*, January/February, http:// www.motherjones.com/cgi-bin/print_article.pl?url=http://www.motherjones.com/news/feature/2004/01/12_405.html.

81. John Pike, quoted in Borger, J., (2003), "The Spies Who Pushed for War," *Guardian*, July 17, http://www.guardian.co.uk/print/0,3858,4714031-103550,00.html.

82. Ibid.

83. Shulsky, quoted in Hersh (2003), 3.

84. Cheney, quoted in Hersh (2003), 2.

85. Caldicott, H., (2004), *The New Nuclear Danger: George W. Bush's Military-Industrial Complex* (New York: New Press).

86. Fetzer, J., (2007), *The 9/11 Conspiracy: The Scamming of America* (Chicago: Open Court/Catfeet Press).

87. Mandell, W., (2003), "The Press, the Press, the Freedom to Suppress," http://theory andscience.icaap.org/content/vol004.002/11_letter_mandel.html.

88. Shane, S., (2005), "Vietnam War Intelligence 'Deliberately Skewed,' Secret Study Says," *New York Times*, December 2, 2005. Posted on *Common Dreams* news center. http://www.commondreams.org/headlines05/1202-06.htm (accessed January 19, 2006).

89. Herman, E., (2006), "U.S. Willing to Talk, with Conditions, and the Media Bites Once Again," *Znet*, June, http://www.zmag.org/sustainers/content/2006-06/10herman.cfm.

90. Herman, E. S., and R. B. DuBoff, (1966), *America's Vietnam Policy: The Strategy of Deception.* (Washington DC: Public Affairs Press); Schurmann, F., P. D. Scott, and R. Zeinik, (1966), *The Politics of Escalation in Vietnam* (Boston: Beacon Press).

91. Herman (2006).

92. Ibid.

93. Schechter, D., (2005), *The Death of Media and the Fight to Save Democracy* (Hoboken, NJ: Melville House); Schechter, D., (2006), *When News Lies: Media Complicity and the Iraq War* (New York: SelectBooks).

94. Victoria Clarke, quoted in Schechter (2006), 173.

95. Wolff, M., (2003), "Live from Doha," *New York Magazine*, April http://nymag.com/nymetro/news/media/columns/medialife/n_8545/.

96. Massing, M., (2003), "The Doha Follies," *Nation*, April http://www.thenation.com/doc/20030421/massing.

97. Robert Young Pelton, quoted in Schechter (2006), 193.

98. Rich, F., (2006a), *The Greatest Story Ever Told: The Decline and Fall of Truth from 9/11 to Katrina* (London: Penguin Press); Rich, F., (2006), "The Peculiar Disappearance of the War in Iraq," *New York Times*, July 30, http://select.nytimes.com/gst/abstract.html?res=F40E17FF385B0C738FDDAE0894DE404482&n=Top%2fOpinion%2fEditorials%20and%20Op%2dEd%2fOp%2dEd%2fColumnists%2fFrank%20Rich.

99. Nichols, J., and R. McChesney, (2005), *Tragedy and Farce: How the American Media Sell Wars, Spin Elections, and Destroy Democracy* (New York: New Press).

100. McChesney (2004).

101. Nichols and McChesney (2005).

102. Ibid, 26.

103. Hollar, J., and P. Hart, (2005), "When 'Old News' Has Never Been Told," *Extra!* July/August, http://www.fair.org/index.php?page=2612.

104. Ibid.

105. Ibid.

106. Klein, N., (2004), "You Asked for My Evidence, Mr. Ambassador: Here It Is in Iraq; the U. S. Does Eliminate Those Who Dare to Count the Dead," *Guardian*, December 4, http://www.guardian.co.uk/Iraq/Story/0,2763,1366349,00.html.

107. Roberts. L., R. Garfield, J. Khudhairi, and G. Burnham, (2004), "Mortality Before and After the 2003 Invasion of Iraq, a Cluster Sample Survey," *Lancet* 364: 9445, http://www.thelancet.com/journal/vol364/iss9445/full//llan.364.9445.early_online_PUBLICATION.3113.

108. Ireland, D., (2006), "Why U.S. Media Dismissed the *Lancet* Study of 100,000 Iraqi Civilian Dead," Common Dreams, http://www.commondreams.org/cgi-bin/print.cgi?file=/views05/0127-23.htm.

109. Ibid.

110. David R. Meddings, quoted in Ireland (2006).

111. Burnham, G., R. Lafta, S. Doocy, and L. Roberts, (2006), "Mortality after the 2003 Invasion of Iraq: A Cross-Sectional Cluster Sample Survey," *Lancet*, DOI:10.1016/SO140-6736 (06) 6949, 1–9.

112. Roberts et al. (2004).

113. *Time* magazine, quoted in Anderson, R., (2003), "'That's Militainment!' The Pentagon's Media-Friendly 'Reality' War," *Extra!* May/June, http://www.fair.org/indexphp?page=1141&printer_friendly=1.

114. Chinni, D., (n.d.), "Jessica Lynch: Media Myth-Making in the Iraq War," http://www.journalism.org/node/223.

115. *London Times*, quoted in Anderson (2003).

116. Rush Limbaugh, quoted in Remnick, D., (2004), "Hearts and Minds," *New Yorker*, May 17, http://www.newyorker.com/printables/talk/040517ta_talk_remnick.

117. Hersh, S., (2004a), "Torture at Abu Ghraib," *New Yorker*, May, http://www.newyorker.com/archive/2004/05/10/040510fa_fact?currentPage=1.

118. Hersh, S., (2004c), "The Grey Zone: How a Secret Pentagon Program Came to Abu Ghraib," *New Yorker*, May, http://www.newyorker.com/archive/2004/05/24/040524fa_fact.

119. Hersh (2004a).

120. Ibid.

121. International Committee of the Red Cross, (2004), "Report of the International Committee of the Red Cross on the Treatment by Coalition Forces of Prisoners of War and Other Protected Persons by the Geneva Conventions in Iraq During Arrest, Internment, and Interrogation," http://www.globalsecurity.org/military/library/report/2004/icrc_report_iraq_feb2004.htm.

122. Human Rights Watch, (2004), "The Road to Abu Ghraib," http://hrw.org/reports/2004/usa0604/.

123. Ibid.

124. Ibid.

125. Ibid.

126. Program on International Policy Issues, (2003), "Study Finds Direct Link Between Misinformation and Public Misconception," http://truthout.org/docs_03/printer_100403F.shtml.

127. Ibid.

128. Ibid.

129. Ibid.

130. Milbank, D., and C. Deane, (2003), "Hussein Link to 9/11 Lingers in Many Minds," *Washington Post*, September 6, http://www.washingtonpost.com/ac2/wp-dyn/A32862-2003Sep5?language=printer.

131. Solomon, N., (2003), "Linking the Occupation of Iraq with the 'War on Terrorism,'" *Media Beat*, November, http://www.fair.org/index.php?page=2385&printer_friendly=1; Solomon, N., (2005), *War Made Easy: How Presidents and Pundits Keep Spinning Us to Death* (Hoboken, NJ: J. Wiley).

132. Rich (2006a).

133. David Brooks, quoted in Bacon, J., (2005), "Saying What They've Been Thinking: Racial Stereotypes in Katrina Commentary," *Extra!* November/December, http://www.fair.org/indexphp?page=2795&printer_friendly=1.

134. Bill O'Reilly, quoted in Bacon (2005).

135. Ibid.

136. Wolf Blitzer, quoted in Yassin, J. O., (2005), "Demonizing Victims of Katrina: Coverage Painted Hurricane Survivors as Looters, Snipers, and Rapists," *Extra!* November/December, http://www.fair.org/index.php?page=2793&printer_friendly=1.

137. Allen Breed, quoted in Yassin (2005).

138. *Washington Post*, quoted in Yassin (2005).

139. Yassin (2005).

140. Bacon (2005); Price, D., (2005), "Workers Get Hit Twice: Hurricane Katrina and Davis-Bacon Profiteering," *Counterpunch*, September, http://www.counterpunch.org/price09232005.html.

141. Ibid.

142. Bacon (2005).

143. Donaghy, T., J. Freeman, F. Grifo, K. Kaufman, T. Maassarani, and L. Shultz, (2007), "Atmosphere of Pressure," Report of Union of Concerned Scientists and Government Accountability Project.

144. Ibid.

145. Revkin, A., (2005), "Bush Aide Softened Greenhouse Gas Links to Global Warming," *New York Times*, June 8, http://www.nytimes.com/2005/06/08/politics/08climate.html?pagewanted=1&ei=5090&en=22149dc70c0731d8&ex=1275883200.

146. Center for Responsive Politics, (2006), "Oil and Gas: Top 20 Recipients," http://www.opensecrets.org/industries/recips.asp?Ind=E01.

147. Suskind, R., (2004), "Without a Doubt," *New York Times*, October 17, http://www.truthout.org/docs_04/101704A.shtml;Lincoln Group, (n.d.), http://www.lincolngroup.com.

Chapter 8

1. Parenti, M., (1995), *Democracy for the Few*, sixth edition (New York: St. Martin's Press); Chomsky, N., (1993), *The Prosperous Few and the Restless Many* (Berkeley: Odonian Press); Korten, D. C., (1995), *When Corporations Rule the World* (West Hartford, CT: Kumerian Press Inc. & San Francisco: Berrett-Koehler Publishers); Klare, M.T., (2002) *Resource Wars: The New Landscape of Global Conflict* (New York: Henry Holt).

2. Pilisuk, M., and T. Hayden, (1965), "Is There a Military-Industrial Complex Which Prevents Peace? Consensus and Countervailing Power," *Journal of Social Issues* 21 (3): 67–117.

3. Bello, W., S. Cunninhan, and B. Rau, (1999), *Dark Victory: The United States and Global Poverty* (London: Pluto).

4. Wolf, E., (1999), *Peasant Wars of the Twentieth Century* (Norman: University of Oklahoma Press).

5. Pilisuk, M., (1982), "Games Strategists Play," *Bulletin of the Atomic Scientists* 38 (9): 13–17.

6. Reiber, R. W., and R. J. Kelly, (1991), "Substance and Shadow: Images of the Enemy," in *The Psychology of War and Peace: The Image of the Enemy*, ed. R. W. Reiber, 3–39 (New York: Plenum); Herman, E. S., and N. Chomsky, (1988), *Manufacturing Consent* (New York: Pantheon Books)

7. Pilisuk, M, and A. Wong, (2002), "State Terrorism: When the Perpetrator Is a Government," in *Psychology and Terrorism*, ed. C. Stout, 105–132 (Westport, CT: Praeger).

8. Pillar, C., (2007), "Report: Gates Foundation Causing Harm With the Same Money It Uses to Do Good," *Los Angeles Times* reporter interview on *Democracy Now,* Tuesday, January 9.

9. Macy, J. R., and M. Y. Brown, (1998), *Coming Back to Life: Practices to Reconnect Our Lives, Our World* (Gabriola Island, BC, Canada: New Society Publishers).

10. Avnery, U., (2006), "Shhhhhh! Avnery on What Is Missing in the Election Campaign," Gush Shalom, March 12.

11. Chomsky, N., (1993), *The Prosperous Few and the Restless Many* (Berkeley: Odonian Press).

12. Monbiot, G., (2006), *Heat: How to Stop the Planet from Burning* (New York: Doubleday).

13. Lewis, E., (1998), *The Buying of the Congress* (New York: Avon); Domhoff, G. W., (1990), *The Power Elite and the State: How Policy Is Made in America* (Hawthorne, NY: Aldine de Gruyter).

14. Palast, G., (2004), *The Best Democracy Money Can Buy* (New York: Penguin).

15. Silverstein, K., (1998), *Washington on Ten Million Dollars a Day* (Monroe, ME: Common Courage Press).

16. Nossiter, B. D., (1970), *Soft State: A Newspaperman's Chronicle of India* (NewYork: Harper & Row), 32.

17. McChesney, R. W., (1997), *Corporate Media and the Threat to Democracy* (New York: Seven Stories Press); Webb, G., (2001), "The New Rules for the New Millennium," in *The Disinformation Guide to Media Distortion, Historical Whitewashes, and Cultural Myths,* ed. R. Kick, 38–39 (New York: Disinformation Company, Ltd).

18. Goldberg, E., and L. Evans, (1998), *The Prison Industrial Complex and the Global Economy* (Berkeley: Agit Press).

19. Kanner, A., and M. Gomes, (1995), "The All-Consuming Self," in *Ecopsychology,* ed. T. Roszak, M. Gomes, and A. Kanner, 77–91 (San Francisco: Sierra Club Books).

20. Pilisuk, M., J. McAllister, and J. Rothman, (1996), "Coming Together for Action: The Challenge of Contemporary Grassroots Organizing," *Journal of Social Issues* 52 (1): 15–37.

21. Turnbull, C., (1962), *The Forest People* (New York: Simon and Schuster).

22. Pilisuk, M., and M. Joy, (2001), "Humanistic Psychology and Ecology," in *Handbook of Humanistic Psychology,* ed. K. Schneider, J. Bugental, and F. Pierson, 101–114 (Thousand Oaks, CA: Sage Publications).

23. Misra, G., and K. J. Gergen, (1993), "On the Place of Culture in Psychological Science," *International Journal of Psychology* 28 (2): 225–243.

24. Bredemeir, H. C., and J. Toby, (1972), *Social Problems in America: Costs and Casualties of an Acquisitive Society* (New York: Wiley).

25. Pilisuk, M., and J. Zazzi, (2006), "Toward a Psychosocial Theory of Military and Economic Violence in the Era of Globalization," *Journal of Social Issues* 62 (1): 41–62.

26. Postman, N., (1992), *Technopoly: The Surrender of Culture to Technology* (New York: Knopf).

27. Seager, J., (1993), *Earth Follies: Coming to Feminist Terms with the Global Environmental Crisis* (New York: Routledge; Bredemeir & Toby).

28. Pilisuk and Zazzi (2006).

29. Norquist, G., (1994), *Rock the House* (Austin: Texas Policy Foundation).

30. Garfinkle, N., (2006), *The American Dream vs. the Gospel of Wealth: The Fight for a Productive Middle-Class Economy,* part of *The Future of American Democracy* series (New Haven, CT: Yale University Press).

31. Cox, H., (1999), "The Market as God," *Atlantic Monthly*, March, 18–23; McGloin, S. J., (1999), "The Market as God: Living in the New Dispensation," Jesuit Center for Theoretical Reflection Bulletin No. 41, September, http://www.jctr.org.zm/bulletins/market%20as%20god.htm.

32. Perelman, M., and S. Sandronsky, (2006), "When Economists Didn't Buy the Free Market: An Interview with Michael Perelman," *Z Magazine Online*, October 29, http://www.zmag.org/content/showarticle.cfm?ItemID=11287.

33. Peterson, Evan Augustine III, (2005a), "American Idols: From Petro-theism to Empire-theism," AxisOfLogic.com essay, October 5, http://www.axisoflogic.com/cgibin/exec/view.pl?archive=135&num=19757.

34. Simon, M., (2006), *Appetite for Profit: How the Food Industry Undermines Our Health and How to Fight Back* (New York: Nation Books).

35. Lakoff, G., and M. Johnson, (2003), *Metaphors We Live By* (Chicago: University of Chicago Press).

36. Chomsky (2003).

37. Dunlop, R., K. Van Liere, A. Mertig, and R. E. Jones, (2000), "Measuring Endorsement of the New Ecological Paradigm," *Journal of Social Issues* 56 (3): 425–442.

38. Dunlop, R., G. H. Gallup, and A. M. Gallup, (1993), *Health of the Planet: A George H. Gallup Memorial Survey* (Princeton, NJ: Gallup International Institute).

39. Lace, Sosin & Snell Assoc., (1997), *US Opinion Poll Commissioned for the Abolition 2000 Network* (New York: Global Resource Action Center).

40. Pilisuk, M., S. H. Parks, and G. R. Hawkes, (1987), "Public Perception of Technological Risk," *Social Science Journal* 24: 403–413.

41. Chomsky (1993).

42. Perelman and Sandonsky (2006).

43. Klein, N., (2005), "The Rise of Disaster Capitalism," *Nation*, May 2, http://www.thenation.com/doc.mhtml?i=20050502&s=klein.

44. Beard, C. A., (1902), *The Industrial Revolution* (London: G. Allen & Unwin).

45. Zinn, Howard, (2006), "America's Blinders," *Progressive*, April http://progressive.org/mag_zinn0406.

46. Kiesling, J. B., (2006), *Diplomacy Lessons: Realism for an Unloved Superpower* (Washington, DC: Potomac Press).

47. Garfinkle (2006).

48. Parenti (1995).

49. Zinn (2006).

50. Alterman, E., (2004), *When Presidents Lie: A History of Official Deception and Its Consequences* (New York: Viking).

51. Carroll, J., (2005), "The Day After the Fireworks," CD/BG essay, July 5, http://www.commondreams.org/views05/0705-24.htm; Peterson, Evan Augustine III, (2005b), "American Militarism, Part 2: On Celebrating Militaristic Nationalism," July 7, 6:51 A.M.

52. Giles, quoted in Andreas, J., (2004), *Addicted to War—Why the U.S. Can't Kick Militarism* (Oakland, CA: AK Press), 3.

53. Mander, J., (1996), "The Rules of Corporate Behavior," in *The Case Against the Global Economy: And for a Turn Toward the Local*, ed. J. Mander and E. Goldsmith, 309–422 (San Francisco: Sierra Club Books).

54. Hartmann, T., M. C. Miller, and G. Palast, (2007), *Screwed: The Undeclared War Against the Middle Class—and What We Can Do About It*, second revised edition (San Francisco: Berrett-Koehler Publishers).

55. Moreton, B. E., (2007), "It Came from Bentonville: The Agrarian Origins of Wal-Mart Culture," in *Wal-Mart: The Face of Twenty-First-Century Capitalism*, ed. N. Lichtenstein (New York: New Press).

56. Ibid.

57. Ibid.

58. Ibid.

59. Ibid.

60. Wal-Mart Watch, (2006a), "Tale of Two WalMarts," http://walmartwatch.com/blog/archives/tale_of_two_wal_marts_retailers_legacy_future_collide_in_transition_era/; Wal-Mart Watch, (2006b), "Betty v, Goliath: A history of *Dukes vs. WalMart*," http://walmartwatch.com/blog/dukesWalMart backgrounder-1.#0.

61. Ibid.

62. Westheimer, Joel, ed. (2007), *Pledging Allegiance: The Politics of Patriotism in American Schools* (New York: Teachers College Press).

63. Hedges, C., (2004), "The Christian Right and the Rise of American Fascism: The Rise of the Religious Right in the Republican Party," a Public Information Project of the Center for Religion, Ethics, and Social Policy at Cornell University, November 15, http://www.theocracywatch.org/chris_hedges_nov24_04.htm retrieved 1/18/07.

64. Fernandes, D., (2007), *Targeted: Homeland Security and the Business of Immigration* (New York: Seven Stories Press).

65. Quoted in Scott, P. D., (2006), "Homeland Security Contracts for Vast New Detention Camps," Global, Pacific News Service, February 6.

66. Yassin, J. O., (2005), "Demonizing the Victims of Katrina," Fairness & Accuracy In Reporting (FAIR), November/December http://www.fair.org (accessed June 16, 2007).

67. Scott (2006); Fernandes (2007).

68. Helvarg, D., (1994), *The War against Greens: The "Wise-Use" Movement, the New Right and Anti-Environmental Violence* (San Francisco: Sierra Club Books).

69. Kennedy, D., (2007), "Chiapas: Reflections on Trade, Immigration, and the Global Economy," Global Exchange, http://www.globalexchange.org/tours/ChiapasReflections.html (accessed May 5, 2007).

70. Bacon, D., (2006), *Communities without Borders: Images and Voices from the World of Migration* (Ithaca, NY: ILR Press).

71. Fernandes (2007).

72. Southern Poverty Law Center, (2007), "Close to Slavery: Guest Worker Programs in the United States," Montgomery, Alabama.

73. Britt, L. W., (2004), "Fascism Anyone," *Free Inquiry Magazine* 23(2), http://www.secularhumanism.org/library/fi/britt_23_2.htm (accessed March 11, 2007).

74. Griffin, D. R., J. B. Cobb, Jr., R. A. Falk, and C. Keller, (2006). *The American Empire and the Commonwealth of God: A Political, Economic, Religious Statement* (Louisville, KY: Westminster John Knox Press).

75. North, G., (1983), *Christianity and Civilization* (Tyler, TX: Geneva Ministries).

76. Griffin et al. (2006).

77. Birchall, J., and H. Yeager, (2006), "A Purchase on Psephology," *Financial Times*, August 17, 9 (U.S. edition).

78. Robertson, P., (1991), *The New World Order* (Dallas, TX: Word Publication).

79. Fernandes (2007).

80. Hedges (2004).

81. Flanders, L., (2007), *Blue Grit: True Democrats Take Back Politics from the Politicians* (New York: Penguin).

82. Quoted in Hartmann, T., (2006), "Reclaiming the Issues: Islamic or Republican Fascism?" *Common Dreams,* August 28.

83. Schell, J., (2005), "The Fall of the One-Party Empire," *Nation* and TomDispatch, November 24.

84. Pilisuk, M., and S. H. Parks, (1986), *The Healing Web: Social Networks and Human Survival* (Hanover, NH: University Press of New England).

References

Adams, P. (2005). The beginning of the end to a coherent U. S. drug strategy. Council on Hemispheric Affairs. http://www.coha.org/NEW_PRESS_RELEASES/_2005/05.82 (accessed November 25, 2005).

Adler, M. (2006). Sometimes, government is the answer. *Los Angeles Times,* March 4. http://www.latimes.com/news/opinion/commentary/la-oe-adler4mar04,0,515451.story?coll=la-news-comment-opinions (accessed March 7, 2006).

Afghanistan: A history of turbulence. (2001). *MSNBC online.* http://www.msnbc.com/news/6555554146.asp (accessed November 20, 2001).

Aguilera Peralta, G., and J. R. Imery. (1981). *Dialectica del tierra in Guatemala.* San Jose: EDUCA.

AIUS (Australian-Asian Union Support Group). (2000). Solidarity speaking tour: The fight for union rights in Indonesia. May 10, 2000. http://intranet.usc.edu.au/wacana/isn/pakpahan_visit.html (accessed March 26, 2006).

Alaimo, K., R. R. Briefel, E. A. Frongillo, and C. M. Olson. (1988). Food, insufficiency exists in the United States: Results from the third national health and nutrition examination survey (NHANES III). *American Journal of Public Health* 88 (3): 419–425.

Alden, E., and N. Buckley. (2004). Wal-Mart becomes largest corporate political investor. *Financial Times,* February 24, 2004. http://reclaimdemocracy.org/articles_2004/walmart_largest_political_donor_investor.html (accessed November 14, 2006).

Alterman, E. (2004). *When presidents lie: A history of official deception and its consequences.* New York: Viking.

America's Second Harvest. (2001). Hunger study 2001 fact sheet. http://www.secondharvest.org/learn_about_hunger/hunger_study_2001_Fact_sheet.html (accessed November 6, 2005).

Americas Watch. (1982). *Human rights in Guatemala: No neutrals allowed.* New York: Americas Watch.

Amnesty International. (1982). *Guatemala: Massive extrajudicial executions in rural areas under the government of General Efrain Rios Montt.* London: Amnesty International.

Amnesty International. (1989). *Guatemala: Human rights violations under civilian governments.* London: Amnesty International.

Amnesty International. (1993). *Getting away with murder: Political killings and "disappearances" in the 1990s.* New York: Amnesty International.

Andersen, R. (2003). That's militainment!: The Pentagon's media-friendly "reality" war. *Extra!* May/June 2003. http://www.fair.org/index.php?page=1141&printer_friendly=1 (accessed May 31, 2006).

Andreas, J. (2004). *Addicted to war: Why the U.S. can't kick militarism.* Oakland, CA: AK Press.

Arendt, H. (2004). *The origins of totalitarianism.* New York: Schocken Press.

Argetsinger, A. (2005). Immigration opponents to patrol U.S. border. *Washington Post,* March, A.03.

Associated Press. (2005). More troops developing latent mental disorders. *Associated Press Online,* July 28, 2005. http://www.msnbc.msn.com/id/8743574/ (accessed September 19, 2005).

Augustine, E. (2007). The Philippines, the World Bank and the race to the bottom. In *A game as old as empire: The secret world of economic hit men and the web of global corruption,* ed. S. Hiatt, 175–196. San Francisco: Berrett-Koehler.

Avnery, U. (2006). Shhhhhh! Avnery on what is missing in the election campaign, Jerusalem: Gush Shalom. http://zope.gush-shalom.org/home/en/channels/avnery/1142114960/ (accessed June 20, 2006).

Bacevich, A. J. (2005). *The new American militarism: How Americans are seduced by war.* New York: Oxford University Press.

Bacon, D. (2006). *Communities without borders: Images and voices from the world of migration.* Ithaca, New York: ILR Press.

Bacon, J. (2005). Saying what they've been thinking: Racial stereotypes in Katrina commentary. *Extra!* November/December. http://www.fair.org/index.php?page=2795&printer_friendly=1 (accessed June 5, 2006).

Bagdikian. (2004). *The new media monopoly.* Boston: Beacon Press.

Bales, K. (2000). *Disposable people: New slavery in the global economy.* Berkeley: University of California Press.

Bales, K. (2005). *Understanding global slavery: A reader.* Berkeley: University of California Press.

Ball, P., P. Kobrack, and H. F. Spirer. (1999). *State violence in Guatemala, 1960–1996: A quantitative reflection.* Washington DC: American Association for the Advancement of Science.

Bamford, J. (2005). The man who sold the Iraq War: John Rendon, Bush's general in the propaganda war. Interview with Amy Goodman. Democracy Now! http://www.democracynow.org (accessed April 3, 2006).

Bandura, A., B. Underwood, and M. E. Fromson. (1975). Disinhibition of aggression through diffusion of responsibility and dehumanization of victims. *Journal of Personality and Social Psychology* 9: 253–269.

Bandura, A. (1988). Mechanisms of moral disengagement. In *Origins of terrorism: Psychologies, ideologies, theologies, states of mind,* ed. W. Reich, 161–191. New York: Cambridge University.

Barash, D. P., and C. P. Webel. (2002). *Peace and conflict studies.* London: Sage Publications.

Barber, B. R. (2000). Challenge to the common good in the age of globalism. *Social Education* 64: 8–13.

Barlow, M. (1999). The global water crisis and the commodification of the world's water supply. International Forum on Globalization. http://www.ifg.org/bgsummary.html (accessed December 23, 2001).

Barnaby, W. (1999). *The plague makers: The secret world of biological warfare.* London: Vision.

Barnes, J., and A. M. Jaffe. (2006). The Persian Gulf and the geopolitics of oil. *Survival* 48 (1): 143–162.

Barnet, R. J., and J. Cavanaugh. (1994a). *Global dreams: Imperial corporations and the new world order.* New York: Simon and Schuster.

Barnet, R. J., and J. Cavanaugh. (1994b) The sound of money. *Sojourners*, January 12.

Barry, K. (1995) *Prostitution of sexuality.* New York: New York University Press.

Bastien, B., J. W. Kremer, J. Rivers-Norten, and P. Vickers. (1999). The genocide of the Native-Americans. *ReVision* 22 (1): 13–20.

Batstone, D. B. (2007). *Not for sale: The return of the global slave trade and how we can fight it.* New York: Harper.

BBC News. (2006). Forbes reports billionaire boom. *BBC*, March 10, 2006. http://news.bbc.co.uk/2/hi/business/4791848.stm.

Beard, C. A. (1902). *The industrial revolution.* London: G. Allen & Unwin.

BearingPoint Inc. (n.d.). Company Web site. http://www.bearingpoint.com/portal/site/bearingpoint/menuitem.a4977774bdb00c911dba0624826106a0/ (accessed May 7, 2006).

Bechtel. (2006). *Wikipedia*, September 2006. http://en.wikipedia.org/wiki/Bechtel (accessed December 12, 2006).

Bellamy, C., ed. (1997). *The state of the world's children, 1996.* UNICEF. Oxford University Press, Oxford, England.

Bello, W. (1998). The end of a "miracle": Speculation, foreign capital dependence and the collapse of the Southeast Asian economies. *Multinational Monitor* 19:10–16.

Bello, W., S. Cunningham, and B. Rau. (1999). *Dark victory: The United States and global poverty.* London: Pluto Press.

Benedict, H. (2007). The private war of women soldiers. *Salon.* http://www.salon.com/news/feature/2007/03/07/women_in_military/index.html (accessed March 12, 2007).

Berkman Center for Internet and Society. (2004). Diebold v. the bloggers. *Berkman Briefings.* Harvard Law School. http://cyber.law.harvard.edu/briefings/dvb (accessed November 13, 2006).

Berkman, L., and S. L. Syme. (1979). Social networks, host resistance and mortality: A nine year follow-up study of Alameda county residents. *American Journal of Epidemiology* 109 (2): 186–204.

Berkowitz, B. (2006). Lincoln Group: Unethical weapon of mass deception. *WorkingForChange*, December 7, 2006. http://www.workingforchange.com/printitem.cfm?itemid=21727 (accessed January 2, 2007).

Bernays, E. L. (1928). *Propaganda.* New York: Liveright.

Bernays, E. L. (1934). *Crystallizing public opinion.* New York: Liveright.

Bernays, E. L. (1955). *The engineering of consent.* Norman: University of Oklahoma Press.

Berrigan, F. (2001). U.S. "supplier of choice" for weapons sale. *Common Dreams.* http://www.commondreams.org/views01/0821-02.htm (accessed July 13, 2002).

Bertell, R. (2004). Health and environmental costs of militarism. Presented in Barcelona, Thursday, June 24, 2004.

Big media companies want to get bigger, again. Kintera. http://www.kintera.org/TR.asp?ID=M716791106742986729756865 and http://www.kintera.org/TR.asp?ID=M717426746742986729756865 (accessed May 7, 2007).

Billings, E. (2002). Hearts and minds: The Rendon Group's top-secret spin machine for the Pentagon is big business. *Washington Business Forward Magazine, May, 2002.* www.sourcewatch.org/index.php?title=Rendon_Group (accessed May 4, 2006).

Bilmes, L., and J. Stiglitz. (2006). War's stunning price tag. *Los Angeles Times*, January 17, 2006. http://www.latimes.com/news/opinion/commentary/la-oe-bilmes17jan17,0,7038018.story?coll=la-news-comment-opinions (accessed March 7, 2006).

Bimbaum, J. H. (2005). Hill a steppingstone to K Street for some: More ex-lawmakers who join private sector are becoming lobbyists, study says. *Washington Post*, Wednesday, July 27, A19.

Biotechnology Industry Organization. (2005). Biotechnology industry facts. http://www.bio.org/speeches/pubs/er/statistics.asp (accessed November 3, 2005).

Birchall, J., and H. Yeager. (2006). A purchase on psephology. *Financial Times*, August 17, 9. (U.S. edition).

Bissel, T. (1997). Campaign for labor rights. Nike packet, parts 1–7. Personal correspondence, April 24, 1997.

Black, G. (1984). *Garrison Guatemala.* New York: Monthly Review Press.

Blanck, E., and R. M. Castillo. (1998). El palacio de las intrigas. *Crónica*, October 10. shr.aaas.org/guatemala/ ciidh/org_rep/english/biblio.html (accessed November 15, 2006).

Blanding, M. (2005). Coke: The new Nike. *Nation.* http://www.thenation.com/doc.mhtml?i=20050411&s=blanding (accessed May 6, 2005).

Bloch, E. (1993). Psychologists in Croatia work to ease trauma among young war victims. *Psychology International* 4 (3): 1–7.

Blum, B. (2004). *Killing hope: US military and CIA interventions since World War II.* Monroe, ME: Common Courage Press.

Bohart, A. C., R. Elliott, L. Greenberg, and J. C. Watson. (2002). Empathy. In *Psychotherapy relationships that work*, ed. J. R. Norcross, et al. New York: Oxford University Press.

Boly, W. (1990). Downwind. *In Health*, July/August, 58–69.

Borger, J. (2003). The spies who pushed for war. *Guardian*, July 17, 2003. http://www.guardian.co.uk/print/0,3858,4714031-103550,00.html (accessed April 12, 2006).

Borjesson, K. (2004) *Into the buzzsaw: Leading journalists expose the myth of a free press.* Amherst, NY: Prometheus.

Borjesson, K., ed. (2005). *Feet to the fire: The media after 9/11, top journalists speak out.* Amherst, NY: Prometheus.

Bourke, J. (1996). *Dismembering the male: Men's bodies, Britain and the Great War.* Chicago: University of Chicago Press.

Brauer, J., and N. Anglewitz. (2005). Two thirds on defense. *Live Journal*, June 13, 2005. http: www.mparent7777 TwoThirds%20On%20Defense.html (accessed December 5, 2006).

Bredemeir, H. C., and J. Toby. (1972). *Social problems in America: Costs and casualties of an acquisitive society.* New York: Wiley.

Britt, L. W. (2004). Fascism anyone? *Free Inquiry Magazine* no. 23:2. http://www.secularhumanism.org/library/fi/britt_23_2.htm (accessed March 11, 2007).

Bronfenbrenner, U. (1961). The mirror image in Soviet-American relations: A social psychologist's report. *Journal of Social Issues* 17 (3): 45–56.

Brooks, R. (2006). Good people; evil deeds. *Los Angeles Times*, June 9, B.11.

Browne, A., and S. S. Bassuk. (1997). Intimate violence in the lives of homeless and poor housed women. *American Journal of Orthopsychiatry* 67 (2): 261–275.

Brownmiller, S. (1975). *Against our will: Men, women and rape.* NewYork: Ballantine Books.

Broyles, W., Jr. (1990). Why men love war: Socialization and masculinity. In *Making war/making peace: The social foundations of violent conflict*, ed. F. M. Cancian and J. W. Gibson, 29–37. Belmont, CA: Wadsworth.

Bruno, K., and J. Valette. (2001). Cheney & Halliburton: Go where the oil is. *Multinational Monitor* 22: 22–25.

Brush, S. B. (1999). Bioprospecting the public domain. *Cultural Anthropology* 14: 535–555.

Bstan-'dzin-rgya-mtsho, Dalai Lama. (1999). *Ethics for the new millennium: His Holiness the Dalai Lama XIV.* New York: Riverhead Books.

Burma Economic Watch. (2001). Battered economy sees kyat on the ropes. *South China Morning Post*, October 12, 2001. http://www.ibiblio.org/obl/docs3/BEW-2006-01.pdf and http://www.scmp.com (accessed May 5, 2006).

Burnham, G., R. Lafta, S. Doocy, and L. Roberts. (2006). Mortality after the 2003 invasion of Iraq: A cross-sectional cluster sample survey. *The Lancet* 369 (556): 101–102.

Business Roundtable. (2007). About business roundtable. http://www.businessroundtable.org:80/aboutUs/index.aspx (accessed April 24, 2007).

Buzuev, A. (1985). *Transnational corporations and militarism.* Moscow: Progress Publishers.

Caldicott, H. (2002). *The new nuclear danger: George W. Bush's military-industrial complex.* New York: New Press.

Calle, F. (2000). The children's movement for peace in Colombia. *Social Justice* 27: 158–159.

Canadian Auto Workers. (1997). Indonesian fight of human rights. http://www.caw.ca/news/videonews/archives/indonesian_fight_of_human_rights.asp (accessed May 5, 2005).

Cancian, F. M., and J. W. Gibson, eds. (1990) *Making war/making peace: The social foundations of violent conflict.* Belmont, CA: Wadsworth, 29–37.

Cardinale, M. (2006). Diebold added secret patch to Georgia e-voting systems in 2002, whistleblowers say. *Atlanta Progressive News*, September 28, 2006. http://www.atlantaprogressivenews.com/news/0091.html (accessed November 2, 2006).

Carr, C. (2002). *The lessons of terror: A history of warfare against civilians: Why it has always failed and why it will fail again.* New York: Random House.

Carroll, J. (2005). The day after the fireworks. *Common Dreams*, July 5, 2005. http://www.commondreams.org/views05/0705-24.htm (accessed October 7, 2005).

Center for Arms Control and Non-Proliferation. (2006). Highlights of the FY '06 budget. http://www.armscontrolcenter.org/archives/001658.php (accessed February 7, 2005).

Center for Defense Information. (1996). Nuclear leakage: A threat without a military solution. *Defense Monitor* XXV (6): 1–7.

Center for Public Integrity (2005). Post-war contractors ranked by total contract value in Iraq and Afghanistan from 2002 through July 1, 2004. http://www.publicintegrity.org/wow/resources.aspx?act=total (accessed March 7, 2006).

Center for Responsive Politics. (2005). Campaign finance reform: What's the issue? http://usgovinfo.about.com/gi/dynamic/offsite.htm?zi=1/XJ&sdn=usgovinfo&zu=http%3A%2F%2Fwww.opensecrets.org%2F (accessed November 15, 2006).

Center for Strategic and International Studies and the Massachusetts Institute of Technology. (2004). Astroturf: Interest group lobbying and corporate strategy. *Journal of Economics & Management Strategy,* Winter 2004, 563–573.

Centro Internacional para Investigaciones en Derechos Humanos (CIIDH) and Grupo de Apoyo Mutuo (GAM). (1999). En Pie de Lucha: Organizacion y Represion en la Universidad de San Carlos, Guatemala 1944-1996. Guatemala: CIIDH y GAM. In *State violence in Guatemala, 1960–1996: A qualitative reflection,* ed. P. Ball, P. Kobrack, and H. F. Spirer. Washington, DC: American Association for the Advancement of Science.

Chandrasekaran R. (2007). *Imperial life in the Emerald City: Inside Iraq's Green Zone.* New York: Alfred A. Knopf.

Chang, J., and J. Halliday. (2005). *Mao: The unknown story.* NewYork: Knopf.

Chang, S. J., and D. Ha. (2001). Corporate governance in the twenty-first century: New managerial concepts for supernational corporations. *American Business Review* 19: 32–44.

Chatterjee, P. (1992). World bank failures soar to 37.5% of completed projects in 1991. *Third World Economics,* December 16, 31–32.

Chatterjee, P. (2000). The earth wrecker. *San Francisco Bay Guardian.* http://www.sfbg.com/News/34/35/bech1.html (accessed December 23, 2001).

Chatterjee, P. (2004). Information warriors: Rendon Group wins hearts and minds in business, politics, and war. *CorpWatch,* August 4, 2004. http://www.corpwatch.org/print_article.php?id=11486 (accessed April 4, 2006).

Chelala, C., and C. Beyrer. (1999). Drug use and HIV/AIDS in Burma. *Lancet* 354:1119.

Chester, J. (2007). *Digital destiny: New media and the future of democracy.* New York: New Press.

Ching Yoon Louie, M. (2001). *Sweatshop warriors: Immigrant women workers take on the global factory.* Boston: South End Press.

Chinni, D. (n.d.). Jessica Lynch: Media myth-making in the Iraq War. Project for Excellence in Journalism. http://www.journalism.org/resources/research/reports/war/postwar/lynch.asp (accessed May 31, 2006).

Chomsky, N. (1993). *The prosperous few and the restless many.* Berkeley: Odonian Press.

Chomsky, N. (2002). *Media control: The spectacular achievements of propaganda.* 2nd ed. New York: Seven Stories Press.

Chomsky, N. (2004). *Hegemony or survival: America's quest for global dominance.* New York: Holt & Co.

Chomsky, N. (2005). *Imperial ambitions: Conversations on the post 9/11 world.* New York: Metropolitan Books.

Christie, D. (1996). Peacebuilding: The human needs approach locally and globally. Division 48 (Peace Psychology) Presidential Address, 104th Annual Convention of the American Psychological Association. August 1996.

Christie, D. (1997). Reducing direct and structural violence: The human needs theory. *Peace and Conflict: Journal of Peace Psychology* 3: 315–332.

Churchill, W. (1929). *The world crisis, 1911–1918. The aftermath.* London: Simon & Schuster.

Churchill, W. (1951). *Second World War, Vol. IV. The hinge of fate.* London: Houghton Mifflin.

Cirincione, J. B., J. B. Wolfsthal, and M. Rajkumar. (2005). *Deadly arsenals: Nuclear, biological and chemical threats.* Rev. ed. Washington DC: Carnegie Endowment for International Peace.

CNN. (1997). Criminal warrants sought in Texas standoff. *CNN,* April 1997. http://www.cnn.com/US/9704/28/texas.militia (accessed April 29, 2005).

Cobain, I., and E. MacAskill, E. (2005). MI5 unmasks covert arms programmes. *Guardian,* October 8, 2005. http://www.guardian.co.uk/nuclear/article/0,2763, 1587752, 00.html (accessed October 8, 2005).

Cockburn, A. (2001). Meet the secret rulers of the world: The truth about the Bohemian Grove. *Counterpunch,* June 19, 2001. http://www.counterpunch.org/bohemian.html (accessed October 16, 2001).

Coday, D. (2001). Burma. *National Catholic Reporter* 37:12.

COHA (Council on Hemispheric Affairs). (2006a). Washington's faltering anti-drug strategy in Colombia, and Bogotá's evaporating extradition policy. Thursday, April 13, 2006.

COHA (Council on Hemispheric Affairs). (2006b). Report on Nicaragua: How the United States continues to manipulate Nicaragua's economic and political future. Thursday, June 22, 2006.

COHA (Council on Hemispheric Affairs). (2007). School of the Americas: A black eye to democracy. Thursday, June 21, 2007.

Cohen, A., and G. P. O'Driscoll, Jr. (2003). Achieving economic reform and growth in Iraq. Heritage Foundation WebMemo #236. http://www.heritage.org/research/middleeast/wm236.cfm (accessed May 5, 2006).

Cohn, C. (1987). Sex and death in the rational world of the defense intellectuals. *Journal of Women in Culture and Society* 12: 687–718.

Coleman, J. R. (2004). Constraining modern mercenarism. *Hastings Law Journal* 55:1493–1538.

Coleman, P. (2006). *Flashback: Posttraumatic stress disorder, suicide, and the lessons of war.* Boston: Beacon Press.

Coleridge, G. (2004). Closing the circle: The corporatization of elections. *Free Press.* http://www.freepress.org/departments/display/19/2004/875 (accessed November 2, 2006).

Coles, R. (1983). The need for scapegoats causes war. In *War and human nature,* ed. D. L. Bender and B. Leone, 60. St. Paul, MN: Greenhaven Press.

Coletta, L. (2007). MySpace refused our ad! Common Cause. January 10, 2007. Email from Lauren Coletta. http://www.commoncause.org/.

Coll, S. (2001). *Ghost wars: The secret history of the CIA, Afghanistan, and Bin Laden, from the Soviet invasion to September 10, 2001.* New York: Penguin.

Colley, L. (2005). The US is now rediscovering the pitfalls of aspirational imperialism. *Guardian,* December 17, 2005.

Columbia Journalism Review. (2006). Who owns what. http://www.cjr.org/tools/owners/?tr=y&auid=1742649 06/27/06.

Comas-Diaz, L., and M. A. Jansen. (1995). Global conflict and violence against women. *Peace and Conflict: Journal of Peace Psychology* 1 (4): 315–331.

Common Cause. (2006). Wolves in sheep's clothing: Telecom industry front groups and Astroturf. August. http://www.commoncause.org/site/pp.asp?c=dkLNK1MQIwG&b=1499059 (accessed August 10, 2006).

Connors, M. (1995). Unraveling the epidemic among poor women in the US. In *Women, poverty and AIDS: Sex, drugs and structural violence,* ed. P. Farmer, M. Connors, and J. Simmons, 98. Monroe, ME: Common Courage Press.

Consultative Group on International Agricultural Research. (2004). Who we are: The CGIAR mission. http://www.cgiar.org/who/index.html (accessed December 6, 2005).

Consumers Union. (n.d.). FCC covers up publicly funded reports. http://cu.convio.net/site/R?i=wvzGnXDfnCdUzwhTKPHZGg (accessed March 3, 2006).

Cooper, Phillip, J. (2002). By order of the President : The use and abuse of executive direct action. Lawrence: University Press of Kansas.

Cordesman, A. H. (2002). *Terrorism, asymmetric warfare, and weapons of mass destruction: Defending the U.S. homeland.* Westport, CT: Praeger.

Corporate Accountability International (formerly Infact). (2000). Challenging corporate abuse, building grassroots power since 1997. Infact Web site. http://www.infact.org (accessed December 23, 2001).

CorpWatch. (2005). UK: Patents on flowers: Profits to blossom. http://www.corpwatch.org/article.php?id=11874 (accessed June 5, 2007).

CorpWatch. (2006). General Electric. http://www.corpwatch.org/print_article.php?list=type&type=16 (accessed May 4, 2006).

Cortwright, D. (1975). *Soldiers in revolt: GI resistance during the Vietnam War.* Chicago: Haymarket Books.

Council on Foreign Relations. (2003a). Iraq: The day after. Task Force Report, March 2003. http://www.cfr.org/publication/5682/president_bush_should_stay_the_course_in_postwar_iraq_to_ensure_battlefield_victory_is_not_lost_says_council_task_force.html?breadcrumb=default (accessed October 4, 2006).

Council on Foreign Relations. (2003b). Iraq: The day after—Chairs' update. Task Force Report, June. http://www.cfr.org/publication/6075/iraq.html?breadcrumb=default (accessed October 4, 2006),

Council on Foreign Relations. (2006). History of CFR. http://www.cfr.org/about/history/ (accessed September 24, 2006).

Cowles, D. (2005). 2 BR., 1.5 BATH, All the defense contracts you can handle. *New Republic,* no. 4 (July): 8.

Cox, H. (1999). The market as God. *Atlantic Monthly,* March, 8–23.

Cray, C. (2000). The U-wa-Oxy standoff. *Multinational Monitor* 21: 7–8.

Cummings, J. (2006). Business owners hedge their bets: Many increase their donations to Democrats, evening war chests in final days. *Wall Street Journal,* October 27, A.4. (Eastern Edition). ABI/INFORM Global.

Daily, J., P. Farmer, J. Rhatigan, J. Katz, and J. Furin. (1995). Women and HIV Infection—a different disease? In *Women, poverty and AIDs: Sex, drugs and structural violence,* ed. P. Farmer, M. Connors, and J. Simmons. Monroe, ME: Common Courage Press.

DeFrank, N. M., J. M. Gholke, E. A. Gribble, and E. M. Faustman (2005). Value of information approaches to evaluate models of low dose radiation effects on neurons in the developing brain. Society for Risk Analysis annual meeting, 2005. http://birenheide.com/sra/2005AM/program/singlesession.php3?sessid=M4.

Democracy Center. (2006). Bechtel vs Bolivia. http://www.democracyctr.org/bechtel/bechtel-vs-bolivia.htm (accessed March 12, 2007).

Democracy Now! (2007). Part II—Blackwater: The rise of the world's most powerful mercenary army. Democracy Now! Interview with Amy Goodman, March 21.

Department of Defense. (2004). *Report of the Defense Science Board Task Force on Strategic Communication.* Washington DC. September, 2004.

Diamond, L. J. (2005). *Squandered victor: The American occupation and the bungled effort to bring democracy to Iraq.* New York: Times Books.

Domhoff, G. W. (1970). *The higher circles.* New York: Random House.

Domhoff, G. W. (1974). *The Bohemian Grove and other retreats: A study in ruling-class cohesiveness.* New York: Harper Colophon Books.

Domhoff, G. W. (1990). *The power elite and the state: How policy is made in America.* Hawthorne, NY: Aldine de Gruyter.

Domhoff, G. W. (1996). *State autonomy or class dominance? Case studies on policy making in America.* Hawthorne, NY: Aldine de Gruyter.

Domhoff, G. W. (2005a). The four networks theory of power: A theoretical home for power structure research. http://sociology.ucsc.edu/whorulesamerica/theory/four_networks.html (accessed September 21, 2006).

Domhoff, G. W. (2005b). The corporate community, nonprofit organizations, and federal advisory committees: A study in linkages. *Who Rules America?* http://sociology.ucsc.edu/whorulesamerica/power.fac.html (accessed September 24, 2006).

Domhoff, G. W. (2005c). Social cohesion and the Bohemian Grove: The power elite at summer camp. *Who Rules America?* http://sociology.ucsc.edu/whorulesamerica/power/bohemian_grove.html (accessed September 24, 2006).

Domosh, M. (2006). *Selling civilization American commodities in an age of empire.* New York: Routledge.

Dreiling, M. C. (2000). The class embeddedness of corporate political action: Leadership in defense of the NAFTA. *Social Problems* 47 (1): 21–48.

Dreyfuss, R., and J. Vest. (2004). The lie factory. *Mother Jones*, January/February. http://www.motherjones.com/cgi-bin/print_article.pl?url=http://www.motherjones.com/news/feature/2004/01/12_405.html (accessed May 4, 2006).

Drinkard, J., and M. Kelley. (2005). Bribed ex-congressman's committees review his activities. *USA Today*, December 2, 4a.

DSM-IV (1994). Diagnostic and Statistical Manual of Mental Disorders. 4th ed. Washington, DC: American Psychiatric Association.

d'Souza, D. (2000). *The virtue of prosperity: Finding values in an age of techno-affluence.* New York: Free Press

DuBoff, R. (2001). Rogue nation. *Znet Daily Commentaries*, December 21, 2001. http://www.zmag.org/roguenation.htm (accessed June 6, 2005).

Dudley, S. (2000). The Colombia quagmire. *American Prospect* 11: 32–37.

Dunlop, R., G. H. Gallup, and A. M. Gallup. (1993). *Health of the planet: A George H. Gallup memorial survey.* Princeton, NJ: Gallup International Institute.

Dunlop, R., K. Van Liere, A. Mertig, and R. E. Jones. (2000). Measuring endorsement of the new ecological paradigm. *Journal of Social Issues* 56 (3): 425–442.

Easterly, W. (2002). *The elusive quest for growth: Economists' adventures and misadventures.* Cambridge: MIT Press.

Ehrenreich, B. (1997). *Blood rites: Origins and history of the passions of war.* New York: Henry Holt.

Eisenhart, R. W. (1975). You can't hack it little girl: A discussion of the covert psychological agenda of modern combat training, *Journal of Social issues* 31 (4): 13–23.

Ekirch, A. A., Jr. (1999). *Militarism and antimilitarism: The Oxford companion to American military history.* Oxford: Oxford University Press.

Elich, G. (2006). *Strange liberators: Militarism, mayhem, and the pursuit of profit.* Valparaiso, IN: Lumina Press.

Elliott, I. (2001). Pulling a fast one. *Ecologist* 31: 36–37.

Ellwood, D. (1996). Welfare reform in name only. *New York Times*, July 22, A15.

Elshtain, J. B. (1987). *Women and war.* New York: Basic Books.

Emerich, T. (2001). PTSD and child abuse among Salvadoran refugees: The after-effects of war. Unpublished doctoral dissertation, Saybrook Graduate School, San Francisco.

Engdahl, F .W. (2004). *A century of war: Anglo-American oil politics and the new world order.* London: Pluto Press.

Englehart, T. (2005). Bases, bases everywhere: It's a Pentagon world and welcome to it. *Common Dreams.* http://www.commondreams.org/views05/0602-28.htm (accessed March 2, 2006).

Ensign, T. (2005). *America's military today.* New York: New Press.

Erlbaum, M. (2005). Review of *The forbidden book: The Philipine American war in political cartoons,* by Abe Ignacio, Enrique de la Cruz, Jorge Emmanuel, and Helen Toribio. *Socialism and Democracy Journal* #37, 19 (1), Spring 2005. http://www.sdonline.org/index2.htm (accessed March 7, 2007).

Fabbro, D. (1990). Equality in peaceful societies. In *Making war/making peace: The social foundations of violent conflict,* ed. F. M. Cancian and J. W. Gibson, 127–142. Belmont, CA: Wadsworth.

Falla, R. (1983). *Masacre de la Finca San Francisco, Huehuetenango, Guatemala.* Copenhagen: International Work Group for Indigenous Affairs.

Farmer, P. (1999). *Infections and inequalities: The modern plagues.* Berkeley: University of California Press.

Farmer, P. (2005). *Pathologies of power: Health, human rights, and the new war on the poor.* Berkeley: University of California Press.

Farsetta, D. (2006). The devil is in the lack of details: The Defense Department's media contracts. *PR Watch,* February 21, 2006. http://www.prwatch.org/node/4481 (accessed April 3, 2006).

Farsetta, D., and D. Price. (2006). Fake TV news: Widespread and undisclosed. *PR Watch,* April 6, 2006. http://www.prwatch.org/fakenews/execsummary (accessed February 1, 2007).

Fergusen, N. (2006). *The war of the worlds: Twentieth–century conflict and the descent of the west.* New York: Penguin Books.

Fernandes, D. (2007). *Targeted: Homeland security and the business of immigration.* New York: Seven Stories Press.

Ferraro, K. J. (2005). The culture of social problems: Observations of the Third Reich, the Cold War, and Vietnam. *Social Problems* 52 (1): 1–14.

Fischetti, M. (2001). Drowning New Orleans. *Scientific American,* October 2001.

Fisher, R. (1993). Grassroots organizing worldwide. In *Mobilizing the community: Local politics in a global era,* ed. R. Fisher and J. Kling. Thousand Oaks, CA: Sage Publishers.

Fisher, R. (1994). *Let the people decide: Neighborhood organizing in America.* Rev. ed. Boston: Twayne.

Fitzsimmons, A. (2004). Mourning people on Santa Monica Beach: Arlington West. *Veterans for Peace,* July 18, 2004. http://www.veteransforpeace.org/ (accessed February 7, 2007).

Flanders, L. (2007). *Blue grit: True democrats take back politics from the politicians.* New York: Penguin.

Fleming, D. F. (1961). *The Cold War and its origins: 1917–1960.* Garden City, NY: Doubleday.

Fleming, D. F. (1967). *The Western intervention in the Soviet Union, 1918–1920.* New York: New World Review

Floyd, C. (2007). Claiming the prize: War escalation aimed at securing Iraqi oil. *Information Clearing House.* http://www.alternet.org/waroniraq/46602/ (accessed January 14, 2007).

Foerstel, L., ed. (2004). *War, lies and videotape: How media monopoly stifles truth.* New York: International Action Center.

Food Research and Action Center. (2005). Hunger and Food Insecurity in the United States. http://www.frac.org/html/hunger_in_the_us/hunger_index.html (accessed November 6, 2005).

Ford, N., and A. Davis. (2001). Chaos in Afghanistan: Famine, aid and bombs. *Lancet* 358:1543–1544.

Foreman, C. (2003). An Asian youth as offender: The legacy of the Khmer Rouge. In *The psychological impact of war trauma on civilians,* ed. S. Krippner and T. M. McIntyre, 95–106. Westport, CT: Praeger.

Fortson, D. (2007). Iraq posed to end drought for thirsting oil giants. *Independent,* January 7, 2007. http://news.independent.co.uk/business/news/article2132467.ece (accessed January 14, 2007).

Francona, R. (1999). *Ally to adversary: An eyewitness account of Iraq's fall from grace.* Annapolis, MD: Naval Institute Press.

Frank, J. (1982). *Sanity and survival in the nuclear age: Psychological aspects of war and peace.* New York: Random House.

Fraser, D. (2001). The "new perception" of animal agriculture: Legless cows, featherless chickens, and a need for genuine analysis. *Journal of Animal Science* 79: 634–641.

Fratepietro, S. (2001). Plan Columbia: The hidden front in the U.S. drug war. [Electronic version], *Humanist* 61:18–21.

Freire, P. (1968). *Pedagogy of the oppressed.* New York: Seabury Press.

Freud, S. (1949). *Why War? Collected Papers,* Vol. 4. London: Hogarth Press.

Friedman, M. (1984). The nuclear threat and the hidden human image. *Journal of Humanistic Psychology* 24 (3): 65–76.

Friedman, M., and J. Jarenson. (1994). The applicability of the post-traumatic stress disorder concept to refugees. In *Amidst peril and pain: The mental health and well-being of the world's refugees,* ed. A. J. Marsella, T. Bornemann, S. Ekblad, and J. Orley, 327–339. Washington DC: American Psychological Association.

Friedman, T. L. (1999). A manifesto for the fast world. In *Globalization,* ed. K. Sjursen. New York: H. W. Wilson Company.

Fromm, E. (1964). *Escape from Freedom.* New York: Holt Rinehart and Winston.

Fukuda, K., R. Nisenbaum, G. Stewart, W. W. Thompson, L. Robin, and R. M. Washko. (1998). Chronic multisymptom illness affecting Air Force veterans of the Gulf War. *JAMA* 280: 981–988.

Gabel, M. (1997). What the world wants and how to pay for it. What the World Wants Project. World Game Institute. Philadelphia, PA.

Galbraith, P. W. (2006a). *The end of Iraq: How American incompetence created a war without end.* New York: Simon & Schuster.

Galbraith, P. W. (2006b). The True Iraq Appeasers. *Boston Globe,* August 31, 2006. http://www.boston.com/news Commondreams.org (accessed September 20, 2006).

Galtung, J. (1996). *Peace by peaceful means: Peace and conflict, development and civilization.* London: Sage Press.

Ganser, D. (2004). *NATO's secret armies. Operation Gladio and terrorism in Western Europe.* London: Frank Cass.

Gardner, W., and K. Preator. (1996). Children of seropositive mothers in the U.S. AIDS Epidemic. *Journal of Social Issues* 52 (3): 177–195.

Garfinkle, N. (2006). *The American dream vs. the gospel of wealth: The fight for a productive middle-class economy.* The Future of American Democracy Series. New Haven, CT: Yale University Press.

Gelles, R. (1976). Demythologizing child abuse. *Family Coordinator* 25:135–141.

Gerace, M. P. (2004). *Military power, conflict and trade: Military tower, international commerce and great power rivalry.* New York: Routledge.

Gil, D. (1971). Violence against children. *Journal of Marriage and the Family* 33: 639–648.

Gil, D. (1975). Unraveling child abuse. *American Journal of Orthopsychiatry* 45: 336–346.

Gilmore, I., and T. Smith. (2006). If you start looking at them as humans, then how are you gonna kill them? *Guardian*, March 29, 2006. http://www.guardian.co.uk/Iraq/Story/0,,1741942,00.html (accessed April 20, 2006).

Giraldo, J. (1996). *Colombia: The genocidal democracy.* Monroe, ME: Common Courage Press.

Glendinning, C. (1990). *When technology wounds: The human consequences of progress.* New York: William Morrow & Co.

Global Policy Forum. (2006). Hurricane Halliburton: Conflict climate change and catastrophe. http://www.globalpolicy.org/security/issues/iraq/contractindex.htm (accessed May 19, 2007).

Goering, P., H. Norberg-Hodge, and J. Page. (1998). Industrial agriculture in context. *IFG News* 3: 4–5.

Goff, F., and M. Locker. (1971). The violence of domination: U.S. power and the Dominican Republic. In *The triple revolution emerging: Social problems in depth,* ed. R. Perrucci and M. Pilisuk. Boston: Little, Brown.

Gofman, John W. (1996). *Preventing breast cancer: The story of a major, proven, preventable cause of this disease.* Egan O'Connor, ed. San Francisco, CA. C.N.R. Book Division, Committee for Nuclear Responsibility, Inc.

Gofman, J. W., and A. R. Tamplin. (1971). *Poisoned power: The case against nuclear power plants.* Emmaus, PA: Rodale Press.

Goldberg, E., and L. Evans. (1998). *The prison industrial complex and the global economy.* Berkeley: Agit Press.

Golden, T. (2001). A war on terror meets a war on drugs. *New York Times,* November 25, 2001. http://www.nytimes.com (accessed November 26, 2001).

Goldman Environmental Prize. (2001). Prize recipients. http://www.goldmanprize.org/recipients/recipients.html (accessed December 23, 2001).

Goldsmith, E. (1997). Can the environment survive the global economy? *Ecologist* 27 (6): 47.

Gomes, L. (2003). *The economics and ideology of free trade: An historical review.* Cheltenham, UK: Edward Elgar.

Goodall, J. (1986). *The chimpanzees of Gombe: Patterns of behavior.* Cambridge: Harvard University Press.

Goodhand, J. (2000). From holy war to opium war? A case study of the opium economy in North Eastern Afghanistan. *Central Asian Survey* 19 (2): 265–280.

Goodhand, J. (2005). Frontiers and wars: The opium economy in Afghanistan. *Journal of Agrarian Change* 5 (2): 191–216.

Goodman, A. (2007). Chiquita's slipping appeal. *Truthdig.* http://www.truthdig.com/report/item/20070320_chiquitas_slipping_appeal/ (accessed March 26, 2007).

Gould, J. M., and B. A. Goldman. (1993). *Deadly deceit: Low-level radiation high-level cover-up.* NewYork: Four Walls Eight Windows Press.

Gould, J. M., E. J. Sternglass, J. J. Mangano, and W. McDonald. (1996). *The enemy within: The high cost of living near nuclear reactors : Breast cancer, AIDS, low birthweights, and other radiation-induced immune deficiency effects.* New York: Four Walls Eight Windows Press.

Government Accountability Project. (2006). Systemic injustice: Hanford's workers' compensation program review of conditions and prescription for remedies. August 2006. Government Accountability Project Nuclear Oversight Program. Washington, DC. http://www.whistleblower.org.

Grain. (2005). Field trials and commercial releases of Bt cotton around the world. http://www.grain.org/research/btcotton.cfm?id=306 (accessed December 6, 2005).

Grandin, G. (2006). *Empire's workshop: Latin America, the United States, and the rise of the new imperialism.* New York: Metropolitan Books.

Greider, W. (1998). *Fortress America: The American military and the consequences of peace.* New York: Public Affairs.

Griffin, D. R., J. B. Cobb, Jr., R. A. Falk, and C. Keller. (2006). *The American empire and the commonwealth of God: A political, economic, religious statement.* Louisville, KY: Westminster John Knox Press.

Griscom, A. (2004). Industry flaks learn how to snooker the public with their not-so-friendly messages. *Grist,* January 1, 2004. http://www.grist.org/news/muck/2004/01/21/spin/index.html (accessed April 24, 2007).

Grohols, J. (2005). Facts about PTSD from National Center for PTSD. http://www.google.com/search?hl=en&q=National+Center+for+PTSD+&btnG (accessed March 12, 2007).

Grossman, R., T. Lindzey, and D. Brannen. (n.d.). *Model brief on corporate personhood.* Program on Corporations, Law, and Democracy. http://www.poclad.org/ModelLegal Brief.cfm (accessed November 15, 2006).

Grossman, Z. (2001). A century of U.S. military interventions: From Wounded Knee to Afghanistan. Revised September 20, 2001. http://zmag.org/CrisesCurEvts/interventions.htm (accessed June 6, 2007).

Grusky, S. (2001). Privatization tidal wave: IMF/World Bank water policies and the price paid by the poor. *Multinational Monitor* 22:14–19.

Guatemalan Commission for Historical Clarification. (n.d.). Guatemala: Memory of silence. Report of the Commission for Historical Clarification. http://shr.aaas.org/guatemala/ceh/report/english/toc.html (accessed March 22, 2007).

Gusterson, H. (1991). *Rituals of renewal among nuclear weapons scientists.* Washington DC: American Association for the Advancement of Science.

Gusterson, H. (1998). *Nuclear rites: A weapons laboratory at the end of the Cold War.* Berkeley: University of California Press.

Hacker, A. (1997). *Money: Who has how much and why?* New York: Scribner.

Hagen, K., and I. Beckerton. (2007). *The unintended consequences of war.* Chicago: University of Chicago Press.

Hamilton, R. F. (1991). *The bourgeois epoch: Marx and Engels on Britain, France, and Germany.* Chapel Hill, NC: University of North Carolina Press.

Hartmann, T. (2004). *Unequal protection: The rise of corporate dominance and the theft of human rights.* New York: St. Martin's Press.

Hartmann, T. (2006). Reclaiming the issues: Islamic or Republican fascism? http://www.commondreams.org/views06/0828-23.htm (accessed January 2, 2007).

Hartmann, T., M. C. Miller, and G. Palast. (2007). *Screwed: The undeclared war against the middle class and what we can do about it.* San Francisco: Berrett-Koehler Publishers.

Hawk, D. (1989). The photographic record. In *Cambodia, 1975–1978: Rendezvous with death,* ed. K. D. Jackson. Princeton, NJ: Princeton University Press.

Hayward, M. (1999). Globalized mergers and acquisitions: The dangers of a monoculture. *Competitiveness Review* 9: i–iv.

Hedges, C. (2003). *War is a force that gives us meaning.* Woodston, Peterborough, UK: Anchor.

Hedges, C. (2004). The Christian right and the rise of American fascism. The rise of the religious right in the Republican Party: A public information project of the Center for Religion, Ethics and Social Policy at Cornell University. http://www.theocracywatch.org/chris_hedges_nov24_04.htm (accessed January 18, 2007).

Hedges, S. J. (2005). Firm helps U.S. mold news abroad. *Chicago Tribune,* November 14, 2005. http://www.mediachannel.org/blog/node/1860 (accessed May 4, 2006).

Helvarg, D. (1994). *The war against greens: The "wise-use" movement, the new right and anti-environmental violence.* San Francisco: Sierra Club Books.

Henderson, K. (2006). *While they're at war: The true story of American families on the home-front.* Boston: Houghton Mifflin.

Herman, E. (2005). U.S. willing to talk, with conditions, and the media bites once again. *Znet,* June 10, 2005. http://www.zmag.org/sustainers/content/2006-06/10herman.cfm (accessed April 12, 2006).

Herman, E. S., and N. Chomsky. (1988). *Manufacturing consent.* New York: Pantheon Books.

Herman, E. S., and R. B. DuBoff. (1966). *America's Vietnam policy: The strategy of deception.* Washington, DC: Public Affairs Press.

Hersh, S. M. (2003). Selective intelligence. *New Yorker,* May 12, 2003.

Hersh, S. M. (2004a). Torture at Abu Ghraib. *New Yorker,* May 10, 2004. http://www.newyorker.com/printables/fact/040510fa_fact (accessed May 4, 2006).

Hersh, S. (2004b). Chain of command. *New Yorker,* May 17, 2004. http://www.newyorker.com/printables/fact/040517fa_fact2 (accessed May 4, 2006).

Hersh, S. (2004c). The gray zone. *New Yorker,* May 24, 2004. http://www.newyorker.com/printables/fact/040524fa_fact (accessed May 4, 2006).

Hiatt, S., ed. (2007). *A game as old as empire: The secret world of economic hit men and the web of global corruption.* San Francisco: Berrett-Koehler.

Hillman, A., and M. Hitt. (1999). Corporate political strategy formulation: A model of approach, participation, and strategy decisions. *Academy of Management Review* 4 (24): 825–842.

Hitchens, C. (2001). *The trial of Henry Kissinger.* London: Verso Press.

Hitchens, C. (2002). Kissinger's green light to Suharto. *Nation,* February 2002. http://www.thenation.com/doc/20020218/hitchens.

Hochschild, A. R., and B. Ehrenriech. (2004). *Global woman: Nannies, maids, and sex workers in the new economy.* New York: Owl Books/Harpers.

Hoge, C. W., C. A. Castro, S. C. Messer, D. McGurk, D. I. Cotting, and R. L. Koffman. (2004). Combat duty in Iraq and Afghanistan, mental health problems, and barriers to care. *New England Journal of Medicine* 351:13–22.

Hollar, J., and P. Hart. (2005). When "old news" has never been told. *Extra!* July/August 2005. http://www.fair.org/index.php?page=2612 (accessed May 31, 2006).

Holthouse, D. (2006). Extremism and the military: A timeline. Southern Poverty Law Center. http://www.splcenter.org/intel/news/item.jsp?aid=66 (accessed July 13, 2006).

Hopey, D. (2000). An inextricable link: Human and environmental rights. *Pittsburgh Post-Gazette*, September 25, A-6.

House, J. S., K. R. Landis, and D. Umberson. (1988). Social relationships and health. *Science* 241: 540–545.

Huber, P. (2003). The palm pilot-JDAM complex. *Forbes* 171 (10): 88.

Human Development Report. (1997). E.98.III.B.38, United Nations Development Programme. Oxford: Oxford University Press.

Human Rights Watch. (2003a). Off target: The conduct of the war and civilian casualties in Iraq. http://www.hrw.org/reports/2003/usa1203.

Human Rights Watch. (2003b). U.K. military practices linked to Iraqi civilian casualties. December 12, 2003. http://www.hrw.org/press/2003/12/uk-iraq-press.htm (accessed March 14, 2004).

Human Rights Watch. (2003c). Background on the crisis in Iraq. http://www.hrw.org/reports/2003/usa1203/4.htm#_ftnref79 and http://www.hrw.org/campaigns/iraq/ (accessed March 20, 2006).

Human Rights Watch. (2004). The road to Abu Ghraib. June 2004. http://www.humanrightswatch.org (accessed June 3, 2006).

Human Rights Watch. (2005). Displaced and discarded: The plight of internally displaced persons in Bogota and Cartagena. http://www.hrw.org/english/docs/2005/10/14/colomb11864_txt.htm (accessed December 13, 2005).

Ignacio, A., E. de la Cruz, J. Emmanuel, and H. Toribio. (2004). *The forbidden book: The Philippine American war in political cartoons.* San Francisco: T'Boli Publishing and Distribution.

Institute for Food and Development Policy. (2001). The global banquet: Politics of food. Film. Maryknoll Productions.

International Campaign to Ban Landmines. (2005a). http://www.icbl.org/treaty (accessed September 11, 2005).

International Campaign to Ban Landmines. (2005b). http://www.icbl.org/problem/what (accessed September 11, 2005).

International Committee of the Red Cross. (2004). Report of the International Committee of the Red Cross (ICRC) on the treatment by the Coalition Forces of prisoners of war and other protected persons by the Geneva Conventions in Iraq during arrest, internment and interrogation. February 2004. http://www.globalsecurity.org/military/library/report/2004/icrc_report_iraq_feb2004.htm (accessed June 5, 2006).

International Labour Organization. (2005). Facts on child labour. http://www.ilo.org/public/english/bureau/inf/fact/index.html (accessed December 16, 2005).

International Solidarity Mission (ISM). (2005). Report back and discussion on the continuing human rights violations in the Philippines. UTLA Headquarters, Los Angeles, CA. October 21, 2005.

Ireland, D. (2004). The Cheney connection: Tracing the Halliburton money trail to Nigeria. *Los Angeles Weekly*, June 17, 2004. http://www.laweekly.com/news/news/the-cheney-connection/1601/ (accessed June 10, 2007).

Ireland, D. (2005). Why U. S. media dismissed the Lancet Study of 100,000 Iraqi civilian dead. *Common Dreams*. http://www.commondreams.org/cgi-bin/print.cgi?file=/views05/0127-23.htm (accessed June 2, 2006).

ISAAA. (2006). International Service for the Acquisition of Agri-biotech Applications ISAAA Brief 35-(2006): Executive Summary. Global Status of Commercialized Biotech/GM Crops. http://www.isaaa.org/resources/publications/briefs/35/default/executive.summary.html (accessed March 14, 2007).

Ismail, M. A. (2006). *Investing in war: The Carlyle Group profits from government and conflict.* Center for Public Integrity. http://www.publicintegrity.org/pns/report.aspx?aid=424 (accessed September 22, 2006).

Ivins, M. (1997). So much for putting people first. *Houston Chronicle Interactive,* April 14, 1997.

Jackson, J., and P. Hart. (2000). How power shapes the news. Fear & Favor 2000. *Extra!* http://www.fair.org/index.php?page=2013&printer_friendly=1 (accessed April 3, 2006).

Jamail, D. (2005) Dahr Jamail's Iraq dispatches. http://dahrjamailiraq.com 8/5/05 (accessed September 7, 2006).

James, C. (2004). *Executive summary preview: Global status of commercialized biotech/GM crops: 2004.* International Service for the Acquisition of Agri-biotech Applications (ISAAA).

James, W. (1995/1910). The moral equivalent of war. *Peace and Conflict: Journal of Peace Psychology* 1: 17–26.

Jardine, M. (2000). East Timor: Up from ground zero. *In These Times,* October 5, 12–14.

Johnson, C. (2004). *The sorrows of empire: Militarism, secrecy, and the end of the republic.* New York: Metropolitan Books.

Johnson, D. (2000). Solving water scarcity. *Journal of Family and Consumer Sciences,* 92: 17.

Jones, P. B. C. (2003). US files SOS with WTO: End EU's GM moratorium ASAP. *Information systems for biotechnology news report,* August 2003. http://www.isb.vt.edu/news/2003/artspdf/aug0306.pdf (accessed January 11, 2007).

Jonas, S. (1991). *The battle for Guatemala: Rebels, death squads and U.S. power.* Boulder, CO: Westview Press.

Juhasz, A. (2006). *The Bush agenda: Invading the world, one economy at a time.* New York: Regan Books, HarperCollins.

Kagen, D, G. Schmidt, and T. Donelly. (2000). Rebuilding America's defenses: Strategy, forces and resources for a new century, September 2000. Washington DC: Project for a New American Century.

Kampfner, J. (2003). The Pentagon basks in triumph. *New Statesman,* April 28, 23.

Kanner, A., and M. Gomes. (1995). The all-consuming self. In *Ecopsychology,* ed. T. Roszak, M. Gomes, and A. Kanner, 77–91. San Francisco: Sierra Club Books.

Keen, S. (1988) *Faces of the enemy: Reflections of the hostile imagination.* San Francisco: Harper & Row.

Keen, S., and A. Valley-Fox. (1989). *Your mythic journey.* Los Angeles: Jermey Tarcher.

Kelly, G. A. (1963). *A theory of personality: The psychology of personal constructs.* New York: W. W. Norton.

Kelman, H. (1973). Violence without moral restraint. *Journal of Social Issues* 29 (4): 25–61.

Kennan, G. F. (1983). *Nuclear delusion: Soviet American relations in the nuclear age.* New York: Pantheon.

Kennedy, D. (2007). Chiapas: Reflections on trade, immigration, and the global economy. Global Exchange, May 5, 2007. http://www.globalexchange.org/tours/Chiapas Reflections.html (accessed June 6, 2007).

Kesan, J. P. (2000). Intellectual property protection and agricultural biotechnology. *American Behavior Scientist* 44: 464–503.

Khor, M. (1997). Communities countering the negative consequences of aquaculture. http://www.earthisland.org/map/w95-nwbriefs.html (accessed October 12, 2005).

Kick, R., ed. (2001). *You are being lied to: The disinformation guide to media distortion, historical whitewashes, and cultural myths.* New York: Disinformation Company.

Kiesling, J. B. (2006). *Diplomacy lessons: Realism for an unloved superpower.* Washington DC: Potomac Press.

Kimmel, P., and C. E. Stout., eds. (2006). *Collateral damage: The psychological consequences of America's war on terror.* Westport, CT: Praeger.

King, G. (2004). *Woman, child for sale: The new slave trade in the 21st century.* New York: Penguin Group.

Kinzer, S. (2003). *All the Shah's men: An American coup and the roots of Middle East terror.* Hoboken, NJ: Wiley & Sons.

Kinzer, S. (2006). *Overthrow: America's century of regime change from Hawaii to Iraq.* New York: Times Books.

Kinzer, S. (n.d.). How to overthrow a government, pt. 1: The 1953 U.S. coup in Iran. *Democracy Now!* http://www.democracynow.org/article.pl?sid=04/03/05/1542249&mode=thread&tid=25.

Klare, M. T. (2002). *Resource wars: The new landscape of global conflict.* New York: Henry Holt.

Klare, M. T. (2004). *Blood and oil: The dangers and consequences of America's growing petroleum dependency.* New York: Metropolitan Books/Henry Holt & Co.

Kleff, R. (1993). Terrorism: The Trinity Perspective. In *Terrorism & political violence: Limits & possibilities of legal control,* ed. H. H. Han. New York: Oceana.

Klein, N. (2004).You asked for my evidence, Mr. Ambassador. Here it is in Iraq, the US does eliminate those who dare to count the dead. *Guardian.* http://www.guardian.co.uk/Columnists/Column/0,,1366348,00.html (accessed December 5, 2004).

Klein, N. (2005). The rise of disaster capitalism. *Nation,* May 2, 2005. http://www.thenation.com/doc.mhtml?i=20050502&s=klein (accessed October 5, 2006).

Klein, N. (2005). Torture's part of the territory. *Los Angeles Times,* June 7, B13.

Klinenberg, E. (2007). *Fighting for air: The battle to control America's media.* New York: Henry Holt & Co.

Kloppenburg, J. (1994). Scientific poaching and global biodiversity. *Elmwood Quarterly* 10 (2&3): 7–11.

Knott, A. (2004). Who gives the most money: Financial corporations and law firms dominate career patrons list. Center for Public Integrity. http://www.publicintegrity.org/bop2004/report.aspx?aid=168 (accessed November 2, 2006).

Koenigsberg, R. A. (2005). The soldier as sacrificial victim: Awakening from the nightmare of history. http://home.earthlink.net/~libraryofsocialscience/as_the_soldier.htm (accessed November 8, 2005).

Korten, D. (1998). *Globalizing civil society: Reclaiming our right to power.* New York: Seven Stories Press.

Korten, D. C. (2001). *When corporations rule the world.* West Hartford, CT: Kumerian and San Francisco: Berrett-Koehler.

Koufa, K. (2001). Terrorism and human rights. United Nations Economic and Social Council. Commission on Human Rights. Sub-Commission on the Promotion and Protection of Human Rights, June 27, 43, 45, and 46.

Krieger, D. (2007). Nuclear disarmament. In *Handbook of peace and conflict studies.* ed. C. Webel and J. Galtung, 106–122. London: Routledge.

Krippner, S., and T. M. McIntyre, eds. (2003). *The psychological impact of war trauma on civilians an international perspective.* Westport, CT: Praeger.

Kyle, D., and R. Koslowsky. (2001). *Global human smuggling: Comparative perspectives.* Baltimore, MD: John Hopkins University Press.

Lace, Sosin, and Snell Assoc. (1997). *U.S. opinion poll commissioned for the Abolition 2000 Network.* New York: Global Resource Action Center.

Lakoff, G., and M. Johnson. (2003). *Metaphors we live by.* Chicago: University of Chicago Press.

Lamison-White, T. (1997). Poverty in the United States: 1996. Current Population Report, Series P60-198. Washington DC: U.S. Government Printing Office.

Landmine Monitor Report. (2003). Toward a mine-free world. *Landmine Monitor,* August 2003. http://www.icbl.org/lm/2003 (accessed May 16, 2005).

Lando, B. (2007). *Web of deceit: The history of Western complicity in Iraq, from Churchill to Kennedy to George W. Bush.* New York: Other Press.

Lang, T., and M. Heasman. (2004). *Food wars: The global battle for mouths, minds and markets.* New York: Earthscan Publications.

Langer, S. (1942). *Philosophy in a new key: A study of the symbolism of reason, rite, and art.* Cambridge: Harvard University Press.

Langewiesche, W. (2007). *The atomic bazaar: The rise of the nuclear poor.* New York: Farrar, Straus and Giroux.

LaVine, S., and D. Pearl. (2001). As the Taliban recede, opium blooms again—until Afghanistan gets a new government, growers are planting. *Wall Street Journal,* A15.

Lawrence, B. (2006). *Messages to the world: The statements of Osama bin Laden.* London and New York: Verso Press.

Leach, W. (1993). *Land of desire: Merchant's power and the rise of the new American culture.* New York: Pantheon.

Lederman, D. (2005). Inside higher ed "Coke: The new Nike." *Campaign to stop killer Coke.* http://www.corporatecampaign.org/killer-coke/who.htm (accessed May 6, 2005).

Lee, M., P. G. Zimbardo, and M. Berthof. (1977). Shy murderers. *Psychology Today* 11 (November): 69 ff.

Leiss, W., and C. Chociolko. (1994). *Risk and responsibility.* Buffalo, NY: McGill-Queens University Press.

Le Shan, L. (2002). *The psychology of war: Comprehending its mystique and its madness.* New York: Helios Press.

Lewis, E. (1998). *The buying of the Congress.* New York: Avon.

Lewis-Horne, J. (2000). Review of *School for rape: The Burmese military and sexual violence,* by Betsy Apple. *Violence Against Women* 6: 1174–1178.

Lewontin, R. (1991). *Biology as ideology: The doctrine of DNA.* New York: HarperCollins.

Lifton, R. J. (1967). *Death in life: Survivors of Hiroshima.* New York: Simon & Schuster.

Lincoln Group. (2006). Lincoln Group Web site. http://www.lincolngroup.com. (accessed April, 11, 2006).

Litterer, J. (1997). ICE case studies: Belize logging conflict. *Inventory of Conflict and Environment.* http://www.american.edu/ted/ice/belize.htm (accessed April 29, 2005).

Litz, B. T. (2005). A brief primer on the mental health impact of the wars in Afghanistan and Iraq. A National Center for PTSD Fact Sheet file, updated April 7, 2005. http://www.ncptsd.va.gov/facts/veterans/fs_iraq_afghanistan_lay_audience.html (accessed September 12, 2005).

Logan, J. R., and H. Molotch. (1987). *Urban fortunes: The political economy of place.* Berkeley: University of California Press.

Longley, R. (2006). Political Action Committees. *About.com.* http://usgovinfo.about.com/od/thepoliticalsystem/a/aboutpacs.htm (accessed November 13, 2006).

Lorenz, K. (1966). *On aggression.* New York: Bantam.

Lyderson, K. (2000). The truth is out there. *In These Times,* October 10, 7.

Lynch, A. (2005). U.S.: The media lobby. *AlterNet*, March 11, 2005. http://www.corpwatch.org/print_article.php?id=11947 (accessed May 4, 2006).

MacCannell, E. D., and J. White. (1984). Social costs of large-scale agriculture: The prospects of land reform in California. In *Land reform American style*, ed. C. C. Giesler and F. J. Popper, 35–54. Totawa, NJ: Rowman and Allenheld.

MacDonald, S. B. (1992). Afghanistan's drug trade. [Electronic version] *Society, 29*, 61–66.

Machel, G. (2001). *The impact of war on children*. Cape Town: David Philip.

Macy, J. R. (1983) *Despair and personal power in the nuclear age*. Philadelphia: New society.

Macy, J. R., & Brown, M. Y. (1998). *Coming back to life: Practices to reconnect our lives, our world*. Gabriola Island, BC, Canada: New Society Publishers.

Makhijani, A. (1992). *From global capitalism to economic justice: An inquiry into the elimination of systematic poverty, violence and environmental destruction in the world economy*. The Council of International and Public Affairs. New York: Apex Press.

Makhmalbaf, M. (2001). Limbs of no body. Opinion. *Iranian*, June 20, 2001. http://www.iranian.com/Opinion/2001/June/Afghan/index.html (accessed November 15, 2001).

Makison, L. (2006). Outsourcing the Pentagon: Who benefits from the politics and economics of national security? Center for Public Integrity. http://publicintegrity.org/pns/report.aspx?aid=385 (accessed August 12, 2006).

Mander, J. (1996). The rules of corporate behavior. In *The case against the global economy: And for a turn toward the local*, ed. J. Mander and E. Goldsmith, 309–422. San Francisco: Sierra Club Books.

Mander, J., and E. Goldsmith. (1996). *The case against the global economy*. San Francisco: Sierra Club Books.

Mann, J. (2004). *Rise of the Vulcans: The history of Bush's war cabinet*. New York: Viking.

Mann, M. (1984). The autonomous power of the state: Its origins, mechanisms, and results. *Archives of European Sociology* 25: 185–213.

Mann, M. (1993). *The sources of social power: The rise of classes and nation-states, 1760–1914*, vol. 2. New York: Cambridge University Press.

Manning, R. (2001). Hunger speaks. *Forum for Applied Research and Public Policy* 16: 48–53.

Maquila Solidarity Network. (2005). Asia-Latina Women's Exchange: Mapping the impacts of the quota phase-out on workers' lives. Maquila Solidarity Network, October 2005. http://www.maquilasolidarity.org/resources/post_mfa/AWID%20exchange/index/htm (accessed March 28, 2006).

Markusen, A., and J. Yukden. (1992). *Dismantling the war economy*. New York: Basic Books.

Marlay, R., and B. Ulmer. (2001). Report on human rights in Burma: Background and current status. *Journal of Third World Studies* 18: 113–128.

Marrow, A. J. (1977). *The practical theorist: The life and work of Kurt Lewin*. New York: Teachers College Press.

Martinez, R., Jr. (1996). Latinos and lethal violence: The impact of poverty and inequality. *Social Problems* 43 (2): 131–143.

Marty, D. (2006). Alleged secret detentions and unlawful interstate transfers involving Council of Europe member states. Council of Europe, Committee on Legal Affairs and Human Rights, Restricted. Doc. 16 2006 Part 2. http://www.globalsecurity.org/intell/library/reports/2006/secret-detentions_pace_060607-10.htm (accessed June 7, 2007).

Matthews, B. (2001). Myanmar: Beyond the reach of international relief? *Southeast Asian Affairs*, 229–248.

May, R. (1984). The problem of evil: An open letter to Carl Rogers. In *American politics and humanistic psychology*, ed. T. Greening, 12–23. San Francisco: Saybrook Publishing Company.

Mayer, J. (2006). The hidden power: The legal mind behind the White House's war on terror. *New Yorker*, July 3, 2006. http://www.newyorker.com/archive/2006/07/03/060703fa_fact1 (accessed October 10, 2006).

Mazzetti, M., and B. Daragahi. (2005). The conflict in Iraq: U.S. military covertly pays to run stories in Iraqi press. *LA Times*, November 30, A1.

McCarthy, S. (2000). Ten year of chaos in Burma: Foreign investment and economic liberalization under the SLORC-SPCD, 1988 to 1998. *Pacific Affairs* 73: 233–262.

McChesney, R. W. (1997). *Corporate media and the threat to democracy.* New York: Seven Stories Press.

McChesney, R. W. (1999). *Rich media, poor democracy: Communication politics in dubious times.* Chicago: University of Illinois Press.

McChesney, R. W. (2004). *The problem of the media: U. S. communication politics in the 21st Century.* New York: Monthly Review Press.

McCoy, A. (2006). *A question of torture: CIA interrogation, from the Cold War to the War on Terror.* New York: Metropolitan Books/Henry Holt.

McGill, C. (2003). *Human traffic: sex, slaves and immigration.* London: Vision Paperbacks.

McGloin, S. J. (1999). *The market as God: Living in the new dispensation.* Jesuit Center for Theoretical Reflection Bulletin, no. 41, September 1999. http://www.jctr.org.zm/bulletins/market%20as%20god.htm (accessed June 5, 2005).

McIntyre, T. M., and M. Ventura. (2003). Children of war: Psychlogical sequeuelae of war trauma in Angolan adolescents. In *The psychological impact of war trauma on civilians*, ed. S. Krippner and T. M. McIntyre, 19–24. Westport, CT: Praeger.

McKay, F. J. (2006). Propaganda: America's psychological warriors. *Seattle Times*, February 19, 2006.

McKay, S. (1998). The effects of armed conflict on girls and women. *Peace and Conflict: Journal of Peace Psychology* 2: 93–107.

McNamara, R. S. (2005). Apocalypse soon. *Foreign Policy Magazine*, May/June 2005. http://www.foreignpolicy.com/story/cms.php?story_id=2829 (accessed September 9, 2005).

McQuaid, J. (2005). The Drowning of New Orleans: Hurricane devastation was predicted. *Democracy Now!* Archives, September 1, 2005. http://www.democracynow.org/search.pl?query=mcQuaid.

McSherry, J. P. (2005). *Predatory states: Operation Condor and covert war in Latin America.* Lanham, MD: Rowman & Littlefield Publishers.

Meade, C., and R. Molander. (2005). W11.2 Analyzing the economic impacts of a catastrophic terrorist attack on the Port of Long Beach. RAND Corporation. http://birenheide.com/sra/2005AM/program/singlesession.php3?sessid=W11 and http://www.ci.olympia.wa.us/council/Corresp/NPTreportTJJohnsonMay2005.pdf (accessed May 1, 2006).

Meadows, D. (1992). Corporate run schools are a threat to our way of life. *Valley News*, October 3, 22.

Mearsheimer, J. J., and S. M. Walt. (2003). An unnecessary war. *Foreign Policy*, January/February 2003.

Melville, T., and M. Melville. (1971). *Guatemala: The politics of land ownership.* New York: The Free Press.

Mendenhall, P. (2001). Afghanistan's cash crop.*MSNBC*. http://www.msnbc.com/news/564809.asp (accessed November 15, 2001).

Mendez, A. (n.d.). An uncommon view of the birth of an uncommon market. *Bilderberg.* http://www.bilderberg.org/bildhist.htm#Mendez (accessed August 12, 2006).

Merari, A. (1990). The readiness to kill and die: Suicidal terrorism in the Middle East. In *Origins of terrorism: Psychologies theologies, states of mind,* ed. W. Reich. New York: Cambridge University Press.

Merton, K., and P. Lazersfeld. (1950). *The American soldier,* vol. 2. Glencoe, IL: Free Press.

Mexican Action Network on Free Trade. (n.d.). (Réseau Mexicain d'Action Sur le Libre-Échange). NAFTA and the Mexican Economy. Excerpted from Espejismo y realidad: el TLCAN tres años después, Análisis y propuesta desde la sociedad civil, by the Mexican Action Network on Free Trade (RMALC). http://www.developmentgap.org (accessed June 9, 2000).

Milbank, D., and C. Deane. (2003). Hussein link to 9/11 lingers in many minds. *Washington Post,* September 6, 2003. http://www.washingtonpost.com/ac2/wp-dyn/A32862-2003Sep5?language=printer (accessed June 5, 2005).

Milgram, S. (1974). *Obedience to authority.* New York: Harper & Row.

Miller, R. D. (2006). The energy employees occupational illness compensation program: Are we fulfilling the promise we made to these veterans of the Cold War when we created the program? Testimony by Richard D. Miller, Government Accountability Project. Committee on Judiciary. U.S. House of Representatives, March 1, 2006.

Milliard, T. S. (2003). Overcoming post-colonial myopia: A call to recognize and regulate private military corporations. *Military Law Review,* no. 176: I-2.

Mills, C. W. (1956). *The power elite.* New York: Oxford University Press.

Misra, G., and K. J. Gergen. (1993). On the place of culture in psychological science. *International Journal of Psychology* 28 (2): 225–243.

Mokhiber, R. (2003). Politics of Chemistry 101. *Multinational Monitor* 24 (10). http://www.multinationalmonitor.org/mm2003/03october/front.html (accessed May 6, 2005).

Mokhiber, R., and R. Weissman. (1997). Beat the devil: The 10 worst corporations in 1997. *Multinational Monitor* 18: 9–18.

Molotch, H. (1999). Growth machine links: Up, down, and across. In *The urban growth machine: Critical perspectives, two decades later,* ed. A. Jonas and D. Wilson, 247–265. Albany, NY: State University of New York Press.

Monbiot, G. (2006). *Heat: How to stop the planet from burning.* New York: Doubleday.

Monteil, C. J. (2001). Toward a psychology of structural peacebuilding. In *Peace, conflict, and violence: Peace psychology for the 21st Century,* ed. D. Christie, R. Wagner, and D. Winter, 282–294. Englewood, NJ: Prentice Hall.

Montgomery, B. P. (2005). Congressional oversight: Vice President Richard B. Cheney's executive branch triumph. *Political Science Quarterly* 120: 581–617.

Moore, M. (1994). *TV Nation.* NBC Television, August 2, 1994.

Moreton, B. E. (2007). It came from Bentonville: The agrarian origins of Wal-Mart culture. In *Wal-Mart: The face of twenty-first-century capitalism,* ed. N. Lichtenstein. New York: New Press.

Morgan, R. (2001). *The demon lover: The roots of terrorism.* New York: Washington Square Press.

Morgan, R. (2006). Rape, murder, and the American GI. Women's Media Center. Posted August 17, 2006. http://www.alternet.org/waroniraq/40481/ (accessed May 10, 2007).

Moss, M. (2005). Struggle for Iraq: Troop shields; Pentagon study links fatalities to body armor. *New York Times,* March 7, A1.

Moyers, B. (1987). The secret government: The constitution in crisis. PBS TV program. http://video.google.com/videoplay?docid=-8536707153900925247.

Moyers, B. (2003). U.S. big media gets bigger. *NOW with Bill Moyers* on PBS, October 10, 2003. http://www.corpwatch.org/print_article.php?id=7836 (accessed May 4, 2006).

Moyers, B. (2007). On digital destiny at the 2007 media reform conference.

MSNBC (2005). Report: U.S. paying Iraqi journalists. *MSNBC Hardball,* December 1, 2005. http://msnbc.msn.com/id/10285246.

Mueller, J. (2006). *Overblown: How politicians and the terrorism industry inflate national security threats, and why we believe them.* New York: Free Press.

Murphy, S. (2001). The global food basket. *Forum for Applied Research and Public Policy* 16: 36–42.

Nairn, A. (1983). Guatemala bleeds. *New Republic,* April 11, 1983.

NAM. (2007a). About us. National Association of Manufacturers. http://www.nam.org/s_nam/sec.asp?CID=4&DID=2 (accessed April 24, 2007).

NAM. (2007b). Bottom line policy achievements for manufacturers. National Association of Manufacturers. http://www.nam.org/s_nam/doc1.asp?CID=24&DID=201889 (accessed April 24, 2007).

NAM. (2007c). Official policy positions: Global climate change. National Association of Manufacturers. http://www.nam.org/s_nam/sec.asp?TRACKID=&SID=1&VID=1&CID=43&DID=41&RTID=0&CIDQS=&Taxonomy=False&specialSearch=False (accessed May 2, 2007).

NAM. (2007d). National Association of Manufacturers. Talking points for manufacturers: Energy security for American competitiveness. http://www.nam.org/s_nam/doc1.asp?CID=202556&DID=238282 (accessed May 2, 2007).

National Adolescent Health Information Center. (1995). *Fact sheets on adolescent homicide, mortality, suicide and injury.* San Francisco: University of California.

National Center for Post-Traumatic Stress Disorder. (1991a). The Project National Center for Post-#C8191. http://www.ncptsd.va.gov/facts/veterans/fs_native_vets.html (accessed October 5, 2005).

National Center for Post-Traumatic Stress Disorder. (1991b). The legacy of psychological trauma of the Vietnam War for Native Hawaiian and American of Japanese ancestry military personnel. A National Center for PTSD Fact Sheet.

Natural Resources Defense Council. (2001). *The U.S. nuclear war plan: A time for change.* http://www.nrdc.org/nuclear/warplan/index.asp, last revised June15, 2001 (accessed September 16. 2005).

National Security Council. (2006). The National Security Strategy, March 2006. The White House, Washington DC. http://www.whitehouse.gov/nsc/nss/2006 (accessed June 6, 2006).

Neale, T. (2006). On the hot seat. *Audobo,* January-February, 17.

Nelson-Pallmeyer, J. (1997). School of Assassins. New York: Orbis Books. Quoted in David Mericle. *Impact Press.* http://www.impactpress.com/articles/aprmay99/soa4599.html.

Netzer, O. (2005). The real causes of war discovered. Interactivist Info Exchange. http://info.interactivist.net/article.pl?sid=05/08/13/2232239 (August 13, 2005).

Nichols, J., and R. W. McChesney. (2005). *Tragedy and farce: How the American media sell wars, spin elections, and destroy democracy.* New York: The New Press.

Niebuhr, R. (1952). *The irony of American history.* New York: Scribners.

Nikolic-Ristanovic, V. (1996). War and violence against women. In *The gendered new world order*, ed. J. Turpin and L. A. Lorentzen, 195–210. New York: Routledge.

Nikolic-Ristanovic., V. (1999). *Women, violence and war: Victimization of refugees in the Balkans.* Budapest: Central European University Press.

Nord, M., S. Andrews, and Carlson. (2005). Household food security in the United States, 2004. Economic Research Service, U.S. Department of Agriculture. http://www.ers.usda.gov/Publications/err11 (accessed November 6, 2005).

Norquist, G. (1994). *Rock the house.* Austin, TX: Texas Policy Foundation.

North, A. (2005). Losing the war on Afghan drugs. *BBC News.* Lashkar Gah, Helmand, December 4, 2005. http://news.bbc.co.uk/2/hi/south_asia/4493596.stm (accessed February 2, 2006).

North, G. (1983). *Christianity and civilization.* Tyler, TX: Geneva Ministries.

Nossiter, B. D. (1970). *Soft state: A newspaperman's chronicle of India.* New York: Harper & Row.

Nunberg, G. (2001). Terrorism: The history of a very frightening word. *San Francisco Chronicle*, October 28, C5.

Nunberg, G. (2006). *Talking right: How conservatives turned Liberalism into a tax-raising, latte-drinking, sushi-eating, Volvo-driving, New York Times-reading, body-piercing, Hollywood-loving, left-wing freak show.* New York: Public Affairs Press.

Øberg, J. (2006). Does the European Union promote peace? Transnational Foundation for Peace and Future Research. Lund, Sweden, October 6, 2006.

O'Kane, R. H. T. (1996). Terror as government and its causes, Cambodia, April 1975–January 1979. In *Terror, force, and states: The path from modernity.* Cheltenham, UK: Edward Elgar.

O'Neill, B. E. (1993). The strategic context of insurgent terrorism. In *Terrorism & political violence: Limits & possibilities of legal control*, ed. H. H. Han. New York: Oceana Publications, Inc.

Osofsky, J. D. (1995). The effects of exposure to violence on young children. *American Psychologist*, September 1995, 782–788.

Oxford Analytica. (2006). WTO: EU food ban violated agreement. *Forbes.* http://www.forbes.com/business/2006/10/11/genetically-modified-food-biz-cx_1012oxford.html (accessed January 10, 2007).

Packer, G. (2005). *The assassins' gate: America in Iraq.* New York: Farrar, Straus & Giroux.

Padron, M. S., and M. G. Uranga. (2001). Protection of biotechnological inventions: a burden too heavy for the patent system. *Journal of Economic Issues* 35: 315–322.

Palast, G. (2004). *The best democracy money can buy.* New York: Penguin.

Parenti, M. (1969). *The anti-communist impulse.* New York: Random House.

Parenti, M. (1995). *Democracy for the Few.* 6th ed. New York: St. Martin's Press.

Parrenas, R. C. (2001). *Servants of globalization: Women, migration and domestic work.* Palo Alto, CA: Stanford University Press.

Paul, R. (2003). National Endowment for Democracy: Paying to make enemies of America, October 11, 2003. http://www.antiwar.com/paul/paul79.html (accessed August 29, 2006).

Peace Pledge Union. (2005). War and peace. Peace Pledge Union. http://www.ppu.org.uk/war/facts.

Pelletiere, Stephen C. (2004). *Iraq and the international oil system: Why America went to war in the Gulf.* Washington DC: Maisonneuve Press.

Perelman, M., and Sandronsky, S. (2006). When economists didn't buy the free market: An interview with Michael Perelman. *Z Magazine Online*, October 29, 2006. http://www.zmag.org/content/showarticle.cfm?ItemID=11287.

Perry, A. (2001). Hunger and despair in the camps. *Time*, 158 (December 3): 33.

Persian Gulf Veterans Coordinating Board. (1995). Unexplained illnesses among Desert Storm veterans: A search for causes, treatment, and cooperation. *Archives of Internal Medicine*, 155: 262–268.

Peters, M. (2001). The Bilderberg Group and the project of European unification. http://www.xs4all.nl/~ac/global/achtergrond/bilderberg.htm (accessed August 12, 2006).

Peterson, Evan Augustine III. (2005). Of Militarism, fascism, war and national consciousness. NFPNZ essay, February 6, 2005. http://nuclearfree.lynx.co.nz/of.htm (accessed February 4, 2006).

Peterson, Evan Augustine, III. (2005a). American idols: From petro-theism to empire-theism. AxisOfLogic.com essay, October 5, 2005. http://www.axisoflogic.com/cgibin/exec/view.pl?archive=135&num=19757 (accessed February 6, 2006).

Peterson, Evan Augustine, III. (2005b). American militarism, Part 2: On celebrating militaristic nationalism. Essay received from author by e-mail, July 7, 2005, 6:51 A.M.

Peterson, L. (2006).*The windfalls of war: Bechtel Group, Inc.* Center for Public Integrity. http://www.publicintegrity.org/wow/bio.aspx?act=pro&ddlC=6 (accessed September 21, 2006).

Phillips, P. (1994). A relative advantage: Sociology of the San Francisco Bohemian Club. Doctoral dissertation, Sonoma State University. http://libweb.sonoma.edu/regional/faculty/phillips/bohemianindex.html (accessed August 12, 2006).

Physicians for Human Rights. (2005). Break them down: Systematic use of torture by U.S. forces. Cambridge, MA. http://physiciansforhumanrights.org (accessed June 9, 2006).

Physicians for Social Responsibility. (2004). Cancer and the environment. http://Cancer_and_ the _ envir#11D668.pdf (accessed March 13, 2007).

Pilisuk, M. (1972). *International conflict and social policy.* Englewod, NJ: Prentice Hall.

Pilisuk, M. (1975). The legacy of the Vietnam veteran. In Soldiers in and after Vietnam, ed. D. Mantell and M. Pilisuk. *Journal of Social Issues* 31 (4): 3–12.

Pilisuk, M. (1982). Games strategists play. *Bulletin of the Atomic Scientists* 38 (9): 13–17.

Pilisuk, M. (1998). The hidden structure of contemporary violence. *Peace and Conflict: Journal of Peace Psychology* 4 (3): 197–216.

Pilisuk, M. (1999). Addictive rewards in nuclear weapons development. *Peace Review: A Transnational Journal* 11 (4): 597–602.

Pilisuk, M. (2001). Globalism and structural violence. In *Peace, conflict, and violence: Peace psychology for the 21st century 2001*, ed. D. Christie, R. Wagner, and D. Winter. Englewood, NJ: Prentice Hall.

Pilisuk, M. (2005). Unprofessional warriors: Lesson small and large. *Peace and Conflict: Journal of Peace Psychology* 11 (1): 95–100.

Pilisuk, M. (2007). Disarmament and survival. In *Handbook of peace and conflict studies*, ed. C. Webel and J. Galtung, 94–105. London: Routledge.

Pilisuk, M., and A. Wong. (2002). State terrorism: When the perpetrator is a government. In *Psychology and Terrorism*, ed. C. Stout, 105–132. Westport, CT: Praeger.

Pilisuk, M., and J. Zazzi. (2006). Toward a psychosocial theory of military and economic violence in the era of globalization. *Journal of Social Issues* 62 (1): 41–62.

Pilisuk, M., and M. Joy. (2001). Humanistic psychology and ecology. In *Handbook of Humanistic Psychology*, ed. K. Schneider, J. Bugental, and F. Pierson, 101–114. Thousand Oaks, CA: Sage Publications.

Pilisuk, M., and S. H. Parks. (1986). *The healing web: Social networks and human survival.* Hanover, NH: University Press of New England.

Pilisuk, M., and T. Hayden. (1965). Is there a military-industrial complex which prevents peace? Consensus and countervailing power. *Journal of Social Issues* 21 (3): 67–117.

Pilisuk, M., J. McAllister, and J. Rothman. (1996). Coming together for action: The challenge of contemporary grassroots organizing. *Journal of Social Issues* 52 (1): 15–37.

Pilisuk, M., S. H. Parks, and G. R. Hawkes. (1987). Public perception of technological risk. *Social Science Journal* 24: 403–413.

Pillar, C. (2007). Report: Gates foundation causing harm with the same money it uses to do good. *Los Angeles Times* reporter Interview on *Democracy Now!* Tuesday, January 9, 2007.

Pimentel, D., and M. Pimentel. (1999). Population growth, environmental resources and the global availability of food. *Social Research* 66: 417–428.

Pinter, H. (2005). The Nobel lecture: Art, truth and politics. *Guardian*, December 7, 2005.

Pitt, W. (2003). The project for the new American century. http://www.information clearinghouse.info/article1665.htm (accessed March 8, 2006).

Piven, F. F. (2004). *The war at home: The domestic costs of Bush's militarism.* New York: New Press/W. W. Norton.

Postman, N. (1992). Technopoly: The surrender of culture to technology. New York: Knopf.

Posttraumatic stress disorder and acute stress disorder. (2000). In *Diagnostic and statistical manual of mental disorders DSM-IV-TR*, 4th ed., American Psychiatric Association, 463–472. Washington, DC: American Psychiatric Association.

Price, J. L. (2004). Effects of the Persian Gulf War on U.S. Veterans. A National Center for PTSD Fact Sheet, updated December 15, 2004. http://www.ncptsd.va.gov/facts/veterans/fs_gulf_war_illness.html (accessed Aprile 6, 2007).

PR Newswire Associates. (1997). McDonald's Happy Meals Promotion. March, 19.

Program on International Policy Issues. (2003). Study finds direct link between misinformation and public misconception. http://truthout.org/docs_03/printer_100403F.shtml (accessed June 2, 2006).

Project for the New American Century. (2000). Rebuilding America's defenses: Strategy, forces, and resources for the new century. www.newamericancentury.org/defensenationalsecurity.htm.

Public Citizen-Congress Watch. (2005). Congressional revolving doors: The journey from Congress to K Street. http://www.lobbyinginfo.org/documents/RevolveDoor.pdf (accessed May 10, 2006).

Quinn, K. M. (1989). Explaining the terror. In *Cambodia 1975–1978: Rendezvous with death*, ed. K. D. Jackson, 215–240. Princeton, NJ: Princeton University Press.

Raddatz, M. (2005). The making of heroes: Lincoln Group and the fight for Fallujah. *ABC News online*, December 14, 2005. http://abcnews.go.com/WNT/story?id=1406342 (accessed December 15, 2005).

Rainforest Action Network. (1986). Coca Cola to convert 50,000 acres of rainforest to frozen orange juice. *Rainforest Action Network Alert*, May, 3.

Rainforest Action Network. (1987). Belize Update. *Rainforest Action Network Alert*, February, no. 11.

Rajiva, L. (2005) The language of empire: Abu Ghraib and the American media. *Monthly Review Press*, http://www.amazon.com/exec/obidos/ASIN/1583671196/commondreams-20/ref=nosim (accessed May 4, 2006).

Rajiva, L. (2005). The Pentagon's "NATO option." *Common Dreams*, February 10, 2005. http://www.commondreams.org/views05/0210-22.htm (accessed November 6, 2006).

Rajiva, L. (2005). The torture-go-round. *Counterpunch*. http://www.counterpunch.org/rajiva12052005.html (accessed May 1, 2006).

Rampton, S., and J. Stauber.(2003). *Weapons of mass deception: The uses of propaganda in Bush's war on Iraq*. New York: Tarcher/Penguin.

Rampton, S., and J. Stauber. (2006). *The best war ever: Lies, damned lies, and the mess in Iraq*. New York: Jeremy P. Tarcher/Penguin.

Rapoport, Anatol. (1964). *Strategy and conscience*. New York: Harper & Row.

Reiber, R. W., and R. J. Kelly. (1991). Substance and shadow: Images of the enemy. In *The psychology of war and peace: The image of the enemy*, ed. R. W. Reiber, 3–39. New York: Plenum.

Reich, R. (1997a). *Locked in the Cabinet*. New York: Alfred A. Knopf.

Reid, T. R. (1998). Feeding the planet. *National Geographic* 194: 56–74.

Reinsborough, P. (2001). Colombia's U'Wa people: The real price of oil. *NACLA Report on the Americas* 34: 44.

Rejali, D. (in press). *Torture and Democracy*. Princeton, NJ: Princeton University Press.

Remnick, D. (2004). Hearts and minds. *New Yorker*, May 17, 2004. http://www.newyorker.com/printables/talk/040517ta_talk_remnick (accessed May 17, 2004).

Renner, M. (1990). Converting to a peaceful economy. In *State of the world: 1990*, ed. L. R. Brown, 154–172. New York: W. W. Norton.

Renner, M. (1991). Assessing the military's war on the environment. In *State of the world: 1991*, ed. L. R. Brown, C. Flavin, and H. French, 139. New York: W. W. Norton.

Renner, M. (1998). Curbing the proliferation of small arms. In *State of the World: 1998*, ed. L. R. Brown, C. Flavin, and H. French, 131–148. New York: W. W. Norton.

Reynolds, P. (2005). White phosphorus: Weapon on the edge. *BBC News*, November 16, 2005. http://news.bbc.co.uk/2/hi/americas/4442988.stm (accessed May 9, 2007).

Rhodes, M. (1997a). Nike workers strike! Analysis, resources. Personal correspondence, May 1, 11: 46.

Rhodes, M. (1997b). Disney and McDonald's linked to $.06/hour sweatshop in Vietnam. Personal correspondence. May 1, 16: 48.

Rhodes, M. (1997c). Day 1 Nike worker tour. Personal correspondence. May 6.

Rich, F. (2006a). *The greatest story ever told: The decline and fall of truth from 9/11 to Katrina*. New York: Penguin Press.

Rich, F. (2006b). The peculiar disappearance of the war in Iraq. *New York Times*, July 30.

Richards, J. F. (1981). The Indian empire and peasant production of opium in the nineteenth century. *Modern Asian Studies* 15 (1): 59–62.

Richards, P. (2005). *No peace no war: An anthropology of contemporary armed conflicts*. Oxford: James Currey.

Ricks, T. (2006). *Fiasco: The American military adventure in Iraq*. New York: Penguin Group.

Ricks, T. E. (1997). *Making the corps.* New York: Scribner.

Robbins, A. (2002). *Secrets of the Tomb: Skull and Bones, the Ivy League, and the hidden paths of power.* Boston: Little, Brown.

Roberts, K. (2006). Iraq propaganda program legal: Pentagon report. Reuters, October 19, 2006. Center for Media and Democracy, www.prwatch.org/taxonomy/term/101?page=4Reuters.html (accessed July 5, 2007).

Roberts. L., R. Garfield, J. Khudhairi, and G. Burnham. (2004). Mortality before and after the 2003 invasion of Iraq: A cluster sample survey. *Lancet* 364: 9445. http://www.thelancet.com/journal/vol364/iss9445/full//llan.364.9445.early_online_PUBLICATION.3113.

Roberts, P. (2004). *The end of oil: On the edge of a perilous new world.* Boston: Houghton Mifflin.

Robertson, P. (1991). *The new world order.* Dallas, TX: Word Publication.

Robichaud, C. (2005). Focusing on the wrong number. Century Foundation, October 28, 2005. http://www.tcf.org/list.asp?type=NC&pubid=1125.

Robinson, L. (2004). *Masters of chaos: The secret history of special forces.* New York: Public Affairs Press.

Roche, D. (2002). Rethink the Unthinkable. *Globe and Mail,* March 12, A19.

Rogers, C. (1984). Notes on Rollo May. In *American politics and humanistic psychology,* ed. T. Greening, 11–12. San Francisco: Saybrook Publishing Company.

Rosenfeld, S. (1997). Women suffer brutal captivity. *San Francisco Examiner,* April 6, A1, A16.

Ross, M. H. (1990). Childrearing and war in different cultures. In *Making war/making peace: The social foundations of violent conflict,* ed. F. M. Cancian and J. W. Gibson, 51–63. Belmont, CA: Wadsworth.

Ross, R. G., Sr. (2004). *Who's who of the elite.* U.S.: RIE.

Roth-Douquet, K., and F. Schaeffer. (2006). *AWOL: The unexcused absence of America's upper classes from military service and how it hurts our country.* New York: HarperCollins.

Rubin, B. R., and O. Zakhilwal. (2005). A war on drugs, or a war on farmers? *Wall Street Journal* (Eastern Edition), A20.

Santos, R., and M. Alejandro. (2003). *Crime of empire: A case against globalization and Third World poverty as a world system.* Los Angeles: Sidelakes Press and Literary Agency.

Savage, C. (2006). Bush challenges hundreds of laws. *Boston Globe,* April 30, 2006. http://www.boston.com/news/nation/washington/articles/2006/04/30/bush_challenges_hundreds_of_laws (accessed May 12, 2006).

Scahill, J. (2007). *Blackwater: The rise of the world's most powerful mercenary army.* New York: Nation Press.

Scahill, J. (2007). Bush's Shadow Army. *Nation,* April 2, 2007.

Schanberg, S. H. (1996). On the playgrounds of America, every kid's goal is to score: In Pakistan, where children stitch soccer balls for six cents an hour, the goal is to survive. *Life,* June, 38–48.

Schechter, D. (2005). *The death of media and the fight to save democracy.* Hoboken, NJ: Melville House.

Schechter, D. (2006). *When news lies: Media complicity and the Iraq war.* New York: SelectBooks.

Scheer, R. (2001). Bush's Faustian deal with the Taliban. *Los Angeles Times,* May 22, 22.

Schell, J. (2003). *The unconquerable world: Power, nonviolence, and the will of the people.* New York: Henry Holt.

Schell, J. (2005). The fall of the one-party empire. *Nation* and TomDispatch, November 24, 2005. http://www.lewrockwell.com/engelhardt/engelhardt136.html (accessed May 24, 2006).

Schirmer, J. (1998). *The Guatemalan military project: A violence called democracy.* Philadelphia: University of Pennsylvania Press.

Schlesinger, S., and S. Kinzer. (1999). *Bitter fruit: The story of the American coup in Guatemala.* Harvard: Harvard University.

Schneider, K. (1990a). U.S. admits A-plant released harmful radiation in the 50s. *San Francisco Chronicle,* July 12, A1, A14 (from the *New York Times*).

Schneider, K. (1990b). Thousands exposed to radiation in '40s. *San Francisco Chronicle,* July, A2 (from the *New York Times*).

Schou, N., and C. Bowden. (2006). *Kill the messenger: How the CIA's crack-cocaine controversy destroyed journalist Gary Webb.* New York: Nation books.

Schrepel, W. (2005). Paras and centurions: Lessons learned from the battle of Algiers *Peace and Conflict: Journal of Peace Psychology* 11 (1): 71–90.

Schuman F. L. (1928). *American policy toward Russia since 1917.* New York: International Publishers.

Schurmann, F., P. D. Scott, and R. Zelnik. (1966). *The politics of escalation in Vietnam.* Boston: Beacon Press.

Schwartz, A., and J. Watson. (2004). The law and economics of costly contracting. *Journal of Law, Economics, and Organization* 20 (1): 2–31.

Schwartz, P. (2005). Military recruits by high school, county and more. National Priorities Project Bulletin, Personal correspondence by email, November 1, 2005.

Schwartz, S. I., ed. (1998). *Atomic audit: The costs and consequences of U.S. nuclear weapons since 1940.* Washington DC: Brookings Institution Press.

Schweizer, P., and R. Schweizer. (2004). *The Bushes: Portrait of a dynasty.* New York: Doubleday.

Scientists Committee for Radiation Information. (1962). The effects of a twenty-megaton bomb. *New University Thought,* Spring, 24–32.

Scott, P. D. (2006). Homeland security contracts for vast new detention camps. Global Research, *Pacific News Service,* February 6, 2006.

Scott, P. D., and J. Marshall. (1991). *Cocaine politics: Drugs, armies, and the CIA in Central America.* Berkeley: University of California Press.

Seager, J. (1993). *Earth follies: Coming to feminist terms with the global environmental crisis.* New York: Routledge

Shah, A. (2006). Media manipulation. http://www.globalissues.org/HumanRights/Media/Manipulation.asp?p=1 (accessed April 3, 2006).

Shah, A. (2006). High military expenditure in some places. http://www.globalissues.org/Geopolitics/ArmsTrade/Spending.asp (accessed March 7, 2006).

Shane, S. (2005). Vietnam war intelligence "deliberately skewed," secret study says. *New York Times,* December 2, 2005. Posted on *Common Dreams* News Center. http://www.commondreams.org/headlines05/1202-06.htm (accessed January 19, 2006).

Shanker, T. (2005). Weapons sales worldwide rise to highest level since 2000. *New York Times,* November 30, 2005. http://www.nytimes.com/2005/08/30/politics/30weapons.html (accessed February 2, 2006).

Shen, F. (2001). Hard lives: People of Afghanistan face war and poverty. *Washington Post,* October 3, C16.

Shiva, V. (2000). Monsanto's expanding monopolies. http://www.purefood.org/Monsanto/waterfish.cfm (accessed December 23, 2001).

Shultz, J. (2000a). Bolivians take to the streets over the price of water. http://www.inthesetimes.com/issue/24/10/shultz2410.html (accessed December 23, 2001).

Shultz, J. (2000b). Water fall out: Bolivians battle globalization. http://www.inthesetimes.com/issue/24/12/shultz2412.html (December 23, 2001).

Shultz, J. (2001). Update: World Bank and multinational corporations seek to privatize water. Project Censored. http://www.projectcensored.org/stories/2001/1.html (accessed December 23, 2001).

Shultz, J. (2005). Launching the final battle in Bolivia's water war. Democracy Center. http://www.democracyctr.org/blog/2005_11_01_democracyctr_archive.html (accessed December 8, 2005).

Shultz, J. (2007). Bolivia pulls out of World Bank trade court. Democracy Center. http://www.democracyctr.org/blog/2007/05/bolivia-pulls-out-of-world-bank-trade.html (accessed May 16, 2007).

Silverstein, K. (1998). *Washington on ten million dollars a day.* Monroe, ME: Common Courage Press.

Simmons, J., P. Farmer, and B. Schoepf. (1995). A global perspective. In *Women, poverty and AIDS: Sex, drugs and structural violence,* ed. P. Farmer, M. Connors, and J. Simmons. Monroe, ME: Common Courage Press.

Simon, M. (2006). *Appetite for profit: How the food industry undermines our health and how to fight back.* New York: Nation Books.

Singer, P. (2002). *One world: The ethics of globalization.* New Haven, CT: Yale University Press.

Sivard, L. (1996). *World military and social expenditures.* Washington DC: World Priorities.

Slater, Mike, Laura Kyser, and JoAnne Chasnow. (2006). New barriers to voting: Eroding the right to vote. *National Voter.* 55 (3). http://findarticles.com/p/articles/mi_m0MLB/is_3_55/ai_n16689802 (accessed November 15, 2006).

Snow, N. (1998). *Propaganda, Inc.: Selling America's culture to the world.* New York: Seven Stories Press.

SOAWATCH. (2004). What is the SOA? http://www.soaw.org/type.php?type=8 (accessed September 6, 2006).

Solomon, N. (2003). Linking the occupation of Iraq with the "War on Terrorism." *Media Beat,* November 20, 2003. http://www.fair.org/index.php?page=2385&printer_friendly=1 (accessed June 1, 2006).

Soltani, A., P. Reinsborough, and J. Carwil. (2001). Colombia's U'wa tribe and supporters celebrate Oxy's failure to find oil. Amazon Watch, July 31, 2001. http://www.amazonwatch.org/newsroom/newsreleases01/jul31_uwa.html (accessed October 21, 2001).

Sorenson, R. E. (1978). Cooperation and freedom among the fore of New Guinea. In *Learning non-aggression,* ed. Ashley Montage. New York: Oxford.

SourceWatch. (2006a). Planting fake news in Iraq. http://www.sourcewatch.org/index.php?title=Lincoln_Group#Planting_Fake_News_in_Iraq (accessed April 11, 2006).

SourceWatch (2006b). Project for the new American century. http://www.sourcewatch.org/index.php?title=Project_for_the_New_American_Century#PNAC_Documents (accessed March 8, 2006).

SourceWatch (2006c). Think tanks. http://www.sourcewatch.org/index.php?title=Think_tanks (accessed September 30, 2006).

SourceWatch (2006d). Defense policy board advisory committee. http://www.sourcewatch.org/index.php?title=Defense_Policy_Board (accessed September 30, 2006).

SourceWatch (2006e). Council on Foreign Relations. http://www.sourcewatch.org/index.php?title=Council_on_Foreign_Relations (accessed September 24, 2006).

SourceWatch. (n.d.)(a). Rendon Group. http://www.sourcewatch.org/index.php?title=Rendon_Group (accessed April 3, 2006).

SourceWatch (n.d.)(b). Office of strategic influence. http://www.sourcewatch.org/index.php?title=Office_of_Strategic_Influence (accessed April 3, 2006).

Southern Poverty Law Center. (2007). Close to slavery: Guestworker programs in the United States. Southern Policy Law Center, Montgomery, AL.

Specter, M. (1998). Contraband women: A special report: Traffickers' new cargo: Naïve Slavic women. *New York Times*. http://archives.nytimes.com/archives/search (accessed January 11, 2006).

Sperry, R. (1995). The riddle of consciousness and the changing scientific worldview. *Journal of Humanistic Psychology* 35 (2): 8.

Sproule, J. M. (1997). *Propaganda and democracy: The American experience of media and mass persuasion*. Cambridge, UK: Cambridge University Press.

Staub, E. (2001). Genocide and mass killing: Their roots and prevention. In *Peace, conflict, and violence: Peace psychology for the 21st century*, ed. D. Christie, R. Wagner, and D. Winter, 76–86. Englewood, NJ: Prentice Hall.

St. Clair, J. (2005). *Grand theft Pentagon*. Monroe, ME: Common Courage Press.

Steinberg, L. D., R. Catalano, and D. Dooley. (1981). Economic antecedents of child abuse and neglect. *Human Development* 52: 975–985.

Stiglitz, J. (2002). *Globalization and its discontents*. New York: W. W. Norton.

Stouffer, S. A. (1949). *Studies in social psychology in World War II: The American soldier*. Princeton, NJ: Princeton University Press.

Strassler, R. B., ed. (1996). *The landmark Thucydides: A comprehensive guide to the Peloponnesian War*. New York: Free Press.

Straus, S. (1997). Eritrea: a do-it-yourself nation. *San Francisco Chronicle*, June 11, C2, C16.

Stumo, M. (2000). Down on the farm. *Multinational Monitor* 21: 17–22.

Suskind, R. (2004). What makes Bush's presidency so radical—even to some Republicans—is his preternatural faith-infused certainty in uncertain times. Without a doubt. *New York Times*, October 17, 44.

Suskind, R. (2006). *The one percent doctrine: Deep inside America's pursuit of its enemies since 9/11*. New York: Simon & Schuster.

Syme, S. L. (1989). Control and health: An epidemiological perspective. In *Stress, personal control and health*, ed. A. Steptoe and A. Appels. New York: Wiley and Sons.

Syme, S. L., and L. Berkman. (1976). Social class, susceptibility and illness. *American Journal of Epidemiology* 104 (1): 1–8.

Tan, G., M. Ray, and R. Cate. (1991). Migrant farm child abuse and neglect within an ecosystem framework. *Family Relations* 40 (1): 84–92.

Taylor, M. (2004). Community issues and social networks. In *Social networks and social exclusion: sociological and policy perspectives*, ed. C. Phillipson, G. Allan, and D. Morgan, 205–218. Hauts, England: Ashgate.

Technology, Entertainment, Design (TED). (n.d.). Nike shoes and child labor in Pakistan. http://www.american.edu/TED/nike.htm#r1.

Teitel, M. (1994a). Ownership of the seed of life. *Elmwood Quarterly* 10 (2&3): 2–6.

Teitel, M. (1994b). Selling cells. *Elmwood Quarterly* 10 (2&3): 12–14.

Thomson, J. E. (1990). State practices, international norms and the decline of mercenarism. *Int. Studies Quarterly* 34 (1): 23–47.

Tuchman, B. W. (1984). *The march of folly: From Troy to Vietnam*. New York: Random House.

Turnbull, C. (1962). *The forest people.* New York: Simon & Schuster.

UN High Commissioner for Refugees. (2004). Trends in unaccompanied and separated minors in industrialized countries (2001–2003), Geneva, Switzerland. http://www.UNHCR.CH/Statistics (accessed July 10, 2007).

UN High Commissioner for Refugees. (2005). 2004 Global refugee trends: Overview of refugees, new arrivals, durable solutions, asylum seekers, stateless and other persons of concern to UNHCR. UNHCR, June 17, 2005. http://www.UNHCR.CH/Statistics (accessed July 10, 2007).

Useem, M. (1984). *The inner circle: large corporations and the rise of business political activity in the U.S. and U.K.* New York: Oxford University Press.

Useem, M. (1996). *Investor capitalism: How money managers are changing the face of corporate America.* New York: Basic Books.

Van der Zee, John. (1974). *The greatest men's party on earth: Inside the Bohemian Grove:* New York: Harcourt Brace Jovanovich.

Vicary, A. (2006). Employment and poverty in Mae Hong Son Province, Thailand: Burmese refugees in the labour market. *Burmese Economic Watch*, no. 1: 47–87.

Vyner, H. (1988). *Invisible trauma: The psychosocial effects of invisible environmental contaminants.* Lexington, MA: Heath & Co.

Wallis, J. (1992). Violence, poverty and separation. *Public Welfare* 50 (4): 14–15.

Wallis, J. (2006). Christmas in the trenches. From editor-in-chief of *Sojourners Magazine.* http://www.beliefnet.com/blogs/godspolitics/2006/12/jim-wallis-christmas-in-trenches.html (accessed December 27, 2006).

Wal-Mart Watch. (2006a). Tale of two WalMarts. http://walmartwatch.com/blog/archives/tale_of_two_wal_marts_retailers_legacy_future_collide_in_transition_era/ (accessed February 10, 2007).

Wal-Mart Watch. (2006b). Betty v. Goliath: A history of *Dukes v. WalMart.* http://walmartwatch.com/blog/ dukes_WalMart backgrounder-1.#0 (accessed June 17, 2007).

Warr, P. G. (2000). The failure of Myanmar's agricultural policies. *Southeast Asian Affairs*, 219–237.

War Resisters League. (2007). Where your income tax money really goes. http://www.warresisters.org/piechart.htm (accessed June 6, 2007).

Washington Technology. (2005). Top 100 federal prime contractors—2005. http://www.washingtontechnology.com/top-100/2005/82.html (accessed March 7, 2006).

Watson, J. R. I. (1973). Investigation into de-individuation using a cross-cultural survey technique. *Journal of Personality and Social Psychology* 25: 342–345.

Watson, P. (2006). Some say India deal ignores another energy need: Food. *Los Angeles Times*, Times Staff Writer, March 7, A3.

Webb, G. (2001). The new rules for the new millennium. In *The disinformation guide to media distortion, historical whitewashes and cultural myths*, ed. R. Kick, 38–39. New York: Disinformation Company.

Weiner, T. (2001). With Taliban gone, opium farmers return to their cash crop. *New York Times*, November 26, 1.

Wessells, M. (1995). Social-psychological determinants of nuclear proliferation: A dual process analysis. *Peace and Conflict: Journal of Peace Psychology* 1: 49–96.

Wessells, M. G. (1998). Children, armed conflict and peace. *Journal of Peace Research* 35: 635–646.

Westheimer, Joel, ed. (2007). *Pledging allegiance: The politics of patriotism in American schools.* New York: Teachers College Press.

Whitlock, C. (2006). European probe finds signs of CIA-run secret prisons *Washington Post,* Foreign Service, June 8, A16. http://projects.washingtonpost.com/staff/email/craig+whitlock (accessed February 10, 2007).

Wilson, S. (2001). Paramilitary troops massacre villagers in Colombia. *Washington Post,* October 12, A29.

Wolf, E. (1999). *Peasant wars of the twentieth century.* Norman: University of Oklahoma Press.

Woodward, C. (2005). Nixon blanched at "horror option." Associated Press, *San Francisco Chronicle,* November 25, A12.

World Bank. (2001). World Development Indicators, CD-ROM Version. International Bank for Reconstruction and Development. From University of California at Berkeley Library Network.

World Bank. (2005). Philippines country brief. http://www.worldbank.org.ph. (accessed April 30, 2005).

Wright, S. (2003). Rethinking the biological warfare problem. *GeneWatch* 16 (2). http://www.gene-watch.org/genewatch/articles/16-2wright.html (accessed July 29, 2007).

Yassin, J. O. (2005). Demonizing the victims of Katrina: Coverage painted hurricane survivors as looters, snipers, and rapists. *Extra!* November/December. Fairness & Accuracy in Reporting (FAIR). http://www.fair.org/index.php?page=2793&printer_friendly=1 (accessed June 5, 2006).

Yulsman, T. (2005). Political interference with science real, troubling. *Denver Post.* http://www.denverpost.com/opinion/ci_2954217 (accessed May 12, 2006).

Zarate, J. C. (1998). The emergence of a new dog of war: private international security companies, international law and the new world disorder. *Stanford Journal of International Law* 34: 75–76.

Zepernick, M. (2004). The impact of corporations on the commons. Address at the Harvard Divinity School's Theological Opportunities Program, October 21, 2004. http://www.poclad.org/articles/zepernick02.html (accessed November 13, 2006).

Zepezauer, M., and A. Naiman. (1996). *Take the rich off welfare.* Tucson, AZ: Odonian Press.

Zimbardo, P. G. (2004). A situationist perspective on the psychology of evil. In *The social psychology of good and evil: Understanding our capacity for kindness and cruelty,* ed. A. Miller. New York: Guilford.

Zinn, H. (1990). *A people's history of the United States.* New York: Harper Perennial.

Zinn, H. (2006). America's blinders. *Progressive,* April 2006. http://progressive.org/mag_zinn0406 (accessed February 2, 2007).

Index

About the Series

The Praeger Series in Contemporary Psychology

In this series, experts from various disciplines peer through the lens of psychology telling us answers they see for questions of human behavior. Their topics may range from humanity's psychological ills—addictions, abuse, suicide, murder, and terrorism among them—to works focused on positive subjects including intelligence, creativity, athleticism, and resilience. Regardless of the topic, the goal of this series remains constant—to offer innovative ideas, provocative considerations, and useful beginnings to better understand human behavior.

Recent Titles in Contemporary Psychology

Redressing the Emperor:
Improving Our Children's Public Mental Health System
John S. Lyons

Havens: Stories of True Community Healing
Leonard Jason and Martin Perdoux

Psychology of Terrorism, Condensed Edition: Coping with the Continuing Threat
Chris E. Stout, editor

Handbook of International Disaster Psychology, Volumes I–IV
Gilbert Reyes and Gerard A. Jacobs, editors

The Psychology of Resolving Global Conflicts: From War to Peace, Volumes 1–3
Mari Fitzduff and Chris E. Stout, editors

The Myth of Depression as Disease: Limitations and Alternatives to Drug Treatment
Allan M. Leventhal and Christopher R. Martell

Preventing Teen Violence: A Guide for Parents and Professionals
Sherri N. McCarthy and Claudio Simon Hutz

Making Enemies Unwittingly: Humiliation and International Conflict
Evelin Gerda Lindner

Collateral Damage: The Psychological Consequences of America's War on Terrorism
Paul R. Kimmel and Chris E. Stout, editors

Terror in the Promised Land: Inside the Anguish of the Israeli-Palestinian Conflict
Judy Kuriansky, editor

Trauma Psychology, Volumes 1 and 2
Elizabeth Carll, editor

Beyond Bullets and Bombs: Grassroots Peace Building between Israelis and Palestinians
Judy Kuriansky, editor

About the Authors

MARC PILISUK teaches at the Saybrook Graduate School and is Professor Emeritus of Community Psychology in the Department of Human and Community Development at the University of California at Davis. He is a former president of the Society for the Study of Peace, Conflict, and Violence and a steering committee member of Psychologists for Social Responsibility. Pilisuk is the author of six earlier books and more than 120 articles and reviews on topics including military-industrial power, conflict resolution, globalization, torture, poverty, and perceptions of a contaminated world. His continuing focus has been on the role of ordinary people facing an often uncaring, sometimes violent, global technological society, which is the topic of the book at hand.

JENNIFER ACHORD ROUNTREE is a doctoral student at Saybrook Graduate School in San Francisco. She is researching restorative agricultural community development projects in Latin America and the tensions between the attendant goals of ecological health, economic development, and cultural sovereignty within the context of the global marketplace.

CPSIA information can be obtained at www.ICGtesting.com
Printed in the USA
LVOW04*2143160914

404424LV00012B/280/P

9 780275 994358